Freedom through Inner Renunciation

McGill studies in the History of Religions,
A Series Devoted to International Scholarship

Katherine K. Young, Editor

Freedom through Inner Renunciation

Śaṅkara's Philosophy in a New Light

ROGER MARCAURELLE

STATE UNIVERSITY OF NEW YORK PRESS

Published by
State University of New York Press, Albany

Printed in the United States of America

For information, address State University of New York Press,
State University Plaza, Albany, NY 12246

Production: Laurie Searl
Marketing: Nancy Farrell

Library of Congress Cataloging-in-Publication Data

Marcaurelle, Roger.
Freedom through inner renunciation : Śaṅkara's philosophy in a new light / Roger Marcaurelle.
p. cm. — (McGill studies in the history of religions)
Includes bibliographical references and index.
ISBN 0-7914-4361-2 (hc. : alk. paper). — ISBN 0-7914-4362-0 (pbk. : alk. paper)
1. Śaṅkarācārya. 2. Renunciation (Philosophy). 3. Advaita. 4. Vedanta. I. Title. II. Series.
B133.S5M35 2000
181'.482—dc21 99-20738
CIP

10 9 8 7 6 5 4 3 2 1

In homage to

all masters

in the art of awakening

to the infinite, blissful Self.

Contents

Chapter Six
THE MAIN OPPOSITION BETWEEN STEADFASTNESS IN ACTION AND STEADFASTNESS IN SELF-KNOWLEDGE
83

Chapter Seven
THE YOGA OF ACTION AND THE MEANS OF SELF-KNOWLEDGE
105

Chapter Eight
SELF-KNOWLEDGE AND PHYSICAL RENUNCIATION
131

PART THREE RENUNCIATION IN POST-ŚAṄKARA *ADVAITA VEDĀNTA* AND HINDUISM

Chapter Nine
POST-ŚAṄKARA *ADVAITA VEDĀNTA* AND RENUNCIATION
165

Chapter Ten
ŚAṄKARA AND THE VALUE OF RENUNCIATION IN HINDUISM
209

Notes 217

Bibliography 255

Index 261

Preface

Whether emphasized in its inner and psychological forms, or external and physical dimensions, renunciation is a key concept and practice in world religions. Believers are asked to give up wrong actions and attachment to worldly objects in order to purify themselves and thus be more in tune with the divine dimension of reality. Similarly, in modern psychology of personal development, a key role is played by the art of "letting go" or the art of "bereavement," by the skill of renouncing concepts, images, and expectations that impair creative, harmonious, and fulfilling interaction of a person with the environment.

Indian spirituality places enormous importance on the theme and practice of renunciation. In its internal or external forms, renunciation runs through all Indian religions with a startling impact. It provides crucial themes to the reflection on the relationships between the individual and society, knowledge and action, metaphysical truth, and practical reality, as well as between the ultimate spiritual goal and the means of attaining it. Louis Renou calls Hinduism "a religion of renunciation" (1966, 123). Many Indologists hold a similar view. Karl H. Potter (1982, 118) believes that a history of Indian thought could easily be written on the basis of the opposition between active functioning in the world (*pravṛtti*) and turning away from the world (*nivṛtti*). In his famous paper on "World Renunciation in Indian Religions," Louis Dumont also considers that "the secret of Hinduism may be found in the dialogue between the renouncer and the man-in-the-world" (1980, 270).

It is also significant that most of the religious traditions in India have been founded by monks. It seems reasonable to believe with Patrick Olivelle that monks represent, with respect to the primary religious concerns, "the most creative element of intellectual history of India" (1975, 83).[1]

Among these monks, Śaṅkara (between 650 and 800 C.E.) was probably the most influential in Hinduism. He is known as the greatest exponent of *Advaita Vedānta*, which can fairly be called the most prominent spiritual tradition of India. This tradition holds that the ultimate teaching

(*Vedānta*) of the Vedic tradition is the essential identity or non-duality (*advaita*) between the individual self, the world and the absolute Self or *Brahman*. Śaṅkara played a major role with respect to the understanding and practice of internal (mental) and external (physical) renunciation. Whether in agreement or disagreement with him, it is often against the background of his works that Hindu spiritual leaders clarified and developed their own positions on that theme as well as on others in succeeding centuries.

Śaṅkara's thought has been studied extensively by both modern Indologists and traditional Indian scholars. Especially within the last twenty years, several works have dealt in whole or in part with renunciation in Hinduism and in Śaṅkara's doctrine. Why then a new study on Śaṅkara and renunciation? My contention is that a major misinterpretation of Śaṅkara's position on this theme has occurred in the past and continues to prevail. Most traditional Indian scholars as well as Indian and Western Indologists hold Śaṅkara to be the herald of the monastic way of living as a sine qua non for complete knowledge of the absolute Self and spiritual freedom from the limitations of life. But the results of our study show that this understanding about Śaṅkara is rooted in a significant misinterpretation of his position. Olivelle (1986–1987) already brought to light the debate on renunciation between the traditions of *Advaita Vedānta* (non-dualism) and *Viśiṣṭādvaita Vedānta* (non-dualism between distinctions); yet a complete evaluation of the controversial situation concerning this theme within the *Advaita Vedānta* tradition itself is still needed. This evaluation will be our task here.

The first part of this study will detail the various aspects of the issue and will explain the methodology used. Chapter 1 will mainly provide an overview of the present scholarship on renunciation in Śaṅkara's works and in the *Advaita Vedānta* tradition. Confusion and inconsistency regarding typology and terminology of renunciation are still frequent in secondary literature (see Marcaurelle 1994). Hence, chapter 2 will propose a systematic definition of the basic types of renunciation in Śaṅkara's commentaries and the *Advaita Vedānta* tradition. This chapter is based on my article "The Basic Types of Renunciation in Hinduism with Special Reference to Śaṅkara's Gītā-Bhāṣya" (*Hermeneutical Paths to the Sacred Worlds of India*, edited by Katherine K. Young. Atlanta: Scholars Press, 1994). Chapter 3 will clarify the basic doctrinal points against the background of which Śaṅkara's treatment of renunciation must be approached. Chapter 4 will refute two explanations often invoked in the *Advaita Vedānta* tradition in order to solve apparent inconsistencies on the theme of renunciation in Śaṅkara's works, for they do not agree with the author's exegetical principles.

Part two will be devoted to Śaṅkara's position on renunciation. Chapter 5 will propose a new interpretation of the well-known sequence toward liberation (spiritual freedom) mentioned by him in his commentary on the *Bhagavadgītā*: yoga of action (*karmayoga*), purity of mind (*sattvaśuddhi*), attainment of knowledge (*jñānaprāpti*), renunciation of all actions (*sarvakarmasaṃnyāsa*) and steadfastness in Self-knowledge (*jñānaniṣṭhā*). Here renunciation of all actions will appear as a *result* rather than as a mandatory means of complete Self-knowledge. In the light of this new interpretation, we will try in chapter 6 to understand in what ways Śaṅkara distinguishes two basic notions of his doctrine often associated with renunciation, namely, steadfastness in action (*karmaniṣṭhā*) and steadfastness in knowledge (*jñānaniṣṭhā*), and how he opposes them as two distinct paths leading to completely different goals, respectively, transmigratory existence and liberation from rebirth and its limitations. If Śaṅkara did not consider physical renunciation of rites and monasticism to be indispensable for complete Self-knowledge, then how did he envision the attainment of that knowledge and of the ensuing spiritual liberation without recourse to physical renunciation? This will be the main question of chapter 7. In contrast, chapter 8 will deal with Śaṅkara's rationale on physical renunciation and monasticism as a means for gaining Self-knowledge. Part 2 will conclude with a survey of the author's terminology on renunciation.

Part three, consisting of chapters 9 and 10, will first explore the various ways later followers of *Advaita* (Advaitins) understood—and often misunderstood—Śaṅkara's position on renunciation and will identify the authors who exerted the greatest influence on the interpretation of this theme within the tradition up to the eighteenth century. Chapter 10 will conclude by outlining how these findings provide a new perspective on the history of renunciation in Hinduism as a whole.

Hopefully the results of this research will provide not only a larger area of agreement on renunciation among interpreters of Śaṅkara, a more accurate angle for the critical assessment of his interpretations, but also a solid basis for a detailed understanding of the development of renunciation in the post-Śaṅkara period.

Since *Advaita Vedānta* is also an art of living, may this new interpretation bear concrete spiritual benefits in the life of those for whom Śaṅkara's teaching is valuable.

Acknowledgements

My foremost gratitude goes to the late Pandit T. S. Srinivasa Sastri, Deccan College, and to K. S. Arjunwadkar, retired Professor and Head, Department of Marathi, University of Bombay. In their own profound and outstanding ways, each has guided me through the intricacies of Śaṅkara's commentaries and literally made this work possible. Although I take full responsibility for the ideas expressed in this book, my debt to them is immeasurable.

I am also most appreciative for the precious critical advice of Professor Arvind Sharma of McGill University, Montreal.

I would like to offer my grateful thanks to four Indian scholars who, often on a daily basis, helped me generously, during months of textual analysis and discussions: Professor P. G. Lalye, formerly Professor and Head of Sanskrit Department, Osmania University, Hyderabad; the late Pandit K. Balasubrahmania Sastrigal, Principal, Madras Sanskrit College; Dr. Ram Sankar Bhattacharya, Varanasi; and Professor M. A. Mahendale, Bhandarkar Oriental Research Institute for his help in reading German articles.

My gratitude also goes to Dr. N. Veezhinathan, retired Professor and Head of Sanskrit Department, University of Madras, and to Dr. S. Revathy, now Professor and Head of this Department, for their critical advice and kind assistance during the first months of my first stay in India. I feel particularly thankful to Professor S. D. Laddu, Director, Post-Graduate and Research Department, for his dedicated efforts in providing me with the best resources with respect to all aspects of my stay at the Bhandarkar Oriental Research Institute, Poona. I also owe much to the diligence of Mr. P. N. Malik of the Shastri Indo-Canadian Institute in ensuring maximum comfort during one of my two-year stays in India.

I am thankful to the following scholars who discussed with me various aspects of my research: Dr. Kamalakar Mishra, Professor of Philosophy, Banares Hindu University; Pandit S. Subrahmanya Sastri, Varanasi; Swami

Santananda Sarasvati, Allahabad; and Dr. R. Balasubramanian, retired Professor and Head, Department of Philosophy, University of Pondicherry.

To Dr. Katherine K. Young, Professor, Faculty of Religious Studies, McGill University, I owe more than I can say for her invaluable comments in the early stages of this research, for her sustained encouragement and her judicious advice.

I want to express all my appreciation to the friends who helped me during this endeavor, above all, to Victoria LeBlanc and Duart Maclean for their careful editing. I am also thankful to Dr. Jan Huben, Parimal Patil, and Jörg Tuske for their useful suggestions. My brother Gérard, Pierre and François Montpetit, Jean-Paul LaPointe, Denis Cauchon, and Allen Faguy also deserve my warm thanks for their timely help at various stages.

I am sincerely thankful to the Shastri Indo-Canadian Institute and to the Social Sciences and Humanities Research Council of Canada for their financial support toward the completion of this work, and to the Fonds pour la Formation de Chercheurs et l'Aide à la Recherche of the Government of Quebec for its two-year postdoctoral scholarship.

Abbreviations of Works by Śaṅkara

N.B. 1. Almost all Sanskrit editions of Śaṅkara's commentaries given below contain one or more subcommentaries. We shall always specify in the running text which commentary is pointed out by the reference.
2. When one of the English translations given below is quoted, the reference will include the abbreviation "transl." In all other cases, the translation will be the author's; the reference will be to the Sanskrit version of the text.
3. The Sanskrit version will be given in addition to the translation only for the more important passages.

AiU *Aitareya Upaniṣad Bhāṣya*
—*Upaniṣadbhāṣyam*. Vol. 1. Edited by S. Subrahmanya Shastri. MountAbu/Varanasi: Mahesh Research Institute, 1979.
—*Eight Upaniṣads, with the Commentary of Śaṅkarācārya*. Vol. 2. Translated by Swāmī Gambhīrānanda. Calcutta: Advaita Ashrama, 1986.

BhG *Bhagavadgītā Bhāṣya*
—*Śrīmadbhagavadgītā, with the commentaries of Śaṅkara, Ānandagiri, Nīlakaṇṭha, Dhanapati, Śrīdhara, Abhinavagupta, Madhusūdana Sarasvatī and Śrīdharmadattaśarmā*. Edited by Wasudev Laxman Śāstrī Panśīkar. Delhi: Indological Book House, 1984.
—*Gita Bhashya*. Translated by C. V. Ramachandra Aiyar. Bombay: Bharatiya Vidya Bhavan, 1988.

BṛU *Bṛhadāraṇyaka Upaniṣad Bhāṣya*
—*Upaniṣadbhāṣyam*. Vol. 3. *Bṛhadāraṇyakopaniṣad*. Edited by S. Subrahmanya Shastri. MountAbu/Varanasi: Mahesh Research Institute, 1986.
—*The Bṛhadāraṇyaka Upaniṣad, with the Commentary of Śaṅkarācārya*. Translated by Swāmī Mādhavānanda. 6th Ed. Calcutta: Advaita Ashrama, n.d.

BS *Brahmasūtra Bhāṣya*

—*Brahmasūtrabhāṣya, with the commentaries of Govindānanda, Vācaspatimiśra and Ānandagiri*. Edited by J. L. Shastri. Delhi: Motilal Banarsidass, 1980.

—*Brahmasūtrabhāṣya*. Translated by Swāmī Gambh¥rānanda. 4th ed. Calcutta: Advaita Ashrama, 1983.

ChU *Chāndogya Upaniṣad Bhāṣya*

—*Upaniṣadbhāṣyam*. Vol. 2. *Chāndogyopaniṣad*. Edited by S. Subrahmanya Shastri. MountAbu/Varanasi: Mahesh Research Institute, 1982.

—*Chāndogya Upaniṣad, with the Commentary of Śrī Śaṅkarācārya*. Translated by Swāmī Gambhīrānanda. Calcutta: Advaita Ashrama, 1983.

ĪU *Īśā Upaniṣad Bhāṣya*

—*Upaniṣadbhāṣyam*. Vol. 1. Edited by S. Subrahmanya Shastri. MountAbu/Varanasi: Mahesh Research Institute, 1979.

—*Eight Upaniṣads, with the Commentary of Śaṅkarācārya*. Vol. 1. Translated by Swāmī Gambhīrānanda. Calcutta: Advaita Ashrama, 1986.

KaU *Kaṭhā Upaniṣad Bhāṣya*

—*Upaniṣadbhāṣyam*. Vol. 1. Edited by S. Subrahmanya Shastri. MountAbu/Varanasi: Mahesh Research Institute, 1979.

—*Eight Upaniṣads, with the Commentary of Śaṅkarācārya*. Vol. 1. Translated by Swāmī Gambhīrānanda. Calcutta: Advaita Ashrama, 1986.

KeU-P *Kena Upaniṣad Padabhāṣya*

—*Upaniṣadbhāṣyam*. Vol. 1. Edited by S. Subrahmanya Shastri. MountAbu/Varanasi: Mahesh Research Institute, 1979.

—*Eight Upaniṣads, with the Commentary of Śaṅkarācārya*. Vol. 1. Translated by Swāmī Gambhīrānanda. Calcutta: Advaita Ashrama, 1986.

KeU-V *Kena Upaniṣad Vākyabhāṣya*

Upaniṣadbhāṣyam. Vol. 1. Edited by S. Subrahmanya Shastri MountAbu/Varanasi: Mahesh Research Institute, 1979.

MāU *Māṇḍūkya Upaniṣad Bhāṣya*

—*Upaniṣadbhāṣyam*. Vol. 1. Edited by S. Subrahmanya Shastri. MountAbu/Varanasi: Mahesh Research Institute, 1979.

—*Eight Upaniṣads, with the Commentary of Śaṅkarācārya*. Vol. 2. Translated by Swāmī Gambhīrānanda. Calcutta: Advaita Ashrama, 1986.

MāU-K *Māṇḍūkya Upaniṣad Kārikā Bhāṣya*
Ibid.

MuU *Muṇḍaka Upaniṣad Bhāṣya*
—*Upaniṣadbhāṣyam*. Vol. 1. Edited by S. Subrahmanya Shastri. MountAbu/Varanasi: Mahesh Research Institute, 1979.
—*Eight Upaniṣads, with the Commentary of Śaṅkarācārya*. Vol. 2. Translated by Swāmī Gambhīrānanda. Calcutta: Advaita Ashrama, 1986.

PU *Praśna Upaniṣad Bhāṣya*
—*Upaniṣadbhāṣyam*. Vol. 1. Edited by S. Subrahmanya Shastri. MountAbu/Varanasi: Mahesh Research Institute, 1979.
—*Eight Upaniṣads, with the Commentary of Śaṅkarācārya*. Vol. 2. Translated by Swāmī Gambhīrānanda. Calcutta: Advaita Ashrama, 1986.

TU *Taittirīya Upaniṣad Bhāṣya*
—*Upaniṣadbhāṣyam*. Vol. 1. Edited by S. Subrahmanya Shastri. MountAbu/Varanasi: Mahesh Research Institute, 1979.
—*Eight Upaniṣads, with the Commentary of Śaṅkarācārya*. Vol. 1. Translated by Swāmī Gambhīrānanda. Calcutta: Advaita Ashrama, 1986.

Upad *Upadeśasāhasr¥*
—*Śaṅkara's Upadeśasāhasrī*. Edited by Sengaku Mayeda. Tokyo: The Hokuseido Press, 1973.
—*A Thousand Teachings. The Upadeśasāhasrī of Śaṅkara*. Translated by Sengaku Mayeda. Tokyo: University of Tokyo Press, 1979.

PART ONE

The Issue and the Methodology

CHAPTER ONE

Śaṅkara and Renunciation: The Controversy

Śaṅkara's contribution to the theme of renunciation can be understood only in the context of Hindu sacred literature which includes texts of divine origin known collectively as *Veda* (Knowledge) or *Śruti* (the Heard), and texts of human origin known as *Smṛti* (given to Memory). The theme of renunciation appears in various forms of inner and outer withdrawal as early as the oldest texts of the *Veda* (1500–800 B.C.E.). In the four collections of hymns known as the *Vedas* as well as in books connected with them such as the *Brāhmaṇas* and the *Āraṇyakas*, one finds methods pertaining to renunciation such as asceticism (*tapas*) and inner sacrifice (*antaryajña*), as well as references to ascetic sages (*munis*), hermits (*vānaprasthas*) and "laborious" spiritual seekers (*śramaṇas*). However, it is only later on, roughly between the tenth and the fifth century B.C.E., that the *Upaniṣads*, known as the *Vedānta* or "final part" of the *Veda*, started to emphasize inner and outer renunciation as the most determining aspects of spiritual endeavor.[1]

Then, between the fourth century B.C.E. and the fourth century C.E., the Great Epics were written, namely, the *Rāmāyaṇa* and the *Mahābhārata* which includes the *Bhagavadgītā*. The very plot of the *Bhagavadgītā* was based on the opposition between respecting one's duty in society and abandoning it in favor of the life of a wandering mendicant: this famous dialogue between the God Kṛṣṇa and the warrior Arjuna starts when, bewildered at suddenly finding himself face-to-face with his own cousins in the opposing army, Arjuna chooses to drop his bow and arrows and to abandon his soldier's duty. Commented upon by hundreds of Hindus, including many eminent representatives of the main schools of Hindu thought which developed later, the seven hundred verses of the *Bhagavadgītā* are, in fact, an ethical and metaphysical answer to the question of renunciation.

The oldest commentary on the *Bhagavadgītā* that has reached us is from Śaṅkara. According to recent scholarship, Śaṅkara lived somewhere between 650 and 800 C.E.[2] He attempted a synthesis of the main Vedāntic texts, that is, the *Brahmasūtras*, the *Upaniṣads* and the *Bhagavadgītā* in terms of a complete non-dualism (*advaita*). According to this doctrine, liberation from limitations in this life as well as from rebirth is attained through direct experience of the ultimate identity between the individual self (*ātman*) and the attributeless *Brahman* (the absolute unmanifest principle which is the source of the whole universe). This specific interpretation has deeply influenced the development of Hindu thought up to the present. After Śaṅkara, a major concern of many medieval thinkers has been to prove or to refute his position on various themes including renunciation. Concerning the latter, the issues can be summarized as follows: Is renunciation really enjoined by sacred texts? If so, what kind(s) of renunciation are prescribed, to which person(s), at what time(s) in life, and for what purpose(s) in the context of the many means proposed for Self-knowledge by sacred texts?

We know from two of the most popular *Advaita* compendiums, namely, the *Vedāntasāra* (around 1500–1550) and the *Vedāntaparibhāṣā* (around 1550–1600), that the concept of renunciation was already controversial even within the *Advaita* tradition many centuries ago. Both these compendiums mention the existence of opposite opinions among Advaitins as to whether monastic life preceded by physical renunciation of Vedic rites is necessary for liberation. Here the divergence concerns the term *uparati* or *uparama* (quietness),[3] one of the six "qualities" (*ṣaṭkasampatti*) within the fourfold requirement (*sādhanacatuṣṭaya*) defining qualification for the *Advaita* discipline of knowledge,[4] which leads to liberation. In BS 1.1.1, Śaṅkara simply writes that the fourfold requirement is: "[1] discernment between the eternal and the ephemeral; [2] disinterest for enjoyment of the rewards [of rites and duties] in this life and hereafter; [3] the group of qualities conducive [to Self-knowledge], such as control of mind and control of senses; and [4] a desire for liberation" (BS 1.1.1, 36–37). According to the *Vedāntasāra* (Sadānanda 1949, 11) and to the tradition as a whole, the remaining qualities of the third requirement—which are left unsaid by Śaṅkara in the passage just quoted—are *uparati* (quietness), endurance (*titikṣā*), collectedness (*samādhāna*) and faith (*śraddhā*). As mentioned by the *Vedāntasāra* and the *Vedāntaparibhāṣā*, some *Advaitins* believe that *uparati* means the cessation of the mind's movement towards external objects and does not imply the monastic way of living; others believe that *uparati* consists of physical renunciation of Vedic rites as part of the initiation into monastic life.

Since names of authors are often left unmentioned in these compendiums, it is quite difficult to know exactly who and how many amongst followers of *Advaita* were on either side of the debate. However, references to the *Vivaraṇa* and *Bhāmatī* Schools of *Advaita* in the *Siddhāntaleśasaṅgraha* (around 1550–1593) suggest that the controversy was understood at that time to go back as far as the division of the *Advaita* tradition into these two schools, led respectively by Padmapāda, a pupil of Śaṅkara, and Vācaspati Miśra (around 850). But there may very well have been differing opinions even within each school. In any case, the various interpretations of renunciation in the *Advaita* tradition can be properly assessed only by first understanding Śaṅkara's exact position on the issue.

The viewpoint that the monastic way of living represents a sine qua non for complete Self-knowledge and liberation is expressed most radically by the late Śaṅkarācārya Candraśekhara Bhāratī, who died in 1954 and who was pontiff of the *Śṛṅgerī Maṭha*, one of the seats of spiritual learning allegedly founded by Śaṅkara himself. First, in the same manner as Śaṅkara, Candraśekhara Bhāratī states in his commentary on the *Vivekacūḍāmaṇi* that Brahmins alone have access to physical renunciation of rites (*karmasaṃnyāsa*) and to the monastic life which follows. But, still representing Śaṅkara and referring to all other possible aspirants, Candraśekhara adds: "As they are disqualified for saṃnyāsa, which alone invests one with the right for Vedāntic inquiry, in their present life itself, they cannot know and realize Brahman" (Candraśekhara 1988, 6). Thus, for this modern representative of Śaṅkara's tradition, monasticism is undoubtedly a sine qua non for liberation. Following his recent field research on the *Śṛṅgerī Maṭha*, Yoshitsugu Saway comes to a similar conclusion: "For Śaṅkara, *mokṣa* [liberation] is not possible without *jñāna* [Self-knowledge], and the road *par excellence* to *jñāna* is *karma-saṃnyāsa*.[5] This *saṃnyāsa*, in turn, is possible only for *brāhmaṇas*. It was they for whom Śaṅkara's instruction was intended" (1992, 133).[6] Sengaku Mayeda writes along the same lines that "Śaṅkara's teachings were meant only for selected *saṃnyāsins*" (1989, 199). Olivelle goes so far as to declare that "by limiting renunciation to Brahmins, Śaṃkara has in effect restricted enlightenment and even the aspiration to enlightenment to Brahmins" (1993,

197).[7] In *Theology after Vedānta*, a comment on *Vedānta* from the viewpoint of interreligious dialogue, Francis X. Clooney also understands that "actual competence is extended to just about no one" (1990, 150) and sees a kind of transgression in approaching *Vedānta* within the context of interreligious dialogue without having taken up physical renunciation of rites and monasticism as a necessary requirement for entitlement to the study of *Vedānta* (1990, 150–152).

According to this interpretation of Śaṅkara's works, any aspirant to liberation must go through the following steps in the course of either one or many lives: [1] the yoga of action (*karmayoga*), that is, performance of regular (*nitya*) and occasional (*naimittika*) rites without attachment to their rewards; [2] purity of mind brought about by the yoga of action and giving rise to the intellectual conviction that the means to liberation is not ritual action, but direct knowledge of the actionless Self; [3] physical renunciation of all rites as part of initiation into monastic life; [4] full-time practice of the discipline of knowledge consisting of hearing (*śravaṇa*), reflection (*manana*) and meditation (*nididhyāsana*) applied mainly to the Upaniṣadic literature. In other words, as summarized by Kalyanasundara Sastri, "one has to practice *karma-yoga* for the purpose of attaining the purification of the mind. This is the preliminary discipline, the ground work for spiritual progress. After attaining the purification of the mind, and after renouncing all *karma*, one treads the path of knowledge" (1989, 299).[8]

Given this prevailing understanding about Śaṅkara, some scholars accused him of holding inflexibly to a biased notion of mandatory physical renunciation when interpreting sacred texts. T. G. Mainkar and P. M. Modi have been his most elaborate critics in this respect. Mainkar claims that the *Bhagavadgītā* teaches a combination of action, devotion, and knowledge as the means to liberation, and that it advocates activism rather than monasticism. He then concludes:

> Śaṅkara has laid quite an undue emphasis on Knowledge, even at the cost of Karman and Bhakti [devotion]; and in order to achieve this, he has understood additional words, reversed the sense of verses and finally changed the spirit of the entire poem. . . . It would not be an exaggeration to say that he is the least faithful interpreter of the Bhagavadgītā (1969, 65).

In a more detailed critique of Śaṅkara's commentary, Modi tries to show that although the *Bhagavadgītā* accepts both monasticism and disinterested action, it favors the latter (1955, 82). Modi then accuses Śaṅkara of using "a variety of interpretational jugglary [*sic*]" (1955, 83) to bypass the textual evidence of the *Gītā*. As a consequence, "a great number of verses in the *Gītā* which Shankara takes as dealing with Sannyasa have nothing to do with renunciation. In fact they are in favor of Yoga or Disinterested Action" (1955, 86–87).

When understood in this way, Śaṅkara does appear dogmatic and sectarian. This kind of picture emerges for instance from Michel Hulin's comparison between Śaṅkara and Maṇḍana Miśra (670–720), a philosopher of the same period:

> Maṇḍana's "method," which is coordinated strategy rather than mere eclectism, allows one to privilege the particular means which best agrees with one's social situation, character, and so forth. Presented by the tradition as a life-time householder, Maṇḍana is far from any sectarian inflexibility and thus on the opposite side from, say, Śaṅkara and his "no salvation outside of *saṃnyāsa*."[9]

Similarly, Suryanarayana Sastri holds that Śaṅkara resorted to a demoralizing doctrine of illusion and "worked up" a dualism between action and contemplation as well as a divorce between practical life and philosophy. The whole thing leads to the "most disastrous effects," namely, "the lethargy of Indians" and their "spirit of false resignation" (1961, 140–141).

While coming to a similar conclusion, Maharishi Mahesh Yogi, a contemporary Advaitin well-known for his teaching of Transcendental Meditation, attributes the fault to Śaṅkara's followers. Maharishi Mahesh Yogi is himself a close disciple of Swāmī Brahmānanda Sarasvatī who, between 1941 and 1953, was pontiff (Śaṅkarācārya) of *Jyotirmaṭha,* one of four or five major seats of knowledge allegedly founded by Śaṅkara himself. The Maharishi writes in his commentary on the *Bhagavadgītā*:

> The sanyasi [*sic*], or recluse orders, of Shankara's tradition have been interpreting Shankara-Vedanta as being completely closed to householders, who form the main section of society, and open only to themselves. This has resulted in spiritual decadence and in the moral downfall of Indian society (1969, 257).

Owing to the tradition's overemphasis on reclusive contemplation, the Maharishi holds, "the teaching became one-sided and, deprived of its wholeness, eventually lost its universal appeal. It came to be regarded as mayavada, a philosophy of illusion, holding the world to be only illusory and emphasizing the detached way of life" (1969, 13).

Kokileswar Bhattacharya, a scholar of the early twentieth century, tried to rectify the understanding that monasticism is necessary according to Śaṅkara. In his *Introduction to Adwaita Philosophy*, first published in 1924, he explains that if, for Śaṅkara, action and Self-knowledge are contradictory, it is because they "cannot *both* be the ultimate ends of life" (1979, 195). One leads to transient mundane prosperity and pleasure, the other to liberation from such transience. He then states that, for Śaṅkara, ritual actions must be performed until one has reached liberation (1979, 202). After interpreting a few passages which recommend monasticism and are likely to be confusing, he argues that they refer only to the enlightened, that is, the liberated man (1979, 226–227). Thus, the author does not account for monasticism when advocated by Śaṅkara for the seeker-after-liberation.

The more recent work by Kapil N. Tiwari suffers from the same shortcoming. Tiwari rightly notes that while a section of the *Advaita* tradition resists the interpretation of renunciation as a "life-negating principle," many scholars, including people who consider themselves *Advaitins*, misunderstand Śaṅkara's position as upholding such a negative principle (1977, 141). But Tiwari holds that whereas in the *Dharmaśāstras* (the texts which expound the rules of conduct) renunciation consists of one of the four modes of living, in *Vedānta*, it means only the consequence of the state of liberation through knowledge of the Self (1977, 47). "By non-performance of action or *karma-saṃnyāsa*," Tiwari says, "the *advaitins* only mean that the *Brahmavid* or *Brahmasaṁstha* [i.e. the liberated person] acts but automatically or spontaneously without any strain or struggle, due to the realization of the cosmic consciousness outside of which nothing remains" (1977, 139). Certainly, this description of the meaning of *saṃnyāsa* is a good attempt at accounting for the inner renunciation of all identification with mental activity, to which Śaṅkara gives much more attention and value than is usually realized. But again, while properly stressing the value of inner renunciation in Śaṅkara's eyes, it wrongly suggests that he did not *also* strongly recommend physical renunciation and monasticism as a means for Self-knowledge.

Karl H. Potter also draws attention to the misinterpretation of Śaṅkara's emphasis on renunciation. First, he notices that "Śaṃkara, when speaking of saṃnyāsa, frequently describes it in terms that seem appropriate only to the liberated person" (1981, 35). He concludes on this ground that in the author's peculiar usage of the term, *saṃnyāsa* is almost invariably "identical with liberation while living" (Ibid.). He explains that when Śaṅkara insists on the idea that one can obtain liberation only from the stage of *saṃnyāsa*, it is not, as usually understood, in the sense that every aspirant has to travel through the monastic mode of living (*saṃnyāsāśrama*), but rather that he can be liberated only if he reaches the state of complete inner renunciation from action through direct Self-knowledge. Potter understands, namely, from Śaṅkara's ChU 2.23.1, that one can reach this state of inner renunciation from the stage of householder or from any of the other modes of living in the usual sense of the term (1982, 120). He argues that since, for Śaṅkara, renunciation of all actions (*sarvakarmasaṃnyāsa*) is the effect of direct Self-knowledge and is internal only, for all practical purposes, it amounts to direct Self-knowledge itself and to the ensuing liberation. According to Potter,

> it is evident that Śaṅkara does not teach withdrawal from the world [that is, physical renunciation of rites and monasticism] at any point along the path of spiritual progress, even at the *saṃnyāsa* or *jīvanmukta* stage [*saṃnyāsa* being here identical with liberation-in-life or *jīvanmukti*] (1981, 35).

Along the age-old chain of *Advaita* commentators, Potter finds the climax of the complete reversal of Śaṅkara's perspective with Vidyāraṇya (fourteenth century). Vidyāraṇya was pontiff of the *Śṛṅgeri Maṭha*, author of the famous *Jīvanmuktiviveka*, and was often identified with Mādhava, the author of Śaṅkara's most popular hagiography called *Śaṅkaradigvijaya*. Potter summarizes the reversal as follows: "For Vidyāraṇya, one gives up actions and gains knowledge. Śaṃkara's position is diametrically opposed. As he sees it, an agent cannot have knowledge, and a true knower cannot act. Thus, it is knowledge which leads to the abandonment of action, not the reverse" (1982, 118). Hence, Potter adds, the imputation of an elitistic social philosophy would suit Vidyāraṇya rather than Śaṅkara (1982, 120).

Although Potter's study provides some significant material for a proper understanding of renunciation in Śaṅkara, it seems to overlook the importance *also* given by Śaṅkara to physical renunciation as a means for the seeker-after-liberation. Reevaluating Śaṅkara's interpretation must involve the description of the respective functions of inner and outer renunciation in his doctrine of Self-knowledge and liberation. But Potter does not account for the passages where Saṅkara values monasticism as a significant means in the context of the path of knowledge. Although in various places Śaṅkara does recommend physical renunciation of rites to the seeker-after-liberation, Potter seems to make no room for it, nor see any use in it: ". . . someone who does not have that knowledge of the reality of nondifference . . . must continue to act. If he refrains from performing certain kinds of acts he may purify himself and become worthy for pleasurable sojourns in heaven, or for high-status rebirth, but he gets no closer to liberation" (1982, 115).

Thus, according to Potter, in Śaṅkara's commentaries, renunciation of all actions is to be understood only in the light of the "thesis that Self-knowledge necessarily renders action of any kind impossible" (1981, 35). Since what is referred to here is an inner renunciation through immediate Self-knowledge, it would be fair to interpret the impossiblity of acting only on the level of the experience of one's identity with *Brahman*, and not on the level of the mind-body complex, which persists even after liberation and which represents, through its daily actions, the *jīvan*, or living aspect of, *jīvanmukti* (liberation-in-life). But when Potter tries to make a case for the incongruity of viewing Śaṅkara as the historic founder of the monastic tradition which has been attached to his name for centuries, he erroneously applies the internal absence of activity characteristic of Self-experience alone, to the physical dimension of renunciation:

> . . . we may well doubt that the philosopher Śaṃkara had anything at all to do with the founding of the *Daśanāmins*. It would have been out of character for him to form a social institution around what he considered to be a *saṃnyāsin*, since he insisted that they were incapable of action and thus entirely outside of society (1982, 121).

The fact that the enlightened person is "incapable of action," because of his renunciation of the sense of doership of mental and physical actions, does not necessarily imply that he has abandoned social activities on the physical level as well. Absence of action and of the sense of doership on the level of direct knowledge of the actionless Self does not necessarily mean absence of activity and undertakings on the level of mind and body as such. Elsewhere Potter himself puts one on guard against committing such a metaphysical error; he specifies about the enlightened person: ". . . from the 'higher standpoint' (*pāramārthika*) he is liberated and thus incapable of ordinary knowledge, action and experiences, but from the 'lower standpoint' (*vyāvahārika*) he is a *saṃnyāsin* or renunciate, capable of all such things" (1981, 34). Thus, Potter's interpretation of Śaṅkara's position is neither complete, nor entirely consistent.

In another attempt at proper contextualization of Śaṅkara's position on renunciation, Sarvapelli Radhakrishnan also considers that "the emphasis in Śaṁkara is not on retirement from the world, but on renunciation of the self" (1929, 633). He understands from Śaṅkara that "to gain salvation, one need not become saññyāsin [*sic*]. . . . Saññyāsins, however, are best entitled to it, since it is easier for them to acquire it than for others, since they are not called upon to undertake active worship, household duties or Vedic rites" (1929, 617). Radhakrishnan sees in Śaṅkara's works an "unnecessary emphasis" on Self-knowledge as the only means to liberation, but he justifies the author's attitude by presenting it as a rather fair reaction to the ritualists' overemphasis on the necessity to perform rites for liberation (1929, 627–628). After noting that the ambiguous use of the word *karman* can lead to a misunderstanding of the relationship between Self-knowledge and action, he clarifies the matter as follows: "If *jñāna* [knowledge] and *karma* are opposed as light and darkness, it is *karma* in the sense of selfish activity and *jñāna* in the sense of unselfish wisdom" (1929, 630).

In the midst of these arguments and counterarguments, some fundamental questions remain unanswered regarding Śaṅkara's standpoint on renunciation. First of all, what did he say exactly about renunciation? Are his writings too unclear for us to identify a univocal and consistent position? If so, many of his Advaitin interpreters would not have misunderstood him. Simply, they would have brought what each of them saw as the proper solution to problems left unresolved by the founder of their tradition. Or, on the contrary, can we reconstruct Śaṅkara's thinking on this theme in terms of clear enough and consistent interpretations? If so, this would allow us to sort out his real interpretations from those superimposed on him.

As will be shown in this book, Śaṅkara's works contain enough material for such a consistent reconstruction. My basic contention is as follows: while Śaṅkara placed emphasis above all on renunciation of doership (*kartṛtvasaṃnyāsa*) through direct Self-knowledge, and did not consider physical renunciation of rites indispensable both before and after enlightenment, early custodians of his tradition and, later on, modern Indologists, often understood from his works that physical renunciation is necessary for one who aspires to Self-knowledge and liberation.

How could such a deep hermeneutical disorientation on such a fundamental theme take place? How could semantic shifts on the part of interpreters of Śaṅkara occur in a way that looked often legitimate, in other words, in the name of Śaṅkara himself? These are questions whose significance many Indologists have not even glimpsed and which no one has yet tried to answer in a rigorous and exhaustive manner.

This book is the result of a systematic analysis of *all* the semantic data related to the theme of renunciation in Śaṅkara's works and of the respective roles of the various types of renunciation in *all* contexts. We shall focus on the works usually considered by modern scholars to be authentic (Upad, transl., 6): the autonomous treatise entitled *Upadeśasāhasrī*, the commentaries on the *Brahmasūtra*, the *Bhagavadgītā*, and those on the *Aitareya, Bṛhadāraṇyaka, Chāndogya, Īśā, Kaṭha, Kena, Māṇḍūkya* (with the *Kārikā*), *Muṇḍaka, Praśna*, and *Taittirīya Upaniṣads*.[10] It must be noted, however, that the authenticity of these works is also not completely beyond doubt. So there always remains the possibility of reaching certain conclusions on Śaṅkara's viewpoint regarding renunciation on the basis of unauthentic works. But we must start with the present level of our knowledge. We will first study the above works as if they were all really authored by Śaṅkara. When needed, due consideration will be given to the possibility that discrepancies are due to false ascription of a work to Śaṅkara.

We do not intend to tackle the even more complex problem of the validity of Śaṅkara's interpretation in relation to the texts he commented upon. Our aim is to clarify what Śaṅkara said on the subject of renunciation, whatever its validity. Only after carrying out a complete *intratextual* analysis of this theme in his works, will a proper assessment of Śaṅkara's interpretation be possible.

The misunderstanding regarding Śaṅkara's teaching on renunciation could be due to his own terminology. Most of the key words he uses in the context of renunciation are polysemous and can designate either a means to reach direct Self-knowledge, or a natural characteristic attached to that knowledge. In his BhG 2.55,[11] Śaṅkara notes that this situation is found in the Vedāntic texts:

> Everywhere indeed in the science of the supreme Self, the characteristics of the man who has achieved the goal are taught also as means, because [the latter] have to be cultivated through effort. The Lord now specifies these means which are to be cultivated through effort and which [later on] become characteristics (BhG 2.55, 114–115).

Polysemy should be distinguished from ambiguity proper, as the latter may entail a defect, that is, the author's failure to check polysemy even when he intends a single specific meaning. While a polysemous word may be more liable to create ambiguity due to its potential reference to at least two meanings, it is not necessarily ambiguous, since a proper evaluation of the context may show without doubt that only one of the possible meanings is proper in that specific case. Whether Śaṅkara's terminology was polysemous, ambiguous or inconsistent is still to be assessed.

Śaṅkara's basic hermeneutical postulate is that the sacred texts commented on by him are possessed of both internal and intertextual consistency. For him, the goal of exegesis is to bring to light the knowledge expressed by these texts in the context of this concordance (*samanvaya*). Therefore, we must identify and be always aware of Śaṅkara's own perspective on how the various scriptural statements on renunciation can be harmonized. We must first verify to what extent Śaṅkara's statements on renunciation can be consistent within the framework of his self-understanding.

Scholars such as Tilmann Vetter have tried to solve inconsistencies in Śaṅkara's works by positing a historical development in his thinking and therefore a change in opinion regarding various topics. But in the course of this analysis there was never enough evidence to bring forward the hypothesis that a change in Śaṅkara's opinion during his lifetime may have led to polysemous, ambiguous, or inconsistent statements on renunciation. On the contrary, with respect to this theme, one meets with the same kind of semantic phenomena throughout the thirteen works listed above as authentic. This comes in support of Wilhelm Halbfass's critique of Vetter's hypothesis that chronological development of Śaṅkara's thought is responsible for significant changes and inconsistencies in his treatment of the methods of liberation (Halbfass 1991, 139–143).[12] Although the possibility of a chronological development is theoretically plausible, evidence for it is lacking notably with respect to renunciation.

Having set out the controversy, let us now further clarify the methodological basis of this analysis by defining the basic types of renunciation in *Advaita Vedānta*, by identifying reference points for a consistent interpretation within Śaṅkara's paradigm, and by presenting a critique of two major arguments usually given within the *Advaita* tradition to explain apparent inconsistencies regarding renunciation in Śaṅkara's works.

CHAPTER TWO

The Basic Types of Renunciation in *Advaita Vedānta*

As a first step towards a systematic study of renunciation in Śaṅkara's works, we must establish a proper typology of renunciation. The main intent of the typology proposed here is to establish a clear, univocal, and consistent working terminology which agrees with the doctrine of *Advaita Vedānta*.

The types of renunciation will be determined on the basis of the *object* being abandoned by the renunciant. Four basic kinds of renunciation can be identified within the framework of *Advaita Vedānta*: physical renunciation—where the object consists of rites and other visible activities or material things; renunciation of the rewards of action—the object being, in this instance, the results of action; meditative renunciation—where the object is either a wrong notion about the Self or a layer of mental activity; and finally renunciation of doership—where the object consists of the sense of being the doer of mental and physical actions.

Although physical renunciation should normally involve some mental abandonment of worldly pursuits, it is more typically associated with the observable, physical cessation of at least some kinds of activities and/or the abandonment of material possessions. The term "renunciation of actions" (*karmasaṃnyāsa*) is commonly used to refer to this type of renunciation. Here the word "actions" means not only rites, but everything that is prescribed by the scriptures for those who pursue a socially active life, usually centered around family ties and obligations. Thus, in "renunciation of actions," the notion of action includes all of the individual's *dharma* or duty prescribed, according to caste (*varṇa*), for the first three modes of living (*āśrama*), that is, for the state of a student (*brahmacarya*), the state of a householder (*gārhastya*) and the state of a forest-dweller (*vānaprastha*). In the case of a householder of the *Kṣatriya* caste, for instance, the duty could include fighting a war to protect his people in addition to performing the daily obligatory sacrificial rites.

Olivelle points out that, in the Upaniṣadic period, physical renunciation was defined as homeless wandering and mendicancy, whereas later on, it became characterized first of all by the abandonment of ritualistic activity and the rite of initiation into formal renunciation (1981, 268). This renunciation consists mainly of the abandonment of all accessories of the ritual, such as the sacrificial thread and the sacrificial ustensils. It allows entry into the fourth, monastic mode of living (*saṃnyāsāśrama*). Thus, somewhat technical definitions of renunciation are found in classical writers, for instance, in the later *Advaitin* Vāsudeva: "Renunciation is the abandonment of rites known through injunctions—the *śrauta* and *smārta*, the permanent, occasional, and optional—after reciting the *praiṣa* ritual formula" (Olivelle 1976–1977, 2:2).

On the other hand, in the fourteenth century, Vidyāraṇya makes a clear distinction between a formal and an informal physical renunciation, the latter having no connection with the monastic mode of living (Vidyāraṇya 1919, 3.5.37–38, 698). Thus, physical renunciation can be either formal—when it includes the rite of initiation into the monastic mode of living—or informal—when it simply leads to wandering mendicancy and is not connected with a monastic initiation and a specific way of living.[1]

Generally speaking, physical renunciation is therefore, in the case of a householder, the physical abandonment of possessions and/or cessation of rites and duties prescribed for him; in the case of a student (*brahmacārin*), it is non-adoption of rites, duties, and possessions pertaining to the householder's stage, their renunciation leading in both cases to the life of a formal or informal renunciant (*saṃnyāsin*).[2]

Renunciation of the rewards, meditative renunciation, and renunciation of doership—the three other types of renunciation—typically involve mental rather than physical relinquishing. Renunciation of the rewards of actions is commonly known as the basic feature of the yoga of action (*karmayoga*). As stated by *Bhagavadgītā* 6.1, the *karmayogin* is "he who performs the prescribed actions without leaning to their reward" (BhG 6.1, 282). Among the various types of rites taught by scriptures,[3] the *Gītā* recommends only the obligatory regular and occasional rites (*nitya* and *naimittika karmans*) without attachment to them and to their result, an attitude which is intended to purify the mind: "O Arjuna, renunciation is considered pure when, having abandoned attachment as well as the reward, one does the obligatory action merely because it ought to be done" (BhG 18.9, 684). Other passages of the *Gītā* suggest that non-attachment applies to the rewards of one's *dharma* as a whole. After describing the social function of each *varṇa*—Brahmin, *Kṣatriya, Vaiśya* and *Śūdra*—Kṛṣṇa declares that one attains perfection by being devoted to the duty prescribed for one's *varṇa* (BhG 18.41–45). In his comment on verse 45, Śaṅkara mentions that the mere performance of one's duty leads to results such as heaven (*svarga*); but doing this duty without minding such rewards prepares the mind and body for steadfastness in Self-knowledge (*jñānaniṣṭhā*). Thus, in the same way as physical renunciation applies to all rites previously carried on according to scriptural injunctions, renunciation of the rewards of actions concerns the results of all undertakings which are part of one's *dharma*.[4]

Both the *Gītā* and Śaṅkara also describe renunciation of the rewards as the offering of *all* actions and results to the Lord, Īśvara, whether they are prescribed or not by scriptures. In *Gītā* 9.27, Kṛṣṇa advises Arjuna as follows: "Whatever you do, whatever you eat, whatever you offer in sacrifice, whatever you give, whatever austerity you practice, O son of Kuntī, do that as an offering to Me" (BhG 9.27, 435). Śaṅkara specifies here that "whatever you do" refers to actions done "of your own accord" (*svataḥ*), that is, not prescribed by scriptures. He also comments as follows about the unenlightened *karmayogin*: *"He who does all actions, having resigned them to Brahman,* deposited them in Īśvara, with the thought that he does them for His sake, as a servant does for his master, *having given up attachment* for the reward—even for liberation—*he is not soiled,* not bound, *by evil, like a lotus-leaf by water*" (BhG 5.10, 255-256).[5] The attitude of the *karmayogin* must be: "I perform action for the sake of the Lord alone, not for my benefit" (BhG 5.11, 256). Even the intent of pleasing the Lord must be discarded (BhG 2.48, 108). It follows that, in Śaṅkara's eyes, the yoga of action (*karmayoga*) is at the same time a yoga of devotion (*bhaktiyoga*), the latter being defined as "the worship of the Lord through one's action" (BhG 18.56, 744).[6]

Thus, renunciation of the rewards of action implies the absence of a motive of self-interest. Since the absence of a selfish motive will leave room in the active psyche for another, more detached, affective and cognitive relationship towards one's mental and physical actions, this type of renunciation is typically related to the emotional and mental structure of the individual self and can be called an attitude. But being unconcerned for the results of one's actions on oneself does not necessarily mean that one is free from all the boundaries of activity, free from the sense of being an ego (*ahaṃkāra*) and a doer (*kartṛ*) limited by time, space, and contingencies.

In fact, as we shall see, this freedom is rather typical of renunciation of doership.

Meditative renunciation—the third type proposed here—brings us to an even deeper form of mental relinquishing. The process of enlightenment can be summarized as the correction of all misapprehensions about one's Self. This correction obviously involves the abandonment of incorrect apprehensions, that is, of any knowledge of the Self which does not hold the Self to be pure non-dual consciousness free from action and its results. Here giving up can apply to intuitive as well as to rational apprehensions. At the rational level, meditative renunciation can be defined as the abandonment of an understanding of the Self which, after due reflection, turns out to be a wrong notion. At the intuitive level, it can be defined as the abandonment of a level of mental activity (*vṛtti*) in favor of a more subtle level. In this second dimension, meditative renunciation gradually withdraws the attention from the gross to the finest level of mental activity, allowing the meditator to reach previously unconscious levels of the mind and to experience the whole range of his or her individual self. Ultimately, according to *Advaita Vedānta*, when applied at the intuitive level, meditative renunciation allows one to discard the impression that one's individual self is merely subject to fluctuations of ordinary pleasure and pain, and opens individual awareness to its own deepest layer of existence which is made of bliss (*ānandamayakośa*). But this does not correct the fundamental intuitive misapprehension according to which the Self is an ego bound by mental and physical limitations, whatever their degree of felicity.

The fundamental intuitive misapprehension of the Self as bound by form and activity can be discarded, that is, corrected, only through the intuitive apprehension of the Self as absolutely unlimited. In other words, only intuitive knowledge of the Self as it really is, namely, infinite and free from all the boundaries of action, can discard ignorance (*avidyā*) concerning the true nature of the Self, and all erroneous superimpositions made on it. The most fundamental superimpositions on the Self are the sense of ego and doership. Since doership shares the notion of activity with the objects of the first three types of renunciation, it seems appropriate, for our purposes, to refer to the correction of the most basic intuitive misapprehension of the Self as renunciation of doership rather than renunciation of the sense of ego. But abandonment of doership and of the sense of ego are both typical results of direct knowledge of the Self as infinite and actionless.

Renunciation of doership is different from meditative renunciation in that it gives up even the mental action of giving up. When, for instance, the meditator abandons the finest level of mental activity and attains the absorption devoid of any mental constructs (*asaṃprajñātasamādhi*), he is neither a meditator, nor a doer of the action of renouncing mental activity: he has become himself a non-doer. His giving up of all activity and sense of doership corresponds to the absence of action (*karmābhāva*) and of doership (*kartṛtvābhāva*) and not to the practice or the movement of their abandonment. Similarly, when the liberated-in-life is said to have renounced doership, it means that he is permanently devoid of the sense of being a doer and naturally experiences his Self as the infinite, actionless and free witness (*sākṣin*) of all mental and bodily activities.

Since, according to our definition, renunciation of doership is not an *action* of renunciation, it cannot be practiced. Practice for the sake of abandoning doership can never be abandonment of doership as such. Exertion aiming at abandonment of doership falls under the category of other types of renunciation. And when renunciation of doership is presented as already acquired by a Self-knower, his Self-knowledge must be direct in nature and his renunciation is equivalent to absence of doership.

Secondary literature sometimes confuses renunciation of the rewards of actions with renunciation of doership. Śaṅkara certainly makes a clear distinction between them. He writes, for instance, in his BhG 12.12, that the abandonment of rewards presented as a means to immortality in verse 12.11, at the end of a hierarchical list, is addressed to the unenlightened man who cannot resort to the preceding higher means: "Renunciation of the rewards of all actions is not recommended first as the means of the supreme good, but [only] when the unenlightened man engaged in action is not capable of taking up the means taught previously" (BhG 12.12, 510). Then, to substantiate the idea that the fruition of renunciation of rewards into immortality applies to the enlightened man alone, Śaṅkara quotes *Kaṭha Upaniṣad* 2.3.14: "When all desires clinging to one's heart fall off, then the mortal becomes immortal; he attains *Brahman* in this very life" (KaU 2.3.14, 123). And his actual comment on this verse of the *Upaniṣad* reads:

> *When*, at the time when, *all desires* of the one who thus perceives the supreme Reality *fall off*, are dissolved, because of the absence of anything else to be desired . . . *then*, he who was *mortal* before enlightenment, *becomes immortal* after enlightenment, by virtue of the elimination of death characterized by ignorance, desire and action (Ibid.).

Thus, Śaṅkara clearly differentiates between renunciation of the desire for rewards, which is based on the Self-knowledge of the enlightened person, and that which is performed by the unenlightened. In the case of the enlightened, renunciation of desire is simultaneous with the complete giving up of spiritual ignorance and, consequently, of doership. Śaṅkara suggests elsewhere that, in fact, it is the abandonment of doership that finally ensures full renunciation of the rewards: "...I am not a doer, [hence] I have no longing for the reward of action..."[7]

From a practical viewpoint, however, on the path to liberation, renunciation of the rewards of action becomes progressively inseparable from that of doership. The value of the object of abandonment gradually shifts from the motive of self-interest to *all* motives or desires; that is, to the total de-identification from even the act of desiring itself, whatever its content. Selfish desires tend to be the characteristic objects of renunciation of rewards. On the other hand, in as much as all desires taken together constitute forms of mental activity to which one gets attached as a doer and experiencer, they can be said to represent the specific sphere of renunciation of doership. And, since one continues to identify with the limitations of the individual self when carrying out renunciation of rewards, it follows that renunciation of doership alone can deliver from bondage.

The ultimate criterion by which to ascertain that one has indeed abandoned all selfish motives is renunciation of the sense of doership. In renunciation of doership, one experiences the Self as the silent blissful witness of all activities and desires of the mind. The body and the individual self cannot be subject to selfish motives since they are guided by Nature (*prakṛti*) alone. In this state, Nature works out its cosmic beneficial motives within its active field (*kṣetra*), unobstructed by identification of consciousness with an ego.

The following chart (Table 2.1) summarizes the types of renunciation we just defined on the basis of the object and nature of the abandonment.

TABLE 2.1
Major Types of Renunciation

Type of Renunciation	Object of Renunciation	Nature of Renunciation
Physical renunciation	A prescribed action or a possession	Physical, whether formal or informal
Renunciation of the rewards of action	Rewards of action (particular selfish desires)	Mental (renunciation in attitude)
Meditative renunciation	A wrong notion about the Self or a layer of mental activity	Mental
Renunciation of doership (equivalent to absence of action, i.e. *karmābhāva*)	Doership of action, i.e. *kartṛtva* (all desires, selfish and unselfishness)	Based on direct Self-knowledge (renunciation in Self)

CHAPTER THREE

Five Reference Points for Proper Interpretation

In order to contextualize Śaṅkara's position on renunciation from his own perspective, it will be first useful to outline his doctrinal statements which are both basic to this topic and as much as possible free from ambiguity. Five points seem to correspond to this requirement. To our knowledge, three of them have been unanimously and duly attributed to Śaṅkara: the notion that immediate Self-knowedge is the only direct means of liberation, the interpretation that Brahmins alone are qualified for physical renunciation, and the idea that the enlightened person is beyond the scope of scriptural injunctions. These correspond to points one, four and five in the following discussion. The two other points are: the understanding that Self-knowledge is accessible, irrespective of modes of living; and the recognition that liberation is possible while not being a physical renunciant. As mentioned in our introduction, opinions contrary to these have been expressed at least by Candraśekhara Bhāratī of *Śṛṅgerī Maṭha*. But we contend that these two points can be shown quite clearly to be part of Śaṅkara's basic outlook. They correspond to items two and three in the following discussion.

IMMEDIATE SELF-KNOWLEDGE IS THE ONLY DIRECT MEANS OF LIBERATION

The nature, role, and relationship of action and knowledge as means of liberation is dealt with by Śaṅkara mainly in terms of whether action and Self-knowledge have to be combined or whether only one of them can lead to liberation, and if so, which of the two. A great deal of Śaṅkara's hermeneutical skill was used to contradict the views that the direct means of liberation consists of obligatory rites alone, or of their combination with Self-knowledge.

The theme of liberation was not even considered by early authors from the hermeneutical and ritualistic school of *Pūrvamīmāṃsā* such as Jaimini, Śabara, and Prabhākara. It was developed later on, by the followers of Prabhākara and by Kumārila.[1] Thus, some commentators of *Pūrvamīmāṃsā* held that obligatory rites alone lead to liberation. On the other hand, some *Vedāntins* of Śaṅkara's time (or of a somewhat earlier period), such as Brahmadatta, Maṇḍana Miśra, and Bhartṛprapañca advocated a combination of Self-knowledge and obligatory rites (*jñānakarmasamuccaya*).[2] Let us briefly review their standpoints and summarize Śaṅkara's argument against them.

According to *Pūrvamīmāṃsā*, the Self (*ātman*) is distinct from the body, the sense organs, and the mind. The Self is that which proceeds to a different world, such as heaven (*svarga*), when the body ceases to function at the time of death. The Self is eternal and omnipresent. But it is also an agent or doer (*kartṛ*) and an experiencer (*bhoktṛ*): it performs actions and experiences external as well as internal objects (such as pleasure and pain) through contact with the mind, the sense organs, and the body.[3]

Kumārila and followers of Prabhākara hold that liberation from transmigratory existence comes at the time of death only when merits and demerits resulting from actions, which are the cause of further embodiment, all become exhausted by the mere process of having been experienced by their doer on account of the law of *karman*.[4] Proscribed actions and desire-prompted rites—which lead only to limited goals in this world or hereafter—are understood to be the cause of bad and good births respectively, while obligatory rites, prescribed for a general well-being and according to modes of living, have no positive result and simply allow to avoid the sin of not doing something enjoined by the scriptures. Are the obligatory rites not supposed to result in purification? Not according to these thinkers. Because if purification were considered a merit resulting from action, it would never cease to be produced by the sustained practice of these ritual actions; accordingly, it could never cease to be experienced and could never bring cessation of further births meant to ensure the perpetual reaping of this purification. Thus liberation would not be possible, which contradicts the scriptures. So, by avoiding the prohibited and desire-prompted actions, and by doing the obligatory ones merely because the scriptures prescribe them, the seeker-after-liberation will be liberated from further births simply when all the effects of his past actions will have been experienced and therefore exhausted. Thus, liberation results from automatic cessation, and mere absence of, further subjection to experiencing the results of action. Contrary to Śaṅkara, *Pūrvamīmāṃsā* holds that knowledge of the Self taught by the scriptures cannot cancel the results of past actions. In fact, Self-knowledge has no independent result of its own, because it stands in a subordinate relation to ritual action. It can only inform the individual about the everlasting nature of his Self and thus motivate him to do the actions prescribed to him for rewards such as heaven after the death of the body.

Vedāntins such as Bhartṛprapañca and Maṇḍana Miśra held that Self-knowledge in the form of meditation—referred to as *prasaṃkhyāna* and other terms—is also necessary for liberation and should be combined with obligatory rites. According to them, the cognition which arises from hearing the Upaniṣadic statements such as, "Thou art That" is as mediate and relational as any other verbal knowledge. By itself, it can never give the direct, nonverbal, intuition—i.e. experience—of *Brahman*. Only meditation on that verbal knowledge can transform it into an intuition. Even if, for some of the advocates of this doctrine, liberation can be attained in this very life, Self-knowledge is always subject to be forgotten due to the operation of karmic residues of past actions. Therefore, even the liberated-in-life has to pursue the practice of meditation and rites that are the means to render karmic residues inoperative. One always remains under the jurisdiction of Vedic injunctions and should never abandon the combined practice of rituals and meditation.

On the contrary, for Śaṅkara, direct knowledge of the Self as taught by the *Upaniṣads* is the sole cause of liberation. The Self or *ātman* is identical with *Brahman*, the non-dual pure consciousness which forms the source and the substratum of the universe, which is without boundaries and attributes, and therefore devoid of any modification whether due to doership (*kartṛtva*) or experiencing (*bhoktṛtva*). When mind and body have been completely purified, *Brahman-Ātman* can be known once and for all by direct intuition through the scriptural statements conveying the non-dual nature of the Self. Ignorance about the Self is then immediately and completely annihilated. So is, as a consequence, the superimposition on the Self of all limiting adjuncts (*upādhis*) such as doership and experiencing. As *Brahman-Ātman* manifests its unsurpassable bliss in the mind, all attachment to anything else, which is the seed of further births, is "burnt" and rendered inoperative.

To know by direct experience that the Self or *ātman* is identical with *Brahman*, the mind requires no action, according to Śaṅkara. The intuitive knowledge of the Self is distinct from the action of meditation, which involves the deliberate activity of reproducing the thought of the object meditated upon. Intuitive Self-knowledge is of the nature of any knowledge, that is, dependent on the object (*vastutantra*), whereas meditative activity is dependent on man's will and action (*puruṣatantra*). As Śaṅkara explains in his BS, "even though meditation, *i.e.*, pondering over, is mental, yet because it is dependent on man, it can be done, not done, or done in different ways by him. But knowledge arises from a valid means and this means has for its object the thing as it already is" (BS 1.1.4, 83). In other words, once the proper conditions of knowledge have been created (for instance, opening the eyes in the case of a visual perception), knowledge arises in the form of the object as it already exists, without any scriptural injunction, effort, or action to maintain it. And this also applies to direct Self-knowledge when the requirement of complete purity of mind has been acheived. On the contrary, action is based on will, effort and on the various modalities through which it can be accomplished. Thus, Śaṅkara's theory of knowledge justifies the notion that immediate knowledge of the Self is independent of action.

Not only is Self-knowledge distinct and independent of action (whether mental or physical) in terms of its cognitive nature, but also in terms of its role in leading to liberation. The independence of Self-knowledge in bringing about liberation is often justified by Śaṅkara on the basis of his interpretation of the Self as nonactive. Direct knowledge of the Self as nonactive is said to be the sole means of liberation because action, more precisely, the experience of the Self as a performer of actions, cannot coexist with experience of the Self as inactive at the same time in the same person. In other words, a man cannot at the same time attribute to himself both the sense of doership, and absence of doership. Since immediate Self-knowledge is apprehension of oneself as devoid of doership and mental fluctuations superimposed on the Self due to ignorance, it cannot possibly exist at the same time with apprehension of oneself as doer and experiencer (TU 1.9.4, transl., 277). Śaṅkara illustrates his position with the following allegory: "For when the knowledge that fire is hot and luminous has arisen in a person, there cannot arise in that same person the false cognition that fire is cold or not luminous" (ĪU 18, 15). Inasmuch as rites and other actions presuppose that one attributes to oneself notions pertaining to duality, such as doership, means and reward, they cannot be said to coexist in the same person and at the same time with direct knowledge of the Self as devoid of any limiting adjuncts and duality. Therefore, according to Śaṅkara, even before considering what the *Upaniṣads* say on the results of direct Self-knowledge and action (either ritualistic or meditative), the combination of direct Self-knowledge and action for the sake of liberation is simply not possible from a logical viewpoint based on the Upaniṣadic descriptions of the Self.

Given his standpoint on knowledge, action, and the true nature of Self, Śaṅkara develops his doctrine of liberation according to a purely functional principle: one can reach a goal only through its proper means. Scriptures prescribe various means for many goals other than liberation. Verse 1.5.16 of the BṛU reads for instance: "There are indeed three worlds, the world of men, the world of manes and the world of gods. The world of men is to be won only through a son, and by no other action; the world of manes, through rites; and the world of gods, through meditation" (BṛU, 130). These three worlds are said to be opposed to liberation for example in verse 4.4.11 of the same *Upaniṣad*: "Miserable are the worlds enveloped by a blinding darkness. To them, after death, go the people who are unenlightened and unwise" (BṛU, 365). In contrast, referring to the knowers of the Self, verse 4.4.14 declares: "Those who know it become immortal, while others only attain suffering" (BṛU, 366). According to Saṅkara, such statements clearly indicate that while birth of a son, rites and meditation serve as means for the three worlds, they do not free one from ignorance, rebirth, and sorrow to which these worlds are said to amount. Self-knowledge alone is given as the means of liberation from the cycle of death and rebirth. Various kinds of prescribed actions, on the one hand, and direct Self-knowledge, on the other, are described as two distinct means leading respectively to the two distinct results of temporary sojourn in some heavenly world, and liberation from limitation, rebirth and sorrow. Therefore, Śaṅkara holds there is no reason to advocate their combination.

But on what account does Śaṅkara say that direct knowledge of the Self does not need any help to result in liberation? According to him, on the path to spiritual freedom, the mind must be purified through rituals, proper understanding of the scriptural means of knowledge (*śabdapramāṇa*) concerning the Self, and various forms of meditation. Once complete purity has been attained, the mind fully understands—verbally and experientially—the purport of the scriptures on the Self. The mind becomes spontaneously and fully open to the immutable Self, to the self-effulgent pure consciousness, of which it is but a semblance of modification. This rediscovery of the mind's real nature is called the "emergence of knowledge" (*jñānotpatti*). As a spontaneous and immediate result of this emergence comes the destruction of ignorance (*avidyānivṛtti*) of the real nature of one's Self. And with annihilation of ignorance also immediately ensues the eradication of its effect, that is, the erroneous superimposition on the Self of limiting adjuncts such as doership and experiencing. Then the whole apparent multiplicity of doer, means and rewards are seen as modes of the *Brahman-Ātman*, leaving no room for something other than the infinity of the Self, and for something that would have to be achieved through action.[5] Therefore, once direct Self-knowledge has been established, it leads spontaneously to liberation, without the need of any other means.

Śaṅkara's theory of qualification for, and prescription of, rites also comes in support of the independence of knowledge as a means to liberation. Awareness of the multiplicity of doership, means and rewards is the basis of qualification for rituals and meditation, as well as the condition for the relevance of a scriptural prescription with respect to a particular person. Indeed, to be applicable, the theory and praxis of these prescriptions need the knowledge of oneself as a doer, the recognition of an object of desire to be enjoyed by the doer and an action prescribed to the doer in order to obtain the object of his desire. Now, for Śaṅkara, doership, desire, and active enjoyment do not apply to the enlightened man whose intellect rather identifies with the actionless, desireless, and silently witnessing Self. Therefore, any action prescribed for enjoying whatever object of desire is no longer relevant in his case. By annulling the erroneous awareness of the Self as active and limited through knowledge of the silent, infinite *Brahman-Ātman*, there is no more room for any prescription of actions and for any obligation to observe it. Therefore, action is not needed along with Self-knowledge for the purpose of liberation.

Moreover, according to Śaṅkara, the state of liberation is such that action has no role in maintaining it. Through the absolute contentment found in one's own Self, the mental residues of past actions (*sañcitakarmans*) fail to create further desires for objects. While residues of past actions that have already begun to fructify in the present life (*prārabdhakarmans*) continue until exhaustion, the actions performed for the rest of the present life (*kriyamāṇakarmans*) by the liberated-in-life have no more binding power, since doership and experiencing are no longer attributed to the Self and since nothing is seen as different from the ever-free *Brahman-Ātman*. Hence comes also, immediately after the destruction of ignorance, the state of simply remaining established in Self-knowledge, which is identical with liberation from all limitations in this life as well as after the death of the body. And once complete purification of the mind, emergence of Self-knowledge and annihilation of ignorance have been ensured, remaining established in the Self needs no practice or effort. Indeed, explains Śaṅkara, because liberation is of the very nature of the Self "like the heat of fire . . . it cannot be said to be a consequence of human activity" (BṛU 4.4.6, 358). Thus, in terms of post-enlightenment also, action cannot be a means of liberation.

Śaṅkara summarizes his position in the following lines:

> The emergence of knowledge cannot be imagined for a person hindered by accumulated sins. On the wearing away of those hindrances, knowledge will emerge; from that will follow the cessation of ignorance, and from that, the complete cessation of unending becoming (*saṃsāra*).
>
> Moreover, a man who perceives [something as] non-Self desires that non-Self. And the man of desire performs actions. From that follows unending becoming—which consists of appropriating things such as the body—for the sake of enjoying the rewards of these [actions]. On the contrary, by reason of the absence of any object, there can be no desire in a man who perceives the unity of the Self. And since, given the absence of any "other," there can be no desire for oneself, there ensues liberation which is remaining in one's own Self . . .[6]

Insofar as ignorance of the Self has to be removed for liberation to occur, and insofar as Self-knowledge alone can remove such ignorance, that knowledge is a completely independent means to liberation. Once Self-knowledge has emerged, no other causal factor enters into play to remove ignorance and to ensure liberation:

> The [Self's] real nature being forever attained, it is simply ignorance that obstructs it. The non-perception of a mother-of-pearl which, though being cognized through its real nature, appears on the contrary as silver by way of misapprehension, just amounts to obstruction by misapprehension. So also, its [subsequent] perception just amounts to knowledge, because the purpose of knowledge is in removing the obstruction produced by misapprehension. Similarly, here also the non-attainment of the Self is simply obstruction produced by ignorance. Therefore it is reasonable that the attainment [of the Self] be simply the removal of that [ignorance] by knowledge, and nothing else whatsoever.[7]

As light alone can remove darkness, so also knowledge alone can remove ignorance. Thus, it is insofar as action belongs to the sphere of ignorance, that it is said to be a means contradictory to direct Self-knowledge.

Moreover, from Śaṅkara's viewpoint, the analysis of the effects of action shows that, by itself, action cannot bring about direct knowledge of the *Brahman-Ātman*. The four possible effects of any action are: creation (*utpatti*), transformation (*vikāra*), acquisition (*āpti*) and purification (*saṃskāra*). First, knowledge of the Self cannot be *produced*: being consciousness itself, it preexists any effect of action, unlike, for instance, attainment of heaven which comes into existence only as a result of appropriate sacrifices.[8] If Self-knowledge and liberation could be produced, they would then be as impermanent as all products found in the world. But both are said by the *Upaniṣads* to be eternal. Second, if liberation were a transformation of something, it would also have the defect of impermanence. Third, *Brahman-Ātman* cannot be acquired or attained, for it is all pervasive, ever-attained by everyone (although erroneously apprehended in the condition of ignorance). Finally, since purification amounts to addition or removal of some quality, it cannot apply to *Brahman-Ātman*, which is ever the same, ever pure, neither improvable nor damageable.[9]

Let us summarize Śaṅkara's doctrine on the relationship between Self-knowledge and action by identifying the main possible cases of combination between them. Let us first consider the possibility of combination in the light of Śaṅkara's position on the nature of action and Self-knowledge, without even considering the usefulness of the combination as a means of liberation. Simply from a logical viewpoint, based on the characteristics of action and *immediate* Self-knowledge, these cannot be combined, because awareness of the Self as active cannot even coexist in the same person and at the same time with awareness of the Self as a silent witness of all actions. But there is no logical inconsistency in the combination of action and *mediate* Self-knowledge—rites and the discipline of knowledge, for instance—because both belong to the realm of activity, whether physical or mental. Śaṅkara's exact position on the latter type of combination is to be further examined in his commentaries. Now considering the possibility of their combination as a means of liberation, action and *immediate* Self-knowledge cannot unite for the same reason that they cannot coexist. Neither can action and *mediate* Self-knowledge succeed in bringing about liberation, since they both pertain to activity and, consequently, cannot eradicate the superimposition of activity on the Self.

A major hermeneutical consequence follows from these considerations: when Śaṅkara states that a given knowledge leads to liberation, the said knowledge must include a direct intuition of the Self. It must be immediate in nature, as opposed to a Self-knowledge which would be only mediate—being merely rational or meditative—and which can never be said to lead to liberation by itself.

In the light of this, the question of whether physical renunciation is necessary or not, pertains to the domain of indirect means of liberation.

Some of these indirect means, such as discernment between the eternal and the ephemeral realities (*nityānityavastuviveka*), disinterest for enjoyment of the rewards [of rites and duties] in this life and hereafter (*ihāmutrārthaphalabhogavirāga*), and the desire for liberation (*mumukṣutva*), can be said to be logically necessary, since direct Self-knowledge and liberation are impossible to imagine without them. The main issue before us is therefore: according to Śaṅkara, is physical renunciation a necessary indirect means for liberation? This question cannot be properly answered without adding a few other basic reference points to our critical apparatus.

SELF-KNOWLEDGE IS ACCESSIBLE IRRESPECTIVE OF MODES OF LIVING

Prescriptions given in the scriptures are always directed toward an addressee. The addressee is determined in terms of the concept of *adhikāra*—a word which has many shades of meanings.[10] For our immediate purposes, let us define *adhikāra* in a way similar to Laugākṣi Bhāskara in his *Arthasaṅgraha*,[11] that is, as the qualification(s) required of a person for the right to engage in a practice prescribed by the scriptures, and to get its reward(s). In this sense, *adhikāra* may be translated as "eligibility," "competence," "entitlement," or "qualification."

The means of Self-knowledge are found mainly in the discipline of knowledge, that is, hearing (*śravaṇa*) the scriptural passages concerning *Brahman-Ātman*, the individual self and its liberation; discursive reflection (*manana*) on the meaning of these passages; and repeated meditation on them (*nididhyāsana*) to transform the concept of *Brahman-Ātman* into a direct experience. In BS 3.4.36, a doubt is raised as to whether widowers,[12] women, *Śūdras* and others who are not qualified for Vedic rites, are nevertheless qualified for Self-knowledge and for the discipline of knowledge. Commenting on this aphorism and the following one, Śaṅkara answers that people unqualified for rites may be qualified for Self-knowledge, because various scriptures talk about people who were *not* qualified for Vedic rites but did obtain Self-knowledge and liberation, such as Raikva (a widower),[13] Vācaknavī (a woman), Gārgī (a woman) and Saṃvarta (an ascetic who roamed about naked). In aphorism 38, he concludes as follows: "And knowledge—which has a perceptible result—allows anyone who desires it to be qualified for hearing and so forth, by reason of mere absence of prohibition. Therefore nothing stands in the way of the qualification of widowers and others."[14] Two aspects need clarification here: the fact that knowledge is said to have a perceptible result (eradication of ignorance and liberation therefrom) and the "mere absence of prohibition." Having "a perceptible result" seems to define fruition of immediate Self-knowledge into annulment of ignorance and into the ensuing liberation, as wholly different from fruition of rites into results, which are out of immediate perception such as attainment of heaven after death. Since the result of rites is quite different from the result of Self-knowledge, lack of qualification for receiving the result of action does not imply failure to obtain the result of knowledge. Śaṅkara then states that anyone who wishes to obtain the result of knowledge is qualified for the discipline of knowledge and its result. Only a scriptural prohibition could restrict such a universal qualification. But there is none as noted by Śaṅkara.

In accordance with aphorism 3.4.39, Śaṅkara then states that, in comparison to being outside a mode of living (*āśrama*), as is the case of widowers and the like, belonging to one gives qualification for the practice of rites and is "better" (*jyāyas*) in that it provides a more complete means for the emergence of Self-knowledge. Thus, in this non-monastic context, Śaṅkara agrees with the aphorism on the idea of combining the discipline of knowledge with rites. If this is true of people outside a mode of living, it goes without saying that householders also are qualified for the discipline of knowledge and that their continued practice of rites and duties does not exclude them from hearing, reflection, and meditation through the Upaniṣadic knowledge. In his BS 4.1.18, Śaṅkara also states that remote and proximate means can work together to bring about Self-knowledge. According to him, "regular obligatory rites such as the *agnihotra* become the cause of the attainment of *Brahman*, provided [they are accompanied by] proximate means such as hearing, reflection, faith, dedication; [thus] they contribute to the same result as knowledge of *Brahman*."[15] Nothing in the comment on this aphorism indicates that rites have to be abandoned before one starts to use the proximate means, consisting of the discipline of knowledge.

The same viewpoint is clearly expressed in the commentaries on the *Upaniṣads*. Answering a doubt as to whether the statement, "I have realized it myself" (from BṛU 4.4.8) means that only one person ever obtained knowledge of *Brahman*, Śaṅkara replies that it is not so, "because *Śruti* states that it is for the sake of everybody" (BṛU 4.4.8, 923). In the comment on TU 1.12.1, an opponent claims that the rise of immediate Self-knowledge depends on rites and that, as a consequence, scriptures allow only the householder mode of living, precluding the *saṃnyāsa* or monastic mode which has none of these rites. Śaṅkara then recalls that the hermit's (*vānaprastha*) and monk's modes of living are said to include other means which are *also* conducive to Self-knowledge: "Practices (*karmāṇi*) such as the *agnihotra* [ritual] are not the only ones. There are also celibacy, austerity, truthfulness, control of mind, control of senses, noninjury, and similar practices, which are commonly associated with other modes of living, and particularly meditation, sustained attention and the like . . ."[16] Then, answering the objection that liberation comes, not from knowledge, but simply from the mechanical wearing away of accumulated results of actions, Śaṅkara concludes the whole discussion as follows:

> There is surely no such rule that knowledge arises from the mere elimination of obstructions, and not from causes such as the grace of God or the practice of austerity and meditation. Because noninjury, celibacy and the like assist knowledge, and hearing, reflection and meditation are its direct causes. Hereby is established the existence of other modes of living. It is also established that everyone is qualified for knowledge, and that the supreme good is by way of knowledge alone.[17]

Śaṅkara's purpose in this context is to prove that rites are not a unique and necessary prerequisite for arriving at immediate Self-knowledge, and that people in modes of living other than the householder's who do not perform them also have access to that knowledge. The conclusion that "everyone is qualified for knowledge" mainly aims at establishing that people in the *saṃnyāsa* mode of living *also* have access to it through the proximate means of knowledge. Needless to say, the word "everyone" (*sarva*) also qualifies householders still engaged in rites for these proximate means of Self-knowledge.

Although, according to Śaṅkara, whatever one's mode of living and caste, one is qualified for the proximate means, consisting in the discipline of knowledge, some restrictions given by the scriptures bring about the subdivision of the latter into two types. We shall call them the discipline of knowledge based on *Śrauta* scriptures—mainly the *Upaniṣads*—(*śrautajñānayoga*), and that based on *Smārta* scriptures such as the epics and the *Purāṇas* (*smārtajñānayoga*). In his BS 1.1.1, Śaṅkara states that the study of the ritualistic portions of the *Śruti* is not necessary for that of the *Upaniṣads*, "as it is logically possible for one who has studied *Vedānta* to undertake a deliberation on *Brahman* even without deliberation on the religious rites" (transl., 7). There is only a slight indication that, according to Śaṅkara, this may also apply to women, who do not have access to *Śrauta* scriptures connected to rites: he gives as an argument in his introduction to BṛU 2.4, the fact that, as part of the story of this *Upaniṣad*, "the knowledge of *Brahman* as a means to immortality has been imparted to

Maitreyī, who was without the means to perform rites" (transl., 243). But, respecting the scriptural statements that forbid *Śūdras* to study the *Śruti,* Śaṅkara holds in his BS 1.3.38 that *Śūdras* are entitled to a discipline of knowledge[18] based only on epics and *Purāṇas*. This is "because the *Smṛti* declares that the four castes are qualified for the study of the *Itihāsas* and the *Purāṇas*.[19] However, it stands confirmed that a *Śūdra* has no qualification [for knowledge] through the *Vedas*."[20]

On the other hand, a few passages in Śaṅkara's works seem to declare that the discipline of knowledge is available only to Brahmins who have taken up physical renunciation. These statements apparently contradict what we have established so far concerning the universal availability of the discipline of knowledge in its *śrauta* or *smārta* forms. The most categorical statements are found in the *Upadeśasāhasrī*. According to this work, knowledge of *Brahman*

> should be repeatedly related to the pupil until it is firmly grasped, if he is dispassionate toward all things non-eternal which are attained by means [other than knowledge]; if he has abandoned the desire for sons, wealth and worlds and reached the state of a *paramahaṃsa* wandering ascetic . . . if he is a Brahmin . . . (Upad 2.1.2, transl., 211).[21]

As also said in Upad 1.13.27, "the meaning of the *Veda* herein determined, which has been briefly related by me, should be imparted to serene wandering ascetics by one of disciplined intellect" (transl., 134).[22] Finally, in another passage of the same work, the prescription of renunciation is found juxtaposed to—yet not explicitly paired with—the injunction of going and receiving Self-knowledge from a teacher:[23]

> 49. Actions result in things being produced, obtained, changed, or purified. There are no results of action other than these. Therefore one should abandon [actions] together with [their] requisites.
>
> 50. Concentrating upon *Ātman* the love which is [now set] on external things . . . a seeker after the truth should resort to a teacher (Upad 1.17.49-50, transl., 165).[24]

These are the passages from the Upad that could be interpreted as defining physical renunciation in terms of a necessary condition for entering the discipline of knowledge. Even if this interpretation were correct, these passages would be the only ones in all of Śaṅkara's works to present physical renunciation as a necessary prerequisite for Self-knowledge. And our contention is that their status is more ambiguous than contradictory in relation to Śaṅkara's typical viewpoint.

Let us show evidence in support of our contention. Immediately after mentioning the requirement of being a wandering ascetic and a Brahmin in Upad 2.1.2 (quoted above), Śaṅkara substantiates his position with an excerpt from MuU 1.2.12–13. Verse 12 reads: "Having examined the worlds acquired through action, a Brahmin should become indifferent to wordly pleasures. . . . For knowing that [*Brahman*], he should indeed go, with sacrificial faggots in hand,[25] to a master versed in the *Vedas* and steadfast in *Brahman*" (MuU 1.2.12, 139). Śaṅkara specifies in his commentary on this verse that "the word Brahmin is used because he alone is distinctly (*viśeṣataḥ*)[26] qualified for the knowledge of *Brahman* by renouncing everything."[27] In the light of Śaṅkara's various statements cited above on the availability of the discipline of knowledge for all, this comment may simply mean that the kind of discipline of knowledge, which is preceded by physical renunciation, concerns Brahmins alone, a situation which does not forbid other people from resorting to the discipline of knowledge without physical renunciation. Moreover, in the introduction to KeU-P, where Śaṅkara also quotes MuU 1.2.12, the latter's prescription of physical renunciation appears as one possible application of the more general virtue of detachment (*vairāgya*) which could then be understood as the really universal prerequisite intended here for the discipline of knowledge. Śaṅkara first introduces the topic in the following manner: ". . . the desire to know the inner Self arises only in that desireless (*niṣkāma*) man of pure mind who is detached (*virakta*) from all connections with transitory, external means and ends by virtue of the rise of a special kind of mental disposition in this life or in previous ones."[28] Then, after citing KaU 2.1.1, which talks of a discriminative man who turns his attention toward the Self, Śaṅkara quotes MuU 1.2.12. He then specifies his understanding of these two passages: "In this way alone and not otherwise, does a man of detachment acquire the competence to hear, meditate on, and experience the knowledge of the inner Self."[29] Following his citation of MuU 1.2.12, in the rest of his introduction to KeU-P, Śaṅkara seems to waver between the general condition of detachment for everyone and the specific condition of physical renunciation for the Brahmins. But at the end of the introduction, he mentions only the requirement of detachment:

> Therefore the Vedic text beginning with "Willed by whom" describes the desire to know *Brahman*—the inner Self—on the part of a man who is detached from all seen and unseen [rewards] attainable by external means. . . . It can be imagined that finding no refuge except in the domain of the inner Self . . . someone properly approached a master established in *Brahman*, and asked:[30]

As pointed out by Boyd Henry Wilson in his dissertation on Śaṅkara's use of scriptures, when Śaṅkara quotes many passages, "there is seldom any explanation of these multiple citations: the common theme easily discerned from the citations is in itself sufficient explanation" (1982, 177–178). Hence, as suggested by the reference to the "detached man" (quoted above) in the presentation and conclusion of this topic in the introduction to KeU, the common theme here does not seem to be the prerequisite of physical renunciation as stated in MuU 1.2.12, but rather a detachment (*vairāgya*) that does not necessarily entail physical renunciation. In his commentary on BS, Śaṅkara also identifies qualification for receiving Self-knowledge from a teacher, by bringing in and interpreting MuU 1.2.12 in terms of detachment or reversal of attention toward the Self, without reference to physical renunciation: "And after finding fault with the lower knowledge [which concerns the non-Self], it is shown that one is qualified for the higher knowledge when one has no attachment for that [lower one]" (BS 1.2.21, 190).

This manner of interpreting the value given by Śaṅkara to the prerequisite of being a Brahmin and a formal renunciant for access to the discipline of knowledge can be substantiated by his comment on ChU 5.11.7. There, householders rather than *saṃnyāsins* are said to duly approach the teacher—himself a king rather than a *saṃnyāsin*. These householders are identified as Brahmins by both the ChU (in 5.11.1) and Śaṅkara. The commentator seems thereby to contradict the requirement of Upad 2.1.2, as much because the king has already gained Self-knowledge without satisfying the criterion of being a Brahmin, as because the Brahmins receiving knowledge from him are not formal renunciants. Yet Śaṅkara's comment on verse 5.2.7 reads:

> Therefore, although they were great householders, deeply versed in the *Vedas*, and Brahmins, they abandoned their pride of being great householders etc., and, desiring knowledge, they approached the king, who was lower in caste, according to the rules, faggots in hand. Other seekers after knowledge should behave in the same manner. And he imparted the knowledge *even without initiating them*, even without doing the initiation. The meaning of the story is that, in the same way as he imparted knowledge to competent persons, so also should others do.[31]

Either this is in obvious contradiction with the conditions given in Upad 2.1.2, or the prerequisite of being a Brahmin and a formal renunciant for access to the discipline of knowledge is in some way restricted in Śaṅkara's eyes.

There is evidence from the Upad itself that the requirement of physical renunciation for entry into the discipline of knowledge is not intended to be universal. Immediately after commenting upon the citation from MuU 1.2.12–13, Śaṅkara quotes ChU 3.11.6 to support the idea that knowledge should be obtained through a teacher. In ChU 3.11.4—two verses before—the *Upaniṣad* states that Āruṇa taught his son Uddālaka Āruṇi about *Brahman*, and the verse preceding the one quoted by Śaṅkara reads: "Of this *Brahman*, a father should speak to his eldest son or to a resident pupil fit to be taught,"[32] which Śaṅkara glosses in his commentary on the *Upaniṣad* without any reservation concerning the fact that the two men are not physical renunciants. Moreover, in the second chapter of the prose part of the Upad, Śaṅkara introduces a man of the student mode of living (*brahmacārin*) in the role of a disciple: "A certain student, who was tired of transmigratory existence characterized by birth and death and was seeking after final release, approached in the prescribed manner a knower of *Brahman* who was established in *Brahman* and sitting at ease . . ." (Upad 2.2.45, transl., 234). It must also be noticed that the Upad contains another elaborate description of the requirements for the discipline of knowledge that does not mention physical renunciation:

> This [highest means of purification] should be always taught to the seeker after final release whose mind has been calmed, whose senses have been controlled, whose faults have been abandoned, who is acting as prescribed [in the scriptures], who is endowed with virtues, and who is always obedient [to his teacher] (Upad 1.16.72, transl., 156).

How are we to explain these seemingly conflicting statements concerning the requirements for the discipline of knowledge? Are they simply self-contradictions on Śaṅkara's part, or can they be understood consistently on the basis of his own exegetical approach? It must first be noted that, when commenting on the *Upaniṣads* and the *Bhagavadgītā*, Śaṅkara does not express any reservation concerning the fact that on many occasions these texts imply the possibility of commencing the discipline of knowledge without physical renunciation. In fact, the scriptures' statements towards this are often so evident and treated so much so by Śaṅkara, that one can hardly argue on any reasonable ground that their commentator just overlooked them whenever he could—especially in the Upad—without noticing that he was contradicting his own tacit agreement with the obvious standpoint of the scriptures. As an example, we can start with a passage from the MuU itself which says in verse 1.1.3: "Śaunaka, a great householder, having approached Aṅgiras according to the rules, asked . . ."[33] According to Śaṅkara's comment on BS 1.3.35, the Śaunaka family belongs to the caste of *Kṣatriyas*. Besides, as stated by the comment on the preceding verse of the MuU (transl., 143), Aṅgiras received the knowledge from Bhāradvāja as "either his son or disciple" (*svaśiṣyāya putrāya vā*), meaning that Bhāradvāja could have been a Self-knower while being a father, that is, without having adopted physical renunciation although he was a Brahmin. Even when facing this situation, Śaṅkara interprets verse 1.1.3 without any reservation: "*Śaunaka*, the son of Śunaka, '*belonging to a great house*,' that is, a great householder, *having approached*, having gone to, the teacher *Aṅgiras*, disciple of Bhāradvāja, *duly*, in accordance with the scriptures, *asked*, enquired . . ."[34] Thus, Śaṅkara does not seem to see any contradiction between this episode exemplifying an appropriate entry into the discipline of knowledge by a *Kṣatriya* householder, and the prerequisite of being both a Brahmin and a physical renunciant.

This is in fact Śaṅkara's consistent approach with respect to the many similar cases found in the texts he commented upon. One could cite, for example, his comment introducing part three of the TU where the seer Bhṛgu receives knowledge from his father Varuṇa: "The story 'Bhṛghu, the well-known son of Varuṇa' is meant to praise knowledge, as it shows that it was imparted by a father to his cherished son."[35] Thus, in Śaṅkara's mind, far from introducing a deviation with respect to the prerequisite of physical renunciation, this episode of entry into the discipline of knowledge without physical renunciation glorifies Self-knowledge as a kind of universal value. Also, Śaṅkara has no problem with the Brahmin Śvetaketu, receiving instruction from his father Āruṇi in chapter 6 of the ChU, as part of a long and continuing tradition of enlightened householders.[36] A similar lineage of knowledge among householders listed in BṛU 6.5.1–3 is also genuinely recognized by Śaṅkara in his commentary on the same. When, in ChU 4.4.1–5, it is as a member of the student mode of living (*brahmacārin*) that Satyakāma Jābāla is initiated into the Upaniṣadic knowledge by Hāridrumata Gautama, Śaṅkara does not express any reservations either; equally so when, pictured later on as enlightened (4.9.2–3) and married (4.10.2), Satyakāma Jābāla also accepts *brahmacārins* (4.10.1) as his students.

Where even kings are seen teaching the knowledge of *Brahman*, Śaṅkara maintains the same kind of nondefensive comment, namely, in ChU 5.11–24, where king Aśvapati shares his wisdom with three householders, in BṛU 2.1 where Ajātaśatru, king of Vārāṇasī, does the same with the Brahmin Gārgya Dṛptabālāki, as well as in BṛU 6.2, and ChU 5.3-

10 where Pravāhaṇa, king of Pañcāla, instructs Śvetaketu and his father Gautama, as part of "a line of *Kṣatriya* teachers" (*kṣatriyaparamparā*).[37] In addition, Śaṅkara is not seen trying to justify any abnormality when king Janaka is enlightened by Yājñavalkya in BṛU 3.1 and 4.1–4, even if, according to the commentator, the latter section contains (in 4.4.22) the most important Upaniṣadic prescription of physical renunciation; the same attitude is found in ChU 4.1–2 where the Brahmin and widower Raikva teaches king Jānaśruti Pautrāyaṇa.

When in BṛU 3.6 and 3.8, Yājñavalkya expounds his teaching to the woman philosopher Gārgī and when, even before physically giving up the practice of rites, he reveals the knowledge of *Brahman* to his wife Maitreyī (2.4 and 4.5), Śaṅkara does not try to diminish the liberal significance of these episodes. Finally, in BṛU 4.5.6, it is to a woman, his wife Maitreyī, that Yājñavalkya states the very nature of the discipline of knowledge, namely, that the Self "should be heard of, reflected on and meditated upon," a dialogue which again Śaṅkara does not try to reduce in scope or to justify as an exception in relation to a supposedly universal prerequisite of physical renunciation for entrance into the discipline of knowledge.

The *Upaniṣads* commented upon by Śaṅkara thus feature a striking liberality concerning access to the discipline of knowledge. This brief survey already brings forward strong evidence that, according to these scriptures, if physical renunciation is to play a role for knowledge of the Self, it is not mandatory. My contention is that Śaṅkara's authentic commentarial works explicitly agree with this position, and that the independent work Upad is *at the most* ambiguous rather than contradictory in relation to the other works, simply because its own text features opposite standpoints: while stating that being a Brahmin and a formal renunciant is necessary for access to the discipline of knowledge, it tells on the other hand the story of a student (*brahmacārin*) receiving knowledge from an enlightened teacher.

For Śaṅkara, physical renunciation is a subsidiary (*aṅga*) for Self-knowledge addressed to Brahmins alone.[38] Therefore, it could be that when Śaṅkara presents physical renunciation as a necessary condition for the discipline of knowledge, it is because, in his eyes, the addressee of the statement or of the whole text is a Brahmin. Since Śaṅkara seems to endorse the *Upaniṣads'* liberality in terms of access to Self-knowledge, the requirement of being a Brahmin and a monk stated in the Upad probably means that *if* one is a Brahmin, one has to become a physical renunciant in order to have access to the discipline of knowledge, and not that one *has to be* a Brahmin and a physical renunciant. As a consequence, this requirement would be valid only for Brahmins and would not preclude any person from the discipline of knowledge, which is confirmed in the Upad itself when a student (*brahmacārin*) is said to be instructed on the Self. The stipulation of physical renunciation given by the Upad would be part of the qualification (*adhikāra*) needed to study this specific text, rather than part of a requirement applicable to everyone with respect to all Vedāntic scriptures, which deal with Self-knowledge. Thus, the apparent contradiction found in the Upad between the Brahmin-physical renunciant requirement and the dialogue between a teacher and a student (*brahmacārin*) can be solved in a manner consistent with Śaṅkara's own basic way of interpretating qualification for Self-knowledge and for formal physical renunciation.

Mayeda believes that since the Upad is non-commentarial, it is more likely to represent the free expression of Śaṅkara's real personal position on renunciation:

> If the *Upad* were a commentary, like the *Brahmasūtrabhāṣya*, on some text or other, Śaṅkara might have been compelled to recommend *karman* though it was against his will. However, the *Upad* is not a commentary on any text. Therefore, it is certainly an expression of his own view that Śaṅkara insists on a complete renunciation of *karman* . . . (1964–66, 70)

According to Mayeda's interpretation of the requirement of being a Brahmin and a physical renunciant as stated in the Upad, "it should be kept in mind in order to understand Śaṅkara's doctrine that he accepts as qualified for his teaching a Brahmin who is in the state of *paramahaṃsa* wandering ascetic" (Upad, transl., 228). But, as we saw, such a conclusion raises the problem of consistency within the Upad itself. Mayeda also implies this when, noticing that *a student* is said to be taught in verse 2.2.45, he reflects that "the requirement of being a *paramahaṃsaparivrājaka* [wandering mendicant] might not be very strict" (Upad, transl., 97). Hence, to determine Śaṅkara's position on the matter, one must take all of his works into consideration rather than focusing on one only as does Mayeda.

But the question remains as to why Śaṅkara did not state generously the universal availability of Self-knowledge in his Upad if he really meant it? It could be argued that the work is inauthentic or partly so. But according to Mayeda's research on this (1965), there is no reason to doubt its authenticity. So this hypothesis seems untenable. At least three other explanations can be proposed. First, Śaṅkara may have followed the common tendency of dharmaśāstric works to be addressed mainly to Brahmins, as observed by Madeleine Biardeau: "A careful reading of the first four chapters of the *Manu-smṛti*, for instance . . . reveals that the "twice-born" for whom prescriptions are meant is in fact the Brahmin."[39] Second, it may be that Śaṅkara had personal reasons to address himself mainly to Brahmins. Having this in mind, Mayeda proposes the following account of the contemporary situation Śaṅkara had to deal with:

> Śaṅkara would not teach his doctrine to city dwellers. In the cities the power of Buddhism was still strong, though already declining, and Jainism prevailed among the merchants and manufacturers. Popular Hinduism occupied the minds of ordinary people while city dwellers pursued ease and pleasure. There were also hedonists in cities, and it was difficult for Śaṅkara to communicate Vedānta philosophy to these people. Consequently he propagated his teachings chiefly among *saṃnyāsins*, who had renounced the world, and intellectuals in the villages, and he gradually won the respect of Brahmins and feudal lords (Upad, transl., 5).

As is often the case in ancient Indian history, it is very difficult to assess such a description. Mayeda's description is at best hypothetical. In the light of what we have established so far, I would rather put it this way: although Śaṅkara understood his teaching to be accessible to all castes, for sociohistorical and/or strategical reasons, in practice, he may have taught mainly to Brahmins, who were probably the most qualified to understand the subtle argumentation of his revival, the most concerned about it, and the most competent to spread it throughout society once converted to his doctrine.[40] This could explain why he sometimes wrote as if his teaching and that of the *Upaniṣads* were addressed only to Brahmins. But this does not mean that, in his eyes, no one else was qualified for Self-knowledge. Additionally, Śaṅkara's specific mention of physical renunciation as a requirement for the discipline of knowledge in the Upad may have been a way to emphasize that, because physical renunciation allows full-time dedication to enquiry into the nature of *Brahman-Ātman*, it is most supportive of Self-knowledge and therefore preferable for those who are qualified for it. Finally, these factors may very well have reinforced each other in the author's mind.

It may be argued that the universal accessibility of Self-knowledge is still contradicted by many passages where Śaṅkara writes that Self-knowledge must be preceded by renunciation. Our contention is that in order to find out if there is indeed a contradiction here, we would have to determine first what is the meaning of renunciation in these passages, that is, to which of the four basic types it refers. To ascertain this would in turn require a detailed textual analysis and therefore the sequence between renunciation and Self-knowledge cannot be given as a general point of reference to start with. The required textual analysis will be carried on in part two.

LIBERATION IS POSSIBLE WHILE NOT BEING A PHYSICAL RENUNCIANT

Śaṅkara acknowledges in various places that one can reach direct Self-knowledge and liberation-in-life even when one has not adopted physical renunciation. In BṛU4.4.23, at the end of the dialogue between Yājñavalkya and king Janaka, Śaṅkara confirms that the latter has now "become *Brahman*" (BṛU 4.4.23, 377) and reached liberation-in-life. Commenting on the famous verse of the BhG which states that "by action only, did Janaka and others attain perfection" (BhG 3.20, 158), Śaṅkara proposes two possible interpretations. The first one is that if Janaka and others continued the performance of actions even after having attained liberation-in-life, then their actions had no other purpose than guiding people (*lokasaṃgraha*). If, on the other hand, they had not yet attained liberation-in-life, then ritual actions helped them in reaching that state through their purifying effect: "Now, if *Janaka and others* had not attained the right perception, then the verse should be explained as follows: *they attained perfection* by steps, *through action* which is the means of attaining purity of mind."[41] The gloss "*perfection*, that is, liberation" (*saṃsiddhiṃ mokṣam*)[42] confirms that Śaṅkara is indeed referring to accessibility of direct Self-knowledge and liberation for people who have not taken up physical renunciation. In addition, quoting verse 3.20 in his comment on BhG 2.10, he suggests that "perfection" can mean either purity of mind or Self-knowledge—which in the light of the comment on verse 3.20 must be immediate in nature: "by means of actions dedicated to *Īśvara, Janaka and others attained perfection*, that is, either purity of mind or the rise of knowledge . . ."[43] Thus these passages suggest that for Śaṅkara liberation is accessible while not being a physical renunciant.

BRAHMINS ALONE ARE QUALIFIED FOR PHYSICAL RENUNCIATION

Throughout his works, Śaṅkara maintains that the addressee of the prescription of physical renunciation is always and only the Brahmin. His clearest statements on the restriction of physical renunciation to Brahmins are found in his comments on BṛU 3.5.1 and 4.5.15. The commentary on verse 3.5.1 specifies that when stating the subject of the verb "having renounced" (*vyutthāya*), the author of the *Upaniṣad* "uses the word Brahmin because they alone are qualified for renunciation."[44] The commentary on verse 4.5.15 even contains a prohibition of renunciation for *Kṣatriyas* and *Vaiśyas*:[45] "Or it may be that [the statement of] the *Śruti* about the lifelong [performance of rites] concerns the other castes [apart from the Brahmin], as the *Kṣatriyas* and the *Vaiśyas* are not entitled to wandering mendicancy."[46] In his commentary on BG 2.10, Śaṅkara also suggests that physical renunciation is not for *Kṣatriyas* when he explains that Arjuna refused to fight according to the *dharma* of his caste (*kṣātradharma*) "and wished to adopt someone else's *dharma*, which consists of living on alms and the like."[47]

THE LIBERATED PERSON IS BEYOND THE SCOPE OF PRESCRIPTIONS

According to Śaṅkara, the enlightened man is beyond the range of injunctions. He knows his Self to be unlimited and unidentifiable with any of the qualifications referred to by the scriptures to define the person entitled to a given practice. "Teachings such as 'A Brahmin should perform a sacrifice' take place [only] when one resorts to superimposition on the Self of particulars such as caste, mode of living, age and circumstance."[48] But the reality of the Self is "devoid of distinctions such as Brahmin and *Kṣatriya*" (BS 1.1.1, 23). Therefore, "when one has destroyed the notion of himself as a Brahmin, a *Kṣatriya* or the like, no prescription—such as 'this is the duty of a Brahmin,' or 'this is the duty of a *Kṣatriya*,'—comes into being, for it has no addressee."[49]

Although Śaṅkara holds that the notion of qualification (*adhikāra*) is irrelevant for the enlightened person, he nonetheless uses the word *adhikāra* with respect to him. Recognizing and understanding this peculiar use is crucial to the proper interpretation of Śaṅkara's position on renunciation. As already mentioned, *adhikāra* commonly means qualification for pursuing a practice and obtaining its result. Given this well-known meaning, when the word *adhikāra* is used by Śaṅkara, one tends to infer that the addressee can only be an unenlightened person. But a proper reading of the context will reveal that it is sometimes otherwise. If Śaṅkara means that the *adhikāra* of the already enlightened person is with respect to renunciation of all actions alone, and one wrongly interprets the addressee to be a seeker-after-liberation, major misinterpretations are bound to occur concerning Śaṅkara's position on the types of renunciation and their respective importance. But then, what does Śaṅkara mean by the *adhikāra* of the enlightened man?

Our contention is that here *adhikāra* does not mean "qualification," but "having to do with." It serves in identifying a sphere or domain which agrees or is consistent with the situation of a given person. Concluding a survey of the meanings of *adhikāra* in the *Pūrvamīmāṃsāsūtras*—among which is the sense of "having to do with"—Francis X. Clooney writes that "for Jaimini *adhikāra* is not so much one's right or personal qualification, but rather one's sphere or domain of competence in intersection with other domains" (1990, 182). Similarly, we contend that Śaṅkara sometimes uses the word *adhikāra* to identify the *relevance* or *non-relevance* of the sphere of action and of the sphere of renunciation and Self-knowledge with respect to a given person. Attribution of an *adhikāra,* in this sense, does not necessarily imply that one has something more to do in order to accomplish some goal. This meaning of *adhikāra* is consistent with the idea that the enlightened person is beyond all considerations pertaining to scriptural prescriptions.

Let us now see concretely how Śaṅkara uses the term *adhikāra* with respect to the enlightened person and how in such cases "having to do with" appears to be its proper meaning. In BG 5.7 (245), Śaṅkara explains that when the verse says "though acting, he is not tainted," it refers to the man who "is not bound by actions," even though he continues to perform ritual actions with a view to guiding people. In the short sentence which follows immediately and which introduces the next verse, Śaṅkara states that "in reality he does not act" (BhG 5.8, 245). A couple of lines below, he again refers in a quite obvious way to the enlightened man, attributing to him *adhikāra* with respect to renunciation of all actions: "Thus the knower of Reality, that man of right perception who, in all the movements of the senses and the mind, sees only inaction in actions, has to do (*adhikāra*)[50] only with renunciation of all actions, because he perceives the absence of action [in himself]."[51] In his subcommentary, Ānandagiri rightly understands here that "even while there is no injunction in the case of the enlightened (*vidvas*) thus described, as a natural outcome of knowledge, he wishes renunciation of actions in terms of a concluding act[52] and a result [of direct Self-knowledge]."[53]

Śaṅkara's comment on *Gītā* 2.21 also uses *adhikāra* with respect to the enlightened man. First, Śaṅkara states that by declaring "O son of Pṛthā, how can that man slay or cause anyone to slay?" (BhG 2.21, 70), "this passage means the sole denial (*pratiṣedha*) of all actions in the case of the enlightened (*vidvas*)" (Ibid., 71). Since only direct knowledge of the Self as actionless can bring about complete cessation of superimposition of doership and action, it follows that the *vidvas* referred to here must be possessed of a Self-knowledge that is immediate in nature. But determined to show that ritual actions are enjoined on the enlightened as well as on the unenlightened, the opponent tries to find fault with Śaṅkara's distinction between what is suitable and not suitable for these two categories of people. Since, as indicated by his very name, the man of knowledge (*vidvas*) is already possessed of Self-knowledge, the opponent argues that it is improper to hold that Self-knowledge unaccompanied by ritual action is intended by scriptures for the man of knowledge:

> Objection: Even knowledge is prescribed to the unenlightened (*avidvas*) alone, because prescribing knowledge to those who already have it would be as useless as grinding flour [over again]. This being so, it is not proper to distinguish between the prescription of ritual actions to the unenlightened and non-prescription of the same to the enlightened (*vidvas*).[54]

Śaṅkara replies that the distinct attribution of prescribed rites to the unenlightened (*avidvas*), and of Self-knowledge without rites to the man of knowledge (*vidvas*) lies in the fact that there is nothing to practice after the understanding of the Self as being beyond doership and action: "It is not so, because the distinction of [respectively] the presence and absence of the need to do something is tenable . . . And . . . nothing needs to be done after understanding the meaning of statements such as '[This Self] is never born' regarding the true nature of the Self."[55] A little further Śaṅkara repeats that verse 2.21 states the denial of action (*karmākṣepa*) in the case of the enlightened (*vidvas*).[56] He then concludes: "Therefore, the enlightened (*vidvas*) who has been distinguished [and] who perceives the immutable Self, as well as the seeker-after-liberation[57] have to do (*adhikāra*) only with renunciation of all actions."[58] Again Ānandagiri's interpretation rightly reflects two values of *adhikāra*, one applying to the seeker-after-liberation, the other to the enlightened:

> Because renunciation consisting of cessation of all activities is not contradictory to knowledge of the actionless Self, one possessed of inducing [indirect] knowledge has to do with prescribed renunciation, while one possessed of the right [direct] knowledge [has to do with] a non-prescribed, natural, resultant [renunciation].[59]

Thus, while the word *adhikāra* can still mean "qualification" when used with respect to the seeker-after-liberation, when employed with reference to the enlightened, it can only serve in pointing out that the latter has nothing to do with action and everything to do with their abandonment followed by simply remaining in direct knowledge of the actionless Self, without anything more to perform and achieve. This peculiar formulation comes out to be yet another way for Śaṅkara to refute the combination of action with Self-knowledge as the direct means of liberation.

Having established these five basic points of reference, we are now equipped with a consistent critical apparatus for a complete study of renunciation in Śaṅkara's works. However, before undertaking this analysis, we still have to examine general explanations provided by many authors to solve the apparent inconsistency raised in their eyes by the attainment of liberation without physical renunciation.

CHAPTER FOUR

Two Unfounded Explanations

In the context of *Advaita Vedānta*, two explanations are often given to solve the apparent contradiction between the Upaniṣadic prescription of physical renunciation as a means of Self-knowledge and Śaṅkara's acknowledgement of attainment of Self-knowledge without being a physical renouncer. The first explanation is that attainment of liberation without physical renunciation is an exception; the second is that one must have taken physical renunciation in a previous life.

Before considering these two explanations, we will first examine the exact function of physical renunciation as the object of a scriptural prescription in Śaṅkara's understanding. First, Brahmins who satisfy the requirements for the discipline of knowledge are not only entitled to resort to physical renunciation, but they also are *prescribed* to do so. According to Śaṅkara, the most explicit injunction of renunciation is found in BṛU 4.4.22. It declares: "Desiring this world [i.e. the Self] alone, wandering mendicants leave everything (*pravrajanti*)" (BṛU 4.4.22, 370). Then the verse justifies this prescription by mentioning that the ancient sages did not desire children and were not concerned with any "world" other then the Self. Śaṅkara considers that no other Upaniṣadic passage provides as clear a combination of both a prescription of renunciation and a eulogy supporting it: "If, however, wandering mendicancy is supposed to be prescribed somewhere, first of all, it is here. It cannot be anywhere else."[1] In his introduction to chapter 3 of the BhG, Śaṅkara recalls that physical renunciation is prescribed by scriptures "as a subsidiary to knowledge" (*jñānāṅgatva*) for the seeker-after-liberation (*mumukṣu*).[2] He then quotes various passages stating the possibility of adopting the monastic mode of living (*saṃnyāsāśrama*) quite early in life, directly after studentship.[3] Thus, according to Śaṅkara, the monastic mode of living is totally justified and applicable, "since wandering mendicancy (*pārivrājya*) is meant as a subsidiary for full maturation[4] of the knowledge of *Brahman*."[5]

Commenting on BṛU 3.5.1, Olivelle clearly defines renunciation's role as a subsidiary (*aṅga*) with respect to knowledge:

> A ritual, according to *Mīmāṃsā*, contains two types of actions and things: principal and subsidiary. The latter has no independent purpose, but serves the principal to attain its object. Here Śaṃkara, using ritual categories, regards knowledge as the principal element that causes liberation, and renunciation characterized by the abandonment of rites and ritual instruments as a subsidiary element within the process of acquiring knowledge and achieving liberation (1986–87, 1:88–89).

According to *Pūrvamīmāṃsā*, the subsidiary is normally considered necessary for completion of the prescribed performance and for obtaining its reward, since "the actualization of the ritual occurs when all the subsidiaries have entered into use" (Clooney 1990, 109).[6] If we apply the same rule to our context, for Brahmins, the process of acquiring Self-knowledge would not be complete, and its effect, namely, liberation, would not be ensured as long as physical renunciation has not been used as a subsidiary.

LIBERATION WITHOUT PHYSICAL RENUNCIATION AS AN EXCEPTION

Some authors explain the apparent inconsistency between this injunction of physical renunciation and attainment of liberation without the latter, by considering such an attainment as an exception. So does G. V. Saroja in her *Tilak and Śaṅkara on the Gītā*: "This is the reason for Śaṅkara's repeated emphasis of *jñāna* [knowledge] prededed by *saṃnyāsa* as the only means to realization. Exceptional cases like Janaka can never be considered as the general case" (1985, 126).

But this explanation has no scriptural or even logical basis. First, it must be noted that neither the *Upaniṣads*, nor the *Gītā*, nor Śaṅkara say that Janaka's process of enlightenment, for instance, is to be taken as an exception. Second, Saroja should have identified the scriptural rule with respect to which Janaka's case is to be considered an exception. She has not. Interestingly, nowhere in her book does she mention that, according to Śaṅkara, only Brahmins are prescribed to renounce physically. The fundamental flaw in the exception argument is this: given that from

Śaṅkara's viewpoint the prescription of physical renunciation as a subsidiary for knowledge concerns Brahmins only, non-Brahmins such as Janaka cannot be exceptions to an injunction that does not even apply to them in the first place. Thus, for non-Brahmins the exception argument explains nothing at all. It could be relevant only for Brahmins. How Śaṅkara deals with the case of Brahmins who reach enlightenment without physical renunciation remains to be studied. This will be done in part two. But one thing is sure at this point: on the basis of our five reference points, the exception argument provides no consistent explanation for all cases of enlightenment without physical renunciation.

LIBERATION THROUGH PHYSICAL RENUNCIATION IN A PREVIOUS LIFE

Other commentarors of Śaṅkara have tried to solve the apparent contradiction of achieving liberation without the subsidiary of physical renunciation, by assuming that it has been resorted to in a previous life. This argument is found as early as Sarvajñātman (eighth–ninth century) who may have been an immediate disciple of Śaṅkara.

According to *Pūrvamīmāṃsā*, rituals enjoined by the scriptures generate an unseen potency (*apūrva*) which continues to operate after performance of the ritual in order to bring about the reward of the latter—heaven for instance. Sarvajñātman understands the unseen potency generated by physical renunciation to be necessary for achieving the result consisting of liberation. As mentioned in his *Saṃkṣepaśārīraka* 3.359–361, and as well summarized by the *Siddhāntaleśasaṅgraha*,

> since the sins that obstruct the rise of knowledge are infinite, some are removable by the practice of sacrifice etc., some are removable by the unseen potency [*apūrva*] from renunciation. . . . And thus, for those householders, who practice hearing (study) etc., in the intervals of karma, there is attainment of knowledge, not in this life, but only after attaining renunciation, in another life. As for those like Janaka and others, who attain knowledge, even while being householders, their attainment of knowledge is due to renunciation in a prior life (Appaya Dīkṣita, 1935–1937, 1:346).[7]

This argument gives to physical renunciation and monastic life not only a necessary role as auxiliary, but also an exclusive power to generate a special kind of merit. It entails a ritualization of the role of physical renunciation oddly reflecting the *Pūrvamīmāṃsā*'s mentality in the *Advaita* context.

Similarly, A. G. Krishna Warrier, a modern interpreter of *Advaita*, gathers the notions of exception and of the unseen potency of physical renunciation from a previous life:

> . . . those who had their renunciation and Vedāntic studies in prior lives but failed to win success may, in the present life, achieve it in any station of life; indeed, a fresh act of renunciation would be superfluous for them. Such exceptions apart, the injunction to renounce actions associated with *varṇas* and *āśramas* is deemed compulsory; renunciation is an indispensable auxiliary in the pursuit of Self-knowledge (1981, 442).

Thus, through unseen potency and unseen lives, some post-Śaṅkara Advaitins have constructed a rationale for physical renunciation as a sine qua non of Self-knowledge.

Let us first observe that, from a logical viewpoint, the question of whether or not one must assume an unseen potency from renunciation in a previous life would arise, if ever, only with respect to Brahmins. The fact that a non-Brahmin attains Self-knowledge and liberation without physical renunciation in a given life can never contradict the fact that a Brahmin is prescribed physical renunciation for Self-knowledge in a given life. The reason is simply that these facts are not said of the same person, belonging to the same caste and so forth. Since, to start with, no prescription of physical renunciation is ever addressed to a non-Brahmin in a given life, there is no need to justify his enlightenment without physical renunciation during that life, by his renunciation in a previous one. The argument of the previous-life renunciation is simply useless in the case of non-Brahmins, as no contradiction awaits to be solved as far as they are concerned.[8] Therefore, even before considering its validity with respect to Brahmins, this argument cannot support physical renunciation as a sine qua non for all cases of enlightenment.

Let us now evaluate the argument of the previous-life renunciation as a possible solution in the case of Brahmins attaining liberation without physical renunciation. First of all, Śaṅkara does not even accept the concept of unseen potency. "And there is no valid proof of its existence" says he in his commentary on BS 3.2.38 (666). Second, when he refers to the effect of practices in previous lives leading to enlightenment in a future one, he never talks of the production of unseen potency but only of mind purification. Even more important, he gives as examples of these practices the remote as well as the proximate means, and connects them only once with a context of physical renunciation. The terms referring to practices done in previous lives in Śaṅkara's works are: "practice of yoga" which, according to Śaṅkara, is presented by the *Gītā* itself in the context of physical renunciation (*yogābhyāsa*; BhG 6.44–45, 336–38); "prescribed actions such as sacrifices" (*kriyāṇāṃ yajñādīnām*; BhG 3.4, 144); "obligatory rites such as *agnihotra*, associated or not with meditation" (*vidyāsaṃyuktaṃ nityam agnihotrādi vidyāvihīnaṃ ca*; BS 4.1.18, 853); "action" (*karman*; BṛU 1.4.2, 59); "actions prescribed for one's mode of living" (*āśramakarman*; BS 3.4.38, 810); remote as well as proximate practices referred to by the word *karman* (TU 1.12.1, 437); "means" (*sādhana*; BS 3.4.51, 822); the type of meditation known as *prasaṃkhyāna* (Upad 1.18.15–16, 148). Therefore, nothing in Śaṅkara's works suggests that physical renunciation is necessary in a previous or future life to ensure direct Self-knowledge and liberation.

It may be argued that the valid means of knowledge known as postulation (*arthāpatti*) allows one to infer renunciation in previous lives because of its absence in the one where enlightenment has been reached. Postulation is assuming the existence of a fact or principle in order to explain an *undeniable fact* which otherwise cannot be accounted for. A stock example of postulation goes as follows: "Devadatta is fat. But he does not eat during the day. So it must be assumed that he eats at night." Most important to note here is that the first two statements (before the conclusive postulation as such) are understood to be visible, undeniable facts.

Now, here is how one would construe the postulation of renunciation in a previous life. "Physical renunciation is necessary for enlightenment. But some people attain enlightenment in a given life without physical renunciation. So it must be assumed that they took up physical renunciation in a previous life." One cannot but notice here that the first statement is not an undeniable fact or injunction. It is simply an unproven statement. So the assumption of physical renunciation in a previous life is not even formally acceptable as a postulation. Rather it amounts to a circular argument.

Even if it were possible to properly construe a postulation in favor of physical renunciation in a previous life, it would not be valid from Śaṅkara's viewpoint since, contrary to later *Advaitins*, he does not use and even accept postulation as a valid means of knowledge (see Wilson 1982, 37–38). Unconvinced by an opponent's recourse to postulation, Śaṅkara retorts: "But this is not logical. This queer assumption of something unknown is sheer dogmatism" (BS 3.2.32, transl., 635).[9] He also points out elsewhere that when something is known from scriptures, postulation can have no claim.[10]

If we wish to understand in Śaṅkara's own terms the relationship between prescription of physical renunciation as a subsidiary, and acquisition of direct Self-knowledge, we have to use something else than postulation or unseen potency. Śaṅkara never directly addressed the question as to why the *Upaniṣads* prescribe physical renunciation to Brahmins seeking Self-knowledge, and yet depict instances where Brahmin householders receive Self-knowledge—implying that the Upaniṣadic injunction of renunciation has not been followed. However, the possibility that a Brahmin attains enlightenment without physical renunciation can be accounted for from a rule provided by *Pūrvamīmāṃsāsūtra* 6.3.1–2:[11]

> [Opponent:] The act should be undertaken (*pravṛttiḥ syāt*) only when the performer has the capacity to perform all [the accessory details]; as the act has been laid down as such. [Reply:] No. There should be performance (*pravṛtti*) even if only a part [of the accessory details] can be performed. For the fulfilment of the purpose (*arthanivṛtti*) proceeds from the principal action. All the rest is [simply not essential],[12] because it subserves the purpose of the act (Clooney 1990, 108).[13]

Applying this rule to physical renunciation as a subsidiary for Self-knowledge, we could say that if, as an exception, a Brahmin cannot take to physical renunciation, he can still fully actualize Self-knowledge (the main means, corresponding to the "principal action") and obtain liberation (its "purpose"), because the latter does accrue mainly from Self-knowledge. Being indirect means, other factors are "simply not essential."

Let us pursue our attempt to resolve, from Śaṅkara's own viewpoint, the apparent contradiction between prescription of physical renunciation and attainment of Self-knowledge without the latter. We may also take recourse to the manner in which Śaṅkara explains the fact that people are reported to reach Self-knowledge and liberation without having practiced the rites prescribed as remote subsidiaries (*bahiraṅga*) for the discipline of knowledge. According to Śaṅkara's interpretation of *Brahmasūtra* 3.4.36–37, the claim that people are qualified for Self-knowledge even when deprived of qualification for rites is explained by the fact that *Śrauta* and *Smārta* texts provide indicatory marks (*liṅga*) suggesting that, even though unqualified for rites, some people, among whom the widower Raikva and women such as Gārgī, did acquire immediate knowledge of the Self. Applying the same exegetical rule to the subsidiary consisting of physical renunciation, we may infer from indicatory marks found in passages we referred to in a preceding section, that Brahmins are said by the scriptures to reach mediate as well as immediate Self-knowledge without fulfilling the auxiliary requirement of physical renunciation.

But this does not render the prescription of physical renunciation useless or unimportant. Its value is again analogous to that of the prescription of rites even when Self-knowledge is accessible without them. According to Śaṅkara's understanding of BS 3.4.39, even when Self-knowledge and liberation are available without rites, it is preferable (*jyāyas*) for people of the first three modes of living to carry on with their ritualistic duties. It can be said in a similar fashion that even if direct Self-knowledge is available for Brahmins without physical renunciation, it is preferable for them to adopt the latter. This exegetical principle explains quite simply why Śaṅkara can, on the one hand, very naturally accept that Brahmins are qualified for the discipline of knowledge even without taking to physical renunciation, and, on the other hand, strongly advocate the latter for them. Arguing in favor of physical renunciation as a sine qua non by taking recourse to assumption, hypothetical lives and unseen potency clearly turns out to be out of place in the context of Śaṅkara's hermeneutics.

We now have to see how, in concrete hermeneutical situations, Śaṅkara defines the relationships between ritual actions, the various types of renunciation, and the different levels of Self-knowledge. At the same time, this will allow us to evaluate Śaṅkara's consistency with respect to renunciation.

PART TWO

Śaṅkara and Renunciation

CHAPTER FIVE

The Householder's Path Toward Liberation

A PROPER CONTEXTUALIZATION OF "RENUNCIATION OF ALL ACTIONS"

According to many an interpreter of *Advaita Vedānta*, Śaṅkara teaches that the seeker-after-liberation must physically abandon all rituals and become a formal physical renunciant (*saṃnyāsin*) as a prerequisite to start the *Advaita* discipline of knowledge proper. At first sight, some passages of Śaṅkara's works seem to support such an interpretation of his standpoint, particularly when the author describes the major steps towards liberation and includes renunciation of all actions (*sarvakarmasaṃnyāsa*). Hence, it will be useful to examine these passages that constitute quite complete summaries of the whole path to liberation. When the occasional mention of the practice of *karmayoga* is taken into account, the most elaborate lists include six steps altogether, including liberation. Let us start with the three summaries found in the commentary on chapter 5 of BhG. We will leave a blank space when one of the steps mentioned in other summaries is skipped by Śaṅkara.

A-BhG 5.27

1. "yoga of action" (*karmayoga*)
2. "purity of mind" (*sattvaśuddhi*)
3. "attainment of knowledge" (*jñānaprāpti*)
4. "renunciation of all actions" (*sarvakarmasaṃnyāsa*)

5. "steadfastness in the right perception" (*samyagdarśananiṣṭhā*)
6. "liberation" (*mokṣa*)[1]

B-BhG 5.12

1. "actions for the sake of the Lord" (*īśvarāya karmāṇi*)
2. "purity of mind" (*sattvaśuddhi*)
3. "attainment of knowledge" (*jñānaprāpti*)
4. "renunciation of all actions" (*sarvakarmasaṃnyāsa*)
5. "steadfastness in knowledge" (*jñānaniṣṭhā*)
6. "liberation" (*mokṣa*)[2]

C-BhG 5.17

1.
2.
3. "those whose Self is That" (*tadātmānaḥ*)
4. "having abandoned all actions" (*sarvāṇi karmāṇi saṃnyasya*)
5. "those who are intent on that [Self]" (*tanniṣṭhāḥ*)
   and
   "dwelling in *Brahman* alone" (*brahmaṇy evāvasthānam*)
6. "they go never again to return" (*te gacchanti . . . apunar āvṛttim*)[3]

It is usually understood by commentators that, in these summaries of the path to liberation, "attainment of knowledge" (lists A and B) or the knowledge that one's self is "That" *Brahman* (list C) do not refer to direct Self-knowledge. They mean a deep intellectual conviction—arising usually from both purity of mind and study of the scriptures—that the ultimate goal of life is liberation from all limited and impermanent states (including sojourn in heaven), and that the means of this liberation is not action or its combination with Self-knowledge, but immediate knowledge of the actionless Self alone. This conviction inspires the seeker to take up physical abandonment of rites (*sarvakarmasaṃnyāsa* in the lists), which is considered to be a necessary condition for entry into the discipline of knowledge (level 5 in the lists).

In the introduction to his English translation of Śaṅkara's commentary on the *Bhagavadgītā*, Swāmī Gambhīrānanda provides a typical example of this most common interpretation. To make things clearer, we will mention within brackets the corresponding items of the sequence given in the above summaries, as well as the nature of the different types of knowledge referred to:

> Śaṅkarācārya . . . says that spiritual unfoldment proceeds along the following stages: practice of scriptural rites and duties with a hankering for results; practice of the same as a dedication to God without expecting rewards for oneself [yoga of action]; purification of the mind or moral excellence along with *upāsanā* (devotion to and meditation on the qualified Brahman); acquisition of [mediate] knowledge [attainment of knowledge] from a teacher and the scriptures, followed by renunciation of all rites and duties (monasticism) [renunciation of all actions], which makes one *fit* for steadfastness in that [mediate] knowledge;[4] steadfastness in that knowledge [steadfastness in knowledge]; removal of ignorance and self-revelation [immediate knowledge] of the supreme Brahman, which is the same as Liberation (Śaṅkara 1984, xxi–xxii).

In a similar fashion, Kalyanasundara Sastri states that "from *karma-yoga* there arises the purification of mind; and from that, mediate knowledge; and therefrom renunciation of action; and after that, establishment in immediate knowledge which is known as *jīvan-mukti* . . ." (300) In his work on the contemporary Śaṅkarācāryas, William Chenkner describes the path of the aspirant to liberation in terms quite equivalent:

> The selfless activity sanctioned by the *Bhagavad Gītā* prepares the student for commitment to knowledge (*jñāna-niṣṭhā*) and subsequently for more advanced religious growth. As he observes injunctions from the scripture, duties and rituals, the student gradually learns that knowledge of the Self is beyond human activity. Śaṅkara speaks of the elimination of ritual and religious duties after the rise of knowledge. The *karma yoga* of the *Gītā*, which consecrates activity as selfless and altruistic, is but the initial path in spiritual development. Such activity serves as a means to achieve educational competency, a means prior to advanced religious instruction, a preparatory moment, to perfect intellectual capacity. Once this moment is past, the religious seeker renounces such activity and commits himself wholly to the path of knowledge (1983, 60–61).

It must be brought to notice that if this sequence toward liberation is intended to be universal in its application, if all the items following "yoga of action" are indispensable, and if "renunciation of all actions" (*sarvakarmasaṃnyāsa*) means physical renunciation, then this sequence contradicts three basic points in Śaṅkara's teaching: accessibility of Self-knowledge irrespective of modes of living; the possibility of achieving liberation while not being a physical renouncer; and the fact that Brahmins alone are qualified for physical renunciation. Did Śaṅkara contradict himself or did he have a different understanding of this sequence? This will be the main enquiry of the present chapter.

Let us first contextualize these summaries in more details. When presenting the outline found in his commentary on verse 5.27, Śaṅkara specifies that "on every occasion" (*pade pade*) Kṛṣṇa has mentioned and will be mentioning this sequence. So this summary of the spiritual path seems quite basic in Śaṅkara's eyes. Yet, before giving the sequence, he mentions another possible way of attaining liberation: "It has been said that the renouncers who are steadfast in the right perception obtain liberation directly (*sadyomukti*)."[5] This statement seems to account for those who adopt physical renunciation immediately after their studies, that is, "even before starting with rites" (BhG 4.21, 211), which are part of the duty of a householder. These physical renouncers are contrasted with people who "started with rites" (BhG 4.20, 210), that is, who married after their studies and became householders. It is as an alternative to the direct way of physical renouncers that the sequence given immediately after also leads to liberation, but "through stages" (*krameṇa*). So, according to Śaṅkara, the common sequence of the lists given above account for the liberation of all people who did not take up physical renunciation immediately after studies. We will call it the "householder's sequence toward liberation."

One could argue that renunciation of all actions (*sarvakarmasaṃnyāsa*) does mean physical renunciation in this sequence, and since only Brahmins are allowed to adopt it, these stages are addressed to them only. But we will now see that "renunciation of actions" (*karmasaṃnyāsa*) and "renunciation of all actions" (*sarvakarmasaṃnyāsa*) are *also* attributed by Śaṅkara to non-Brahmins or to Self-knowers in general, although not in the sense of physical renunciation as a prerequisite for the discipline of knowledge.

When, in his commentary on verse 4.19, Śaṅkara describes what happens with action after enlightenment, he refers to two possible cases, that is, that of the man who did not renounce physically and that of the one who did:

> *He*, the one possessing the perception described in the previous verse, *whose undertakings*—they are called undertakings because all actions are undertaken—actions undertaken, *are all*, as many as they are, *devoid of desires and of their incentives*, of desires and of their causes, [and] accomplished without purpose, as mere movements, for the guidance of people if one leads an active life, and for the bare maintainance of life, if one abstains from active life . . .[6]

Since Śaṅkara acknowledges here the possibility that one continues rites after attaining liberation-in-life, in his eyes, at least some people followed the discipline of knowledge and even attained direct Self-knowledge without physical renunciation, that is, without the physical "renunciation of all actions" of the above householder's sequence as usually understood by Śaṅkara's interpreters. And we saw that, if we want to remain consistent with Śaṅkara's own position, neither the notion of exception nor the postulation of physical renunciation in a previous life can justify physical renunciation as a universal requirement. Then the questions are: What people does the sequence proposed by the above summaries really account for? And what is the meaning of "renunciation of all actions" (*sarvakarmasaṃnyāsa*) and of the other steps in the sequence?

The most significant clue is found in the various passages where Śaṅkara accounts for people who attained enlightenment without physical renunciation and who continued the performance of rites even after that. As written in the comment on verse 2.11:

> Now, as for the man who, [after] engaging in actions out of ignorance or out of imperfections such as desire, had his mind purified by sacrifices, gifts, or austerity, and in whom arose knowledge of the supreme truth that all this is simply the One, the *Brahman*, the non-doer, what may appear—even after action and its motive have disappeared—as his involvement in action for the guidance of people and with the same assiduity as before, is no action. . . [7]

A little further, explaining verse 3.20 which says that Janaka and others attained liberation through action alone, Śaṅkara adds that, even though these enlightened men did not renounce physically at any point in time, they did reach a stage which he calls "renunciation of actions":

> If, even though knowers of the Reality, *Janaka and others* of old were engaged in actions, they did so for the guidance of people. *They attained perfection* only through the knowledge that "the *guṇas* act upon the *guṇas*."[8] The idea is that, even though [the stage of] renunciation of actions had been reached (*karmasaṃnyāse prāpte 'pi*), *they attained perfection* through action alone, that is, they did not renounce rites [physically].[9]

What then is the meaning of "renunciation of actions" (*karmasaṃnyāsa*) here? Both the above quotations describe enlightened men who have direct Self-knowledge and are beyond the realm of the *guṇas* and activity. In other words, they are liberated in this very life. Because they have attained direct Self-knowledge and reached the ultimate spiritual goal, all prescribed actions have certainly served their purpose.[10] Therefore the meaning of Śaṅkara's comment is that these liberated men were no doubt justified in renouncing these prescribed actions physically, but they did not, for the sake of providing an examplary behavior to people around them. It also follows that the level of renunciation of actions (*karmasaṃnyāsa*), which they are said to have attained, must refer to the possibility of physical renunciation *after* reaching a Self-knowledge that is already direct in nature.

Śaṅkara comes back with a similar description in his introduction to verse 4.20:

> On the other hand, one having started with action and having gained the right perception of the Self later on, surely abandons actions along with their accessories, as he does not see any purpose in action. If for some reason it is impossible to abandon actions, he remains involved in actions as before, in order to guide people, without attachment to action and its rewards, as he has no purpose of his own. Yet he does nothing at all, because, being burnt by the fire of knowledge, his action turns out to be inaction.[11]

Again the idea conveyed by Śaṅkara is that the most logical behavior after enlightenment is to abandon rites physically. And even when this is impossible, absence of doership ("he does nothing at all") is maintained by the enlightened man. This suggests that absence of doership—or renunciation of doership—is already achieved along with direct Self-knowledge when the stage of "abandonment of actions" (*karmaparityāga*) or physical renunciation referred to in this context is attained.

A little further, Śaṅkara insists that "because the man of knowledge is endowed with the perception of the actionless Self, the action done by him is in reality non-action."[12] He then repeats more or less the same idea as in the introduction to the verse:

> When such a person, having no purpose of his own, has reached the conviction that action and its accessories are only to be abandoned, then, if he finds it impossible to leave [them], *even though he engages in actions* as before—with a view to guide people or to avoid the blame of the virtuous—*he does not do anything*, because he is endowed with the perception of the actionless Self.[13]

Referring to verse 4.20 in his introduction to verse 4.23, Śaṅkara gives a similar description, mentioning again that the enlightened man has reached the stage where he is justified in abandoning actions physically also:

> When a person having started with actions attains the realization that the Self is the actionless *Brahman*, then, seeing no doer, action

> and purpose in the Self, he reaches [the stage of] abandonment of actions (*karmaparityāge prāpte*). If for some reason this [abandonment] is not possible, even though engaged in actions as before, he does not do anything. This absence of action has been shown in the verse "having abandoned attachment to the rewards of actions [4.20]." With respect to the same person who has been shown to be without action . . .[14]

Let us now consider the hypothesis that the "renunciation of all actions" (*sarvakarmasaṃnyāsa*) found in the householder's sequence toward liberation is the same as "renunciation of actions" (*karmasaṃnyāsa* or *karmaparityāga*) in the comments on verses 2.11, 4.20, and 4.23 quoted above. Then "renunciation of all actions" (*sarvakarmasaṃnyāsa*) would refer to physical renunciation of prescribed actions *not before* enlightenment, as is usually interpreted, but *after* it has been attained. And the stage of "attainment of knowledge" (*jñānaprāpti*) would not refer to a mediate knowledge or conviction about the Self, but to a Self-knowledge that is already immediate.

A first observation on this hypothesis is that the meaning it gives to "renunciation of all actions" (*sarvakarmasaṃnyāsa*) and "attainment of knowledge" (*jñānaprāpti*) in the householder's sequence is much more consistent with Śaṅkara's basic doctrinal position. Indeed, when we understand that, in this sequence, "renunciation of all actions" (*sarvakarmasaṃnyāsa*) means physical renunciation *after* enlightenment, the three inconsistencies raised by the usual interpretation of the sequence simply disappear. First, inasmuch as, in the sequence, physical renunciation is done *after* enlightenment, mediate and immediate Self-knowledge have necessarily been gained *before* physical renunciation, which avoids the inconsistency of making the latter a necessary step before mediate or immediate Self-knowledge. Second, since direct Self-knowledge—the first condition for liberation—is present even before physical renunciation, it follows that liberation is attainable while not being a physical renunciant. Third, since the physical renunciation of this sequence pertains to the person who is already enlightened, since the latter is beyond the scope of prescriptions and since he is no more, for instance, the individual self of the non-Brahmin to whom the prohibition of physical renunciation is addressed, it is fair to assume that enlightened non-Brahmins also could physically renounce without violating the principle of this prohibition. Thus, according to our interpretation, the householder's sequence has a universal application with respect to cases of liberation without prior physical renunciation. And this does not contradict any of the five basic reference points presented in chapter 3.

Yet the following objection could be raised: if, in this sequence, "attainment of knowledge" (*jñānaprāpti*) is already immediate in nature, then "steadfastness in knowledge" (*jñānaniṣṭhā*), which follows renunciation of all actions and is the last level before liberation, becomes redundant. Our reply is that although in both "attainment of knowledge" and "steadfastness in knowledge," the said knowledge is immediate, "steadfastness in knowledge" is meant to emphasize that the means of liberation is steadiness in direct Self-knowledge alone, rather than any kind of "steadfastness in action" (*karmaniṣṭhā*) comprising rites alone or their combination with meditation. As we will see in the next chapter, Śaṅkara often uses the terms "steadfastness in action" and "steadfastness in knowledge" to mean respectively the conditions of bondage and liberation. Thus, the term "steadfastness in knowledge" serves mainly in refuting other theories concerning the means of liberation and, by doing so, it brings to the fore the logical consequences of the complete mental and physical renunciation which precedes it. It equally points out that even those who could stop the physical performance of rites after attaining direct Self-knowledge, and who, however, choose to continue with it, are also devoid of all activity and therefore liberated through Self-knowledge alone.

A few commentators of Śaṅkara have favored interpretations which may appear similar to the one proposed here, but which are in fact quite different. After introducing the sequence given in BhG 5.12, Trevor Legget insists, for instance, that the third level, namely, attainment of knowledge (*jñānaprāpti*), "means a direct view of Self; it is not simply an intellectual idea" (Śaṅkara 1978a, 55). Elsewhere he refers as follows to this type of summary in Śaṅkara's commentary on the *Gītā*: "The doctrine is summed up in many places; for instance II.69 says that when they have realized the Self (quoting V.17—tadbuddhayas tadātmanas), their duty (adhikāra) consists in renunciation of all actions and devotion to Knowledge (jñānaniṣṭhā)" (Ibid., 170). However, referring a few lines below to enlightened kings, Legget suggests that he views the steadfastness in knowledge (*jñānaniṣṭhā*) which follows, as a practice rather than a permanent state devoid of any exertion: "In the Gītā commentary, however, Śaṅkara allows certain exceptions to the rule that jñānaniṣṭhā must entail saṃnyāsa. . . . In the commentary to IV.2, several kings who were practicing jñānaniṣṭhā are given as examples" (Ibid.). Legget also understands that the experience referred to by "attainment of knowledge" is not yet stabilized and will ideally be "reinforced, or rather protected from disturbance of remaining prārabdhakarma" (Ibid., 171) through a physical renunciation that will allow full absorption in the discipline of knowledge.

But this does not fit the context of the householder's sequence under consideration, because Legget's interpretation presents *physical* renunciation for liberation as a *universal* rule, and regards the absence of it as an exception. This understanding misses Śaṅkara's point in the sequence, which is to show the *universality of direct Self-knowledge* as the sole means of liberation, even before considering the question of the active and monastic ways of living as means to reach it.

On his part, Karl Potter believes that "*saṃnyāsa is* liberation—so that it is tautologous to say one must pass through it to be liberated" (1981, 35). In the context of the householder's sequence, however, "renunciation of all actions" (*sarvakarmasaṃnyāsa*) cannot be equal to liberation. If Śaṅkara understood "renunciation of all actions" and liberation as synonymous, it would have been redundant and useless to mention them as distinct items in the sequence. True, even when the sequence conveys that one achieves liberation by "starting" with attainment of knowledge (*jñānaprāpti*) and "going through" renunciation of all actions (*sarvakarmasaṃnyāsa*) and steadfastness in knowledge (*jñānaniṣṭhā*), in fact, nothing more happens at the cognitive level, since direct Self-knowledge is already acheived at the level of "attainment of knowledge." But Potter's interpretation does not account for the many descriptions of *physical* renunciation referring to the already enlightened person in Śaṅkara's comments. While Potter takes "renunciation of all actions" in the figurative sense of renunciation of doership alone or even liberation, the context of Śaṅkara's commentary does not allow us to do so with respect to the householder's sequence considered here, as shown by the passages on Janaka and other enlightened people who are seen not to actualize the *physical* aspect of "renunciation of all actions."

Further evidence in favor of our interpretation is found in chapter 5, from which the above three summaries of the householder's sequence have been taken. In BhG 5.19, Śaṅkara states that verses 5.13 to 29 describe the renouncer of all actions (*sarvakarmasaṃnyāsin*): ". . . from '[having] mentally [renounced] all actions' to the end of the chapter, the topic is the renouncer of all actions" (BhG 5.19, 268). Therefore, it would be fair to say that, for all practical purposes, the summaries of 5.12 (list B) and 5.27 (list A) are respectively the introduction (or at least the foreword) and conclusion of this specific section. This is especially valid in view of the fact that the last three verses of the chapter, from 27 to 29, are turned toward the next chapter of the *Gītā*, as a kind of preview of the theme of meditation developed in chapter 6. Now, according to Vedic exegesis, one of the six criteria (*ṣaḍliṅgas*) for finding the purport of a text is the principle of unity of the initial and concluding passages (*upakramopasaṃhāraikya*).[15] It assumes that, a Vedic text being infallible, its introduction (*upakrama*) and conclusion (*upasaṃhāra*) must agree. Hence, if the meaning of a particular statement is not obvious, it can be interpreted with reference to the undubious fact that the text expresses a basic single idea from beginning to end. Śaṅkara does use this very important criterion in a number of places,[16] even adding the notion of harmony with the development (*madhya*),[17] as well as between the introduction and the conclusion. Hence, this criterion can be made use of here.

If Śaṅkara himself wrote according to this rule, then the summaries of the householder's sequence found in the comments on verses 12, 17, and 27 of chapter 5 must agree and convey the same meaning. If, according to Śaṅkara, the main theme of this section is the renouncer of all actions, then what is the nature of his renunciation? As a first indication, a reading of the verses themselves conveys quite clearly that, from 5.13 to 26, the *Gītā* describes the enlightened person in various ways, ascribing to him liberation from birth and death. The brief introductions given by Śaṅkara to some of these verses confirm this purport. Just before verse 13, we read: "But as for the man who sees the supreme reality . . ." (BhG 5.13, 257); then, before verse 18: "Now He explains how the wise men, whose ignorance of the Self has been destroyed by knowledge, see the Reality" (BhG 5.18, 265); again before verse 21: "Moreover, he who rests in *Brahman* . . ." (BhG 5.21, 269); and finally before verse 24: "And what kind of a person, being established in *Brahman*, attains *Brahman*? He answers: . . ." (BhG 5.24, 274). Since all these passages have in common the theme of the enlightened man and also, as stated by Śaṅkara, that of the renouncer of all actions, it is totally consistent with the context of this section of the commentary to interpret "renunciation of all actions" in the householder's sequence toward liberation as that of the enlightened man.

Moreover, after quoting verses 18, 19, 21, 22, 24, 32, 33, 37, and 41 of chapter 4, Śaṅkara specifies in his introduction to chapter 5 that all these refer to renunciation of all actions (*sarvakarmasaṃnyāsa*).[18] And, according to his interpretation of each of these verses, they all refer to various aspects of the already enlightened person. First, verse 18 describes the enlightened man who sees inaction in action and action in inaction; verse 19 provides the occasion for Śaṅkara to describe the two possible courses after enlightenment: either physical renunciation of rites or their continuance for the sake of guiding people; verse 20 refers to the enlightened who, although continuing actions, does nothing at all; verses 21 and 22 describe the enlightened man who has renounced physically and who is also not bound by anything; verses 23, 24, 32, and 33 talk about the "knowledge-sacrifice" of the liberated person for whom everything is *Brahman*; verse 37 eulogizes the fire of direct Self-knowledge which reduces all actions to ashes; finally verse 41 states that one who has renounced actions through yoga and knowledge is not bound by them. Thus, from this larger context also, it appears much more consistent to interpret the term "renunciation of all actions" of the householder's sequence toward liberation, not as a necessary requirement for the seeker-after-liberation, but as the physical renunciation of the already enlightened person.

"RENUNCIATION OF ALL ACTIONS" AS DISTINCT FROM "RENUNCIATION OF ACTIONS"

We already established that the renunciation of all actions (*sarvakarmasaṃnyāsa*) of the householder's sequence toward liberation stated in BhG 5.12, 5.17, and 5.27 refers to the physical renunciation of the enlightened man. Further analysis of the use of this compound in various places of Śaṅkara's commentary on the *Gītā* reveals that it means more precisely renunciation of mental, oral, and bodily actions. We contend that this is the exact meaning of "renunciation of all actions" in the householder's sequence. In addition we hold that inasmuch as giving up all actions can occur only in the absence of doership, in the householder's sequence, renunciation of all actions must refer above all to abandonment of doership. Let us now turn to passages favoring this interpretation.

In his introduction to chapter 5, Śaṅkara explicitly distinguishes between a type of renunciation which is *not free* from the limitation of doership, and another which *is*. He clearly makes a separate case for "the renunciation of actions (*karmasaṃnyāsa*) which, *being accompanied by the sense of doership,*[19] applies to a few actions [only], and which is different from the renunciation of all actions (*sarvakarmasaṃnyāsa*) previously referred to[20] and accomplished by the knowers of the Self."[21] It is quite clear that, in Śaṅkara's eyes, renunciation of actions refers to a partial abandonment of actions because it *is not* accompanied by renunciation of doership, and that renunciation of *all* actions refers to full abandonment of actions because it *is* accompanied by renunciation of doership.

Śaṅkara also distinguishes these two types of renunciation by adding the word *sarva* (all) to the compound intended to mean renunciation devoid of doership. As stated in a discussion on the purport of "renunciation of all actions" (*sarvakarmasaṃnyāsa*) at the end of the comment on verse 2.21 (transl., 57), in this compound, the word "all" conveys that all kinds of actions are included: mental, oral, and bodily. Similarly, when verse 5.13 says that one "has renounced all actions" (*sarvakarmāṇi . . . saṃnyasya*), it means, according to Śaṅkara, that "he has abandoned oral, mental and bodily movements" (*tyaktavāṅmanaḥkāyaceṣṭā*).[22] "And," he adds, "it stands to reason that he renounces mentally, through wisdom, through discriminative knowledge, the actions of the non-Self superimposed on the supreme Self because of ignorance."[23] If renunciation of all actions comes with cessation of superimposition of the non-Self on the Self, it must include abandonment of doership and can be found only in the enlightened man.

Four inadequate interpretations of the contrast between "renunciation of actions" and "renunciation of all actions" must be set aside at this point. First, Śaṅkara does not intend to oppose undue physical renunciation, motivated by tendencies such as laziness or misunderstanding,[24] with proper physical renunciation, motivated by a mediate knowledge concerning the true nature of the Self. Evidence for this is provided by the fact that, while commenting on the statement "renunciation (*saṃnyāsa*) and yoga of action (*karmayoga*) both lead to the highest good" (verse 5.2), Śaṅkara specifies that partial renunciation, referred to by him as "mere renunciation of ritual actions" (*karmasaṃnyāsāt kevalāt*), does lead to liberation in due time. In Śaṅkara's commentary on chapter 5, "renunciation of actions" (*karmasaṃnyāsa*) is never presented as an improper physical renunciation which could never lead to liberation. Rather, it is a proper abandonment which can eventually yield liberation through Self-knowledge.

The interpretation of "renunciation of actions" as an undue abandonment is improper also because, according to it, the "renunciation of all actions" with which it is contrasted would be the prescribed and proper physical renunciation based only on mediate Self-knowledge and therefore accompanied by doership. But, in his definition of the contrast between renunciation of actions and renunciation of all actions, Śaṅkara stipulates that renunciation of actions entails the sense of doership while renunciation of all actions does not.

It should be emphasized here that one cannot experience at the same time mere mediate Self-knowledge and absence of doership. Only direct experience of oneself as identical with the actionless *Brahman* can eliminate the sense of being a doer. When devoid of direct knowledge of the actionless *Ātman-Brahman,* even the act of physically renouncing is characterized by doership. "And because the Self is immutable," writes Śaṅkara, "the fact that things such as doership come from ignorance holds good with regard to all actions alike."[25] Śaṅkara explains in BhG 4.18 how the sense of doership is found in all people who do not know the actionless nature of the Self by direct experience, whether they have physically renounced or are still pursuing an active life in society:

> . . . and, superimposing on the Self actions pertaining to forms such as the body, one thinks: "I am a doer, this ritual action is mine, I am going to enjoy its reward." In the same way, one thinks: "I shall remain quiet, so that I may be without fatigue, free from action, happy;" having thus superimposed on the Self the cessation of activity pertaining to the body and the senses, as well as the ensuing happiness, one imagines: "I am not doing anything," [and later on] "I was quiet and happy."[26]

Commenting on *Gītā* 18.24, Śaṅkara further specifies that "even the doer of a pure (*sāttvika*) action is ignorant of the Self and has the sense of ego (*sāhaṃkāra*)."[27] Whether the renouncer having physically abandoned ritual actions is simply lazy or an ardent seeker-after-liberation totally devoting himself to the discipline of knowledge, his renunciation is not complete and does not involve eradication of ignorance and its effects, because it does not include abandonment of doership. Moreover, in BṛU 4.3.22, Śaṅkara even refers to practices of the unenlightened formal renouncer as specific "*karmans*" (333) which define him as a monk in contrast to people belonging to other modes of living. Thus, the abandonment of "a few actions" pertaining to the yoga of action, and the adoption of those pertaining to the formal renouncer, even when they exclude everything but the discipline of knowledge, is not what Śaṅkara understands by "renunciation of all actions" in his introduction to chapter 5 of the *Gītā*.

According to another possible interpretation, Śaṅkara would be opposing "renunciation of actions" to "renunciation of all actions" in terms of "renunciation of actions" as pure and appropriate physical renunciation *unaccompanied* by mediate Self-knowledge, versus "renunciation of all actions" as "renunciation of actions" *when accompanied* by mediate Self-knowledge. This is also incorrect, because pure and appropriate physical renunciation for the sake of Self-knowledge and liberation implies at least a general mediate knowledge about the true nature of the Self. Thus, the first element of the proposed opposition cannot even exist: by definition, there can be no appropriate and pure physical renunciation as subsidiary to Self-knowledge without general mediate Self-knowledge. As the above proposed opposition includes a term that is not even valid, it is not likely to be the meaning intended by Śaṅkara.

Nor is Śaṅkara discerning, in a third possible interpretation, between proper physical renunciation based only on a general (*āpāta*) mediate

Self-knowledge and the same based on a precise mediate Self-knowledge—a distinction used by later *Advaitins*. This is because he states explicitly that the difference between the two types of renunciation is based on whether one abandons a few or all actions, and whether or not one has the sense of doership. It is not a function of whether one has a general or precise mediate Self-knowledge. Moreover none of Śaṅkara's works contains any clear reference to the distinction between general and precise mediate Self-knowledge.

Finally Śaṅkara is not contrasting even proper physical renunciation by the seeker-after-liberation possessed of mediate Self-knowledge, with the enlightened's physical renunciation accompanied by immediate Self-knowledge. A detailed analysis is needed to point out the shortcoming of this interpretation. Śaṅkara's whole introduction to chapter 5 aims at showing that the question (answered by verse 5.2) as to which of the two, yoga of action or renunciation of action, is superior, does not apply to the liberated-in-life because these options represent two paths for unenlightened people who still have the sense of doership.[28] According to the context of the commentary on chapters 4 and 5, the idea of treading a path rendered necessary by ignorance of the Self—whether yoga of action in the householder's mode of living or full-time discipline of knowledge in the monastic mode of living—is incompatible with both the enlightened man continuing his life in society, and the enlightened physical renouncer. Whether he pursues ritual actions just for guidance of people (*lokasaṅgraha*) or abandons them physically, the enlightened Self-knower remains beyond the obligation of undertaking the yoga of action or physical renunciation, which are enjoined for two types of unenlightened people. Before contrasting renunciation of actions and renunciation of all actions in the passage under discussion (taken from the introduction to chapter 5), Śaṅkara first rejects the possiblity that yoga of action be mandatory for the enlightened Self-knower:

> . . . [for the Self-knower] it is taught that, owing to the contradiction between right and false knowledge as well as between their effects, yoga of action is not possible—the latter being accompanied by the sense of doership based on false knowledge, being made up of a state wherein the Self is active, and being the opposite of the latter [renunciation of all actions].[29] Therefore it is rightly said that, for the Self-knower whose false knowledge has disappeared, yoga of action, which is based on erroneous knowledge, is impossible.[30]

Now, in verse 5.2, the *Gītā* states that yoga of action is superior to renunciation of actions. Because both the enlightened physical renouncer and the monastic seeker-after-liberation have physical renunciation (*karmasaṃnyāsa*) in common, the term "renunciation of actions" might be interpreted here as the enlightened's physical abandonment and therefore be viewed as inferior to the yoga of action of the unenlightened person. To avoid this, in his introduction to the chapter, Śaṅkara distinguishes "renunciation of all actions" from "renunciation of actions," specifying that, in the latter's case, the sense of doership is still prevailing, while it is completely absent in the former by virtue of direct Self-knowledge.[31] Thus, in a context where "renunciation of actions" is as connected with doership as is the yoga of action, the latter can be viewed as superior to the former; but being devoid of doership, renunciation of all actions is uncomparable with both. Renunciation of all actions on the part of the enlightened person still active in society is as opposed to the yoga of action and to renunciation of actions, as is renunciation of all actions on the part of the enlightened physical renunciant. Therefore, renunciation of all actions is opposed to the yoga of action and to renunciation of actions because it refers to abandonment of doership, not because it refers to the combination of abandonment of doership and physical renunciation. It follows that the only valid interpretation of the contrast between renunciation of actions and renunciation of all actions remains the opposition between the following: 1. physical renunciation accompanied by mediate Self-knowledge, and 2. that type of renunciation which, including first of all renunciation of doership, is possible only for the enlightened and leads logically to physical renunciation, but does not always include it from the practical viewpoint.

But Śaṅkara's use of terms related to renunciation is not always consistent. For example, the term "renunciation of all actions" (*sarvakarmasaṃnyāsa*) does not always entail absence of doership, and "renunciation of actions" (*karmasaṃnyāsa*) or "renunciation" (*saṃnyāsa*) sometimes includes it. Among these instances are the passages already quoted where even though the enlightened man "has reached [the stage of] renunciation of action" (*karmasaṃnyāse prāpte* or *karmaparityāge prāpte*), for some reason, he does not abandon them physically. Although the word "all" is not used here, as we saw, Śaṅkara means that the enlightened has indeed attained the stage where renunciation of *all* actions is possible, yet he does not carry out the physical aspect of it.

Śaṅkara's commentaries on verses 4.20 and 4.23–24 even show that in the author's usage, the expression "renunciation of all actions" can mean renunciation of doership alone (i.e., unaccompanied by physical renunciation) as a result of immediate Self-knowledge, and can thus be characteristic even of the enlightened person who has not physically abandoned ritual actions. Śaṅkara interprets the *Brahman*-sacrifice described in verse 4.24 as being performed by a Self-knower who has not carried out physical renunciation. This man, he insists, is "a renouncer of all action" (*sarvakarmasaṃnyāsin*). Thus, Śaṅkara leaves no doubt that here the compound means renunciation of doership alone, as it coexists with the physical performance of rites:

> Thus, even the action performed by one desiring to guide people, is in reality non-action, for it has been annulled by the knowledge of *Brahman*. This being so, it is most appropriate, for the purpose of praising the right perception, to represent as a sacrifice the knowledge of one in whom action has even disappeared and who is a renouncer of all actions. . . . Therefore, all actions cease to exist for the man of knowledge who recognizes that all this is but *Brahman* . . .[32]

Two English translators of Śaṅkara's commentary have clearly missed the purport of this passage, providing yet another example of the misinterpretation still prevailing around such expressions from Śaṅkara's works. Both their renderings suggest that by "renouncer of all actions," Śaṅkara refers to a formal renunciant, that is, to a monk who is here uncharacteristically represented as performing a sacrifice. Ramachandra Aiyar translates the middle part of the above passage as follows: "It thus becomes exceedingly appropriate to represent the Knowledge of even the *saṁnyāsin*[33] who has retired from action and renounced all actions, as *yajña* (sacrifice) . . ." (BhG, transl., 163). Swāmī Gambhīrānanda displays an even more explicit monastic bias: "This being so, in the case of the monk from whom action has dropped off, who has renounced all activity, viewing his Knowledge as (a kind of) sacrifice, too, becomes justifiable . . ." (Śaṅkara 1984, 209).

First, these renderings overlook Śaṅkara's introduction to this verse in which he conveys that the performer of this knowledge-sacrifice is the same person that is clearly depicted in verse 23 as a Self-knower who did not physically abandon ritual actions after his enlightenment. Indeed Śaṅkara links the two verses by saying that the second verse is the explanation given for the situation described in the first: "What is then the reason for saying that an action under way is entirely dissolved, without producing its effect? Because . . ." (BhG 4.24, 216). Second, as is implied in the comment on verse 24 quoted above, attribution of the term "renouncer of all actions" is not determined by the condition of physical renunciation, but by the absence of duality and doership in the enlightened man, which applies to the seemingly active Self-knower as well as to the enlightened physical renouncer. It is also significant that Śaṅkara quotes verse 23 in his comment on verse 24, pointing out again that the subject matter of the latter is the same seemingly active enlightened man:

> . . . no ritual action such as the *agnihotra* is ever found deprived of the knowledge of the distinctions between action, accessories and rewards of action, or devoid of the sense of doership and aiming at rewards. But, in this ritual action, the knowledge of the distinctions between actions such as offerings, rewards, and agent of actions, has been annulled by the knowledge of *Brahman*; hence it is no action at all. . . . As it is mere external movement, the action of the man of knowledge turns out to be inaction. Hence it was said that his action "is entirely dissolved" [4.23].[34]

It is therefore quite clear that, at least once, Śaṅkara uses the concept of renunciation of all actions to mean renunciation of doership alone, a fact which reinforces the idea that, in the householder's sequence toward liberation, renunciation of all actions applies only to the already enlightened and not to the seeker-after-liberation.

The criterion of unity of the initial and concluding passages can help us in further assessing Śaṅkara's overall consistency with respect to the term renunciation of all actions and the householder's sequence toward liberation. This will be done by connecting the summary of the process of liberation in Śaṅkara's *introduction*, with some of his *concluding comments* in chapter 18, which closes the work. Let us first give the summaries found in the introduction and in verse 18.10, which are clearly akin to the ones found in chapter 5:

D-BhG, INTRO[35]

1. "*dharma* consisting of engagement in action" *(pravṛttilakṣaṇo dharmaḥ)* yet practiced with devotion and without attachment to rewards
2. "purity of mind" *(sattvaśuddhi)*
3. "attainment of the ability to be steadfast in knowledge"[36] *(jñānaniṣṭhāyogyatāprāpti)*
   and
   "emergence of knowledge" *(jñānotpatti)*
4. "renunciation of all actions" *(sarvakarmasaṃnyāsa)*

5. "steadfastness in Self-knowledge" (*ātmajñānaniṣṭhā*)
6. "highest good" (*niḥśreyasa*)[37]

E-BhG 18.10[38]

1. "yoga of action" (*karmayoga*)
2. "purified in mind" (*saṃskṛtātman*)
3. "he realizes that he is himself the actionless Self" (*ātmānam ātmatvena saṃbuddhaḥ*)
4. "having mentally renounced all actions" (*sarvakarmāṇi manasā saṃnyasya*)
5. "steadfastness in knowledge which consists of actionlessness" (*naiṣkarmyalakṣaṇā jñānaniṣṭhā*)
6. "highest good" (*niḥśreyasa*)

Let us contextualize our interpretation of these summaries. Commenting on verse 18.17, Śaṅkara first confirms the meaning of the latter: "Therefore, it has rightly been said that, because his awareness is not polluted by the impression that he is a doer, the man of knowledge *neither kills nor is bound*."[39] Śaṅkara then points out that this reference to non-killing through absence of doership echoes verse 2.19 which declares: "he slays not, nor is he slain." Thus, in Śaṅkara's eyes, the *Gītā* comes full circle with the essential message that through experience of the actionless Self, one reaches renunciation or absence of doership and, as a result, freedom from everything, including ritualistic obligations:

> Having declared "he does not slay, nor is he slain" [2.19] . . . having briefly stated at the beginning of the scripture, in "He who knows [the Self] to be indestructible" [2.21], that qualification for actions ceases in the case of the man of knowledge, having developed [this] repeatedly in the middle whenever he found an occasion, here, in order to sum up the purport of the scripture, [the Lord] concludes by saying that the man of knowledge *neither kills, nor is bound*.[40]

The items "emergence of knowledge" (*jñānotpatti*) and "renunciation of all actions" (*sarvakarmasaṃnyāsa*) found in the above sequence of the introduction to the *Gītā* are presented as part of "the *dharma* which constitutes the purport of the *Gītā*" (*gītārthadharma*). [41] According to the criterion of textual unity of beginning and end of the *Gītā* underscored by Śaṅkara, these two terms must convey the same basic message of the *Gītā* that is summed up again in the comment on verse 18.17 (last quotation above) and that focuses on freedom from actions for the enlightened man. Therefore, in the sequence toward liberation given by Śaṅkara in his introduction to the *Gītā*, "emergence of knowledge" and "renunciation of all actions" must mean respectively the rise of immediate Self-knowledge in the enlightened man and the abandonment of all actions—mental and bodily—that logically ensues.

Pursuing his comment on verse 18.17, Śaṅkara adds concerning the synthesis of verse 18.17 that the only persons referred to as not bound by the results of action (in this life and at the time of death of the body) are the "renouncers" (*saṃnyāsin*) who do not see themselves as "embodied" (*dehabhṛt*)[42] and who are therefore enlightened:

> Thus, when the impression of being embodied is untenable, [and] when it is reasonable that the *saṃnyāsins* completely renounce actions generated by ignorance, it is reasonable to say that the three kinds of results of action (the disagreeable ones, etc.) do not accrue to them; and conversely, in the case of others, it is inevitable that the results accrue. Thus is concluded the teaching of the *Gītā* scripture.[43]

It follows from the criterion of textual unity that these *saṃnyāsins* or "renouncers" must be equivalent to the enlightened renouncers of all actions found in the basic sequence toward liberation in Śaṅkara's introduction to the *Gītā* as well as in the householder's sequence of the comment on chapter 5.

In the light of all these passages, let us now summarize the purport of the basic sequence, leading to liberation in the case of householders. First, emergence of knowledge following the practice of the yoga of action, is already direct in nature. Then *sarvakarmasaṃnyāsa* means that type of renunciation which includes all actions, mental as well as oral and bodily. Therefore it includes renunciation—that is, absence—of doership and it is possible only for the enlightened. As far as the latter are concerned, in principle, renunciation of all actions is universal, which agrees with Śaṅkara's contextualization of the sequence. Yet, in practice, the physical aspect of this renunciation is not actualized by all liberated men. Because, by definition, all enlightened people have renounced doership through direct knowledge of the Self as free from activity, and because they ever maintain that steadfastness in knowledge (*jñānaniṣṭhā*), even apparent continuation of rites on their part in no way contradicts the principle that liberation comes from Self-knowledge alone. As a consequence, it is not physical abandonment of rites as a necessary prerequisite for the discipline of knowledge, that is put forward by Śaṅkara in the householder's sequence leading to liberation, but rather renunciation of doership as an essential condition for direct Self-knowledge and liberation.

THE SEQUENCE BETWEEN DIRECT SELF-KNOWLEDGE AND RENUNCIATION

These findings have major consequences for the understanding of Śaṅkara's repeated statement that liberation can only be reached through Self-knowledge accompanied by renunciation. We saw that, according to Śaṅkara's basic soteriological standpoint, Self-knowledge alone can annihilate spiritual ignorance and its binding effect. But, in Śaṅkara's various statements joining Self-knowledge with renunciation for the purpose of liberation, what is the nature of renunciation? Is it physical renunciation, is it abandonment of doership, or both? Is it a means for the experience of the Self or one of its characteristics? And what is the exact relationship between Self-knowledge and renunciation? Does one precede the other (logically or chronologically), are they concomitant, or are they metaphorically presented as identical?

Let us look first at the positive words used by Śaṅkara to express the connection between renunciation and Self-knowledge as the means to liberation.[44] In BhG 2.11 (40), for instance, grief and delusion, which are the causes of transmigratory existence, are said to come to an end "through knowledge of the Self preceded by (*pūrvaka*) renunciation of all actions." In BhG 18.66 (761), "steadfastness in knowledge preceded by (*pūrvika*),[45] renunciation of all actions," is said to pertain to the enlightened man. In BhG 18.55 (743), the word *sahita* (accompanied by) is used to connect the two notions:[46] it is said that knowledge must be "accompanied by renunciation of all actions." In BṛU 4.5.15 (383), the two are coordinated by the particle "and" (*ca*): "complete knowledge and renunciation of everything" represent the means of immortality. In some places, renunciation (*saṃnyāsa*) is said to serve as a subsidiary to knowledge (*jñānāṅgatva*).[47] In the above examples, renunciation precedes or accompanies knowledge. But the reverse is also stated: in the introduction to chapter 5 of the *Gītā*, it is renunciation (*saṃnyāsa*) as "accompanied by knowledge" (*jñānasahita*) that is considered the means to perfection.[48] In BhG 18.8 (684), it is also knowledge that precedes (or accompanies) renunciation, as liberation is said to be "the result of abandonment of all actions preceded by (*pūrvaka*) knowledge." Finally, in his introduction to the *Gītā*, Śaṅkara quotes the *Mahābhārata* as stating that "knowledge is characterized by [or consists of] renunciation" (*jñānaṃ saṃnyāsalakṣaṇaṃ*).[49]

As is evident from these few examples, the various wordings concerning the relationship between renunciation and Self-knowledge in Śaṅkara's commentaries show some ambiguity. One is not always sure as to what precedes what, or if both are concomitant, and if all these expressions always refer to the same type of knowledge and the same kind of renunciation. Undoubtedly, such ambiguity is partly responsible for centuries of misinterpretations about the intent of their author. The now prevailing *Advaita Vedānta* doctrine on the matter is that one must physically renounce in order to have access to the discipline of knowledge which alone opens the awareness to direct experience of the Self and to liberation. But we will now demonstrate that these statements about the relationship between renunciation and Self-knowledge are not meant by Śaṅkara to establish physical renunciation as a mandatory means for direct Self-knowledge.

Let us start by considering the problem from a logical viewpoint. First, when Self-knowledge is said to be the means of liberation, it can only be immediate, because no mediate knowledge, which always amounts to mental activity, can annihilate the superimposition of mental activity on the immutable Self. Second, we can say that, irrespective of which of the two precedes the other, according to the statements quoted above, Self-knowledge and renunciation must be joined at some point. So let us first consider the nature of their conjunction as such. According to Śaṅkara, the yoga of action does not lead to liberation without the emergence of direct knowledge of the Self. This is also true for physical renunciation, as nobody can attain perfection "by mere renunciation, by merely abandoning action, without knowledge" (BhG 3.4, 145). So, if both the yoga of action and physical renunciation—in other words, the monastic way of living in itself—do not yield liberation without emergence of immediate Self-knowledge; if, as also acknowledged by Śaṅkara, the latter can occur without physical renunciation for Janaka and others; and if, in spite of this, Self-knowledge must still be accompanied by renunciation as a means to liberation, then, unless Śaṅkara is self-contradicting, the said renunciation can only be that of doership. Or, as we saw, it could also correspond to the renunciation of all actions which can occur only with the enlightened, and whose physical aspect may not be always actualized.

This logical approach is most useful for solving cases of ambiguity in the relationship between renunciation and Self-knowledge. In BhG 3.20, Śaṅkara explains that if Janaka and others attained liberation, they did it "verily without renouncing ritual action" (*asaṃnyasyaiva karma*).[50] Yet, in BhG 2.70, Śaṅkara writes that "liberation is attained only by the man of knowledge who has abandoned desires, who has a steady intellect and is a renouncer (*yati*), and not by the non-renouncer (*asaṃnyāsin*) *who cherishes desire* . . . "[51] So, within a few pages of the same work, one passage says that liberation can be attained without renunciation and the other says that it cannot, still using the same word: *asaṃnyasya* (merely shifted from the verbal to the nominal form in the second quotation). Does this amount to an elementary contradiction? No, because according to the evidence gathered so far, it can be easily removed by saying that, in the first case, "without renouncing ritual action" means "without taking up physical renunciation," which is consistent with Śaṅkara's basic position about physical renunciation, in that this type of renunciation is *not* mandatory for liberation. In the second case, "non-renouncer" means the one who has not renounced doership, who has not reached the type of renunciation which is concomitant with immediate knowledge of the Self and which in this respect alone is a sine qua non for liberation.

A similar ambiguity as to the status of renunciation is found in the comment on MuU 3.2.4. Glossing the words of the verse which says that *tapas* cannot be attained without *liṅga*, Śaṅkara writes: "*Tapas* here means knowledge. *Liṅga* means renunciation (*saṃnyāsa*).[52] The purport is that [the Self] is not attained through knowledge unaccompanied by (*rahita*) renunciation."[53] Śaṅkara adds that, through the help of knowledge and renunciation, "the man of knowledge, the man of discernment, the knower of the Self"[54] enters the abode of *Brahman*. Since the ideas of attaining the Self and entering the abode of *Brahman* suggest direct experience of *Ātman-Brahman*, the meaning seems to be here that Self-knowledge alone which is direct, and therefore accompanied by renunciation of doership, leads to liberation. If physical renunciation were meant as a necessary companion of knowledge, it would go counter to Śaṅkara's defense of the universal access to liberation through Self-knowledge, whatever the way of life.

On his part, after rendering *saṃnyāsa* by "monasticism" in a footnote to his translation of the commentary on this verse, Swāmī Gambhīrānanda reflects:

> Śaṅkara is very emphatic that external renunciation is necessary (see introductions to this and Aitareya Upaniṣads).[55] But Ānanda Giri seems to differ. Says he, "Why should this be so, since the Vedas mention the attainment of the Self by Indra, Janaka, Gārgī and others? That is a valid objection. Sannyāsa consists in renunciation of everything; and since they [the wise] had no idea of possession, they had the internal renunciation as a matter of fact.[56] The external sign is not the idea intended" (MuU, transl., 163–164).[57]

Does Ānandagiri really interpret here that Śaṅkara holds physical renunciation to be indispensable for liberation? It must be noted first that the opponent's argument ("Why should this be so . . .") does not aim at invalidating Śaṅkara's equation between *liṅga* and renunciation in its widest sense. Neither the opponent nor Ānandagiri himself try to deny this connexion between *liṅga* and *some form* of renunciation—yet to be determined. The issue introduced by the objection is rather: what type of renunciation should be understood as a synonym for *liṅga*? And when raising the objection that some people do achieve Self-knowledge without physical renunciation, the opponent suggests that he understands monasticism to be necessary in Śaṅkara's eyes. By answering "This is a valid objection," Ānandagiri agrees with the opponent that people do achieve enlightenment without physical renunciation. He explains this by the fact that they are possessed of this inner (*antara*) renunciation which is abandonment of "everything," in other words, "absence of the idea of possession" or "ownership" (*svatva*). This renunciation must be equivalent to freedom from doership as it is connected with attainment of full Self-knowledge on the part of Janaka and others. But, contrary to Gambhīrānanda's interpretation, by writing "The external sign is not the idea intended," Ānandagiri departs from the opponent rather than from Śaṅkara. He corrects the opponent's reading of the commentary by underlining that Śaṅkara does not intend physical renunciation and actually agrees with the opponent's view that it is not mandatory. So, what is pointed out as wrong by Ānandagiri is not Śaṅkara's interpretation, nor that of the opponent regarding the nature of renunciation in this verse, but the misinterpretation of the opponent with respect to Śaṅkara. Thus, taking recourse to Ānandagiri's commentary, Swāmī Gambhīrānanda comes to attribute to Śaṅkara himself the very viewpoint that Ānandagiri is trying to refute as a possible misinterpretation about Śaṅkara's commentary! Such is the imbroglio in which the interpretation about Śaṅkara's views on renunciation can culminate.

Other passages clearly show that abandonment of doership is the only form of renunciation that is required by Śaṅkara as a necessary means, along with Self-knowledge, for the purpose of liberation. At the beginning of his introduction to chapter 4 of the *Gītā*, Śaṅkara states that the yoga taught by Kṛṣṇa in the preceding chapters is "accompanied by renunciation and consists of steadfastness in knowledge" (*jñānaniṣṭhālakṣaṇaḥ sasaṃnyāsaḥ*).[58] Then, commenting on verse 4.2, he agrees that "*the royal seers*, those who were both kings and seers, *knew this* yoga *thus handed down in regular succession* among *Kṣatriyas*."[59] If this yoga included physical renunciation as a sine qua non for the discipline of knowledge or direct Self-knowledge, these generations of *Kṣatriyas* who, according to Śaṅkara, do not have access to this type of renunciation, could not have started the discipline of knowledge or reached liberation. They wouldn't even have known and taught the yoga described by Kṛṣṇa, since according to the spirit of the *Gītā* and the *Upaniṣads*, it can be really known only through direct experience of *Brahman-Ātman*.[60] Again, we do not think that Śaṅkara overlooked what, for many modern scholars, would seem to contradict his so-called dogmatic position on physical renunciation. Rather, when the yoga of steadfastness in knowledge, leading to liberation, is qualified by the term *sasaṃnyāsa*, it simply means Self-knowledge as necessarily "accompanied by renunciation [of doership]."

Similarly, in BṛU 4.4.23 (377), at the end of the dialogue between Yājñavalkya and Janaka, Śaṅkara confirms that the latter has now indeed "become *Brahman*" (*brahmabhūta*) and has therefore reached liberation-in-life. As a concluding remark, Śaṅkara adds: "The doctrine of *Brahman* has been completely dealt with, including renunciation, the subsidiary means and the procedures" (Ibid.). It is quite obvious that if physical renunciation were a prerequisite for acquiring complete instruction from Yājñavalkya, Janaka would never have received this teaching, and if it were also a necessary condition for liberation, he could not have reached enlightenment. But since parts of the dialogue (such as 3.5.1 and 4.4.22) deal with physical renunciation, the concluding remark on renunciation refers to it as well as to abandonment of doership.

Interestingly, in some passages, a relation of identity is even established between Self-knowledge and renunciation. In his MuU 3.2.6, Śaṅkara defines *saṃnyāsa* as the very experience of *Brahman*: "*Their minds*[61] *have become purified through the yoga of renunciation* (*saṃnyāsa*), through the yoga marked by abandonment of all actions, through the yoga consisting (*svarūpa*) only of steadfastness in *Brahman* alone."[62] According to Śaṅkara, the same equation is made in verse 5.6 of the *Gītā*: "But renunciation, O mighty-armed, is hard to attain without yoga. The sage equipped with yoga reaches *Brahman* before long."[63] With the understanding that renunciation and *Brahman*, the two objects of attainment stated here, are one and the same, and finding support from a passage of the *Taittirīya Upaniṣad* that equates the two, Śaṅkara holds that "renunciation, the topic under discussion, is termed '*Brahman*,' because it consists of steadfastness in the knowledge of the supreme Self."[64] Thus, these passages provide additional instances where *saṃnyāsa* refers to an inner abandonment based on direct Self-knowledge rather than to physical renunciation.

A gloss from BhG 18.49 shows a significant wavering between the idea that Self-knowledge and renunciation are identical and the notion that the former precedes the latter. Śaṅkara writes that the knower of the Self attains to perfection "*through saṃnyāsa* (renunciation), that is, through the right perception; or through renunciation of all actions preceded by the latter."[65] Śaṅkara seems to feel here that the identification of *saṃnyāsa* with the right perception may be suspected to be too far-fetched, and therefore suggests that Self-knowledge as preceding renunciation could have been left understood by the verse. But the identification of renunciation with the right perception is quite equivalent to that between renunciation and *Brahman* in verse 5.6 of the *Gītā* discussed above. In both cases we seem to have a metaphorical identity between renunciation and direct Self-knowledge, in that the two words are not employed with their primary usage (*mukhyavṛtti*), but rather with one that is secondary (*guṇavṛtti* or *lakṣaṇāvṛtti*).[66] It seems proper to analyze this metaphorical identity in a way similar to Sarvajñātman's when dealing with the fundamental statements (*mahāvākyas*) of the *Upaniṣads* such as "Thou art That." According to Sarvajñātman, this kind of metaphor can be understood either in terms of *guṇavṛtti*, that is, on the basis of a common quality, or in terms of *lakṣaṇāvṛtti*, that is, on the basis of some connection with the primary usage (Kocmarek 1985, 48–50). Using Sureśvara's explanation as presented in *Naiṣkarmyasiddhi* 2.55, Sarvajñātman holds that the individual "I" can be said to be That [supreme Self], because it shares the following qualities with the latter: inwardness, subtlety, and the (apparent) nature of consciousness (Ibid., 49). This equation is thus explained in terms of *guṇavṛtti*. In the same manner, we can understand that renunciation is said to be *Brahman* or its direct knowledge, because it is also characterized by actionlessness. Then Sarvajñātman explains "Thou art That" in terms of *jahadajahallakṣaṇā*, which is, according to him, the only type of *lakṣaṇā* properly accounting for such statements, and in which a part of the usual meaning of both terms is left out and a part of it is retained. In "Thou art That," the primary sense of remoteness implied by "That" is left aside and the primary sense of duality contained in "I" is also abandoned (Ibid.). Yet a portion of the remaining semantic scope of both "I" and "That" remains common, namely, the sense of pure and absolute consciousness (Ibid., 77). Similarly, in the case of renunciation and direct knowledge of *Brahman*, the primary meaning of renunciation as the physical abandonment of a material object or the cessation of an action is left behind, and the primary meaning of knowing something (namely, *Brahman*) as an object is dropped. The remaining common meaning between renunciation and direct knowledge of *Brahman* is then the pure subject as being devoid of action.

Now, coming back to the comment on *Gītā* 18.49, the intent of the second gloss on "through *saṃnyāsa*" seems to present the relationship between Self-knowledge and renunciation no longer in terms of identity but in terms of cause and effect: "or through renunciation of all actions preceded by the latter [right perception]." Renunciation is no longer equal to Self-knowledge, but an effect of it. This statement agrees with the householder's sequence toward liberation that was identified earlier and where renunciation of mental as well as physical actions follows the emergence of immediate Self-knowledge (*jñānotpatti*) and yields a permanent state of being which is as actionless as the Self (*jñānaniṣṭhā*).

Let us now turn to the various quotations given at the beginning of our discussion on the relationship between renunciation and Self-knowledge, and try to summarize Śaṅkara's position on the subject. First, as we saw in the previous chapter, at least some of these statements do enjoin physical renunciation as a means to full absorption in the discipline of knowledge, particularly those passages where renunciation is said to be a subsidiary (*aṅga*) to knowledge. Except for the monosemic usage of *aṅga*, all the other terms expressing the relationship betweeen renunciation and Self-knowledge do not seem to express a single invariable connection between the two notions. For instance, according to context, *pūrvaka* can be used to state that renunciation precedes Self-knowledge or vice versa. Moreover, as stated by Śaṅkara in his BhG 2.55, depending on whether one considers a scriptural statement as applying to a seeker-after-liberation or to an already enlightened person, it can be a means (for the aspirant) or a characteristic (for the enlightened). Because this can also apply to statements on renunciation, the relationship between the latter and Self-knowledge will vary according to the state of consciousness of the person to whom it refers.

Taking into account the various aspects discussed so far, we can summarize Śaṅkara's viewpoint on the relationship between renunciation and immediate Self-knowledge as a means to liberation in the following manner:

If immediate Self-knowledge precedes renunciation, then, according to context, renunciation is [1] above all, abandonment of doership, or [2] possibly, both the latter and physical abandonment of all practices. Here, direct Self-knowledge is the cause of abandonment of doership because it alone can destroy spiritual ignorance and its effects, such as superimposition of doership on the Self (BS 2.3.48, transl., 513).

If renunciation precedes immediate Self-knowledge, then, according to context, renunciation is [1] for Brahmins only, physical abandonment of ritual actions (itself preceded by some mediate knowledge about the real nature of the Self) as a subsidiary to Self-knowledge and/or [2] the inner process of withdrawal (mainly through meditation and available to both the *karmayogin* and the formal renouncer aspiring to liberation) until the cessation of all mental activity in the experience of the Self (*akhaṇḍākāravṛtti*),[67] or [3] "renunciation of all actions," that is, absence of doership accompanied or not by physical renunciation and understood as the middle term between attainment of immediate Self-knowledge (*jñānaprāpti*) and "resting," or being permanently steadfast, in that knowledge of the actionless Self (*ātmajñānaniṣṭhā*).

Finally, *if renunciation "is" immediate Self-knowledge,* it simply represents, in a figurative way, a characteristic of the direct experience of the Self, namely, the absence of the bondage of doership and action.

In the final analysis, for Śaṅkara, abandonment of doership is so intimately related to the actionless and unbounded nature of direct Self-knowledge that, even though a simple characteristic of the latter, it also acquires the status of a sine qua non of liberation. If Śaṅkara insisted so much on "renunciation of all actions," it is at least partly because, for his opponents, Self-knowledge remained in the field of mental activity and doership, while for him, the real Self was free from them and, leading beyond the realm of qualification and prescription, its direct knowledge totally justified physical renunciation as well as that of doership. And this underscored all the more clearly that direct Self-knowledge rather than action or its combination with Self-knowledge was the sole means of liberation.

CHAPTER SIX

The Main Opposition Between Steadfastness in Action and Steadfastness in Self-knowledge

As already shown in our analysis of the basic sequence leading householders to liberation, commentators usually interpret steadfastness in Self-knowledge (*jñānaniṣṭhā*) as the discipline of knowledge. It follows that the opposition frequently highlighted by Śaṅkara between steadfastness in action (*karmaniṣṭhā)* and steadfastness in Self-knowledge is most often understood in terms of two paths or types of practice: one based mainly on rites and the other based on their physical abandonment and full-time practice of the discipline of knowledge. There follows a tendency to center the debate concerning the role of action and Self-knowledge, around the opposition between the means available, on the one hand, to those who remain active in society and, on the other hand, to those who lead a monastic life. My contention is that, although found in Śaṅkara's teaching, this form of polarity between steadfastness in action and in knowledge is secondary as compared to a more basic opposition which these two terms also emphasize and which is often overlooked by interpreters. The *main* opposition stressed by Śaṅkara with these two terms is not between two *paths* polarized by the antagonistic practices of rites and Self-knowledge without rites, but between two *states*: one consisting of steadfastness in the false impression of being the doer of mental and bodily actions, and another consisting of steadfastness in direct knowledge of the Self, which is never bound by doership and action. The contrast is thus very similar to the one between action as defining the sphere of spiritual ignorance and bondage, and knowledge as defining the sphere of experience of the Self's true nature and absolute freedom. Similarly, we contend that, as the last step before liberation in the householder's sequence toward liberation, steadfastness in knowledge does not convey that only physical renunciation and full-time practice of the discipline of knowledge can lead to liberation as opposed to the way of living which involves ritual practices. Rather, it is meant to emphasize that, as the only direct means of liberation, *direct* Self-knowledge cannot coexist with, and is independent from, the Self's involvement with any action and practice.

Our task is therefore to clarify how Śaṅkara views the two types of opposition between steadfastness in action and steadfastness in Self-knowledge, and how, for him, attainment of steadfastness in knowledge as a sine qua non for liberation means obtaining direct knowledge of the Self as free from all activity, whatever the way of living, rather than acquiring it exclusively through the way of living which follows physical renunciation. As a preparation for this discussion, let us now identify the different semantic values of the word *niṣṭhā* in Śaṅkara's works.

THE MEANINGS OF *NIṢṬHĀ*

A first meaning of *niṣṭhā* is provided by the comment on *Gītā* 3.3. Here Śaṅkara glosses *niṣṭhā* by "steady application, dedication to the procedure" (*sthitir anuṣṭheyatātparyam*).[1] As we will see later on, according to Śaṅkara, *niṣṭhā* refers in this verse to a very general line of conduct which can be adopted for one's whole life after the period of studentship. So it seems better translated as "way of living."

The only occurrence of the word *niṣṭhā* in the BS introduces a second sense, that of "culmination." It appears in the last sentence of the commentary on aphorism 2.1.15: "We said that all means of knowledge culminate (*niṣṭhā*) in It [*Brahman*]" (BS, 385). The same meaning is found in the commentary on the *Gītā*. Śaṅkara writes on verse 18.50: "[Here] *niṣṭhā* means culmination, that is, final stage. [Final stage] of what? Of the knowledge of *Brahman*. It is the supreme, final stage" (BhG, 734).

A third meaning of *niṣṭhā* and of its adjectival form *niṣṭha* is provided to Śaṅkara by the *Upaniṣads* themselves. It conveys the notion of devotion in the sense of either dedication or love. In PU 1.1, Śaṅkara reads the compound *brahmaniṣṭha* as follows: ". . . these were *brahmaparāḥ*, approaching the lower *Brahman* as the supreme one, and *brahmaniṣṭhāḥ*, devoted to (*niṣṭha*) practices [conducive] to Him" (PU, 164). Apart from dedication to a practice, *niṣṭhā* can also mean devotion in the sense of a feeling of love directed toward a divinity or a teacher. Verse 3.2.10 of *Muṇḍaka Upaniṣad* says for instance: "To them alone should one teach this knowledge of *Brahman*, who are versed in spiritual practices, versed in the *Vedas*, and devoted to *Brahman* (*brahmaniṣṭhāḥ*) . . ." (MuU, 160). Here Śaṅkara understands *brahmaniṣṭhāḥ* as "devoted to the lower *Brahman*, desirous of becoming the supreme *Brahman*" (Ibid.). The term *niṣṭhā* also occurs in this sense in verse 7.20.1 of *Chāndogya Upaniṣad*: "—'One acquires faith by devoted service alone. Devotion (*niṣṭhā*) is surely to be sought after.'—'O venerable sir, I seek after devotion'" (transl., 555). Śaṅkara comments thereupon: "*Niṣṭhā* is service to the teacher and the like, complete devotion (*tatparatva*) in order to acquire the knowledge of *Brahman*" (Ibid.).

A fourth meaning of *niṣṭhā* or *niṣṭha* is "steadfastness" or "steadfast." It pertains to descriptions of states of consciousness rather than practices. This is exemplified by the comment on *Gītā* 8.24. The verse describes the postmortem destiny of unenlightened people who have meditated on *Brahman* (*brahmavid*) during their life on earth. They are said to reach *Brahman* indirectly, by first going to the world of Brahmā through a celestial avenue called "Northern Path" (*uttarāyaṇa*) or "Path of gods" (*devayāna*). Śaṅkara contrasts these people with those who are liberated without any delay, referring to the latter through the compound *samyagdarśananiṣṭha*, that is, "being *niṣṭha* in right perception [of the Self]." If they are said to be liberated immediately inasmuch as they are steadfast in the right perception of the Self, their Self-knowledge must be direct in nature. No one attains liberation through mere dedication to the *practice* or discipline of right perception but through the right direct Self-perception alone. The "one who fails in yoga" (*yogabhraṣṭa*) referred to by verse 6.41 of the *Gītā* provides the best example for this principle. Being a physical renunciant in Śaṅkara's eyes, the "one who fails in yoga" is fully devoted (*niṣṭha*) to the discipline of knowledge. But somehow he falls short of liberation, dies, and is reborn later on. Since *niṣṭhā* as a practice of Self-knowledge can never secure liberation by itself, it follows that when Śaṅkara states in BhG 8.24 that "being *niṣṭha* in right perception [of the Self]" is a *sure* means of liberation, the compound cannot be interpreted as "devoted to [the discipline of] right perception." The idea is rather that the people who are liberated without any delay are "steadfast" or "well established" in the right immediate perception of the Self. Therefore, we suggest the following translation of the whole passage:

> *Departing*, passing away, *on that*, on that path, *the knowers of Brahman*, those persons who have been devoted to meditation on *Brahman*, *go to Brahman*. "In course of time" is to be added to the sentence. For those steadfast in the right perception, who attain immediate liberation, there is verily no going to, nor any returning from, anywhere . . .[2]

Similarly, in BhG 18.12, Śaṅkara states, "steadfastness in the right perception alone (*kevalasamyagdarśananiṣṭhā*) can never fail to uproot the seeds of unending becoming such as ignorance."[3] Since steadfastness in the right perception is presented here as the unique means of liberation, it must refer to direct Self-knowledge and its translation must suggest "stability" rather than "dedication" and the idea of practice.

The word *niṣṭhā* also appears in the adjectival form *niṣṭha* in a compound of the last sentence of *Muṇḍaka Upaniṣad* 1.2.12, which reads as follows: "For knowing that Reality, with sacrificial faggots in hand,[4] he should go to a teacher who is versed in the *Vedas* and steadfast in *Brahman* (*brahmaniṣṭha*)" (MuU, 139). Śaṅkara comments the passage in the following manner:

> . . . one who, having renounced all actions, remains steadfast (*niṣṭhā*) in the non-dual *Brahman* alone, is a *brahmaniṣṭha*, just as with the words *japaniṣṭha* (steadfast in mental repetition) and *taponiṣṭha* (steadfast in asceticism). Steadfastness in *Brahman* is not possible for the acting man (*karmin*), because action and Self-knowledge are contradictory.[5]

In this instance, does *brahmaniṣṭha* mean "dedicated to [the practice of mediate knowledge of] *Brahman*" or "steadfast in [the direct knowledge of] *Brahman*?" According to the spirit of the *Upaniṣads* as well as to Śaṅkara, the knowledge of *Brahman* will not prove fruitful unless it is taught by a teacher who knows the Self by direct experience and is liberated. Therefore, being attributed to a teacher of the knowledge of *Brahman*, *brahmaniṣṭha* means most likely in this context "steadfast in [the direct knowledge of] *Brahman*." To clarify the meaning, Śaṅkara mentions two other compounds containing the word *niṣṭha*: *japaniṣṭha* and *taponiṣṭha*. But, surprisingly, both words joined here with *niṣṭha* refer to a practice and not to a state: *japa*, consisting in the repetition of one or several *mantras*, and *tapas*, representing some form of asceticism. Since a student goes to an Upaniṣadic teacher not because the latter is involved in practices but rather because he has reached the goal of all practices, the common element between the *brahmaniṣṭha* and the two *niṣṭhas* given as examples cannot be the idea of dedication to a practice. Hence, it can only be the notion of steadfastness. All three people considered here as *niṣṭhas* are understood to be steadfastly absorbed in something. In the first case, it is in knowledge, while in the latter two, it is in practices that consist of actions and are therefore contradictory to direct knowledge of the Self. It must be recalled that Śaṅkara allows people outside the monastic way of living to use the discipline of knowledge and, as a consequence, he does not forbid the combination of ritual actions with *brahmaniṣṭhā* in the sense of dedication to the discipline of knowledge. Therefore, the incompatibility between action and steadfastness in *Brahman* (or Self-knowledge) stated in the last sentence of the MuU 1.2.12 passage quoted above can only be between action and *direct* Self-knowledge. It also follows that Śaṅkara's comparison of *brahmaniṣṭha* with other compounds containing *niṣṭha* holds true only insofar as steadfastness or absorption—rather than practice—is concerned.

Thus, the very example given by Śaṅkara to clarify the meaning of *niṣṭhā* as "steadfastness" in the experience of *Brahman* could be somewhat ambiguous and misleading. Interestingly, this is precisely the kind of ambivalence which is likely to accompany the word *niṣṭhā*, especially in the commentary on the *Gītā*. Such is also the case in MuU 3.2.4, where means of attaining the Self such as strength are described: "*This Self cannot be attained by one who is without strength*, by one devoid of strength, bereft of the vigour created by steadfastness in the Self (*ātmaniṣṭhājanita*) . . ."[6] In this instance does "steadfastness in the Self" refer to the practice of mediate means of Self-knowledge such as meditation, or to the state of naturally remaining established in the direct experience of the non-dual Self? Since, in this context, "steadfastness in the Self" is said to create a strength which is in turn a means for attaining the Self, one could be led to interpret the said steadfastness simply as a mediate means of knowledge. But in KeU-P 2.4, where the same passage is quoted, Śaṅkara specifies that the strength which brings about the liberating Self-knowledge does not come from any practice such as yoga, but from direct Self-knowledge itself:

> . . . the strength produced by wealth, by a friend, a *mantra*, a medicine, asceticism, or yoga cannot overcome death, for it is produced by impermanent things. But the strength produced by Self-knowledge is acquired through the Self alone and not by anything else. Thus, because the strength of Self-knowledge does not come through any other means, that strength alone can overcome death.[7]

Hence, in MuU 3.2.4, it seems more appropriate to understand "steadfastness in the Self" as a kind of adherence of the intellect to direct knowledge of the Self. This adherence would develop a strength consisting of a stable experience of the same Self even in the waking state of consciousness[8] and, in that respect alone, would bring about complete "attainment of the Self."

So far we have been rendering the word *niṣṭhā* by "way of living," "culmination," devotion" (adjective: devoted), and "steadfastness" (adjective: steadfast). The English "steadfastness" seems to be closer to the semantic range of *niṣṭhā*, as it can carry both the meanings of absorption in a practice, and in an object of knowledge. Therefore, unless the context unambiguously suggests that *niṣṭhā* refers to a way of living or to a culmination, we will normally translate *niṣṭhā* and *niṣṭha* respectively by "steadfastness" and "steadfast."

Thus, the compound *jñānaniṣṭhā* or "steadfastness in knowledge" can mean dedication to the discipline of knowledge, or absorption of one's awareness in the immediate knowledge of the Self which alone yields liberation.[9] In contrast with *jñānaniṣṭhā*, *karmaniṣṭhā* or "steadfastness in action" can mean—at least theoretically for now—regular practice of rites and duties, or absorption of one's awareness in the sphere of action, which amounts to spiritual ignorance and bondage.

THE TWO BASIC TEACHINGS OF THE SCRIPTURES

At a few places in his works, Śaṅkara presents steadfastness in action and steadfastness in Self-knowledge as the two basic teachings of the *Veda*. In this context, they appear synonymous with engagement in action (*pravṛtti*) and abstention from action (*nivṛtti*) respectively. Śaṅkara writes for instance in his introduction to the *Gītā* that "the twofold Vedic *dharma* consists of engagement in action (*pravṛtti*) and abstention from action (*nivṛtti*)" (BhG intro, 3). They lead respectively to temporary happiness (*abhyudaya*) and to the highest good (*niḥśreyasa*) of liberation (Ibid.). Further in his introduction, Śaṅkara adds that

> the aim of the famous text of the *Gītā* is, in brief, the supreme and highest good, which consists of the complete cessation of unending becoming with its cause. And it accrues from the *dharma* of steadfastness in Self-knowledge preceded by renunciation of all actions.[10]

Since, as opposed to the other basic *dharma* of the *Veda* which leads only to temporary happiness and transmigratory existence, abstention from action (*nivṛtti*) and steadfastness in knowledge preceded by renunciation of all actions are both said by Śaṅkara to be the means of liberation, they seem quite equivalent from his viewpoint. The same equivalence is suggested in his ĪU 15:

> Scriptures indicate that dissolution into Nature is the ultimate reward attainable through human and divine wealth.[11] Such is the limit of unending becoming. Beyond this . . . is identification with the Self of everything,[12] which is the reward of renunciation of all desires and steadfastness in knowledge. Thus has been brought to light the twofold teaching of the *Vedas* consisting of engagement in action (*pravṛtti*) and abstention from action (*nivṛtti*).[13]

On the other hand, towards the end of his introduction to the *Gītā*, Śaṅkara explains that

> even though it may aim at temporary happiness . . . when practiced in a spirit of dedication to the Lord, without attachment to rewards, the *dharma* of engagement in action (*pravṛtti*) brings about purity of mind. And the man whose mind is pure also attains the condition for the highest good [i.e. liberation] by way of competence for steadfastness in knowledge, and emergence of knowledge.[14]

In this passage, Śaṅkara describes the two forms of engagement in action: either performance of rites and duties with attachment to rewards such as celestial worlds, or their performance without attachment, which consists of the yoga of action (*karmayoga*) and which leads indirectly to liberation. So one type of engagement in action is based on attachment to the rewards of actions and aims at goals different from knowledge of the non-dual Self and liberation. We may call it the "path of desire-prompted action" (*kāmyakarmamārga*). The other type of engagement in action is based on renunciation of the rewards of actions and aims at liberation.[15] We may call it the "yoga of action."[16]

In his introduction to chapter 4, Śaṅkara summarizes the basic teaching of the *Gītā* in a slightly different manner, presenting it as a yoga of knowledge and renunciation (or *nivṛtti*) which is the culmination of the yoga of action (or *pravṛtti*):

> The yoga described in the last two chapters, which consists of steadfastness in knowledge, which involves renunciation and is attained

> through the yoga of action, summarizes the teaching of the *Veda*, consisting of engagement in action (*pravṛtti*) and abstention from action (*nivṛtti*). It is this yoga that is meant by the Lord throughout the *Gītā*.[17]

We can conclude so far that (1) steadfastness in knowledge (*jñānaniṣṭhā*) accompanied by renunciation corresponds to abstention from action (*nivṛtti*), and that (2) steadfastness in action (*karmaniṣṭhā*) is equivalent to engagement in action (*pravṛtti*) and subdivides into the path of desire-prompted action, and the yoga of action.

Now, in chapter 3 of the *Gīta*, Śaṅkara clearly uses steadfastness in action (*karmaniṣṭhā*) and steadfastness in knowledge (*jñānaniṣṭhā*) as synonymous with, respectively, yoga of action (*karmayoga*) and yoga of knowledge (*jñānayoga*), that is, in this context, the discipline of knowledge preceded by physical renunciation. In his introduction to the chapter, he writes for instance: "And the combination of knowledge and action is untenable because [in verse 3.3] the Lord's answer is that steadfastness in knowledge and in action (*jñānakarmaniṣṭhā*) are to be followed by different people" (BhG 3 intro, 139). But in fact, it is the yoga of action (*karmayoga*)—rather than steadfastness in action (*karmaniṣṭhā*)—and the yoga of knowledge (*jñānayoga*)—rather than steadfastness in knowledge (*jñānaniṣṭhā*)—that verse 3.3 ascribes to two distinct classes of people. Hence, for Śaṅkara, steadfastness in action is here equivalent to yoga of action, and steadfastness in knowledge to yoga of knowledge. In his BhG 3.2 (140), Śaṅkara also uses the compound "steadfastness in action" to infer from verse 3.3 the untenability of combining action with Self-knowledge as the means of liberation. Finally, in his introduction to verse 3.4, Śaṅkara provides the following summary by again using steadfastness in action in the sense of yoga of action as stated in verse 3.3, and steadfastness in knowledge in the sense of yoga of knowledge also mentioned in the same verse:

> Or, since steadfastness in knowledge and steadfastness in action (*jñānakarmaniṣṭhā*) are mutually opposed, and thus cannot be practiced simultaneously by one and the same person, one could conclude that either of them can lead to man's goal [liberation] independently of the other. In order to convey the notion that steadfastness in action (*karmaniṣṭhā*) leads to man's goal, not independently, but by being the means of attainment of steadfastness in knowledge (*jñānaniṣṭhā*), and that, steadfastness in knowledge (*jñānaniṣṭhā*), having been gained by way of steadfastness in action

(*karmaniṣṭhā*), leads to man's goal independently, without the need for anything else, the Lord says:[18]

Thus, as found in Śaṅkara's usage, steadfastness in action (*karmaniṣṭhā*) is equivalent to engagement in action (*pravṛtti*). The yoga of action (*karmayoga*) is only one form of steadfastness in action (*karmaniṣṭhā*), the other form being the path of desire-prompted action. But sometimes steadfastness in action (*karmaniṣṭhā*) is used in a restricted sense as synonymous with the yoga of action (*karmayoga*). Steadfastness in knowledge (*jñānaniṣṭhā*) accompanied by renunciation is equivalent to abstention from action (*nivṛtti*) and is sometimes used as synonymous with yoga of knowledge (*jñānayoga*).

TWO OPPOSITE WAYS OF LIVING

Given these lexical clarifications and connexions, we can now bring to light how Śaṅkara understands the opposition between, on the one hand, steadfastness in action or engagement in action and, on the other, steadfastness in knowledge or abstention from action. This opposition subdivides into two major types. The first type of opposition polarizes two ways of living, while the second one sees an incompatibility between two states of consciousness, irrespective of whether a person continues the performance of rites and householder duties or has abandoned them and adopted the monastic way of living.

The first type of opposition—involving ways of living—can be further divided into two perspectives. The first one, which we will call the "start perspective," corresponds to the two major and quite contrasting ways of living one may choose as a young adult after completion of the basic Vedic studies: either [1] marrying and embarking upon the path of rites and duties of the householder, or [2] not marrying, adopting the monastic way of living, and just absorbing oneself in the knowledge of *Brahman*. The second perspective, which we will call the "end perspective," contrasts [1] the *continued performance* of rites and duties of a householder up to the end of life, with [2] *abstention* from them—that is, physical abandonment—at some point in life, in favor of complete absorption in the knowledge of *Brahman*. In both these perspectives pertaining to ways of living, according to context, absorption in knowledge by the physical renouncer can be through a direct experience of *Brahman* or through the discipline of knowledge as a means to reach that experience.

Here is a chart outlining what will be brought to light in this section:

TABLE 6.1
The Contrast Between Steadfastness in Action/Engagement in Action and Steadfastness in Knowledge/Abstention from Action

<table>
<tr><th colspan="3">Ways of Living</th><th>States of Consciousness</th></tr>
<tr><td rowspan="3">Steadfastness in action or engagement in action</td><td colspan="2">With physical performance of rites</td><td rowspan="3">A characteristic of the state of unenlightenment, whatever the way of living</td></tr>
<tr><td>"Start perspective"</td><td>"End perspective"</td></tr>
<tr><td>Marrying immediately after studies and adopting the householder's duties and rites</td><td>Physical performance of rites up to the end of life</td></tr>
<tr><td rowspan="3">Steadfastness in knowledge or abstention from action</td><td colspan="2">Without physical performance of rites</td><td rowspan="3">A characteristic of the state of enlightenment, whatever the way of living</td></tr>
<tr><td>"Start perspective"</td><td>"End perspective"</td></tr>
<tr><td>Not marrying after studies and adopting the monastic way of living for one's whole life</td><td>Physical abstention from rites and adoption of the monastic way of living at some point in life</td></tr>
</table>

Following the spirit of a few verses from the *Upaniṣads* and the *Gītā*, Śaṅkara sees the "start perspective" as rooted in archetypes of the two basic ways of living revealed by the scriptures. His interpretation of *Gītā* 3.3 provides a striking example of this understanding. Kṛṣṇa says in this verse: "As taught by Me of yore, O sinless one, there is in this world two ways of living (*niṣṭhā*): the yoga of knowledge for followers of *Sāṃkhya*[19] and the yoga of action for *yogins*" (BhG 3.3, 141). After mentioning that the first way of living leads to temporary happiness (*abhyudaya*) and the second to the highest good (*niḥśreyasa*) of liberation, Śaṅkara proceeds with their definition:

> *The way of living consisting of the yoga of knowledge*—knowledge itself being yoga—has been taught *for followers of Sāṃkhya*, those who are possessed of the discriminative knowledge between the Self and the non-Self,[20] who have adopted [physical][21] renunciation immediately after studentship, who have well ascertained the meaning of the Vedāntic knowledge, who are wandering mendicants and established in *Brahman* alone. *The way of living consisting of the yoga of action*—action itself being yoga—has been taught *for yogins*, the men of action.[22]

A peculiar element of the description of the yoga of knowledge given here is that the followers of *Sāṃkhya* physically renounce immediately after the stage of studentship. Why does the commentator restrict adoption of physical renunciation to the specific time following studentship, when elsewhere[23] he clearly points out that passages such as *Jābāla Upaniṣad* 4 recommend physical renunciation from any of the first three modes of living? If we assume the above definition of the yoga of knowledge to be holistic, we are led to the odd conclusion that in this famous and fundamental definition of the two basic ways of living by the *Gītā*, the term *jñānayoga* or "yoga of knowledge" does not even account for those who renounce physically *after* the householder's or the hermit's modes of living. But we contend that by specifying this particular time for renunciation, Śaṅkara simply wishes to agree with the archetypal context which, according to him, is suggested by the verse itself. Let us now shed light on this context.

Śaṅkara interprets the expression "as taught of yore" (*purā proktā*) used in verse 3.3 as meaning: taught by Kṛṣṇa "of old, at the beginning of creation" (BhG 3.3, 141). Using the terms "*dharma* of engagement in action" (*pravṛttidharma)* and "*dharma* of abstention from action" (*nivṛttidharma)* as equivalent to the two ways of living of verse 3.3, Śaṅkara states in his introduction to the *Gītā* that they were taught by Kṛṣṇa at the beginning of creation:

> Having created this universe and desirous of ensuring its sustenance, He, the Lord, first created Marīci and other Prajāpatis, and assigned them the *dharma* stated in the *Veda* and characterized by engagement in action (*pravṛtti*). Then He created others such as Sanaka and Sanandana and assigned them the *dharma* of abstention from action (*nivṛtti*), characterized by knowledge and detachment (BG intro, 2–3).

Sanaka and others of his group are known in the scriptures for their lifelong celibacy, that is, for not having engaged in the householder's mode of living after completion of their studies. They are also considered to be the first teachers of *Sāṃkhya* and *Yoga*.[24] If Śaṅkara adds the restriction that, in the way of living based on abstention from action proposed by verse 3.3, physical renunciation occurs immediately after studentship, it is because he has in mind the people typically depicted in this primordial scene of the foundation of the two *niṣṭhās* at the beginning of creation.

Another archetypal setting and exemple of the "start perspective" upon the basic ways of living is found in the contrast emphasized by Śaṅkara between verses 1.4.17 and 4.4.22 of the *Bṛhadāraṇyaka Upaniṣad*. Let us first quote the beginning of verse 1.4.17:

> This [aggregate of desirable objects] was but the self in the beginning—the only entity. He desired, "Let me have a wife, so that I may be born [as the child]. And let me have wealth, so that I may perform rites." This much indeed is [the range of] desire. Even if one wishes, one cannot get more than this. Therefore to this day a man being single desires, "Let me have a wife, so that I may be born. And let me have wealth, so that I may perform rites." Until he obtains each one of these, he considers himself incomplete (BṛU transl., 132).[25]

In this verse, Śaṅkara interprets "in the beginning" as "before marriage"[26] and "the self" as "an unenlightened member of [one of the three upper] *varṇas* identified with the body and senses."[27] The verse's archetypal intent is expressed by "therefore to this day," and commented by Śaṅkara in the light of the creation myth told in verses 1 to 6 of the same section of the *Upaniṣad*:

> In ancient times an ignorant man possessed of desire wished like this, and others before him had also done the same. Such is the way of the world. This creation of Virāj has been like this. It has been said that he was afraid on account of his ignorance; then, prompted by desire, he was unhappy in being alone, and to remove that boredom he wished for a wife; and he was united with her, which led to this creation. Because it was like this, *therefore to this day*, in his creation, *a man being single*, before marriage, *desires*, *"Let me have a wife, so that I may be born. And let me have wealth, so that I may perform rites"* (BṛU 1.4.17, transl., 134).

A sharply contrasting alternative available after studentship is provided also with an archetypal reference to some "ancient men" by verse 4.4.22 of the same *Upaniṣad*:

> Desiring this world [the Self] alone, wandering mendicants leave everything. This is [the reason for it]: the ancient men who knew this [Self], it is said, did not desire children, thinking "What shall we achieve with children [when], for us, the Self is the world."[28]

Obviously, the absence of desire for children on the part of the ancient Self-knowers is exactly opposite to the project of people described in verse 1.4.17. Although Śaṅkara does not say explicitly in his comment on verse 4.4.22 that their decision takes place immediately after studentship, he mentions (transl., 527) that the context has been explained while commenting on a previous verse. This seems to refer to verse 3.5.1 which provides the same kind of description. In his comment thereupon, Śaṅkara mentions that when the verse says, "having renounced the desire for sons" (*putraiṣaṇāyāḥ . . . vyutthāya*) "it means 'not having married.'"[29] Further in the same comment, Śaṅkara clearly connects the archetypal model of the past with the duty of the present time: "Because *ancient men who knew* [this] abstained from actions [done] for the purpose of children and so forth, and did leave everything, therefore people of today also leave everything, that is, should leave everything . . ."[30]

In his BhG 2.10, Śaṅkara mentions that the *Gītā*'s two ways of living—as stated in verse 3.3—are also found in verses 1.4.17 and 4.4.22 of the *Bṛhadāraṇyaka Upaniṣad*. After summarizing the purport of the latter, he uses them to refute the combination of Self-knowledge and action:

> As shown by "He desired . . . " [BṛU 4.1.17], all *Śrauta* rites are for him only who is possessed of ignorance and desire. By "having renounced them, they leave everything," [BṛU 4.4.22][31] renunciation is prescribed for him who seeks the world of the Self alone and is without desire. The assertion of this distinction would be irrelevant if the Lord intended a combination of *Śrauta* rites and knowledge.[32]

The purport of the same two verses from the *Bṛhadāraṇyaka Upaniṣad* is also said to be equivalent to the two ways of living described in the *Īśā Upaniṣad*:

> Here, in the first *mantra*, steadfastness in knowledge through abandonment of all desires is given as the first teaching of the *Vedas*. . . . When, for people who are devoid of knowledge and wish to live [a hundred years], steadfastness in knowledge is not possible . . . steadfastness in action is given as the second teaching of the *Vedas*. These ways of living (*niṣṭhā*) have been distinguished in the *Bṛhadāraṇyaka* as well as in [this] *mantra*.[33]

Yet the "start perspective" is not the only manner through which Śaṅkara accounts for the opposition between engagement in action (or steadfastness in action) and abstention from action (or steadfastness in knowledge) as ways of living. We saw in the previous chapter that Śaṅkara acknowledges the possibility that one may "have started with actions" (*prārabdhakarmā*) and may have physically abandoned actions only later on in life. According to this "end perspective," the opposition is between the way of living which favors continuation of rites and duties for the whole life, and the way of living in which one abstains from them at some point in life. The "start" and "end" perspectives are described side by side in Śaṅkara's commentary on *Gītā* 2.72:

> *O son of Pṛthā, this,* the aforesaid, *is the state of Brahman,* of being in *Brahman.* It is dwelling in the true nature of *Brahman* after having renounced all actions. *Having attained,* having reached, *this* state, *no one is deluded,* falls [again] into delusion. *Remaining established therein,* in the aforesaid state of *Brahman, even at the end,* at the end of life, *one attains the final bliss of Brahman,* the final beatitude of *Brahman,* liberation. It goes without saying that he who, having renounced just after studentship, dwells all his life in *Brahman* alone, attains to the final bliss of *Brahman.*[34]

This passage clearly describes two types of people who have reached direct Self-knowledge and liberation. One of them did not engage in rites after studentship, while the other first engaged in them, to renounce them physically later on. These choices—one in the case of the first type of person and two in the case of the other—allow us to illustrate the "start" and "end perspectives" of the opposition between steadfastness in action and in Self-knowledge as ways of living. From the "start perspective," these two types of people, having different understandings of the Self, of the highest goal of life and of its means, begin their adult life with opposite ways of living. This, in itself, accounts for the opposition between steadfastness in action and in Self-knowledge from the "start perspective." Yet at one point or the other in their life, both these types of people choose the way of living referred to by abstention from action. As a consequence, they both contrast with the other people who kept with the performance of rites and duties for their entire life. It is the latter polarity that accounts for the opposition between steadfastness in action and in Self-knowledge from the "end perspective."

Thus, the "start perspective" sheds light on the choice of a goal, a means and a way of living which is made after completion of studies. This choice expresses one's subjective conviction concerning the highest spiritual goal of man, its proper means and the most favorable way of living to attain it. If the understanding of the Self is right and immediate in nature, the goal is already attained, there is no desire for it and no use in resorting to any means. A life of holy wandering seems the natural expression of this complete absence of anything to do. If the understanding of the Self is right, that is, intellectually in agreement with the *Upaniṣads*, if it involves a deep conviction but is only mediate in nature, the proper means for attaining the goal appears to be full-time practice of the discipline of knowledge, which is allowed by freedom from family and ritualistic obligations. From the "end perspective," the same direct or indirect Self-knowledge can emerge at some point in life and lead to abstention from rites and duties of the householder in favor of absorption in the knowledge of *Brahman*.

It is in the light of this whole context that, from the very start of adult life or later on, one way of living can be said to lead to temporary happiness (*abhyudaya*) and the other to liberation. This certainly means that Śaṅkara presents engagement in action (or steadfastness in action) and abstention from action (or steadfastness in knowledge) as the two basic teachings of the *Vedas* and as opposite means leading to opposite goals. Now, does this also mean for Śaṅkara that physical renunciation must be adopted as an indispensible aspect of abstention from action (or steadfastness in knowledge) which alone leads to direct Self-knowledge and liberation? If so, we are again confronted with the fact that such an interpretation contradicts our reference point according to which liberation is possible while not being a physical renouncer. If it is not so, then the opposition between steadfastness in action/engagement in action (*karmaniṣṭhā/pravṛtti*) and steadfastness in knowledge/abstention from action (*jñānaniṣṭhā/nivṛtti*) must have yet another meaning.

TWO OPPOSITE STATES OF CONSCIOUSNESS

The solution to this apparent contradiction is found in the passages where Śaṅkara uses the terms steadfastness in knowledge (*jñānaniṣṭhā*) or abstention from action (*nivṛtti*) to mean *a state of consciousness* that is independent of ways of living. This state consists of direct knowledge of the Self as devoid of all activity and is opposed to the state where the active and limited dimensions of the non-Self are superimposed on the Self through ignorance. This corresponds to the second—and most important—way in which Śaṅkara understands the opposition between steadfastness in action and in Self-knowledge—or between engagement in, and abstention from, action.

This type of opposition is even found in the connection made by Śaṅkara between verse 2.72 of the *Gītā*—whose comment we quoted above—and the preceding verse. Verses 2.71 and 2.72 are the last ones in the sequence which starts with verse 55 and where Kṛṣṇa describes the man of steady intellect (*sthitaprajña*), that is, the liberated-in-life. After specifying, in his comment on verse 2.71, that the latter refers to a physical renouncer, Śaṅkara concludes: "*He*, such a man, a man of steady intellect, a knower of *Brahman*, *attains to*, reaches, *peace*, which is called "bliss" and which consists of the cessation of all the sorrows of unending becoming. It means that he becomes *Brahman*."[35] Immediately after, he introduces verse 72 as follows: "It is this steadfastness in knowledge (*jñānaniṣṭhā*) that is praised:" (BhG 2.72, 132).[36] Since Śaṅkara uses steadfastness in knowledge to characterize the already enlightened, it cannot refer here to a mere way of living or even to the discipline of knowledge. Actually, in this context, it cannot refer to any practice whatsoever. Since the Self of the enlightened cannot be involved in any practice, the very fact that steadfastness in knowledge is attributed to such a person makes it incompatible with any kind of practice, be it full-time discipline of knowledge. Therefore, although, as we saw, steadfastness in knowledge can possibly refer to the discipline of knowledge as practiced by the physical renouncer, it refers quite clearly in the comment on verse 2.72 to the enlightened's absorption in direct knowledge of the actionless *Brahman*, which is opposed to steadfastness in action only insofar as the latter is identification with the active and limited self.

Thus, inasmuch as steadfastness in Self-knowledge points to a means used in order to reach enlightenment, it can be associated with a way of living. But inasmuch as it points to an experience of, and absorption in, the actionless *Brahman*, it refers to a state of consciousness which is independent of ways of living and practices, and which is the only direct means to liberation, as opposed to steadfastness in action consisting of the experience of, and the absorption in, a self bound by doership and action.

This interpretation of steadfastness in action is supported by Śaṅkara's basic understanding of *karman*. As rightly pointed out by S. Radhakrishnan (1929, 630-631), Karl H. Potter (1982, 115), and Wilhelm Halbfass (1983, 302), for Śaṅkara, the basic meaning of *karman* is an action which is done by one who perceives himself as a doer and which, feeding on the desire to achieve a result, either good or bad for himself, perpetuates the cycle of birth and death. And the definition refers to both profane and religious types of action.

Most significant is the fact that the very passages which are understood by Śaṅkara to convey the idea of opposite ways of living are also seen by him to contrast opposite states of consciousness. In his introduction to BhG 3.17, Śaṅkara paraphrases BṛU 3.5.1—which talks about the physical renunciation of the ancient Brahmins—and states that, through verse 3.17, Kṛṣṇa wants to distinguish the one who is beyond the prescription of yoga of action, and to show that "the teaching of the *Śruti* [including BṛU 3.5.1] is also what is meant to be imparted here in the *Gītā* scripture."[37] Verse 3.17 is a clear description of the enlightened man for whom "there is no duty to perform" (*kāryaṃ na vidyate*) because of his total self-sufficiency with the experience of the Self: "But for that man who rejoices only in the Self and is satisfied with the Self, and is contented only in the Self, there is no duty to perform" (BhG, 155). After quoting this verse in his BS 4.1.2, Śaṅkara contrasts its description of a man who has no more duty to fulfill, with the unenlightened man who must pursue (or repeat) the practice of hearing, reflection, and meditation (transl., 817–818). Thus, according to this passage, even the discipline of knowledge is part of practices which don't have to be pursued anymore by the man described in BhG 3.17. This confirms that, in Śaṅkara's eyes, this man is already liberated. And Śaṅkara describes him in his comment on verse 3.17 (156) as a "follower of *Sāṃkhya* who is steadfast in Self-knowledge" (*sāṃkhya ātmajñānaniṣṭhaḥ*). Thus, according to the context built up by Śaṅkara in his introduction to this verse, it is in such a steadfastness that the common message of the *Gītā* and the *Śruti* on steadfastness in Self-knowledge—as opposed to steadfastness in action—is to be found. As a consequence, the *most significant* opposition between steadfastness in knowledge and in action seems to be between the states of enlightenment and unenlightenment, not between the ways of living of physical renouncers absorbed in the discipline of knowledge, and of people belonging to other stages of life.

In the introduction to BṛU 2.4, Śaṅkara refers to verses 1.4.17 and 4.4.22, which define the two possible ways of living after studentship. But, in this introduction, the contrast between the two types of steadfastness again concerns states of consciousness rather than ways of living. In support of this is the fact that when opposing the knower of *Brahman* of verse 4.4.22 to the people who are portrayed in verse 1.4.17 as desiring a wife and a son, Śaṅkara describes the knower of *Brahman* as having already fulfilled all desires:

> And [means such as sons] are not prescribed for the knower of *Brahman*, being stated by *Śruti* as desire-prompted: "This much

> indeed is [the range of] desire" [1.4.17]. And because the knower of *Brahman* has fulfilled [all his] desires, he cannot have any more desires. And because the *Śruti* says: "For us, the Self is the world" [4.4.22].[38]

This suggests that the opposition between steadfastness in action as expressed in verse 1.4.17, and steadfastness in knowledge as expressed in verses 3.5.1/4.4.22 can also be understood as the polarity between the state of consciousness based on ignorance and desire, and the state of consciousness based on direct Self-knowledge and absence of desire.

The two types of steadfastness proclaimed in *Gītā* 3.3 are also understood by Śaṅkara in terms of a polarity between states of consciousness rather than ways of living. In the comment on verse 18.3 of the *Gītā*, the opponent quotes verse 3.3 to support his opinion that the discussion about obligatory regular rites applies to followers of *Sāṃkhya* as well as to [*karma-*]*yogins*. Śaṅkara refutes this interpretation by stating that followers of *Sāṃkhya*—also called by him the ones who are steadfast in knowledge (*jñānaniṣṭha*)—are not at all concerned with the issue of the yoga of action. This is because "they do not perceive action in the Self" (BhG 18.3, 678), "because the true renunciant (*saṃnyāsin*) has been distinguished in the description of the one who is beyond the *guṇas* [verses14.22-26]" (Ibid.), and because "they have realized the supreme truth" (*paramārthadarśin*) (Ibid., 679). Thus, the followers of *Sāṃkhya*, who are steadfast in knowledge and for whom the yoga of knowledge was prescribed in verse 3.3, are here understood by Śaṅkara to be already enlightened.

Similarly, in BhG 2.69, Śaṅkara clearly connects the question of engagement in, and abstention from, action as well as steadfastness in action and in Self-knowledge with the states of ignorance and enlightenment rather than with ways of living. He first establishes that when ignorance ceases, activity also ceases: "For the man of steady intellect, who has acquired discriminative knowledge, secular and Vedic activities cease on the cessation of ignorance, because they are the result of ignorance" (BhG 2.69, 127). Answering a question as to what is that which the verse refers as the night for all beings, he replies: "It is the supreme Reality, which is the domain of the man of steady intellect" (Ibid.). He then specifies: "*In that*, which consitsts of the supreme Reality, *the self-controlled man*, the *yogin* who is endowed with control, who has conquered his senses, *is awake*, he has woken up from the sleep of ignorance."[39] Śaṅkara later concludes from this: "Therefore actions are enjoined only in the context of the state of ignorance, and not in the context of the state of knowledge" (Ibid., 128). He then states that such a Self-knower has to do (*adhikāra*) only with renunciation of all actions and steadfastness in Self-knowledge, and quotes, as evidence for this, verse 5.17, which also describes steadfastness in direct Self-knowledge:

> But the Self-knower who knows that all this aggregate of differences amounts, like the night, to mere ignorance, has everything to do (*adhikāra*) with renunciation of all actions, and nothing to do with engaging in them (*pravṛtti*). Accordingly the Lord will show by "Those whose intellect is absorbed in That, whose Self is That" [5.17] and similar statements, that such a man has to do with steadfastness in knowledge alone.[40]

Thus, the opposition between steadfastness in action and in Self-knowledge as states of unenlightenment and enlightenment is used to justify the absence of duties and rites for the enlightened man. In his BhG 18.11, Śaṅkara brings in the same opposition but this time as a way to justify the prescription of engagement in rites addressed to the unenlightened man. First, in 18.10, he describes what can only be interpreted as the enlightened person: "'having mentally renounced all actions,' [5.13] remaining 'without acting nor causing to act,' [5.13], he attains steadfastness in knowledge which consists of freedom from action."[41] Indeed, one who has mentally renounced all actions, including mental ones, must also have renounced doership. And this is possible only through direct Self-knowledge. This is confirmed by 'without acting nor causing to act.' Therefore the "steadfastness in knowledge," which also follows, must be equivalent to just remaining in the Self-knowledge which is completely free from action. Then, in BhG 18.11, Śaṅkara introduces the counterpart of the enlightened not mainly in terms of a way of living, but of that state of consciousness which is opposed to the enlightened, and which is based on superimposition of doership and so forth on the actionless Self:

> On the other hand, since complete abandonment of action is not possible for the man who is qualified for rites, who is embodied by reason of regarding the body as himself, who is devoid of knowledge, who has the firm conviction that he is a doer—because his experience of the Self's doership has not been annulled—he has to do (*adhikāra*) only with the performance of actions enjoined by the scriptures [and] accompanied by abandonment of the rewards of actions.[42]

Verse 1.4.10 of BṛU also describes engagement in, and abstention from, rites as based mainly on the opposite states of consciousness, consisting respectively of perception of duality and non-duality:

> And to this day whoever in like manner knows It as "I am Brahman," becomes all this [universe]. Even the gods cannot prevail against him, for he becomes their Self. While he who worships another god thinking, "He is one, and I am another," does not know. He is like an animal to the gods (transl., 100).

In his comment on verse 1.4.16—which immediately precedes the one describing people who marry after studentship—Śaṅkara recalls verse 1.4.10 as follows: "It has been said in this [scripture] that an unenlightened man attributing to himself things such as caste and mode of living, and controlled by righteousness, is dependent on gods and others, like an animal, because [he thinks] he has duties to perform for them" (BṛU, 111). This can only refer to the general condition of the unenlightened person, whatever his way of living, since even an unenlightened wandering mendicant is identified through ignorance with his mode of living (*āśrama*) and, seeking good and avoiding evil, is still "controlled by righteousness." A little further in verse 1.4.16, Śaṅkara envisages the possibility that the same man becomes enlightened and free from this kind of existence. This reminds the reader of the enlightened man described in verse 1.4.10 and contrasted with the unenlightened. Again Śaṅkara states that the *adhikāra* of such an enlightened man is with respect to knowledge alone:

> When he comes to know *Brahman*, he is freed from the animal life which the bondage of duty amounts to. At whose instance, like a slave, can he have something to do (*adhikāra*) with action, which is bondage, and not everything to do (*adhikāra*) with knowledge which is the means of liberation from the latter?[43]

Since, according to Śaṅkara, action as a source of bondage can exist only through a state of being which is based on ignorance and superimposition of doership, it follows that steadfastness in action means first of all a binding "steadfastness" in doership and action, and in the second place only, a practice of prescribed ritual actions. It is quite clear that when, in the passages of the BṛU just quoted, Śaṅkara opposes steadfastness in action and steadfastness in knowledge, he does not contrast the *practice* of ritual actions with the practice of full-time *mediate* knowledge of the Self preceded by physical renunciation. Rather, he opposes two *states of consciousness*: one based on ignorance and one based on immediate Self-knowledge. This is in agreement with Śaṅkara's understanding of the main purport of this *Upaniṣad*: "This whole *Upaniṣad*," he writes, "is solely dedicated to showing the distinction between knowledge and ignorance."[44] Since Śaṅkara understands that the *Upaniṣads*, the *Bhagavadgītā* and the *Brahmasūtras* all teach the same knowledge of the non-dual Self, according to him, this intent of the *Bṛhadāraṇyaka Upaniṣad* can be attributed to all these texts as well as to his own commentaries, and finally to the comparison often made by him between the two fundamental concepts of steadfastness in action and steadfastness in knowledge.

The opposition between the states of enlightenment and unenlightenment is also conveyed by the terms "engagement in action" (*pravṛtti*) and "abstention from action" (*nivṛtti*). Describing the man who does not choose physical renunciation of rites and duties after his enlightenment, Śaṅkara emphasizes: "What may appear—even after action and its motive have disappeared—as his engagement in action (*pravṛtti*) with the same assiduity as before and for the sake of guiding people, is no action."[45] Śaṅkara then specifies that this precludes combining action and Self-knowledge as a means of liberation because, in the same way as Kṛṣṇa himself, such a person "has no sense of ego" (*ahaṃkārābhāva*).[46] In the previous chapter, we came across other passages where the actions of the enlightened man engaged in guiding people are said to be in fact no action (*karmābhāva*). All these expressions are ways to underscore abstention from action (*nivṛtti*) as a state of consciousness which is free from action, whether one continues to perform the duties as before, or one has abandoned them physically.

It follows that a person who has chosen abstention from action (*nivṛtti*) as a way of living and has thus become a physical renouncer, but who, like the *Gītā*'s "man who fails in yoga," has not attained abstention from action as the state of actionlessness coextensive with enlightenment, is still within the range of engagement in action (*pravṛtti*) as a state of consciousness bound by action and transmigratory existence. One could argue that the situation of the physical renunciant "who fails in yoga" can very well correspond to abstention from action as a way of living indispensable for enlightenment, yet short of its culmination in direct Self-knowledge and liberation. But this would mean that direct Self-knowledge is the sole means of liberation only inasmuch as it is the culmination of the monastic way of living—formal or informal. And this would again contradict the basic reference point according to which one can attain liberation without adopting the monastic way of living. The only way Śaṅkara could have understood abstention from action (*nivṛtti*) consistently is by distinguishing two possible and independent values in it: a way of living and a state of consciousness. Consequently, although, according to Śaṅkara, *as a way of living*, abstention from action accomplishes the goal with more focus and speed than its counterpart engagement in action, it is only *as a state of consciousness* incompatible with involvement in doership and so forth, that it leads directly and independently to liberation, whatever one's way of living. Such an understanding of the two types of opposition between steadfastness in action and in Self-knowledge allows each of them to retain its own validity, without contradicting the fundamentals of Śaṅkara's outlook as stated in our reference points.

We can summarize our findings with the following distinctions.

As a way of living, engagement in action/steadfastness in action (*pravṛtti/karmaniṣṭhā*) can correspond to the practice of rites and duties of people who desire temporary happiness; or to the practice of the yoga of action as an indirect means to liberation; or even to the *apparent* practice of enlightened people who pursue their duties as before. *As a way of living,* abstention from action/steadfastness in knowledge (*nivṛtti/jñānaniṣṭhā*) can correspond to physical renunciation—formal or informal—and full-time practice of the discipline of knowledge in the case of the seeker-after-liberation; or to physical renunciation followed by wandering mendicancy in the case of the enlightened person.

As a characteristic of the state of unenlightenment, engagement in action/steadfastness in action (*pravṛtti/karmaniṣṭhā*) can refer to the state of consciouness of unenlightened people who practice rites and duties for temporary happiness; or to the state of consciousness of unenlightened people who practice the yoga of action in view of liberation; or finally to the state of consciousness of unenlightened physical renouncers who strive for liberation through full-time practice of the discipline of knowledge. *As a characteristic of the state of enlightenment,* abstention from action/steadfastness in knowledge (*nivṛtti/jñānaniṣṭhā*) refers exclusively to the enlightened person, whether he has physically abandoned all practices, or he is still pursuing them with a view to guide people.

Therefore, when Śaṅkara describes abstention from action/steadfastness in knowledge as the means of liberation in opposition to engagement in action/steadfastness in action, it is not mainly as a way of living, but as including direct Self-knowledge, whatever the way of living. This allows us to better understand how, to be consistent with Śaṅkara's overall opposition between steadfastness in knowledge and steadfastness in action, the steadfastness in knowledge of the householder's sequence toward liberation cannot mean that only full-time practice of the discipline of knowledge preceded by physical renunciation leads to liberation, but rather that, in bringing about emancipation, immediate Self-knowledge cannot coexist with, and is independent from, all actions and practices.

CHAPTER SEVEN

The Yoga of Action and the Means of Self-knowledge

Since physical renunciation is not a sine qua non on the path to liberation, the question arises as to how exactly Śaṅkara envisioned the way to liberation for those who do not resort to the monastic way of living. Obviously the yoga of action (*karmayoga*) is prescribed for such people. Now, what does it include? Does it comprise only remote subsidiaries to Self-knowledge (*bahiraṅga*), such as rites, or also proximate subsidiaries such as meditation? If it includes both, then what kind of meditation and for the sake of which results? And what is the relationship between the yoga of action and the discipline of knowledge? If their combination is allowed, how does Śaṅkara explain it in the context of his refutation of the combination of action and Self-knowledge as means of liberation (*jñānakarmasamuccaya*)? These are the questions which now need to be answered in order to understand the specific value given by Śaṅkara to inner and outer forms of renunciation in the broad context of the different means and ways of living variously conducive to liberation.

RITES AND THE YOGA OF ACTION

Following *Bhagavadgītā* 3.3 and Śaṅkara's commentary thereupon, we have so far identified *karmayoga* or the yoga of action as one form of steadfastness in action (*karmaniṣṭhā*). Śaṅkara explains that while some rites prescribed by the scriptures are already obligatory by virtue of their purifiying effect even for the man who does not desire liberation (BS 3.4.32, transl., 789–790), they become more purifying and conducive to the rise of Self-knowledge for one who, desirous of liberation, performs them without attachment to their rewards (BS 4.3.34, transl., 792). However, since some people may be aspiring for liberation, yet be unqualified for the sacrifices which are usually attached to *karmayoga*, the latter could provisionally be extended to mean unattached performance of whatever means of purification one is eligible to. Thus, two more types of people who do not practice Vedic sacrifices could be included in our study of *karmayogins*: [1] the unenlightened people who, although normally qualified for Vedic sacrifices, cannot perform them (widowers, for instance) but who, aiming at liberation, can still pursue without attachment practices which are recommended for people in general, such as repetition of mantras (*japa*) and yogic meditation which is available irrespective of any social condition (BS 3.4.38, transl., 794); [2] the unenlightened people belonging to the *varṇa* of *Śūdras* and who, even though not permitted Vedic studies and practices, can nevertheless pursue, for liberation and without attachment, the practices attached to their *varṇa* as well as those recommended for people in general (Ibid.).

But the yoga of action is not merely a function of the performance of a particular type of action. It is also based on the attitude of the performer during the action. "And it is observed in cases such as a desire-prompted *agnihotra*," says Śaṅkara, "that the *agnihotra* ceases to be desire-prompted when the desire [for the reward] is annihilated. Thus, actions produce different results, as they are done with or without expectation" (BhG 4.24, 218). Therefore, when an action formally defined as an obligatory rite is done with a desire for a specific result, it becomes a desire-prompted rite and spoils the spirit of the yoga of action. The latter must therefore be defined as the performance of obligatory rites, duties and non-prohibited actions—excluding desire-prompted rites—without attachment to their rewards.

But what is the purifying effect of rites and duties performed in such a manner? First, with respect to the accomplishment of rites as such, regardless of the doer's attitude, Śaṅkara explains—after the *Gītā*—that the *Vedas* are the expression of how the world revolves according to its Creator, *Īśvara* (BhG 3.16, transl., 117). And when, in accord with this world-vision, the *Vedas* prescribe to man rites that will satisfy gods, Vedic seers and ancestors, it is because, at all levels, the wheel of life is a constant exchange of "food" (BhG 3.11, transl., 113). If man does not maintain his contribution as a giver to the rest of the world, he becomes a thief (BhG 3.12, transl., 114). Thus, we can say that performance of rites purifies man in that it helps in maintaining his individual life in tune with the basic organizing principle of the universe.

How exactly does renunciation of the rewards of all actions also produce in itself a purifying effect? First Śaṅkara remarks that it maintains steadiness of mind: "Therefore the purport is that only such a performer of action *who has renounced the expectation of the reward*, can become a *yogin*, can become a man of composure, one whose mind is not distracted—because the cause of the mind's distraction, namely, *the expectation of the reward*, has been renounced" (BhG 6.2, 286–287). Śaṅkara specifies elsewhere that while performing actions "one should pay more attention to the means rather than to the end" (TU 1.12.1, transl., 282). Thus, this attitude contributes to evenness of mind. In turn, this calmness tends to loosen the grip of bondage on the awareness since "even if they are binding by nature, actions naturally cease to be so by virtue of mental equanimity" (BhG 2.50, 110). Yet, for Śaṅkara, only immediate knowledge of the Self can free from all bondage, and any type of renunciation accomplished by the yet unenlightened man will result in limited freedom.

MEDITATION ON THE QUALIFIED *BRAHMAN* AS PART OF THE YOGA OF ACTION

The Vedāntic doctrine divides the means of Self-knowledge into remote subsidiaries (*bahiraṅgas*) such as rites, and proximate subsidiaries (*antaraṅgas*) such as meditation. It is well established that the proximate subsidiaries are comparatively more direct and efficient for the attainment of immediate Self-knowledge and liberation. Therefore, as part of the assessment of the yoga of action in Śaṅkara's doctrine of liberation, we must determine whether a practice such as meditation is included in the yoga of action and understand its nature and role in comparison with the mediate Self-knowledge available in the yoga of knowledge (*jñānayoga*). Whatever role meditation plays in the yoga of action, it is of major importance in understanding the relationships between the various forms of renunciation in Śaṅkara's doctrine of liberation.

Śaṅkara defines meditation in several places and usually refers to it through the words *upāsana(ā)*, *vidyā*, *dhyāna*, *abhyāsa*, or *nididhyāsana*. Remarkably, in both the contexts of the discipline of knowledge and the yoga of action, Śaṅkara defines the process of meditation in quite the same manner. In his PU 5.1, he understands meditation on *Om* to be "a means of attaining the lower and higher *Brahman*" (PU, 190), that is, a way to raise one's awareness to the personal and qualified aspect of *Brahman*, as well as to its transpersonal and attributeless aspect. Śaṅkara then gives the following definition of that means: "an unbroken flow of self-identification [with the object of meditation], which is not interrupted by other thoughts of a different kind, [and] which is like the [unflickering] flame of a lamp in a windless place."[1]

In his book on the contemporary representatives of Śaṅkara, William Chenkner reports that modern Śaṅkarācāryas prescribe meditation as part of the yoga of action (1983, 170). However, many scholars consider that it does not suit the seeker-after-liberation at this level. Contrasting the *Yoga* of Patañjali and the *Advaita* discipline, with the yoga of action (*karmayoga*) and the yoga of devotion (*bhaktiyoga*), Pandurang V. Kane remarks that "the path of *Karmayoga* (performing good deeds and acts prescribed by Śāstra without hankering for rewards) and *Bhaktiyoga* (in which there is deep devotion to God and self-surrender) appears to me more suitable and practical for ordinary human beings" (1974, 5:1462). According to M. Hiriyanna, meditation is to be adopted "in the later phase" of life, as a preparation for the life of a formal *saṃnyāsin* (1952, 11–12). Mircea Eliade believes on his part that, according to the *Gītā*, yogic meditation is reserved for the monk alone (1954, 164).

Sometimes the scriptures themselves give the impression that the yoga of action includes only rites and duties, and no meditation. After telling Arjuna in *Gītā* 3.7 that one who engages in the yoga of action excels, in the next verse, Kṛṣṇa declares: "Do perform obligatory rites" (*niyataṃ kuru karma tvam*). In 18.3 and 18.5, these obligatory actions are referred to as "sacrifice, gift and austerity" (*yajñadānatapaḥ karma*). The same three terms are used in *Bṛhadāraṇyaka Upaniṣad* 4.4.22 to describe the means through which "Brahmins seek to know the Self." Here Śaṅkara specifies that the term sacrifice (*yajña*) includes "those performed with things and those consisting of knowledge" (transl., 524), which could suggest that the term *yajña* also includes the mental sacrifice consisting of meditation. But in BS 4.1.18, Śaṅkara quotes the same verse in a way that distinguishes its reference to sacrifice, from meditation: "Even so, the *agnihotra* and other rites are not absolutely useless when they are not accompanied by meditation. Why? Because in 'They seek to know this Self through sacrifice' [BṛU 4.4.22], the *Śruti* declares without distinction that rites such as the *agnihotra* are means of knowledge" (BS 4.1.18, 853). Moreover, in his BṛU 6.2.16, Śaṅkara associates the path defined by the same terms (*yajñena danena tapasā*) with "mere ritualists" (*kevelakarmiṇaḥ*) who do not meditate and therefore go only to the path of ancestors. So although some ambiguity remains as to the meaning of the phrase "sacrifice consisting of knowledge" in BṛU 4.4.22, Śaṅkara's main tendency is to exclude meditation from the phrase "sacrifice, gift and austerity."

Following the *Upaniṣads*, Śaṅkara mentions in several places that three possible fates await the unenlightened people at the time of death. They either go to the highest layer of the world of gods, namely, the heaven of the god Brahmā (*Brahmaloka*) through the path of gods (Northern Course), or to inferior heavens such as the world of Indra through the path of ancestors (Southern Course), or they are reborn as small animals. Access to the path of gods and to that of ancestors, says Śaṅkara, come respectively from practice of meditation (here termed *vidyā*) and performance of obligatory rites:

> Meditation and action are mentioned here as opening the paths of gods and of ancestors.... For those who are neither qualified for the path of gods through the practice of meditation, nor for the path of ancestors through the performance of rites, there is the ever-rotating third path involving [birth as] a tiny creature.[2]

Now, in the commentaries on *Chāndogya Upaniṣad* 5.10.3 and *Praśna Upaniṣad* 1.9, the performance of sacrifices, gifts, and austerities is not associated with the path of gods, but with the path of ancestors. This suggests again that it does not include meditation.

On the other hand, the numerous meditations addressed to the *karmayogin* by the *Upaniṣads* as well as by the *Bhagavadgītā* prevents one from concluding that meditation is unavailable outside the monastic way of living.

At least two hypotheses could be put forward to explain why meditation is prescribed for *karmayogins* while not formally included by scriptures and Śaṅkara in what could be considered as the basic list of *karmayoga*'s practices. It could be [1] because the meditations prescribed for *karmayogins* are to be carried on only during the performance of sacrifices; or [2] because sacrifices stand as the most important means in the discipline of the *karmayogin*, meditation being only optional or secondary. Let us now assess these two hypotheses.

The first hypothesis is dealt with by Śaṅkara in BS 3.3.42. The opponent claims that meditations on the letter *om* and the like are necessarily enjoined as part of sacrifices, but never independently. Śaṅkara retorts that meditation cannot always be a mere feature of sacrifices, because *Chāndogya Upaniṣad* specifies that sacrifices are simply rendered *more* effective by meditation and do not need the latter to maintain by themselves a relative degree of efficacy. Thus, concludes Śaṅkara, meditations can be conceived of outside of sacrifices. They have independent existence and results, and can be objects of injunctions unconnected with sacrifices (transl., 722–725). In BS 4.1.7, Śaṅkara also remarks that when considerations about posture of meditation arise in the scriptures, they cannot refer to meditations related to sacrifices, since if it were related, these details would have been regulated as part of the prescriptions connected to rites. And, for instance, the sitting posture is advised to favor an easy flow of awareness toward subtle levels of the object of meditation, which is characteristic of deep meditation unrelated to outward ritualistic activities (transl., 830–831). Śaṅkara goes even further by distinguishing a subtle type of meditation, quite different from those connected with sacrifices. He notices that there are "meditations whose results are proximate to liberation, which relate to the slightly modified non-dual *Brahman* and which are spoken of in such sentences as 'made up of mind and having the vital breath (*prāṇa*) as the body' [MuU 2.2.7], and [other meditations] which enhance the results of rites and rank among ritual subsidiaries."[3] And both these types of meditation are recommended by Śaṅkara as part of the yoga of action for purifying the mind (ChU intro, transl., 6). In his ChU 8.15.1, he confirms that part of the householder's duty is "*withdrawing*, bringing back, *all his organs into the Self*, into his own heart, into *Brahman* in his heart."[4] He then quickly specifies that this is to be accomplished outside of rituals: "and, as indicated by the word 'organs,' abandoning rites . . ."[5] Thus is ruled out the hypothesis that meditation is not formally included in the yoga of action or *karmayoga* because *karmayogins* have to perform it only in sacrifices.

Even if meditation's independence from sacrifices were agreed upon, one could still argue, in terms of the second hypothesis mentioned above, that people retired in the forests (*vānaprasthas*) and formal physical renouncers are usually more fit and have more time for meditation than householders. So that, even when available and enjoined, meditation remains secondary in the life of the householder and therefore in the yoga of action—the householder being the main representative of that path.

Let us explore Śaṅkara's position on this matter. In his introduction to KeU-P, he clearly diminishes mere performance of rites and favors the combination of meditation and rites:

> Properly observed by the desireless seeker-after-liberation, all the above rites and meditations serve in purifying the mind. But mere *Śrauta* and *Smārta* rites lead the desireful person who doesn't meditate to the Southern path [the path of ancestors] and then back[6] to this world.[7]

Śaṅkara's attitude may be related to the fact that in his eyes scriptures deprecate the exclusive practice of either rites or meditation by the *karmayogin.*[8] He explains in his ĪU 9 that "denunciation of the single performance of either [meditative] knowledge or rites is for the sake of their combination, not for mere denunciation" (10).

Elsewhere, as part of the teaching of the *Upaniṣads* on how to avoid developing evil in oneself by one's evil actions, he advocates for the *karmayogins* still destined to the world of gods, the practice of yoga and of *parisaṅkhyāna* meditation:[9] "Therefore, in order to gain sovereignty (*svātantrya*)[10] at the time [of death], the trustful and careful aspirants after the next world should follow the *dharma* of yoga, practice *parisaṅkhyāna* [meditation], and accumulate particular merits."[11]

Similarly, in BṛU 6.2.15, Śaṅkara states that, when yet unenlightened at the time of death, it is as a result of their practice of meditation on the five fires that householders follow the path of gods in the same way as do unenlightened hermits and physical renunciants who practice their own type of meditation:

> Therefore those householders who know as above, that they are thus born of fire, that they are children of fire . . . *and those who meditate with faith*—not on faith—being endowed with faith, *on Truth,* on *Brahman,* on the Self as the Golden Womb[12] (*Hiraṇyagarbha*), *in the forest,* that is, the hermits and wandering mendicants who live in the forest, all *reach the flame deity* [i.e., the Golden Womb].[13]

So it is quite clear from the above passages that, in Śaṅkara's view, meditation is not secondary but basic among the means prescribed to the *karmayogin.*

We presented so far two hypotheses to explain the absence of meditation in formal accounts of *karmayoga*'s practices by scriptures and by Śaṅkara, and we showed that both these hypotheses do not hold. We would like to propose a third hypothesis. In spite of their insistance on the combined use of meditation and rites, at times, scriptures seem to relax the requirements of the path. This is especially true of *Gītā* 12.8–11 where, quite obviously as part of the yoga of action, practices are advocated in descending order of difficulty according to the capacity of the aspirant to perform them, so that, after meditation, which comes first, the last practice consists simply in renunciation of the rewards of actions. Thus, we propose that, according to scriptures and Śaṅkara, when loosely defined, the yoga of action can rest solely on rites and renunciation of its rewards, but its efficacy must normally rely on the additional use of meditation. In the following passage, Śaṅkara even insists that in the yoga of action priority should be given to meditation:

> The purport of the passage is that, giving up as much as possible one's natural action and knowledge, one must therefore try one's best to practice those rites or meditations which are enjoined by the scriptures and which are the means of attaining the Southern or the Northern Path. . . . It is further understood that, among these, greater attention should be given to the means of attaining the Northern Path [i.e., meditation].[14]

Finally, as suggested by the *Muṇḍaka Upaniṣad* and confirmed by Śaṅkara, the very eligibility to the *Advaita* discipline of knowledge is based mainly on previous practice of meditation on the qualified or lower *Brahman*. When the *Muṇḍaka Upaniṣad* states that knowledge of *Brahman* should be given only to those who are engaged in practices, versed in the *Vedas*, and steadfast in *Brahman*, Śaṅkara glosses these terms thus: "Those who are *engaged in practices* (*kriyāvat*), devoted to the performance of duties as mentioned earlier;[15] *versed in Vedic studies; steadfast in Brahman*, devoted to the lower *Brahman* and seeking identity with the supreme *Brahman*" (MuU 3.2.10, 160). It should be noted that, in the context of *Upaniṣads* such as *Muṇḍaka*, "devoted to the lower *Brahman*" typically refers to meditation on a personal god.

It follows from this whole discussion that even though the householder has to devote himself to rites and does not have as much time for meditation as one who has taken up the monastic mode of living, his focus must *also* rest mainly on the proximate means of Self-knowledge which meditation provides. To exclude meditation from the yoga of action, to consider it as secondary or optional for that stage, or to see it as trivial and even unworthy compared to the *Advaita* discipline of knowledge proper, is thus a major misunderstanding of Śaṅkara's teaching concerning the path to Self-knowledge and liberation. By spiriting the inner means of Self-knowledge away from people who remain active in society, such a misunderstanding also contributes in confining Śaṅkara's teaching to the monastic mode of living.

THE ROLE OF MEDITATION ON THE QUALIFIED *BRAHMAN* IN THE YOGA OF ACTION

According to the now prevailing understanding, Śaṅkara teaches that the highest result one can normally expect from practices available to the householder is rather insignificant as compared to the outcome of means accessible in the monastic mode of living. This result consists of a purity of mind that merely ensures the acquisition of the fourfold requirement for the discipline of knowledge, including physical renunciation as a sine qua non for the discipline of knowledge and liberation. It is also understood that combining the yoga of action with the discipline of knowledge would be contradictory to Śaṅkara's refutation of the combination (*samuccaya*) of action and Self-knowledge toward liberation. As stated by S. Revathy: "The stage of life where one is devoted to the meditation upon Brahman is *sannyāsa* [*sic*]. Meditation upon Brahman is not possible in the case of those who are in one of the [first] three stages of life. It is because they have to perform the duties relating to their respective stages of life" (1990, 128).

But, as we will now show in the next two sections, this interpretation represents quite a major departure from Śaṅkara's position. On the contrary, Śaṅkara teaches that [1] meditation on the qualified *Brahman* leads to the very threshold of immediate knowledge of the Self; [2] the discipline of knowledge can be added along with the yoga of action; [3] this combination can lead to immediate knowledge of *Ātman-Brahman*; and [4] this path is not at all in contradiction with the refutation of the combination of action and Self-knowledge as means of liberation.

A close study of Śaṅkara's descriptions of the effects of meditation on the qualified or "lower" *Brahman* (the main characteristic of meditations pertaining to the yoga of action) shows that, not only does it deserve to be practiced by the seeker-after-liberation, but it can actuallly lead him to the threshold of direct Self-knowledge by perfectly preparing the mind to transcend all mental activity.

Meditation on the qualified *Brahman* can have several results: increase efficacy of rites in producing their result;[16] attenuation of sins, which is probably another expression for purification of mind; acquisition of divine powers; and graded liberation,[17] which consists of reaching the world of the Golden Womb after death and obtaining liberation later on from there. A result similar to reaching the world of the Golden Womb is termed as attainment of identity (*āpatti*) with any deity that is meditated upon (ChU 1.11.9, transl, 87). It can be produced either by combination of rites and meditation or by meditation alone in the case of an unenlightened physical renouncer (BṛU 1.3.28, transl., 62).

However, identity with the deity can be attained during human life itself, and it is different from reaching some level of the world of the Golden Womb after death. Referring to a meditation on the qualified *Brahman*, Śaṅkara distinguishes between meditations in which unity with the qualified *Brahman* prevails during the human life of the meditator, and those in which the symbol used remains an obstacle to that immediate identity: "But in the case of [meditation on] symbols, there is no concrete apprehension (*kratutva*)[18] of the [qualified] *Brahman* because, in [such a] meditation, the symbol predominates."[19] In BṛU 1.3.9, Śaṅkara describes this concrete apprehension, resulting from meditation, as "the emergence of the experience of the form of the deity and the like, as one's self, in the same way as one experiences the ordinary self."[20] According to another description, this identity prevails in the perceptions of the waking state even outside meditation proper:

> This *Brahmā* is the Golden Womb in whom these kinds of bliss become unified, and in whom reside *dharma* as caused by that [unified bliss], as well as knowledge of that [bliss], and unsurpassed dispassion. This bliss of His is directly perceived everywhere by one who is versed in the *Vedas*, free from sin, and dispassionate.[21]

Of course Śaṅkara underscores on many occasions that since this bliss is still tainted by doership and experience of the results of actions, it is not the infinite and imperishable felicity of the Self, and therefore cannot eliminate desire, bondage, and suffering. Thus, he specifies: "Therefore, the idea intended here is that even the state characterized by merger in *agni* and other deities—which has been explained and which is the reward of the combined practice of meditation and rites—even this is not enough for the removal of the sorrows of transmigratory existence" (AiU 1.2.1, 646). Commenting on the *Māṇḍukyakārikā*, he also underscores that the goal of meditation on the Golden Womb, that is, experiencing his bliss, is different from the bliss of direct knowledge of *Brahman* and from liberation referred to here as "immortality:"

> Therefore, since [meditation on] the Origin [the Golden Womb] has a different goal, its censure is for the purpose of finding fault in it as compared with knowledge of *Brahman* which is the means of immortality. Because, even though a means of eliminating impurities, it is not [directly] conducive to that [immortality] (MāU-K 3.25, 303).

On the other hand, it should be recalled that, in the final analysis, according to Śaṅkara, all efforts of the seeker-after-liberation serve solely to remove obstacles to the correct knowledge of the Self through purifying body and mind. Śaṅkara often specifies that the condition for direct knowledge of the Self is complete purity of mind. In his BhG 2.52, he clearly equates the condition for eradicating ignorance with purity of mind:

> *When*, at the time when, *your intellect will cross*, pass, *beyond the confusion of delusion*, the turbidness consisting of delusion and of

> lack of discrimination, by which the internal organ turns towards objects of senses, obscuring the discriminative knowledge between the Self and the non-Self, that is, when your intellect will attain purity.[22]

Also referring to the direct experience of *Brahman*, he writes in his MuU 3.1.8:

> What then is the means for its attainment? This is answered: through clarity of intellect. . . . Clarity of intellect would come about when the latter remains transparent and peaceful on having been made clear as a mirror, water or the like. . . . As one's mind, one's internal organ, has become cleansed through this clarity of intellect, one is able to see Brahman; accordingly, therefore, one sees, perceives, experiences, that Self . . .[23]

Śaṅkara writes along the same lines in BṛU 4.4.22: "*Through sacrifices*, sacrifices performed with material things and those consisting of knowledge [i.e., meditation],[24] all of which aim at purity. And one who, being purified, has a pure mind, will attain knowledge without obstruction."[25]

Whatever may be the role of the discipline of knowledge proper—which is not under discussion now—the various passages given above clearly suggest continuity, rather than discontinuity and opposition, between the yoga of action and the process of complete purification that leads to direct experience of *Ātman-Brahman*. This continuity is conveyed quite clearly when *Kaṭha Upaniṣad* 1.3.13 describes a process of withdrawal of awareness from the gross to more and more subtle levels of existence, and in which the man of discrimination should merge the organ of speech into the mind, the mind into the intellect, the intellect into the Golden Womb and the latter into the Self. Śaṅkara comments on the subtler levels of the merger as follows: "*He should settle down knowledge*, i.e., the intellect, *in the Great Soul*, in the First-Born [the Golden Womb]. The idea is that he should make Self-knowledge as clear in its nature as is the First-Born. And *that* Great Soul, *he should settle into the peaceful . . . Self*."[26]

Saying that meditation on the qualified *Brahman* renders knowledge of the Self as pure as the realm of the Golden Womb, that is, of the subtlest phenomenal existence, is attributing to it remarkable power and efficacy. It would even be fair to say that through this comment Śaṅkara suggests that most of the purifying work toward immediate knowledge of the Self is already done when meditation on the qualified *Brahman* has reached its pinacle in the identity with the Golden Womb. Moreover, the last sentence quite obviously describes the passage from identity with the Golden Womb to identity with the non-dual Self, that is, from meditation on the qualified

Brahman (involving doership) to experience of the non-qualified *Brahman* (devoid of doership). And the ability to arrive at the latter is presented in continuity with the gradual process of inner renunciation already started with meditation on the qualified *Brahman* associated with the yoga of action. Of course, according to the tradition, the completion of this conscious integration of the Self may take years and lives. Still the meditative renunciation available in the yoga of action is described as having very significant results in the overall process of withdrawal from the limitations of action.

Other passages describe how meditation on the qualified *Brahman* leads gradually to its own transcendance into experience of the actionless Self. It can therefore be considered as a means of complete inner renunciation marked by a spontaneous culmination/disappearance of meditation on the qualified *Brahman* in the experience of the attributeless Self. Commenting on *Chāndogya Upaniṣad* 3.11.1, Śaṅkara writes that, after practicing meditations on various aspects of the qualified *Brahman* such as the nectar and the sun, "a certain meditator (*vidvas*) who behaved like the *Vasus* and others, who enjoyed pleasures such as the red ambrosia, who had realized his identity with the sun as his own Self by following the process stated above, became absorbed (*samāhita*). Having seen this *mantra*, he arose from his absorption . . .[27] A little further, in verse 3.2.3, Śaṅkara specifies that this absorption corresponds to direct experience of the *Ātman-Brahman*, since the man who knows thus "becomes the eternal and unborn *Brahman* which is not limited by periods of rising up and setting down."[28]

Śaṅkara even acknowledges that one can reach liberation through meditation outside the formal study and contemplation of the *Upaniṣads* (the traditional yoga of knowledge or *jñānayoga*), as he quotes the following passage from *Manu Smṛti*: "Doubtless, a Brahmin can succeed merely through *japa*,"[29] the latter being simply repetition of *mantras*.

Śaṅkara explains that although meditations on the qualified *Brahman* are within the realm of ignorance, they can lead to immediate Self-knowledge inasmuch as their activity is eventually transcended in the experience of the actionless Self. This explanation is provided for instance with reference to *Taittirīya Upaniṣad* 3.2.1, which is part of a sequence where the sage *Bhṛgu* performs meditations (called "*tapas*") meant to gradually recognize subtler and subtler levels of the qualified *Brahman* (the gross level of creation, the vital force, the mind, the intellect) and to finally bring about merger in the non-dual bliss of the Self:

> From such *Śruti* texts as "Seek to know *Brahman* through austerity" [TU 3.2.1], actions such as austerity and service to the master, which

> are means for the rise of knowledge, are called ignorance, since they consist of ignorance. Having brought forth knowledge through them, one transcends death, that is, desire.[30]

Thus, according to Śaṅkara, although pertaining to the yoga of action, meditation on the qualified *Brahman* does purify the mind enough to bring the seeker-after-liberation up to the very threshold of immediate knowledge of the Self. We say "threshold" only, because as long as an attribute of *Brahman* is still binding the awareness of the meditator—a situation characteristic of meditation on the qualified *Brahman*—immediate knowledge of the Self is not available. To have direct knowledge of the attributeless Self, one has to transcend the experience of the binding attribute, and therefore the very meditation on the qualified *Brahman*. At the moment when it is ultimately transcended, the experience of the purely silent Self dawns. Here, achieving transcendence is the key dimension that differentiates between steadfastness in action (*karmaniṣṭhā*) and steadfastness in direct Self-knowledge (*aparokṣajñānaniṣṭhā*): as long as one is bound by the sense of doership that accompanies meditation on the qualified *Brahman*, one remains steadfast in action. But, when, as a culmination of the purity gained through this meditation, transcendence of all binding mental activities of meditation occurs, and the Self is experienced as pure silent consciousness, one has stepped into steadfastness in direct knowledge of the Self.

Moreover, while the *nididhyāsana* type of meditation is usually understood by followers of Śaṅkara to be much superior to meditation on the qualified *Brahman*, from the various definitions of meditation given by Śaṅkara, it can be seen as the culmination of meditation on the qualified *Brahman*, rather than as something wholly opposed to the latter or radically different in nature. This is because in both meditation on the qualified *Brahman* and *nididhyāsana*, the process is essentially the same, that is, repeated experience of a thought, gradually moving from its grosser to its more subtle levels. Śaṅkara characterizes both *nididhyāsana* and meditation on the qualified Brahman (*upāsanā*) as the repetition of mental actions: "Besides, the words *upāsana* and *nididhyāsana* denote an act (*kriyā*) which specifically involves repetition" (BS 4.1.1, 826). He specifies that *Brahman* is meditated upon with attributes because it is not possible for people with less purified minds to know it directly, that is, without attributes:

> Even the statements as to [*Brahman*'s] magnitudes [such as having four feet or sixteen parts] are not meant for establishing the existence of something different from *Brahman*. What are they meant for

> then? They serve the purposes of the intellect, *i.e.*, of meditation. . . . For, as men can be of dull, middling or superior intellect, they are not all capable of fixing it on the infinite *Brahman* that is devoid of modifications.[31]

So there exists a major difference between meditation of the qualified *Brahman* (usually associated with the yoga of action) and *nididhyāsana*—which pertains to the discipline of knowledge and is associated with a more abstract meditation on the *Ātman-Brahman* as being without attributes. Due to purity already acquired, namely, through meditation on the qualified *Brahman*, in *nididhyāsana*, the meditator seems to be able to have his mind more easily absorbed in abstract Upaniṣadic thoughts such as "Thou art That." Yet, the process as such is quite similar in both types of meditation. This similarity is examplified by the following two definitions. The first one refers to meditation on the vital force which is the entity termed here as deity: "Once the form of a deity or the like has been approached mentally as it is presented by the explanatory portions of the *Śruti* relating to the objects of meditation, meditation is dwelling on it, thinking of it with no interruption from ordinary thoughts . . ."[32] In BhG 12.3, Śaṅkara presents a quite similar definition: "Once proximity with the thing to be meditated upon has been reached by making it the object of meditation in the way prescribed by scriptures, meditation is dwelling on it for a long time with a continuous flow of the same thought like a thread of [descending] oil."[33] Most significant, however, is that the context of this second definition specifies the object of meditation as the attributeless *Brahman*. Thus, as far as the meditative process is concerned, meditation on the qualified *Brahman* is quite close to the *nididhyāsana* type of meditation.

Interestingly, in BṛU 4.2.4, Śaṅkara describes the whole range of both these types of meditation within one single process of completely transcending all meditative activity in favor of the experience of the actionless Self: "Thus, by stages, the meditator identifies himself with the vital force which is the self of everything. Having withdrawn this self of everything into the inner Self, the seer then discovers the true condition of the seer, that is, the fourth [state of the] Self which is described as 'neither this, nor that.' "[34]

It follows from these passages that, apart from knowledge of the non-dual Self to be acquired from the scriptures, complete purity remains the key condition for emergence of immediate Self-knowledge. Particular means or ways of living used for increasing purity come second. This seems to be the reason why Śaṅkara states in a manner quite free from dogmatism that even remote means such as faith can in some cases be considered as the single cause of the rise of direct Self-knowledge:

> For, in ordinary life, effects resulting from causes may be considered to be produced separately, from distinct causes in a variety of ways, or from their combination. And these causes operating separately or in combination can again be divided in terms of their efficiency or otherwise. . . . Sometimes, the ritual actions of one's past life are the cause, as in the case of Prajāpati. Sometimes it is austerity. . . . Sometimes . . . faith and the like are a sure cause in attaining knowledge, because they remove obstacles such as unrighteousness. Hearing about, reflection on and meditation upon *Vedānta* scriptures are also causes, as they are directly related to that [*Brahman*] which is to be known. And this is because when obstacles consisting of [the results of] prohibited actions and the like have disappeared, it is of the nature of the Self and the mind to cause the knowledge of things as they are."[35]

Thus, all these passages suggest that the condition for enlightenment through the teaching of scriptures is not purity as an exclusive result of full-time discipline of knowledge following formal renunciation, but simply purity. They also show that meditation on the qualified *Brahman* is quite a significant practice in the process of enlightenment. Moreover the last quotation states that the various means of Self-knowledge can be combined. So how does Śaṅkara view the relationship and combination of the yoga of action with the discipline of knowledge?

THE YOGA OF ACTION AND THE DISCIPLINE OF KNOWLEDGE

The relationship between the yoga of action (*karmayoga*) and the discipline of knowledge is closely related to the issue of physical renunciation. In BhG 3.3, for instance, Śaṅkara makes a clear distinction between the yoga of action and the yoga of knowledge (*jñānayoga*) which consists mainly of the discipline of knowledge preceded by physical renunciation. In this kind of context, he presents the yoga of action as a means which merely prepares to the yoga of knowledge and which is to be abandoned when one is ready for the latter. However, as we saw, other passages suggest that practices available to people outside the monastic way of living can lead to direct Self-knowedge and liberation. So let us try to clarify Śaṅkara's position on the relationship between the yoga of action and the discipline of knowledge.

Owing to its purifying effect, the yoga of action is a subsidiary to direct Self-knowledge (BS 3.4.27, transl., 785; BhG 5 intro, transl., 184). But the rites on which it is based are considered to be only remote subsidiaries (BS 3.4.27, transl., 785). The yoga of action gives mind and body "the ability to be steadfast in [the yoga of] knowledge" (*jñānaniṣṭhāyogyatā*).[36] It is "a means to the yoga of knowledge" (BhG 3.4, 145), "a means to ascend to the yoga of meditation" (BhG 6 intro, 285). Now, according to Śaṅkara's interpretation of *Gītā* 6.3, when one is no more "deprived of the ability to remain steady in the yoga of meditation" (BhG 6.3, 287), then, "abstention from all actions is said to be the means" (Ibid.). This is to say that the yoga of action has to be abandoned physically as a way to complete absorption in the discipline of knowledge.

Now, Śaṅkara considers the discipline of knowledge to be the most proximate means of direct Self-knowledge (TU 1.12.1, transl., 282). He also mentions that enlightenment is achieved only when the process of hearing, reflection, and meditation on the Upaniṣadic knowledge concerning the *Ātman-Brahman* has been completed (BṛU 2.4.5, transl., 247). In addition, this practice seems incompatible with meditation on the qualified *Brahman*—called below the Universal Form—since the discipline of knowledge implies the exclusive meditation on the attributeless *Brahman*—called below the Imperishable:

> The meaning is: *those who are thus ever disciplined* regularly perform rites and the like for the sake of the Lord, in the prescribed manner, with their mind concentrated. Resorting to no other refuge, *those devotees worship Thee*, meditate on Thee, as manifested in the Universal Form; *and those*, others, *also*, who, having abandoned all desires and renounced all rites, meditate on *Brahman*, characterized as *the Imperishable* . . .[37]

Thus, the yoga of action and the yoga of knowledge seem to be opposed in that they are respectively [1] remote and proximate means of direct Self-knowledge, [2] associated and unassociated with meditation on the qualified *Brahman*, [3] to be abandoned and pursued when one has the ability to remain steadfast in Self-knowledge. Authors such as R. Balasubramanian interpret this contrast as meaning that the discipline of knowledge and the yoga of action "cannot be practiced at the same time" (Sureśvara 1988, 344).[38] But, in Śaṅkara's eyes, physical abandonment of rites and of the yoga of action is not required for the discipline of knowledge and is prescribed only for Brahmins. So, in view of this basic reference point, statements such as those found in the commentary on *Gītā* 6.3 would mean that the yoga of action is to be abandoned physically by Brahmins. Yet nothing prevents others from combining the yoga of action with the discipline of knowledge, and we even saw that the scriptures mention instances where Brahmins also combine the two.

Now, what is the evidence accounted by Śaṅkara for this combination and for its efficiency in bringing about liberation? First, he connects the proximate means of meditation and the like referred to by the phrase "those who know it thus," with householders as well as with people who have renounced physically: "But who are 'those who know [it] thus?' The householders, of course . . . *and those in the forest,* hermits and wandering mendicants who always remain in the forest, *who meditate* . . ."[39] Śaṅkara also clearly states that apart from the remote means of Self-knowledge, which are attached to his mode of living, the householder is also prescribed practices more typical of "other modes of living," namely, meditative means such as control of senses:

> This is because the scriptures prescribe for him many duties connected with his mode of living and which require great effort, such as sacrifices. And duties of other modes of living, such as nonviolence and control of senses[40] are [also] there for him inasmuch as possible.[41]

Also as evidence that householders have access to the means of full Self-knowledge are some passages of Śaṅkara's works which clearly describe attainment of direct Self-knowledge without any reference to physical renunciation. The comment on TU 1.10 specifies quite clearly the immediate nature of the Self-knowledge attained outside the monastic context: "It is obvious that the visions of the seers concerning the Self and the like, arise in one who is thus engaged in the daily obligatory duties enjoined in the *Śruti* and the *Smṛti,* who is without desires, and who seeks after the knowledge of the supreme *Brahman.*"[42] Introducing BhG 4.42, Śaṅkara also grants the yoga of action the power to give direct Self-knowledge through purification: ". . . the man who, by virtue of the practice of the yoga of action, has his doubts cut asunder by knowledge which arises from the elimination of impurities, is not bound by actions, solely because they have been consumed in the fire of knowledge . . ."[43] Similarly, in BhG 3.19, Śaṅkara writes: "This is because, performing *action without attachment,* doing it for the sake of *Īśvara, man attains the supreme,* liberation, by means of purity of mind."[44] The next verse (3.20) uses similar terms to describe the way Self-knowers such as king Janaka attained enlightenment—obviously without physical renunciation and full-time involvement in the discipline of knowledge. In another passage, Śaṅkara states that the yoga of action leads to a Self-knowledge which results in freedom from virtue and vice. Since this freedom is possible only through direct Self-knowledge, it is such a knowledge that is caused by the yoga of action: "Hear what reward is obtained by one who performs his duty with evenness of mind. *One who is endued with knowledge*, who is possessed of the knowledge of evenness, *casts off*, abandons, *here*, in this world, *both virtue and vice*, merit and demerit, through purification of mind and attainment of knowledge . . ."[45]

Thus, in these passages, Śaṅkara establishes an unbroken continuity between the yoga of action, its purifying power, and the rise of direct Self-knowledge. Now, since he restricts physical renunciation to Brahmins alone, yet considers qualification for the discipline of knowledge to be both fundamental and independent from modes of living (*āśrama*), when in such passages he mentions that the yoga of action leads to direct Self-knowledge, it can be reasonably presumed that he left understood the combination of the yoga of action with the discipline of knowledge, or the physical abandonment of the yoga of action in the case of Brahmins. But there is no ground to assume that he left understood physical renunciation as a sine qua non for direct Self-knowledge.

Using the terms wisdom of yoga (*yogabuddhi*) and wisdom of *Sāṃkhya* (*sāṃkyabuddhi*), Śaṅkara again clearly states that means available outside the monastic context lead to direct Self-knowledge. In his BhG 2.11, the wisdom of yoga and the wisdom of *Sāṃkhya* are described thus:[46]

> . . . the wisdom of *Sāṃkhya* is the knowledge—arising from the ascertainment of the content of the [said] section—that because the Self is devoid of the six modifications such as birth, it is not a doer; and those knowers to whom it applies are the followers of *Sāṃkhya*. Before the dawn of this knowledge is yoga, defined as the ascertainment of the practice of the means of liberation, based on the notion that the Self is distinct from the body and that it is a doer, enjoyer and the like, [as well as] accompanied by discrimination between good and evil. The knowledge that pertains to it is the wisdom of yoga; and the performers of action to whom it applies are the *yogins*.[47]

It will be useful to further clarify this passage. Let us first specify the meaning of "wisdom of yoga" (*yogabuddhi*). When understood in this context, the word yoga is defined four times in Śaṅkara's BhG as including two elements: yoga of action (or simply actions) and evenness of mind. Evenness of mind is expressed by either of the following terms: yoga of absorption (*samādhiyoga*), evenness of mind (*samabuddhitva*), or wisdom of evenness (*samatvabuddhi*). Yoga of absorption seems to mean the practice of meditation. Unfortunately, the compound is used only twice in Śaṅkara's BhG (2.39 and 4.38), and the author merely mentions it without comment. In the *Gītā* and in Śaṅkara's commentaries, expressions based on the word *samatva* (equanimity, evenness, balance) are used to describe various levels of equanimity. First, they may refer, from a broad perspective, to a quality that is worth developing by the seeker-after-liberation;[48] second, they can be understood as a result of meditation and as a major prerequisite for immediate knowledge of the Self;[49] finally, they will appear as a characteristic of liberation-in-life.[50] Hence, the three terms variously added to the yoga of action in the definition of the wisdom of yoga (*yogabuddhi*) can be understood as follows: evenness of mind (*samabuddhitva*) or wisdom of evenness (*samatvabuddhi*) may refer to a general quality to be developed, to a result of meditation or to a major prerequisite for direct knowledge of the Self; and, because of the well-known meaning of *samādhi* as absorption in meditation, *samādhiyoga* or yoga of absorption can hardly refer to anything else than to the practice of meditation. It probably stands for the discipline of knowledge as included in the "wisdom of yoga," and practiced along with the yoga of action outside the context of physical renunciation.[51]

Most significant for us is that, in the context of all four definitions of yoga in Śaṅkara's comment, yoga is said to lead to direct Self-knowledge. In these passages, the latter is referred to as the wisdom of *Sāṃkhya* (*sāṃkhyabuddhi*). In his BhG 2.39, for instance, Śaṅkara starts with the following gloss on the wisdom of *Sāṃkhya*: "the wisdom, i.e., the knowledge, of *Sāṃkhya*, i.e., pertaining to the discrimination of the supreme reality and which is the direct means for eradication of imperfections such as sorrow and delusion—the latter being the cause of transmigratory existence."[52] Since the wisdom of *Sāṃkhya* is here the direct means for eradicating transmigratory existence, it must correspond to immediate Self-knowledge. The wisdom of *Sāṃkhya* is therefore the direct Self-knowledge that brings about liberation. Śaṅkara then gives the definition of yoga, mentioning that it leads to that wisdom of *Sāṃkhya*:

> *Hear now* about the wisdom *concerning yoga*—the means of attaining the [wisdom of *Sāṃkhya*]—that is, concerning the yoga of action—the detached performance of actions as a way to propitiate the Lord after having discarded the pairs of opposites—and concerning the yoga of meditation (*samādhiyoga*). This is to be told shortly.[53]

In quite the same spirit, Śaṅkara writes in his BhG 4.38: "*Having reached perfection through yoga*, having refined [himself], having reached competence, through yoga, that is, through the yoga of action and the yoga of absorption, the seeker-after-liberation *realizes that* knowledge, after a long *time, in himself, by himself* alone."[54]

It is thus clear that the means available outside the monastic context—which include rites, meditation on the qualified *Brahman* and the discipline of knowledge—are in themselves sufficient for immediate Self-knowledge. But then, it may be asked, how does Śaṅkara reconcile the refutation of the doctrine of combination of action and knowledge (*jñānakarmasamuccayavāda*) for achieving liberation, with the ability of the wisdom of yoga to directly bring about immediate Self-knowledge?

THE REFUTATION OF THE COMBINATION OF ACTION AND SELF-KNOWLEDGE

A frequent misinterpretation of Śaṅkara's refutation of the combination of action and Self-knowledge must first be brushed aside. It goes without saying that the yoga of action as comprising the practice of rites, and the monastic mode of living as characterized by the absence of these and by full-time practice of the discipline of knowledge, cannot be combined at the same time by one and the same person, simply because it is not possible for the same individual to do *and* not to do rites in the same period of time. But, contrary to a common interpretation, this is not the opposition on which Śaṅkara's refutation of combination of action and Self-knowledge as means to liberation is based. The reason is that, in themselves, neither the yoga of action, nor full-time discipline of knowledge preceded by physical renunciation lead to liberation: in terms of postmortem fate, their result can only be either the world of ancestors (*pitṛloka*) or the world of gods (*devaloka*), the latter having the Golden Womb as highest attainment. Both the yoga of action and the discipline of knowledge preceded by physical renunciation lead to liberation only indirectly, that is, inasmuch as, through complete purity of mind, they generate *immediate* knowledge of the Self, which alone is the unaccompanied and independent means to liberation by virtue of being the only element that is opposed to ignorance of the actionless nature of the Self and that can therefore cancel it. So, although the yoga of action and the monastic mode of living as comprising the discipline of knowledge cannot be combined, from Śaṅkara's perspective, this absence of combination is not significant with respect to identification of the real and direct means of liberation.

It is true that, in order to refute the doctrine of the combination of Self-knowledge and action, from time to time, Śaṅkara uses among other arguments the fact that the monastic mode of living—which by definition is without obligatory rites—is prescribed by the scriptures for

Self-knowledge and liberation.[55] But from his perspective, it only proves the following: since there exists an authorized path to liberation which is without rituals, it follows that the latter are not meant by the scriptures to be necessary for liberation. This argument does not claim that because the monastic mode of living is free from obligatory rites and because it allows full-time absorption in the discipline of knowledge, it is the only means to complete Self-knowledge and liberation. This is clearly conveyed, as we saw, when Śaṅkara states in his BhG 2.11 that Janaka and others did attain liberation through Self-knowledge *unaccompanied by rites even if they continued to perform them physically* throughout their life. The same is asserted in the introduction to the MuU. Arguing against the doctrine of combination of Self-knowledge and action, Śaṅkara writes:

> And by mentioning "who go about begging for alms" [Mu 1.2.11] and "through the yoga of renunciation" [Mu 3.2.6], [the *Upaniṣad*] shows that while people in all stages of life are qualified for knowledge as a whole, still it is the knowledge of *Brahman* as founded on renunciation alone and unassociated with action that is the means of liberation. And this is because of the mutual exclusiveness of knowledge and action. Not even in a dream can action coexist with the perception of the unity [of the self] with *Brahman*.[56]

It must be noted here that the mention of "begging for alms" is another example of using the monastic mode of living simply as a proof that rites are not always mandatory for the whole life; it illustrates that rites cannot be said to be necessary along with Self-knowledge for bringing about liberation. Reference to this passage in the above quotation does not mean that the monastic mode of living is the only state in which Self-knowledge can lead by itself to liberation. Evidence for this is found in the fact that, in his commentary on *Muṇḍaka Upaniṣad* 1.2.1, which is cited in the passage we just quoted, Śaṅkara states that this verse merely identifies people belonging to the monastic mode of living, who practice meditation on the Golden Womb and who, not having attained liberation, go at the end of life "along the Northern Path, indicated by the [word] sun" (MuU 1.2.11, 138). Hence, the monastic mode of living is certainly not said here to be the privileged way for the application of knowledge as the only means to liberation. As for the citation "through the yoga of renunciation" (from *Muṇḍaka Upaniṣad* 3.2.6) also given in the above excerpt, we saw that this yoga consists in either renunciation of doership or the latter accompanied by physical renunciation. The compound "with the perception of the unity [of the self] with *Brahman*" used as part of the explanation then given by Śaṅkara in the above excerpt refers quite clearly to direct Self-knowledge since it is contextually connected with "knowledge of *Brahman*" as the sole means of liberation. Thus, it also indicates that the incompatibility is between any action and direct Self-knowledge, not between rites and a discipline of knowledge that would be accessible only after abandoning the yoga of action.

Following the above excerpt from the introduction to the MuU, Śaṅkara refutes the combination of action and Self-knowledge even in the case of enlightened householders. Such a refutation could not make sense if the said combination were between rites and the discipline of knowledge preceded by physical renunciation. The first two verses of the *Upaniṣad* give names of people who handed down Self-knowledge through the ages and among whom were householders. Foreseeing that this could support the doctrine of the combination of Self-knowledge and action, Śaṅkara clarifies:

> But indications such as the fact that among householders some are founders of the tradition of the knowledge of *Brahman*, have no power to annul the established principle. When even a hundred injunctions cannot bring about the coexistence of light and darkness in the same place, how can mere indications do?[57]

Now, at the end of his commentary on the same *Upaniṣad*, Śaṅkara specifies that these founders "directly perceived the supreme *Brahman*," leaving no doubt that in his mind they were all enlightened even though some of them were householders. Thus, in a context obviously referring to enlightened knowers of *Brahman*, who were also householders, the incompatibility between "light" (Self-knowledge) and "darkness" (action) can only stand for the impossibility of combining immediate knowledge of the actionless Self with ignorance of it and with characteristics such as the sense of doership.

It follows that when Śaṅkara argues against the combination of action and Self-knowledge as means of liberation, it is not for the sake of prescribing physical renunciation and the ensuing monastic mode of living as necessary for gaining mediate and immediate knowledge, but simply and repeatedly for the sake of establishing that immediate Self-knowledge alone can annul ignorance of the actionless nature of the Self and thus lead to freedom from change and mortality.

Śaṅkara's rejection of the combination of Self-knowledge and action is most clearly and briefly stated in his BS 3.4.25-26. He says in his comment on verse 3.4.25 that Self-knowledge is independent from action in producing the result of liberation: "*And for this very reason*, because knowledge is the cause of liberation, the ritual actions (such as 'lightening up a fire') of the [various] modes of living, are not needed by knowledge for producing its own result."[58] But he also mentions in the comment on the next verse (3.4.2) that these actions can generate the said knowledge: "Just as, for a consideration of suitability, a horse is not yoked for drawing a plough, but a chariot is,[59] similarly the duties of the modes of living are not needed for the fruition of the result of knowledge, but for the emergence of knowledge."[60]

Thus, Śaṅkara's doctrine about the respective functions of action and Self-knowledge with respect to liberation can be stated as follows. All prescribed actions, that is, all practices (whether meditation on the Upaniṣadic statements as performed by the monk or even sacrifices as performed by the householders) lead to direct Self-knowledge through purification of body and mind; thus the rise of immediate Self-knowledge is dependent upon the (various) purifying powers of all practices, whether they be sacrifices or the discipline of knowledge, whether these are combined by the householder, or uncombined, as in the case of the monk; yet once purity of body and mind is complete and, as a consequence, immediate Self-knowledge is established, then that knowledge needs no other practice or means to bring about liberation, since the latter comes spontaneously as a result of eradication of ignorance and of its effects such as identification with the boundaries of mind and body and transmigratory existence.

It is on the basis of this understanding that Śaṅkara can feel totally consistent in stating, on the one hand, like the *Gītā*, that ritual actions of the yoga of action should be performed (or should not be physically abandoned) for the sake of direct experience of the Self,[61] and on the other hand, that it is impossible to combine ritual actions and Self-knowledge as means of liberation. It is also on the basis of this understanding that, in passages such as the following one, steadfastness in knowledge is to be understood as an already immediate Self-knowledge, and not as the discipline of knowledge:

> . . . in order to convey the idea that steadfastness in action leads to the goal, not independently, but by leading to the attainment of steadfastness in knowledge, whereas steadfastness in knowledge, having been gained through steadfastness in action, leads to the goal by itself, without anything else, the Lord says:[62]

Śaṅkara's position on this question has been deeply misunderstood by many scholars. In the introduction to his translation of Śaṅkara's BhG,

Ramachandra Aiyar first blames a modern tendency to understand Śaṅkara's doctrine as prescribing a combined use of the path of action and the discipline of knowledge: "According to this interpretation the Knowledge-based Activity must be practiced[63] by the spiritual aspirant right up to Liberation, without his ever having to embrace the *saṁnyāsin*'s life of complete renunciation of works" (BhG, transl., xvii). Referring to the advanced aspirant to liberation, the translator then says:

> His total dedication to reflection, ipso facto, implies his complete renunciation of the life of activity. Since it is only the constant reflection on the Self that directly leads to Self-Realization, which is Perfection/Liberation, the Path of Knowledge alone is the proximate means to that Goal.
>
> The Path of Action, according to the Ācārya [Śaṅkara], is only the remote means to the Goal. It is the remote path that leads to the proximate path of Knowledge. . . . By following the path of Action exclusively . . . he gets the competence to take the Path of Knowledge (Ibid., xvii–xviii).

It should be noted first that this statement is partially true from Śaṅkara's viewpoint, in that the yoga of action can lead the Brahmin to a state of detachment that will induce him to abandon all obligatory rites in order to enter the monastic mode of living and devote all his time to the discipline of knowledge. But Ramachandra Aiyar's misinterpretation consists in thinking that when Śaṅkara says that the yoga of action brings about liberation only indirectly, by first leading to steadfastness in knowledge (or the yoga of knowledge), it means that the yoga of action can merely bring the seeker-after-liberation to the threshold of the discipline of knowledge for which physical renunciation is required.

In Sengaku Mayeda's analysis, the misinterpretation about Śaṅkara's doctrine crystallizes in the finding that "Śaṅkara's treatment of action is self-contradictory" (Upad transl., 88-89).[64] Mayeda first observes:

> In the *Upadeśasāhasrī* (I, 17,44) Śaṅkara says that action can take place only before acquisition of knowledge of *Ātman*, since a firm belief that "Thou art That" removes any notions of belonging to a certain caste and so on, which are the prerequistes to the performance of action. This statement is indeed negative, but it implies *paradoxically*[65] the positive meaning that action should be performed before one can achieve cessation of nescience. . . . Practically speaking, therefore, the aspirant should perform actions until his attainment of final release (Ibid., 92).

Mayeda's understanding is made explicit a few lines further. After mentioning practices such as abstinence from injury, austerities, and study recommended in the Upad to students involved in the discipline of knowledge, Mayeda is surprised that Śaṅkara "considers these means to be compatible with knowledge, though they are unquestionably actions" (Ibid.). We can see that, from Mayeda's viewpoint, the absence of combination should be between the discipline of knowledge and any other practice, which is why he sees a contradiction in Śaṅkara's doctrine. But, according to Śaṅkara, the incompatibility is rather between immediate Self-knowledge and any physical or mental activity, including that of the discipline of knowledge.

Mayeda also sees a contradiction between two of Śaṅkara's statements on the practice of *prasaṃkhyāna* or *parisaṃkhyāna* meditation which according to him are not clearly distinguished in Śaṅkara's writings (Ibid., 254). He notices that Śaṅkara

> rejects the opinion of those who assert *jñānakarmasamuccayavāda* [the doctrine of the combination of knowledge and action] that *prasaṃkhyāna* meditation should be observed until *Ātman* is apprehended (Upad. I, 18, 9 ff.), but in the chapter entitled "*Parisaṃkhyāna*" in the *Upadeśasāhasrī* (II, 3, 112–116) he prescribes *parisaṃkhyāna* meditation for those seekers after final release . . ." (Ibid., 88)

But Mayeda misses the fact that if Śaṅkara refutes the opponent's position in Upad 1.18.9 ff., it is because this opponent holds meditation as an activity to be the means of liberation: "So it is *prasaṃkhyāna* meditation that is the means," says the opponent, "and nothing else . . ." (Ibid., 174). To this, Śaṅkara replies with the argument that this kind of means does not pertain to the *Upaniṣads,* which teach a goal that is not attainable through activity—an answer that perfectly agrees with his basic position on this whole issue, namely, that immediate knowledge of the actionless Self alone yields liberation: "Ends to be attained by actions should be stated in the scriptures before [these *Upaniṣadic* doctrines] and final release is not [an end to be attained by actions], since it is ever-existing" (Ibid.).[66]

Therefore, from Śaṅkara's perspective, even though the yoga of action cannot lead directly to liberation by reason of its basic involvement with the sense of doership, nevertheless, since it can be accompanied by the discipline of knowledge, together with the latter, it can produce the purity necessary for the mind to access, through the scriptures, that experiential steadfastness in Self-knowledge (*jñānaniṣṭhā*), which alone is free from doership and yields liberation.

However, from a strict terminological viewpoint, the term yoga of action *(karmayoga)* as used by Śaṅkara does not account for all possible ways of obtaining immediate Self-knowledge without physical renunciation. This is suggested by Śaṅkara's mention that steadfastness in action and steadfastness in knowledge are for the "[first] three *varṇas*" (BhG 3.3, 141). It follows from this indication that, in Śaṅkara's use, these terms refer only to the disciplines of action and of knowledge of people who have access to the *Śruti* literature. Thus, for a more precise and all-including terminology in the description of the relationship between action and Self-knowledge in Śaṅkara's works, I propose the following terms, definitions, and relationships: [1] *karmayoga* or the yoga of action means performance of obligatory rites, preferably along with the practice of meditation on the qualified *Brahman*, by the members of the first three *varṇas* (*dvijas* or twice-borns); [2] caste duty (*varṇadharma*) means all practices related to any one *varṇa*, which include therefore also those prescribed for *Śūdras*, those available for example to widowers from the first three *varṇas*, who cannot perform rites as before; to these can be added proximate means of knowledge such as mental repetition of mantras (*japa*) and those found in Patañjali's Yoga and *Smārta* texts; [3] the discipline of knowledge is the threefold universally available practice of hearing, reflection, and meditation on the doctrine of the non-dual *Ātman-Brahman* based either on the *Śrauta* texts for twice-born people or on the *Smārta* texts for *Śūdras*; [4] when understood as a means to immediate knowledge of the Self, steadfastness in knowledge—or the yoga of knowledge—is the full-time practice of the discipline of knowledge after formal physical renunciation, that is, following adoption of monastic life, and is available to Brahmins alone.

As far as the relationships between these categories and the goal of liberation are concerned, the two most important points are: [1] the yoga of action or the caste duty can be combined with the discipline of knowledge; [2] they can lead to direct Self-knowledge.

These clarifications thus account for the prescription of physical renunciation by scriptures, for the universal availability of Self-knowledge as expressed in Śaṅkara's works and for all possible prescribed ways of attaining immediate Self-knowledge and liberation.

CHAPTER EIGHT

Self-knowledge and Physical Renunciation

Having considered the relationship between the yoga of action and Self-knowledge, let us now examine how Śaṅkara views the links between physical renunciation and Self-knowledge. We will look at the role of physical renunciation after enlightenment, and then before enlightenment.

PHYSICAL RENUNCIATION FOLLOWING ENLIGHTENMENT

Śaṅkara's clearest discussion of physical renunciation as a result of direct Self-knowledge is found in his introduction to the AiU. In this passage, the opponent is an advocate of the combination of Self-knowledge and action for the purpose of liberation. His main argument starts with the idea that reference to renunciation in verses such as *Bṛhadāraṇyaka Upaniṣad* 3.5.1 is not an injunction, but a mere praise of Self-knowledge or a prescription of renunciation for people disqualified from rites by some physical incapacity (AiU intro, transl., 7). Therefore, the opponent holds that there exists no such non-performer (*akarmin*) belonging to a distinct mode of living (*āśramyantara*) for whom knowledge of the Self would be meant (Ibid., transl. 4). Thus, when the *Upaniṣad* prescribes Self-knowledge, it is in the sense of meditation and only for those who also practice rituals (Ibid., transl., 6). Śaṅkara answers thus: "This is not so, because when the supreme knowledge is reached [and] when there is no looking for rewards, action is not possible. . . . When one knows that his Self is *Brahman* . . . action is impossible" (AiU intro, 632). He further specifies that such a man is not subject to scriptural injunctions "because he has realized the Self that is beyond the range of injunctions" (Ibid.). And he declares even more boldly: "Nor can he be impelled by anybody, since even the scriptures emanate from him. No one can be impelled by an injunction issuing out of his own knowledge."[1] Doubtless, this can only refer to the already enlightened person and not to the seeker-after-liberation.

The opponent then claims (Ibid., transl., 10) that if in the case of the Self-knower, there is no goal (*prayojana*) attainable through rites, likewise there will be no aim in the act of renouncing, since *Gītā* 3.18 states that the Self-knower has nothing to achieve "through non-performance" (*akṛtena*). Śaṅkara retorts that this is not so, "since renunciation consists in mere cessation from activity" (Ibid., 634) unlike an action to be performed for accomplishing a goal. It is a characteristic of the person (*puruṣadharma*) rather than a performance on his part (Ibid., transl., 11). Thus, physical renunciation is again presented as a natural consequence of direct Self-knowledge. Thereupon the opponent reiterates the idea that there is, in fact, no injunction of physical renunciation: "As renunciation naturally follows (*arthaprāptatvāt*), it is not to be enjoined. Then, if the supreme knowledge of *Brahman* dawns in the stage of householder, the inactive man may continue in that state [and] there is no need to move away from it" (Ibid., 634). The argument does not hold, responds Śaṅkara, "since the householder mode of living is a product of desire."[2]

Let us clarify this rather condensed reply. We already noted that Swāmī Gambhīrānanda, translator of this commentary, interprets this kind of statement as precluding immediate Self-knowledge from householders. But Śaṅkara's answer here does not mean that a householder cannot obtain knowledge and liberation; it rather refutes the notion implied by the opponent's argument, according to which a householder can be "non-active" (*akurvan*) and at the same time belong to the householder mode of living with all the desires and practices it entails. In other words, Śaṅkara answers from the viewpoint of the ultimate reality that one can either identify with the desireless and actionless Self or with the personality of a householder nourished by desire, but not with both at the same time. It is the desireless state of Self-knowledge, and not the monastic way of living, that is here opposed to the desireful householder mode of living. That Śaṅkara understands the contrast in this way is confirmed when he writes further in the introduction, "the highest reward of duties pertaining to the householder mode of living has been summarized as identification with the deity [namely, the Golden Womb]" (Ibid., 636), which applies only to unenlightened people, and not to enlightened persons who pursue the life of householders without the sense of doership.[3] Thus, holds Śaṅkara, if the householder is really enlightened, he is actionless, desireless and, as a consequence, he can only abandon all practices and attachments, which are based on desire and which even include staying in a particular home, always receiving food from the same person, and so forth (Ibid., transl., 12). The enlightened therefore renounces everything physically "as a matter of course" (*arthāt*; Ibid., 635), and not out of being prescribed to do so.

The opponent then argues that since the physical renunciant has to abide by the regulation (*niyama*) with respect to living on alms, and so forth, it is proper to understand that he should also observe prescribed rites. Śaṅkara answers that the enlightened is outside the range of injunction. The opponent retorts that if this is so these scriptural injunctions become useless, which is untenable. Śaṅkara rejoins that they remain useful for the unenlightened. He then adds that, true, prescriptions of sacrifices like *agnihotra* suppose in the sacrificer the desire of a goal, namely, heaven, for which the scriptures indicate sacrifice as the means. But the regulation with respect to living on alms does not imply any purpose (*prayojana*) for which a prescription would be needed: the only purpose of the physical renouncer is to satisfy the natural desire to eat that is indispensible for the mere sustenance of the body (Ibid., transl., 13). The opponent then comes back with the argument that if it serves no purpose (*prayojana*) the restriction from the scriptures with respect to living on alms will be useless, which is unacceptable (Ibid., transl. 14). Śaṅkara answers that here the injunctive formula is not a prescription but only a sort of confirmation of the renunciant's background in inner and outer renunciation: "No, because that observance is the result of previous practices (*pravṛtti*), and an overriding of the latter involves enormous effort."[4] Śaṅkara then specifies that even when the tendency to simply live on alms naturally results from inner renunciation based on direct Self-knowledge, the explicit injunction of physical renunciation (addressed to Self-knowers for instance in *Bṛhadāraṇyaka Upaniṣad* 3.5.1) just confirms that the spontaneous attitude of the enlightened is indeed to be expressed in the form of physical renunciation: "Because the renunciation that naturally follows (*arthaprāpta*) is restated (*punarvacana*), it is substantiated that the man of knowledge has to do it."[5] But since, in this context, Śaṅkara seems to refer to the already enlightened man, his idea that the scripture is just stating what is already spontaneous and saying what is to be done without really prescribing, is not convincing.

A similar ambiguity pertaining to the relationship between direct Self-knowledge and physical renunciation is that if, as a *Kṣatriya*, a *Vaiśya* or a *Śūdra*, anybody who becomes enlightened is beyond the range of scriptural injunctions and prohibitions, then why should Śaṅkara advocate that only Brahmins are allowed to renounce physically? As we saw, Śaṅkara even mentions with respect to the *Kṣatriya* as well as to the Brahmin, the possibility of being devoid of any identification with the characteristics of their caste and, at least theoretically, their qualification for physical abandonment of rites. So there seems to be no reason to restrict physical renunciation to Brahmins as far as enlightened people are concerned. The same kind of inconsistency is found when, in his BhG, Śaṅkara seems to understand that the *Gītā* prescribes guidance of people even to the already enlightened. Paraphrasing Kṛṣṇa's advice to Arjuna, he states in BhG 3.20 that although Arjuna thinks that rites will not have to be performed after reaching enlightenment, "even then, being dependent on the result of action (*karman*), which has come to fruition [in the form of this life] *and having in view the sole* purpose of *guiding people*—the latter consisting of keeping people back from engaging in a wrong path—*you should perform action*."[6] Thus, it seems that, for Śaṅkara, it is the fruition of the result of action expressed in a birth as a Brahmin or a *Kṣatriya* family, and so forth, that remains the deciding factor of qualification for physical renunciation with respect to enlightened men, even if they experience the Self as the attributeless witness of these results of action and of any other phenomenal reality. But how could something brought about by the force of the law of karma be a matter of prescription or even advice? Śaṅkara didn't address this question.

Let us now turn to another key passage concerning physical renunciation after enlightenment. Verse 2.23.1 of *Chāndogya Upaniṣad* is well-known for its statement on the connection between Self-knowledge and physical renunciation. It runs as follows:

> There are three divisions of *dharma*. The first comprises sacrifice, study, and charity. The second is austerity alone. The third is the student living in the house of his teacher, where he dedicates himself for life. All these attain the worlds of merits; the man established in *Brahman* (*brahmasaṃstha*) attains immortality (75).

Here the issue is centered around the word *brahmasaṃstha*, "the man established in *Brahman*," which represents the main characteristic required for liberation. Karl Potter understands that, according to Śaṅkara, the "man established in *Brahman*" is by definition liberated: "The fourth way, that of being 'fixed in *Brahman*,' belongs to the true wandering mendicant (*parivrājaka*), and it is he alone who is freed from further births and deaths, unlike the other three, who will eventually be reborn" (1982, 116).[7]

The question is whether, according to Śaṅkara, the *brahmasaṃstha* or "man established in *Brahman*" means [1] any enlightened man, whatever his way of living, or [2] the enlightened man after his physical renunciation, or [3] one who reaches enlightenment only after having resorted to physical renunciation and full-time discipline of knowledge. Or, strictly viewed from the angle of types of renunciation, does the "man established in *Brahman*" define [1] any renouncer of doership, whatever his way of living, or [2] the informal physical renouncer that doesn't belong to any mode of living (*āśrama*) or [3] the formal physical renouncer of the fourth mode of living?

In his comment on this verse, Śaṅkara attributes at least three major viewpoints to the opponent (ChU, transl., 146–149): first, "immortality" (*amṛtatva*) is simply excellence (*atiśaya*) within "the virtuous worlds" (*puṇyaloka*); second, this immortality comes from the combination of rites—or any prescribed *dharma*—with knowledge consisting of meditation on *om*; third, people from all four modes of living can reach the said immortality inasmuch as they conform to this combined practice. From the opponent's viewpoint, there exists no such thing as a mode of living based on physical renunciation and conducive to liberation without the combined practice of rites and meditation. This is mainly what Śaṅkara will try to refute.

Interestingly, in all of the *Upaniṣads*, the expression *brahmasaṃstha* or "man established in *Brahman*" occurs only there, so that it is impossible to compare this occurrence with others in the *Upaniṣads* themselves or in Śaṅkara's comments. We saw that the similar compound *brahmaniṣṭha* (steadfast in *Brahman*) can imply either mediate or immediate knowledge of *Brahman*. Thus, it provides no decisive clue for our enquiry.

But two citations of verse 2.23.1 by Śaṅkara in his ChU do suggest that, to him, "the man established in *Brahman*" refers to an already enlightened person. Immediately after describing how, in spite of his enlightenment, the knower of *Brahman* (*brahmavid*) lives on the basis of the result of action that has come to fruition in his present life, Śaṅkara implicitly equates that enlightened man with the man established in *Brahman* of verse 2.23.1: "And concerning the passage "the man established in *Brahman* attains immortality," we said that for a knower of *Brahman* there is no action after the emergence of knowledge."[8] In the introduction of the ChU, Śaṅkara also equates with "the man established in *Brahman*," the person who has been freed from ignorance through knowledge of the non-dual Self: "Therefore ritual actions are enjoined only on one who has imperfections such as ignorance, not on one who has the knowledge of non-duality. Hence [the *Upaniṣad*] will declare: 'All these attain the worlds of merits; the man established in *Brahman* attains immortality.' "[9]

We can certainly recognize Śaṅkara's fundamental position here: immediate Self-knowledge alone leads to liberation. Obviously, even physical renunciants who are completely devoted to meditation on the attributeless *Brahman* but who are yet without direct experience of the actionless Self cannot be liberated. So, from a logical viewpoint, it cannot be that mere full-time absorption in the discipline of knowledge on the basis of physical renunciation ensures immortality. If it be said that the "man established in *Brahman*" as a physical renunciant only attains liberation "eventually," then this will not do justice to the marked difference between him and the other three kinds of people stated in verse 2.23.1, since the first three types of people will also "eventually" attain liberation. If it be said that only the one who is both a physical renouncer and established in direct experience of *Brahman* is liberated, then it contradicts one of Śaṅkara's basic reference points according to which liberation can be attained irrespective of one's mode of living. Therefore it seems fair to say that, as far as *Advaita* logic and the above cross-references are concerned, direct Self-knowledge is the main characteristic of the man established in *Brahman*.

Since BS 3.4.20 refers extensively to *Chāndogya Upaniṣad* 2.23.1, it must also be used to understand Śaṅkara's interpretation of this verse. So let us now look at Śaṅkara's characterization and definition of the man established in *Brahman* in both these passages.

In ChU 2.23.1, Śaṅkara distinguishes the man established in *Brahman* from people merely following the rules of a mode of living: "Austerity (*tapas*) means [practices] such as the "painful" (*kṛcchra*) and the "moon-course" (*cāndrāyaṇa*) fastings. A person possessed of these is called an "ascetic" (*tāpasa*) or a "wandering mendicant" (*parivrāṭ*). Established only in the *dharma* of a mode of living, he is different from the man established in *Brahman* . . ."[10] Let us first clarify an ambiguity here. Does Śaṅkara mean that the "wandering mendicant" (*parivrāṭ*) is synonymous with the "ascetic" (*tāpasa*), or that with the word "austerity" (*tapas*), the verse includes *both* the ascetic (*tāpasa*) mode of living—corresponding to the condition of hermit, or *vānaprastha*—and the wandering mendicant (*parivrāṭ*) stage—corresponding to the monastic mode of living (*saṃnyāsāśrama*)? When discussing the issue of the etymological or conventional meaning of the term "man established in *Brahman*," elsewhere in his comment, Śaṅkara uses as an example the fact that even if the word "wandering mendicant" (*parivrājaka*) is connected with the primary meaning of "wandering" (*pārivrājya*), it is used in the conventional sense of a man belonging to a mode of living (*āśrama*), that is, to the monastic mode of living (ChU 2.23.1, transl.,154). This allusion makes it probable that, when subdividing austerity (*tapas*) into the situations of the ascetic (*tāpasa*) and of the wandering mendicant (*parivrāṭ*), Śaṅkara understands *parivrāṭ* to mean the wandering mendicant (*parivrājaka*) in its conventional sense, that is, the man simply belonging to the monastic mode of living, the physical renouncer without immediate knowledge of the Self as opposed to the enlightened "man established in *Brahman*."

Further in the comment on verse 2.23.1, the opponent advocates that "in the sentence 'The second is austerity alone,' both the wandering mendicant (*parivrāṭ*) and the ascetic (*tāpasa*) are understood by the word 'austerity' (*tapas*)" and that "whosoever among these four [people] is a man established in *Brahman* who meditates on *om*, attains immortality."[11] While replying to this interpretation, Śaṅkara does not refute that the word "austerity" also stands for the person belonging to the monastic mode of living, but he does reject the idea that it includes the man who has overcome duality (called here *"parivrāṭ"*[12] and *"parivrājaka"*) and for whom alone establishment in *Brahman* is possible: "And the claim that by the word "austerity," the wandering mendicant (*parivrāṭ*) also is referred to is wrong. Why? Because being established in *Brahman* is possible for the wandering mendicant (*parivrājaka*) alone whose experience of differences has come to an end."[13] We are again faced here with an apparent contradiction: Śaṅkara attributes to the wandering mendicant (*parivrājaka*) the state of being established in *Brahman* which is distinguished from the four modes of living, even though he defined earlier the wandering mendicant (*parivrājaka*) as the conventional term for the person belonging to the fourth mode of living . . . So we need to further investigate the meaning of "the man established in *Brahman*" (*brahmasaṃstha*), as well as the meaning of "wandering mendicant" (*parivrāṭ* and *parivrājaka*) when associated with the man established in *Brahman*.

The first definition of "the man established in *Brahman*" in the comment on ChU 2.23.1 reads thus: "But the one not [yet] mentioned is the wandering mendicant (*parivrāṭ*), *the man established in Brahman*, i.e., the well-established in *Brahman*."[14] In BS 3.4.20, we also find the following definition: "For the term "the man established in *Brahman*" implies a consummation in *Brahman*, a steadfastness in It, consisting of the absence of any other involvement."[15] There is no clear indication here as to whether the *Brahman*-knowledge of the man established in *Brahman* is direct or not. But in almost all contexts of ChU 2.23.1 where "the man established in

Brahman" is found and where "wandering mendicant" (*parivrāṭ/parivrājaka*) is given as synonymous with it, Śaṅkara associates with these three terms either the knowledge of non-duality and/or the absence of desire in exactly the same way as he does in other, clearer, contexts, with the liberated-in-life. He writes for instance:

> This being so, whoever has annulled the experience of differences (*bhedapratyaya*) from which injunctions of actions come to be observed, he abstains from all actions because their cause ceases to exist as a result of the experience of Unity arising from the valid scriptural means of knowledge. . . . And the one who abstains from actions is said to be established in *Brahman*.[16]

Since Śaṅkara refers here to the eradication of the experience of differences after gaining Self-knowledge from scriptures, the abstention from action which is said to come from this eradication seems to describe physical renunciation on the basis of direct Self-knowledge. By introducing a little further the idea that the obligation to perform rituals applies to those who do not have non-dual Self-knowledge, he also implies that, in contrast, having nothing to do with ritual actions, the man established in *Brahman* is indeed possessed of that non-dualistic Self-knowledge: "We said that the person who is possessed of the experience of differences, whose perception of differences has not been annulled by knowledge, is qualified for duties (*karman*)" (ChU 2.23.1, 81). The opponent concludes that if the wandering mendicant (*parivrāṭ*) is the one with experience of Unity, then people having reached this experience could continue in their respective modes of living (*āśrama*) and be in fact wandering mendicants (*parivrāṭ*). "This is incorrect," retorts Śaṅkara, "because [in their case] the perception of differences such as 'me' and 'mine' has not ceased. . . . Therefore, because of the absence of 'me' and 'mine,' the mendicant (*bhikṣu*) is the only one to be wandering mendicant (*parivrāṭ*), not householders and others."[17] Thus, the contrast here is between people who are, and people who are not, beyond the sense of doership or possession based on the latter, not between people who have, and people who have not, all the time to be absorbed in the discipline of knowledge. Therefore, "the man established in *Brahman*" is better understood as being already enlightened.

But why does Śaṅkara introduce here the outward characteristic of a mendicant (*bhikṣu*) to specify that he is in fact referring to the enlightened man? It is likely in order to establish that when the householder attains this knowledge of Unity and the ensuing inner renunciation, he will spontaneously abandon the householder mode of living with all its practices, as they are of no further use to him. Reference to the mendicant seems to provide Śaṅkara with the clearest symbol of an authorized mode of living that does not require rites and does lead to liberation through Self-knowledge alone. However, while "the man established in *Brahman*" is indeed defined by Śaṅkara as a physical renouncer, his renunciation is by virtue of direct Self-knowledge rather than for the purpose of gaining it. And his attainment of immortality is through immediate Self-knowledge, not through full-time absorption in the discipline of knowledge within the monastic context. It is probably in this very sense that "the man established in *Brahman*" and the "wandering mendicant" (*parivrāṭ*) are said by Śaṅkara to be "beyond modes of living" (*atyāśramin*; ChU 2.23.1, 82), and thus also beyond the monastic mode of living of the seeker-after-liberation fully absorbed in the discipline of knowledge.

The idea that the state of "the man established in Brahman" is based on direct Self-knowledge is quite in accordance with the end of the comment on verse 2.23.1 where Śaṅkara suggests that for the householder who has attained the knowledge of *Ātman-Brahman*'s non-duality, wandering mendicancy (*pārivrājya*) does not come about through an injunction but through the spontaneous effect of Self-knowledge:

> Therefore, it is proven that wandering mendicancy (*pārivrājya*), the state of being established in *Brahman*, characterized by abstention from rites and duties, is only for the man who has the experience of Unity arising from the Vedāntic valid means of knowledge. Hence, when the householder has the knowledge of Unity, wandering mendicancy (*pārivrājya*) follows naturally[18] (*arthasiddha*).[19]

Let us now try to understand Śaṅkara's overall position on *Chāndogya Upaniṣad* 2.23.1. Karl Potter views it as follows:

> As Śaṃkara interprets the *Chāndogya*'s "ways" or stages they are not a series of steps one must mount successively on the way to liberation, but just four kinds of people. Any one of the first three kinds, or for that matter any kind of persons whatsoever, provided he gains true knowledge of the nondifference of things, thereby becomes a person of the fourth kind. But he can't be both at once (1982, 120).

But the picture is more complex than suggested by Potter. As noticed by Patrick Olivelle, in his BS 3.4.20, Śaṅkara treats the topic of the man established in *Brahman* in a way quite different from how he does in ChU 2.23.1 (1993, 226). While in ChU 2.23.1 Śaṅkara considers the man established in

Brahman to be beyond the four modes of living, in BS 3.4.20, he describes him as the representative of the fourth mode and as a follower of its specific duties:

> But his *dharma,* [consisting of means] such as control of mind and senses, strengthens establishment in *Brahman;* it does not go against it. The duty (*karman*) for his order of life is steadfastness in *Brahman* (*brahmaniṣṭhatva*) alone, supported by control of mind and senses [whereas] sacrifices and the like are the duties of other people; and he would incur sin by transgressing his duty.[20]

In his ChU 2.23.1, Śaṅkara denies that means such as control of mind represent mandatory practices when addressed to one who already has the experience of *Brahman.* The opponent argues that because the knowledge of Unity eliminates all injunctions, means such as control of mind and of senses cannot even be enjoined on the wandering mendicant. Śaṅkara replies: "No, because [these rules] are meant for restraining [from some other behavior] a person who may have lost the experience of Unity because of hunger and the like."[21] So, even when corresponding to an unstable direct experience of Self-knowledge, in ChU 2.23.1, the state of the man established in *Brahman* is far more advanced than the use of hearing, reflection, and meditation after physical renunciation in the case of the seeker-after-liberation with no direct experience of the Self at all. But we find no indication in BS 3.4.20 that Śaṅkara understands in the same way the man established in *Brahman* and his recourse to means of control. He merely says that the duties of the man established in *Brahman* "strengthen" his state while the duties of the other modes of living tend to oppose it. In addition, while in ChU 2.23.1 he distinguishes the man established in *Brahman* from the other people only on the basis of knowledge of Unity and non-attachment, in BS 3.4.20, he writes that the term "man established in *Brahman*" implies "no occupation except that" (*ananyavyāpāratārūpa*).[22] "And," says he, "this is not possible for the other three modes of living."[23] Thus, "the man established in *Brahman*" seems depicted here more in terms of the fourth mode of living as such (*saṃnyāsāśrama*). Consequently, Śaṅkara's compared treatment of "the man established in *Brahman*" in ChU 2.23.1 and BS 3.4.20 appears ambiguous.

Olivelle concludes with respect to this problem that "Śaṃkara either changed his views or was inconsistent" (1993, 227). Let us first consider the possibility that he changed his views. According to this hypothesis, he would have thought on the one hand, in ChU 2.23.1, that the only person eligible to liberation is the man established in direct knowledge of *Brah-*

man who would normally renounce physically as a result of his enlightenment; on the other hand, in BS 3.4.20, he would have believed that the only person eligible to liberation is the man established in indirect knowledge of *Brahman* who uses physical renunciation as a means to convert this knowledge into a direct one. But if Śaṅkara means in his BS 3.4.20 that physical renunciation must be resorted to by the seeker-after-liberation in order to attain enlightenment, then he contradicts his own comments on BS 1.3.38 and 3.4.38 where he writes that Self-knowledge is available irrespective of castes and ways of living. So, to hypostatize that Śaṅkara changed his views on *Chāndogya Upaniṣa*d 2.23.1 does not solve his apparent self-contradiction.

In addition to the two hypotheses proposed by Olivelle, another one could be that, of the ChU and the BS, one commentary is not from Śaṅkara. But if the ChU is not authentic, we still face the apparent contradiction within the BS. And if the BS is not authentic, we face the opposite evidence from earlier studies on the matter. Thus, this third hypothesis also does not solve the apparent inconsistency.

I would like to propose a fourth hypothesis. This explanation is to be found in the context of BS 3.4.20. I propose that, here, the reason for Śaṅkara's attribution of physical renunciation to the man established in *Brahman* as a means rather than as a result of enlightenment is given by the general context of the fourth section of the third chapter of this work where aphorism 3.4.20 appears. According to Śaṅkara, in this section, Bādarāyaṇa, the author of the aphorisms, tries to gather evidence in favor of the idea that Self-knowledge is the only direct means of liberation. One argument used is that the *Śruti* does prescribe physical renunciation for those who desire non-dual Self-knowledge; consequently, rites are not necessary for enlightement, and they or their combination with Self-knowledge cannot be the direct means of liberation. According to Śaṅkara, as part of that argument, aphorism 3.4.20 simply states that the monastic mode of living (*saṃnyāsāśrama*) is the object of an injunction by the *Śruti*. In his comment thereupon, Śaṅkara appears to follow the general context set up, according to him, by Bādarāyaṇa. The man established in *Brahman* described in verse 2.23.1 of the *Chāndogya Upaniṣad* is then viewed as an exemplary for the use of physical abandonment of rites as a *means* to enlightenment. But, in his ChU 2.23.1, Śaṅkara suggests that the man established in *Brahman*, who physically abandons all rites, is already enlightened. Perhaps he expresses here a more personal position than in his BS 3.4.20. In any case, Śaṅkara's reference to the man established in *Brahman* in BS 3.4.20 is better understood as part of an argument to prove that physical renunciation is an authentic and significant Vedic means of Self-knowledge, but not that it is a sine qua non.

Overall, Śaṅkara's position on "the man established in *Brahman*" remains ambiguous. And, to that extent, it does not clearly present physical renunciation as indispensible for Self-knowledge. It resembles the ambivalent picture given by the Upad about the requirement of physical renunciation for entering the discipline of knowledge. These two passages appear to be the only ones concerning renunciation in Śaṅkara's works that cannot be interpreted in a completely consistent manner. Consequently, they certainly cannot be representative of his interpretation of physical renunciation as a whole.

PHYSICAL RENUNCIATION FOR ENLIGHTENMENT

Although Śaṅkara didn't hold physical renunciation to be a sine qua non for direct Self-knowledge, he certainly emphasized its prescription by scriptures as a significant means or subsidiary of Self-knowledge. He even states that renunciation is the main (*mukhya*) proximate means of Self-knowledge (BṛU 4.4.22, 373). Referring to the combination of physical renunciation and Self-knowledge he declares, "there is no better means than this for man's goal."[24] We still have to specify the various aspects involved in this form of renunciation according to him: For what kind of seeker-after-liberation is it meant? At what point on his path? What are the objects to be abandoned? And finally, what reasons are given to justify such a renunciation?

It is very important here to understand the main doctrine Śaṅkara was trying to refute while establishing his own. The advocates of *Pūrvamīmāṃsā* argued that the *Śruti* prescribes neither the inner renunciation of doership, nor the monastic mode of living as a means of Self-knowledge. They understood that there was only one real mode of living, namely, the householder's; that physical renunciation was only for the disabled; and that all passages seemingly enjoining it for people qualified for rites were mere praise (*stuti*) of meditation rather than real prescriptions. Mainly against this position, Śaṅkara endeavored on every occasion to prove that scriptures [1] prescribe renunciation of doership as a necessary means, or correlate of direct Self-knowledge which in turn leads to liberation; [2] mention physical renunciation as both a natural consequence of, and a prescribed means to, direct Self-knowledge.[25]

Śaṅkara substantiates his position in various places by quoting passages from the *Śruti* and the *Smṛti*, which allow the seeker-after-liberation to enter the monastic mode of living either immediately after the period of studies,[26] after the stage of the householder, or finally after going through the third stage: "Thus because the four modes of living are enjoined equally, there is an option of belonging to any one of them singly or to all of them successively"[27] (BS 3.4.49, transl., 806).

As already mentioned, according to Śaṅkara, renunciation is for Brahmins only. What then is the inner disposition that qualifies them for it? For the sake of accuracy, it is important here to distinguish qualification for the discipline of knowledge, which is open to all, from qualification for physical renunciation. Their confusion under one single qualification, leading to mandatory physical renunciation, has been a major cause of misinterpretation of Śaṅkara's thought. In BṛU 4.5.15 (388), Śaṅkara recalls, "all rites are a duty for the unenlightened man with desire." Yet, he adds, the absence of the impulsion of desire (*kāmapravṛttyabhāvāt*) is sufficient reason to say that "although the detached[28] seeker-after-liberation is without [immediate Self-] knowledge, statements such as, 'He should renounce even from the student life' [*Nāradaparivrājaka Upaniṣad* 77] hold good for him" (Ibid., 387). In his introduction to the *Aitareya Upaniṣad*, Śaṅkara also states, "the Vedic passages referring to [the performance of rites] throughout life have their purpose served only with respect to the unenlightened who do not seek after liberation" (AiU intro, 638). So it is quite clear that, when a Brahmin has a strong enough desire to know the Self after completing his studies in the student mode of living, since the discipline of knowledge is the most direct means for Self-knowledge, the logical and appropriate conduct is, from Śaṅkara's viewpoint, to enter the monastic mode of living for the sake of devoting himself entirely to that discipline.

Now, as we saw, Śaṅkara views the follower of the yoga of action also as a seeker-after-liberation. But when this *karmayogin* is a Brahmin and a genuine seeker, why does he not immediately take up physical renunciation? It could be that the intensity of the desire for liberation is not strong enough for the *karmayogin* to abandon everything. We also saw that, for some reason, physical renunciation may not be possible even for the enlightened. This could apply to the unenlightened as well, because of family responsibilities and the like before old age.[29]

With respect to objects to be abandoned in the context of physical renunciation, Śaṅkara's view concerning the seeker-after-liberation is not as clear as for the enlightened. In ChU 2.23.1 and BṛU 3.5.1, he distinguishes the physical renunciation of the enlightened man established in *Brahman* (ChU 2.23.1, transl. 154–155) and of ancient enlightened Brahmins (BṛU 3.5.1, transl., 335) from that of people who resort to physical renunciation of householder rites as a way to attain the world of Brahmā—which is equivalent to the Golden Womb. According to Śaṅkara, in the case of those people seeking the world of Brahmā, the scriptures prescribe the sacrificial cord,[30] some ritual instruments, emblems of renunciation such as the triple staff and the water-pot, as well as meditation on the qualified *Brahman* (BṛU 4.4.22, transl., 525–526); but this does not apply to the enlightened who has to do with Self-knowledge alone. "And apart from that [renunciation of the enlightened]," he states, "there exists a wandering mendicancy (*pārivrājya*), which is a mode of living and a means of attaining the world of Brahmā and the like. It is with respect to it that means such as the sacrificial cord and distinguishing signs are enjoined."[31]

Now, according to Olivelle, it is

> unclear whether Śaṃkara assumed the renunciation of a seeker after knowledge to be an *āśrama*, and if so, whether he made a distinction between that and the *āśrama* of renunciation that he had earlier distinguished from the renunciation of the enlightened and characterized as consisting of carrying the emblems of that state and as unrelated to knowledge (1993, 226).

On the other hand, Olivelle (Ibid.) notes that, in BṛU 4.5.15 (transl., 551) and BS 3.4.49 (transl., 805–806), Śaṅkara connects physical renunciation for the sake of Self-knowledge with the monastic mode of living (*saṃnyāsāśrama*). The same association is found in many other passages,[32] so that physical renunciation as a subsidiary to Self-knowledge is most often presented by Śaṅkara as part and parcel of the monastic mode of living. The only passage where Śaṅkara clearly associates the state beyond modes of living with the seeker-after-liberation is found in the introduction to the AiU, where he states that the total observance of disciplines such as continence is possible only for the *atyāśramin*, that is, the man beyond modes of living (transl., 15). But a little further in the introduction, he refers to the same context of physical renunciation in terms of a mode of living (Ibid., 17–18). Thus, Śaṅkara tends to see the physical renunciation of the enlightened as lying beyond modes of living, but that of the aspirant as part of a mode of living. But the physical renunciation of both the enlightened and the seeker have nothing to do with attaining the world of Brahmā, meditation on the qualified *Brahman,* and wearing emblems prescribed for those who aim at his heavenly world. It remains, however, that while Śaṅkara clearly says what the enlightened and the seeker have nothing to do with, he never mentions if the latter has to keep some objects, particularly the single staff (*ekadaṇḍa*) which has been associated for centuries with the followers of *Advaita Vedānta*.[33]

Among the various considerations related to physical renunciation, reasons likely to validate it receive most of Śaṅkara's attention. One argument is that while Self-knowledge succeeds in leading to liberation, ritual actions fail to do so: "And because liberation is not a result, action is of no use for the seeker-after-liberation" (BhG intro 3, 137). Śaṅkara also explains in BhG 2.21 that following hearing of the *Vedas*, two types of understanding can arise: either that the Self is a doer and that it has to perform some action in order to enjoy its result, or that it is a non-doer (*akartṛ*) and that there remains nothing to do after knowing its real nature. He adds that the person qualified for action is the one who perceives himself as a doer and who therefore sees himself as being prescribed some action by the scriptures. He then underscores that both the seeker-after-liberation and the already enlightened do not fall in that category. So, even if the seeker-after-liberation is still bound by the sense of doership, and must still pursue the discipline of knowledge, it seems that for Śaṅkara, his deep conviction about the actionless nature of the Self is enough to qualify him for physical renunciation.

Given its metaphysical background concerning the supreme Self, Śaṅkara's argumentation in favor of physical renunciation then relies on a purely functional principle. Renunciation is to be resorted to, he writes, "also because liberation implies steadfastness in the actionless and true nature of the inner Self. It is indeed not proper for one who wishes to reach the eastern sea [liberation] to face the opposite direction and take the same path [actions] as the man who wishes to reach the western sea [heaven and the like]."[34] Conversely, people who do not desire the actionless Self are not qualified for physical renunciation: "Because of the statement 'Desiring this world alone,' it is understood that those who desire the three external worlds are not qualified for wandering mendicancy, for a resident of the Banares area who desires to reach Hardwar does not head towards east."[35]

Apart from the fact that complete observance of some means such as continence is not possible in the householder mode of living, violence against animals for the sake of sacrifice, and more frequent occasions of sinful acts are additional reasons given by Śaṅkara to suggest that the householder mode of living is less conducive to Self-knowledge and liberation when compared with the three other modes. In contrast with the householders' situation, Śaṅkara writes for example:

> Those qualified persons—students, forest-dwellers and mendicants—in whom imperfections such as crookedness do not exist—there being no reason for them—gain this untainted world of Brahmā through its appropriate means. Such is the destiny of those who combine ritual actions (*karman*) with meditation[36] (*jñāna*).[37]

Here, however, superiority over the householder mode of living is not exclusive to the monastic mode of living; in addition, no mode of living guarantees liberation, since, in the context of the passage just quoted, for instance, people belonging to the other three modes, including the monastic mode of living, are said to go to the world of Brahmā. Therefore, in Śaṅkara's eyes, even this depreciation of the householder mode of living raises only a mitigated polarity between active social life and the *saṃnyāsa* mode of living as far as the means of liberation is concerned. But the contrast is sharper when Śaṅkara comments that the monastic mode of living may be termed as meditativeness (*mauna*), "because it has knowledge as its essential component" (*jñānapradhānāt*).[38] Since the monastic mode of living does not entail the obligation of performing ritual actions as in the other modes, it allows full absorption in the discipline of knowledge and is in this sense more conducive to the goal of liberation. From this perspective, even if all modes can lead a man directly to full Self-knowledge, because ritual actions receive much of the aspirant's attention in the first three modes, by comparison, they appear more conducive to goals such as the world of ancestors and of gods, than to liberation. Thus, from Śaṅkara's viewpoint, injunction of the monastic mode of living brings to light the unique focus of the latter on the means of liberation.

Another major argument in favor of physical renunciation of the seeker-after-liberation is the model offered by ancient Brahmins. Even when their own physical abandonment was the result of a personal choice and therefore unrelated to any scriptural injunction, these ancient Brahmins provide a behavior to be imitated by future generations. They are referred to in verses 3.5.1 and 4.4.22 of the *Bṛhadāraṇyaka Upaniṣad*. Some passages indicate that Śaṅkara undertands these ancient Brahmins to have been already enlightened before their physical renunciation. Such is the comment on aphorism BS 3.4.15 which Śaṅkara reads as, "Moreover some [renounce actions] according to their liking." When introducing the reason given by verse 4.4.22 of the *Bṛhadāraṇyaka Upaniṣad* to justify physical renunciation, Śaṅkara clearly describes these ancient Brahmins as already enlightened and their physical renunciation as unconnected with any injunction:[39]

> Moreover, *some*, men of knowledge who have direct experience of the result of knowledge, relying on that [experience], point out that there is no need for having children and for means conducive to other purposes. As to *"according to their liking,"* there is this *Śruti* passage from the *Vājasaneyins* [the authors of the *Bṛhadāraṇyaka Upaniṣad*] . . .[40]

In BṛU 4.5.15, Śaṅkara explains that the physical renunciation of these sages didn't take place on the basis of an injunction but simply "from the knowledge of the world of the Self" (BṛU 4.5.15, 387). In the introduction of BṛU 2.4, he also interprets verse 4.4.22 of the same *Upaniṣad* as referring to enlightened people who have transcended desire: "And because the knower of *Brahman* has all desires fulfilled, he cannot, with such a fulfillment, have any desire. The *Śruti* also says, '[since] for us, the Self is the world' [4.4.22]."[41] Similarly, before quoting the same passage in BS 4.1.2 (831), he writes: "Thus the *Śruti* . . . shows the absence of any duty (*kartavya*) for the knower of the Self." He then adds that meditation is prescribed for one who has not yet reached that state of knowledge.[42] A Self-knower who does not need meditation anymore must be enlightened. Thus, these passages strongly suggest that Śaṅkara viewed the ancient Brahmins as already enlightened before their physical renunciation.

In BṛU 4.4.22, Śaṅkara recommends that contemporary seekers-after-liberation follow the model embodied by the ancient Brahmins: "Therefore, *desiring [this] world*, the Self, *they leave everything*, they should[43] leave everything . . ."[44] And he reads the same connection in verse 3.5.1:

> Since the ancient *Brahmins, knowing this Self* as different in nature from means and results, *renounced* the whole domain of means and results, which is characterized by desire, *and led a mendicant life*, giving up actions producing visible and invisible results, as well as their means, *therefore* today also *the Brahmin, the knower of Brahman* . . . after renouncing desires . . .[45]

The freely chosen physical renunciation of ancient sages thus becomes the source of authority for prescribing that type of abandonment to the contemporary seeker-after-liberation. Paradoxically, those who physically renounced only *after* enlightenment serve as model and inspiration for taking recourse to physical renunciation *before* enlightenment. Yet the paradox seems consistent with the various arguments describing the nature of Self-knowledge, of actions and of their respective results. Whether the physical renouncer is already enlightened or not, his intent is the same: to remain in Self-knowledge alone, as it constitutes the only means of liberation.

The fact that Śaṅkara viewed the ancient Brahmins as already enlightened before their physical renunciation confirms his main stand on renunciation. Primacy goes to direct Self-knowledge, whether associated or not with physical renunciation as a means for its rise. When physical renunciation has not been necessary even for the enlightenment of people who are presented as models for it, it cannot be considered as a sine qua non for enlightenment.

ŚAṄKARA'S POLYSEMIC TERMINOLOGY ON RENUNCIATION

Having clarified Śaṅkara's position on the various dimensions of renunciation, let us now consider if a systematic account of his terminology on this theme is possible. The endeavor of assigning one single meaning for every occurrence of words such as *saṃnyāsa* or *sarvakarmasaṃnyāsa* is set aside by Śaṅkara himself when pointing out, for instance in his BhG 2.55, that, in the scriptures, the same description can be understood as referring to the *characteristics* of the enlightened person or, in another context, to the *means* that the seeker-after-liberation tries to cultivate in himself in order to reach enlightenment. In the light of this, it is useless to try in establishing the number of times each word related to renunciation is employed with this or that specific meaning. What will be significant on the other hand, is [1] to identify the scope of polysemy or ambiguity for each term related to renunciation; [2] to indicate and employ some semantic devices for recognizing a possible ambiguity, as well as for identifying the most appropriate meaning according to the context and in the light of Śaṅkara's basic position as expressed in clearer passages; [3] to complete the picture of how, based on Śaṅkara's polysemic terminology, interpreters may have misunderstood him.

So we will now proceed to identify all the meanings conveyed in Śaṅkara's comments by the following terms: *saṃnyāsa, saṃnyāsin, karmasaṃnyāsa, sarvakarmasaṃnyāsa, tyāga, tyāgin, karma(pari)tyāga, sarva(pari)tyāga, sarvakarma(pari)tyāga, yati, nivṛtti, uparati, vyutthāna, pārivrājya, parivrāṭ, (paramahaṃsa)parivrājaka, sāṃkhya, bhikṣu, akṣaropāsaka, vidvas*. Except for the word *uparati*, the various meanings of each term will always be presented in a semantic sequence that moves from the more literal and common purports of the term to the less obvious ones, in other words, from the meaning of overt physical renunciation to that which stands for some form of inner renunciation even in the midst of continued performance of rites and of an active social life.

First, concerning Śaṅkara's usage of the word *saṃnyāsa*, the evidence gathered so far makes it quite clear that the following comment by Karl

H. Potter does not hold true for the whole of Śaṅkara's work:

> It is interesting to note that Śaṃkara, the philosopher, regularly avoids using the term *saṃnyāsa*, favoring other, to his mind, less ambiguous, expression. He is quite aware that traditional usage identifies *saṃnyāsa* as the fourth and highest stage of an ideal life, and that there exist varied opinions about what that stage consists in. In the main passages where Śaṃkara confronts the social implications of this thesis [that only the self-knower is a true *saṃnyāsin*], he prefers to utilize an alternative list of "modes of living . . ." (1982, 116).

Again, the situation is more complex and ambiguous than suggested by Potter. To substantiate his point, Potter analyzes Śaṅkara's comment on *Chāndogya Upaniṣad* 2.23.1 and the statement that only the "man established in *Brahman*" reaches immortality. It is true that Śaṅkara does not use the word *saṃnyāsa* in this comment. But, as we saw, the possible ambiguity resides here in the derivatives of *pari/vraj* (to wander). It is also true that in this comment as well as in BṛU 3.5.1, which is also referred to by Potter, Śaṅkara clearly distinguishes, to quote the scholar again, between the way of "the wandering mendicant (*parivrājaka*), the ascetic who is not 'fixed in *Brahman*' " and "the fourth way, that of being 'fixed in *Brahman*,' [which] belongs to the true wandering mendicant (*parivrājaka*)" (Ibid.). But it could be argued by an advocate of mandatory renunciation that the first wandering mendicant is merely taking up *saṃnyāsa* as a way of living based on rules from *Smṛti* literature, while the other is a true seeker-after-liberation following the Upaniṣadic prescription of physical renunciation for gaining Self-knowledge alone. Along Potter's perspective, this could be refuted by the following argument. The *Smṛtis* also enjoin pursuit of liberation as the main duty of the formal *saṃnyāsin*,[46] and therefore the only person who can differ from the formal *saṃnyāsin* following his duty is the "true" wandering mendicant, that is, the enlightened man who has to do only with physical renunciation by virtue of his direct Self-knowledge, but who may not have renounced physically. In spite of this counterargument, one can realize the ambiguity of using the term "wandering mendicant" (*parivrājaka*) to refer to the enlightened person *whatever his way of living*, and therefore to the enlightened householder who *does not* wander about, begging for his food. Moreover, the same word *parivrājaka* is used elsewhere by Śaṅkara in a way that creates even more shades of ambiguity. As we saw, in the BS's comment on *Chāndogya Upaniṣad* 2.23.1, "wandering mendicant" means the monastic seeker-after-liberation. In Upad 2.1.2, one has to be a wandering mendicant of the *paramahaṃsa* type in order to be qualified for knowledge. Finally, in his BhG, Śaṅkara never clearly states if the *paramahaṃsa* mendicant is enlightened or simply an aspirant. According to Potter, in Śaṅkara's works, the term *paramahaṃsa* applies only to the enlightened man. As noticed by Olivelle against Potter, the *Paramahaṃsa Upaniṣad* 46–47 refers to two types of *paramahaṃsa saṃnyāsins*,[47] one without any emblem and the other with emblems such as the loincloth and the single staff (1976–1977, 1:56). But it is not clear whether or not Śaṅkara followed the *Paramahaṃsa Upaniṣad*. So, although Potter is basically right in his understanding of Śaṅkara's emphasis on inner renunciation, his perspective on the Advaitin's terminology is rather sketchy.

Let us start with the semantic pole of the word *saṃnyāsa* that conveys the sense of physical renunciation. The root *saṃ-ni* $\sqrt{}$*as* can mean to deposit, to lay down or lay aside, to give up, to abandon. According to one definition of *saṃnyāsa* identified by Olivelle, it is found in many medieval texts in the sense of "the performance of the rite by which one becomes a renouncer" (1981, 271). Olivelle remarks that "once *saṃnyāsa* became fixed as the title of the rite, the expression *saṃnyāsaṃ karoti* [he accomplishes renunciation] comes to be used with increasing frequency with reference to the performance of the rite . . ." (Ibid., 272). However, Śaṅkara's use of *saṃnyāsa* with the verb $\sqrt{}$*kṛ* seems to convey either formal physical abandonment of ritual actions associated with the recitation of the ritualistic formulation of renunciation (*praiṣa*) and initiation into the monastic mode of living, or physical renunciation in general. As an example of the first meaning, in BhG 4.15, Śaṅkara glosses Kṛṣṇa's advice thus: "*Do you, therefore,* for that reason, that is, because action was performed even by the ancients, *surely perform action*; neither sitting quiet, nor renunciation should be resorted to" (transl., 149).[48] Because mention is already made of simply "sitting quiet," the addition of "nor renunciation should be resorted to" (*nāpi saṃnyāsaḥ kartavyaḥ*) seems to refer to formal entry into the monastic mode of living. Śaṅkara writes elsewhere that people such as Janaka "did not renounce *karmans*" (*na karmasaṃnyāsaṃ kṛtavantaḥ*).[49] Because the physical renunciation of an enlightened person does not have to be associated with adoption of the monastic mode of living, here, "did not renounce *karmans*" does not necessarily mean the rite of initiation into this mode of living.[50] It seems therefore to mean physical renunciation in general.

Śaṅkara's clearest way of suggesting that he refers to renunciation simply as a monastic way of living is when he adds words with the sense of "mere," "only" or "alone" (*eva, mātra,* or *kevala*) after the word *saṃnyāsa* (or *tyāga*): "*Neither through saṃnyāsa alone*, by mere, by simple abandonment of action devoid of knowledge, *does he attain*, does he reach, *perfection*, steadfastness in the yoga of knowledge characterized by actionlessness."[51] It should be noted that in such contexts, Śaṅkara does not refer to people who take up the monastic mode of living in order to run away from social responsibilities, because this type of abandonment is distinctly identified as based on passions (rājasic) and unconducive to direct Self-knowledge (BhG 18.8), whereas the mere *saṃnyāsā* referred to here is said to lead to that knowledge in the same way as the yoga of action (BhG 5.2). Hence, even when *saṃnyāsa* and *tyāga* are followed by particles meaning "mere," "only," or "alone," they refer to the monastic mode of living as including the discipline of knowledge, yet without direct experience of the Self.

When corresponding to *saṃnyāsa* as physical renunciation, the word *saṃnyāsin* (renouncer or renunciant) can of course mean the formal physical renunciant who has entered the monastic mode of living. Responding, for instance, to the viewpoint that rites must be performed to avoid sin, Śaṅkara writes: "For non-performance of the worship of *Agni* and the like, it is as impossible to ascribe sin to the *saṃnyāsin* as it is in the case of students (*brahmacārins*) who are ritualists[52] [and] not even *saṃnyāsins*."[53]

We have so far considered *saṃnyāsa* and *saṃnyāsin* as conveying the sense of physical renunciation without direct Self-knowledge. *Saṃnyāsa* can also refer to physical abandonment on the basis of direct Self-knowledge. Following a long discussion mainly on various aspects of the state of enlightenment, Śaṅkara concludes his comment on *Gītā* 2.21 by stating that the enlightened "who possesses Self-knowledge has to do with *saṃnyāsa* alone."[54] The same can be said of *saṃnyāsin* in passages such as the following: "As for him who sees inaction and the like, by virtue of that very perception of inaction and the like, he is free from action, a *saṃnyāsin*, moving merely for the purpose of maintaining life . . . " (BhG 4.20, 209).

We found earlier that, according to Śaṅkara, when used in a metaphoric sense as in *Gītā* 5.3, *saṃnyāsa* can mean immediate Self-knowledge itself. Similarly, without any reference to physical renunciation, *saṃnyāsin* can simply mean the enlightened man who has automatically renounced doership by virtue of his direct experience of the actionless Self. It is in this sense that Śaṅkara calls the man of steady intellect (*sthitaprajña*) a *saṃnyāsin*, thereby precluding liberation from the non-*saṃnyāsin*: "The attainment of liberation is possible only for the man of knowledge, for the man of steady intellect who has abandoned desires, for the disciplined man, but not for the non-*saṃnyāsin*, the one who cherishes desires . . ."[55]

However, some contexts remain definitely more ambiguous than the latter one. For instance, when commenting on *Bṛhadāraṇyaka Upaniṣad* 4.4.22 which, according to him, validates physical renunciation both before and after direct Self-knowledge, Śaṅkara writes: "Thus for a *saṃnyāsin* who knows *Brahman*, both kinds of *karmans*, whether done in the past or in the present life, are destroyed, and no new ones are undertaken" (BṛU 4.4.22, 376). The reference to destruction of all *karmans* certainly suggest that the one "who knows *Brahman*" is an enlightened person. But what is the relationship between his enlightenment and his being called a *saṃnyāsin*? Śaṅkara gives no clue in the immediate context as to the answer. So, at least four meanings are possible here: either *saṃnyāsin* means that the man became formal *saṃnyāsin* and through this gained enlightenment, or that he informally renounced *karmans* after enlightenment, or that he did the same formally, or finally that by virtue of his direct experience of *Brahman*, he is simply a renouncer of doership, without reference to his way of living. Interestingly, the same situation is found almost word for word in BhG 2.46: "Similarly, *whatever profit*, reward of action, *is found in all the Vedas*, in actions prescribed by the *Vedas*, that is equally found in the reward of knowledge—corresponding to the all-spreading flood—by the Brahmin who is a *saṃnyāsin* and *who knows* the nature of the supreme Reality" (BhG 2.46, 106). Although the four meanings are again possible, it is easier here to verify that Śaṅkara does not make formal physical renunciation a prerequisite of enlightenment, for immediately after this statement, he quotes *Chāndogya Upaniṣad* 4.1.4 which states that anyone can attain the enlightened knowledge that Raikva possessed—even though he was simply a widower[56] and was outside the monastic way of living.[57]

Another and last meaning of *saṃnyāsin* is based on the *Gītā*'s description of the *karmayogin* as "a *saṃnyāsin* and a *yogin*." It is connected by Śaṅkara to the unenlightened's renunciation of the results of action: "His being a *saṃnyāsin*," says he, "is by virtue of the renunciation of the expectation of the rewards of action; and his being a *yogin* is by virtue of his performance of action as a subsidiary to yoga . . ." (BhG 6.2, 285).

In brief, *saṃnyāsa* and *saṃnyāsin* can refer to physical renunciation with direct Self-knowledge, to the same without such knowledge, to renunciation of doership alone, and to giving up the rewards of action. On the other hand, the compound *karmasaṃnyāsa* (renunciation of actions) is found to convey only physical renunciation with or without direct Self-knowledge. *Karmasaṃnyāsa* is frequently used, for instance in the introduction to chapter 5 of the BhG as well as in the comments to its first two verses, to mean the formal physical renunciation without direct Self-knowledge which consists, as we saw in chapter 4, in abandoning only "a few actions" without giving up doership. Mere physical abandonment is also conveyed by the same compound when used to refer to passion-prompted (*rājasic*) and inertia-prompted (*tāmasic*) renunciation in BhG 18.9 (686).[58] However, the same *karmasaṃnyāsa* means physical renunciation based on immediate Self-knowledge when Śaṅkara states, about enlightened people such as Janaka, that, "even though [the stage of] *karmasaṃnyāsa* had been reached" (*karmasaṃnyāse prāpte 'pi*),[59] they did not renounce physically and yet were liberated.

We showed in chapter 4 that, as part of the necessary steps in the householder's sequence toward liberation, *sarvakarmasaṃnyāsa* (renunciation of all actions) means above all renunciation of doership. But, in other contexts, it can also mean formal physical renunciation without direct Self-knowledge. For instance, in the introduction of BhG 3, Śaṅkara says that "*sarvakarmasaṃnyāsa* is enjoined on the seeker-after-liberation as a subsidiary to knowledge" (BhG 3 intro, 136). In some other passages, the statement of renunciation of actions seems to refer to the abandonment of the rewards of action that is typical of the yoga of action. When in verses 3.30, 12.6 and 18.57, the *Gītā* uses the expression *sarvāṇi* (or *sarva-*) *karmāṇi saṃnyasya* in the sense of "having renounced all actions" in Kṛṣṇa, Śaṅkara understands it as part of the yoga of action. In his introduction to BhG 18.66, he addresses the sequence of verses 18.56–65 to the unenlightened *karmayogin*. When introducing verse 18.56, Śaṅkara also contextualizes these verses in terms of a devotional yoga of action: "Now will be praised the yoga of devotion to the Lord" which consists in "worship of the Lord through one's duties."[60] According to this contextualization, the expression "having mentally abandoned (*saṃnyasya*) all actions in Me" found in verse 18.57 (746) describes a practice belonging to the yoga of action. Similarly, when verses 3.30 and 12.6 use "having abandoned all actions in Me," Śaṅkara associates them with the yoga of action. In 3.30, the same expression is understood as a general abandonment to the will of the Lord, yet accompanied by a sense of doership: "Having abandoned all actions . . . in Me . . . with the awareness that I am a doer acting for the Lord as a servant."[61] According to Śaṅkara, in 12.6, the same phrase is spoken in a context of meditation on *Brahman* with attributes,[62] a practice associated for him with the yoga of action. Thus, these usages of *sarvakarmasaṃnyāsa* and the like show that in Śaṅkara's works this compound can refer either to giving up attachment for the rewards of actions (BhG 3.30 and 18.57), or to a process of inner renunciation induced by meditation on *Brahman* with attributes (BhG 12.6), or again to renunciation of doership on the basis of immediate Self-knowledge, whether accompanied or not by physical renunciation.

This semantic overview of the root *saṃ-ni* √*as* and its derivatives thus gives clear indication that its use in Śaṅkara's works is polysemic, at times ambiguous, and always needs careful contextualization. A very similar semantic diversity is found for the root (*pari*) √*tyaj* and its derivatives which also mean "to abandon," the optional prefix *pari* adding the notion "entirely." As pointed out by Olivelle (1981, 270) and myself (1987, 120), the *Bhagavadgītā* tends to use √*tyaj* and its derivatives with reference to the results of action and attachment (*saṅga*). Śaṅkara follows this tendency in his comment on verses 18.1 to 18.12, using these words to define the inner abandonment of the unenlightened *karmayogin*. But elsewhere in his works we find almost the same semantic variations as with *saṃ-ni* √*as*.

First, *tyāga* is glossed with *saṃnyāsa* seemingly in the sense of physical renunciation in the comment on BhG 16.2. *Sarvatyāga*, "abandonment of everything," is used with the same meaning in MuU 1.2.12 when Śaṅkara states that only Brahmins are eligible to it (139). *Sarvakarmaparityāgin* (the abandoner of all actions) is also used with the same meaning in BhG 14.25, as indicated by the fact that the renouncers then keep only the actions necessary for the bare maintenance of the body (605). But soon thereafter, Śaṅkara specifies that the same compound could be understood also as an indication that the person being described is beyond the *guṇas*. This suggests that, in Śaṅkara's eyes, this compound can refer to renunciation of doership alone or combined with physical renunciation. The latter combination is clearly conveyed by the expression *karmaparityāge prāpte* in BhG 4.23 (215), which Śaṅkara uses in the same way as the *karmasaṃnyāse prāpte* of BhG 2.11, meaning that even "when [the stage of] abandonment of rites and duties has been attained" the enlightened person may pursue the latter. In BhG 4.20 also, *karmaparityāga* seems to refer to the enlightened's physical renunciation, since the context attributes this expression to a man who is without action by virtue of his perceiving inaction in action (209) and since, in the same way as in the comment on verse 4.23 and 2.11, even when his abandonment of actions is not possible (*karmaparityāgāsaṃbhave*), he does nothing at all (210). Derivatives of √*tyaj* also present renunciation simply as a quality of the enlightened man, irrespective of his way of living. Without any consideration about ways of living, PU 4.10 (127) states that the *sarvatyāgin* (renouncer of everything) "knows everything" (*sarvajña*)—by knowing the Self which is the source of everything. Finally, *sarvatyāga* is given in MuU 3.1.2 (152) as one of the means on the path of yoga that is said to be accompanied by *karmans*, suggesting thereby that the compound refers here to a process of inner renunciation for the *karmayogin*.[63] Thus, this survey of derivatives of √*tyaj* reaffirms Śaṅkara's polysemic usage of key terms related to renunciation and further clarifies the semantic background out of which later misinterpretations have occurred.

The word *yati* is another term commonly designating the ascetic or the monk. It is, of course, used in this sense by Śaṅkara, for instance in his MuU 3.1.5, where the *Upaniṣad* prescribes means such as truth, austerity, and continence to the *yati* and where Śaṅkara gives *bhikṣu* (mendicant) as a synonym of *yati* (167). *Yati* also conveys the meaning of a monastic aspirant in BhG 14.26 (605) and 18.52 (739), as both verses are contextualized by the comment on the preceding verse in terms of abandoning everything except that which is necessary for bare maintenance of the body. However, in passages such as BhG 4.21–22, *yati* means the enlightened person having taken up physical renunciation. As presented in the introduction to verse 21,

> On the other hand, he who, unlike the above-mentioned person, has realised *Brahman*, the all-pervasive, innermost, actionless Self, even before engaging in ritual actions, who, being bereft of expectation for seen and unseen objects of desire, sees no purpose in action aimed at securing the latter, renounces action with its means, and does merely [what is necessary] for the maintenance of the body, such a *yati*, steadfast in knowledge, is liberated (BhG 4.21, 211).

Finally, *yati* is used by Śaṅkara with reference to the enlightened man irrespective of his way of living. The best example of this is found in his BhG 2.55–68, where the word occurs seven times even though found only once (in verse 60) in this section of the *Gītā* itself. In his introduction to this sequence, Śaṅkara explains that these verses account for the enlightenment of the person remaining active in society as well as of the physical renouncer:

> To the person who got engaged in steadfastness in the yoga of knowledge after renouncing ritual actions from the very first [mode of living], as well as to him who got engaged in the same by way of the yoga of action, the distinctive marks of, and the means [used by], the man of established intellect are taught from "[When a man] completely casts away" [2.55] to the end of the chapter.[64]

In verse 2.60 (120) of this sequence, *yati* is used in the sense of a "persevering aspirant" as it is said that even the persevering wise man (*yatataḥ . . . puruṣasya vipaścitaḥ*) is driven away by senses. From the broad context it can be inferred that *yati* refers here to the seeker-after-liberation, irrespective of his way of life. When the task of controlling the mind and senses has been completed, *yati* is then used for referring to the "self-controlled" man of direct Self-knowledge. It is by virtue of self-control based on direct Self-knowledge, and not by the status of a physical renouncer, that "only the *yati* who has a steady intellect attains liberation" (BhG 2.70, 129).

We saw that the word *nivṛtti* (abstention from action) is not only commonly associated with physical renunciation, but also identifies the universal inner path of liberation as opposed to *pravṛtti* (engagement in action), the universal inner path of transmigratory existence. This is further evidenced by the fact that, in Śaṅkara's works, *nivṛtti* basically covers the same semantic scope as *yati* and derivatives from *saṃ-ni* √*as*, and √*tyaj*. The only difference in the semantic scope is that, in the same way as *yati*, it never refers to renunciation of the rewards of action. A first meaning of *nivṛtti* is abstention from any action while yet retaining the sense of doership: ". . . because *pravṛtti* and *nivṛtti* are both dependent on a doer. All matters involving action, accessories and so forth, exist in the domain of ignorance alone, only as long as Reality has not been attained . . ." [65] Interestingly, the same external dimension of engagement in, and abstention from action is referred to in the next verse (by adjectival forms of these words), although applying here to the enlightened man who did abandon the sense of doership through his direct Self-knowledge. His actions "are performed without motivation, without purpose, as mere bodily movements; when done by one engaged in actions (*pravṛtta*), they are for the guidance of people; when done by one abstaining from actions (*nivṛtta*), they are for the mere maintenance of the body . . ." [66] Thus, with the second meaning, *nivṛtti* still refers to the monastic way of living (as opposed to a socially active one), yet the sense of doership is no longer attached to it, as it is the way of living of the man of direct Self-knowledge. In the comment on BhG 6.3 (287), we come across *nivṛtti* as a process of both inner and outer renunciation when *śama* (calmness) is defined as "*nivṛtti* from all actions." Finally, in some passages, it is the sense of inner renunciation of doership irrespective of the way of living that is conveyed by *nivṛtti* or *nivṛtta*. Like the *sarvakarmasaṃnyāsa* of the householder's sequence toward liberation, *nivṛtti* can mean a renunciation of doership that is normally but not necessarily accompanied by physical renunciation. In KaU 2.2.12, *nivṛtti* consisting of inner renunciation of all activity, is clearly given as a correlate of direct Self-knowledge. In contrast with "those whose intellect is attached to the outside objects" are "*the wise,* the ones who abstain (*nivṛtta*) from external activity, who discriminate, who *see,* who directly experience *Him,* the *Īśvara,* the Self, in accord with the teaching of the master and the traditional texts . . ."[67] Similarly, Śaṅkara states in BhG 18.13 that "as shown by these passages, when Self-knowledge arises there is *nivṛtti* of all actions. Therefore *in* that *Sāṃkhya,* whose aim is Self-knowledge and which is *the end of action, i.e.,* in *Vedānta,* [five causes] *are declared,* are said, *to bring about the completion,* the termination, *of all actions.*"[68] Obviously *nivṛtti* as the termination of all actions cannot simply mean the monastic way of living even when meant solely for Self-knowledge. It can only be abandonment of doership, the only type of renunciation that brings fulfilment and termination to all actions. Referring to the enlightened who does not give up physically the practice of rites, Śaṅkara underscores that "what may appear—even after action and its motive have disappeared—as his engagement in action (*pravṛtti*) for the guidance of people and with the same assiduity as before, is no action . . . "[69] Thus, it is this inner renunciation of all identification to activity that defines *nivṛtti* along with Self-knowledge as the only means of liberation.

It would be a major misunderstanding to believe that in a gloss such as the following, the term *nivṛtti* means for Śaṅkara renunciation through the monastic way of living: "*Pravṛtti,* that is, engagement in action, the cause of bondage, the path of action. *And nivṛtti,* that is, abstaining from action, the cause of liberation, the path of *saṃnyāsa.*"[70] We saw that the semantic scope of *pravṛtti* includes both a way of living and a purely inner dimension of identification with action. Given this scope, the most consistent interpretation of *pravṛtti* here is that it represents the cause of bondage only inasmuch as it entails the sense of doership due to spiritual ignorance. Similarly, the semantic scope of *nivṛtti* reveals that the latter is the cause of liberation only inasmuch as it entails withdrawal from the sense of doership through direct Self-knowledge.[71] Although polysemic and at times ambiguous, Śaṅkara's usage of *saṃ-ni* √*as,* √*tyaj* and *nivṛtti* reveals a soteriology that is based on the sine qua non of Self-knowledge accompanied by inner renunciation of doership, and not on any outer requirement such as physical renunciation.

The word *uparati* (quietness), its synonym *uparama,* or its adjectival form *uparata* also manifest a polysemic and ambiguous character in Śaṅkara's works. Although our author uses them quite rarely in the context of renunciation and does not give them a prominent role, they deserve a close analysis, as they will become a major concept in the way post-Śaṅkara *Advaita* will define the nature and function of renunciation.

Uparati is regarded by the *Advaita* tradition as one of the "six qualities" (*ṣatkasampatti*) which, as a whole, correspond to the third among the four requirements for entry into the discipline of knowledge.

While describing, in his BS 1.1.1, the requirements for beginning the enquiry into the nature of the *Brahman*, Śaṅkara mentions only the first two "qualities" and does not comment on them. Thus, we have no indication here as to how he interprets *uparati* in this context. On the other hand, this list seems to originate from verse 4.4.23 of the *Bṛhadāraṇyaka Upaniṣad* which declares: "Therefore when one thus knows [the *Brahman*], one's mind is controlled, one's senses are controlled, one is quiet (*uparata*), enduring, concentrated, and sees the Self in the [individual] self itself" (376). Here Śaṅkara glosses "quiet" (*uparata*) by "a renouncer (*saṃnyāsin*) who is completely free from all desires" (Ibid., 377). The use of the word *saṃnyāsin* obviously suggests that *uparati* corresponds to physical renunciation. But it can be interpreted that the verse describes an already enlightened person, since it goes on as follows: "Evil does not burn him, he burns away all evil. He becomes sinless, taintless, free from doubts, and a knower of *Brahman*." (Ibid., 376). Equally significant is the fact that Yājñavalkya, the speaker of the verse, then declares to his disciple, king Janaka, that he has attained complete realization of *Brahman*: "This is the world of *Brahman*, O Emperor. You have attained it" (Ibid.). Since Janaka was obviously not a physical renouncer and yet, as certified by Yājñavalkya, fitted the description of the complete knower of *Brahman*, perhaps Śaṅkara understood by *uparata* (quiet) that, whatever his way of living, one who has direct knowledge of *Brahman* is inwardly free from all desires.

The value of *uparati* or *uparama* as an inner quietness withdrawn from external objects is evidenced by the comment on *Bṛhadāraṇyaka Upaniṣad* 4.4.21 which clearly shows that *uparama* does not necessarily refer to physical renunciation when given as part of the means of enlightenment. The verse says: "Once the Brahmin has known this [Self] alone, let him bring about the experience" (369). And Śaṅkara proceeds with the following comment:

> *Once the Brahmin has known* about *this* kind of *Self alone*, through instruction [from a teacher] and through scriptures, *let him bring about the experience*, which was the teaching-subject of the scriptures and the teacher, and which fulfills the desire to know. The meaning is that he should practice the means conducive to the experience, namely, renunciation (*saṃnyāsa*), control of mind, control of senses, quietness (*uparama*), endurance and concentration (Ibid.).

It must be noted first that in this passage the prescription of renunciation comes *after* rather than before the acquisition of the discursive knowledge about the Self. Nothing suggests here that physical renunciation is necessary for starting the enquiry into the nature of the Self, even in a context referring to a Brahmin. Second, *saṃnyāsa* and *uparama* are given as two distinct means. *Saṃnyāsa* seems to refer to the abandonment of rites, which allows full-time practice of the following means given in the enumeration. Since the verse presents the aspirant as a Brahmin, Śaṅkara's statement of *saṃnyāsa* as the first means to be used is proper. *Uparama* can then very well be understood as an inner state of quietness and abstention from objects other than the means leading to the experience of the Self.

However, two citations of the sentence of verse 4.4.23 containing *uparata* suggest that, for Śaṅkara, this word also denotes physical renunciation. After quoting verse 4.4.23 in BṛU 4.4.9 (365), Śaṅkara states, "it will teach the cessation (*uparama*) of all actions." In his introduction to the AiU, he cites the same passage as an authority (*pramāṇa*) to substantiate that "even the unenlightened man who seeks after liberation has to adopt wandering mendicancy" (636). He also uses the expression "cessation (*uparama*) of all actions" to mean physical renunciation in his BṛU 4.4.22 (373).

Thus, *uparati* and its equivalents certainly share the polysemy and ambiguity found in the other terms used by Śaṅkara to refer to renunciation and to the various means of knowledge. It seems that, in Śaṅkara's view, *uparati* and its equivalents can mean, according to context, inner renunciation alone, as well as physical renunciation, before or after enlightenment. Since according to Śaṅkara physical renunciation is for Brahmins alone and qualification for the discipline of knowledge is also accessible without physical renunciation, there is no reason to understand that *uparati* means physical renunciation when given as a necessary "quality" for undertaking the discipline of knowledge. Yet we can see already how the misinterpretation of the word *uparati* as a requirement for the discipline of knowledge by some later *Advaitins* is intimately connected with the problem of polysemy and ambiguity in Śaṅkara's own terminology.

We saw in the previous chapters that the words *vyutthāna* (renunciation), *pārivrājya* (wandering mendicancy), *parivrāṭ* (wandering mendicant), (*paramahaṃsa*) *parivrājaka* (wandering mendicant), *sāṃkhya* (follower of *Sāṃkhya*), and *bhikṣu* (mendicant) can be connected with both the formal physical renunciation of the seeker-after-liberation and the (formal or informal) physical renunciation of the enlightened. Thus, *vyutthāna* and *pārivrājya* are practically synonymous for Śaṅkara. So also are *parivrāṭ*, (*paramahaṃsa*) *parivrājaka*, *sāṃkhya*, and *bhikṣu*.

The word *akṣaropāsaka* (meditator on the Imperishable), which is often associated with physical renunciation, also features polysemy. In *Gītā* 8.3, *akṣara* is said to be the supreme *Brahman*, a designation understood by Śaṅkara to be the attributeless nature of *Brahman* (BhG 8.11, 276). In his BhG 12.1, Śaṅkara distinguishes people who meditate on *Brahman* as the attributeless *akṣara*, from people who meditate on the qualified or attributeful *Brahman*, consisting of a universal form (*viśvarūpa*). Being also presented as pursuing the meditative means of enlightenment, the ones dedicated to the attributeless *Brahman* are quite obviously unenlightened meditators on the Imperishable (*akṣaropāsakas*). But in his introduction to *Gītā* 12.13, Śaṅkara clearly defines the *akṣaropāsaka* in terms of his direct non-dual Self-knowledge, contrasting him with meditators who still see a duality between their Self and the Lord:

> And here, yoga consisting of the deep focus of the mind on *Īśvara* in the universal form [*Brahman* with attributes], and practices such as rites for the sake of *Īśvara*, have been prescribed, based on the distinction between the Self and *Īśvara*. . . . Having said in "They verily reach Me . . ." [12.4] that, with respect to attainment of liberation, the *akṣaropāsakas* are independent, [Kṛṣṇa] has shown, in "I am their emancipator" [12.7], that the others are dependent on someone else, that is, under the control of *Īśvara*. For, when they [*akṣaropāsakas*] are considered as one with *Īśvara*'s Self, it would be inconsistent to speak of the process of their emancipation because, being the *akṣara* itself, they do not perceive any difference [with it].[72]

Similarly, in BhG 18.66, Śaṅkara clearly presents *akṣaropāsakas* as liberated-in-life, since the triple result of action is said not to accrue to them and since "they have obtained refuge in the unity of the real nature of the Self and the Lord" (762).

Vidvas (knower) is another term closely related to renunciation, being often given by Śaṅkara as an addressee (*adhikārin*) of the prescription of renunciation. Its proper understanding is also essential to a faithful account of Śaṅkara's position on renunciation, because it determines whether the commentator addresses the notion of renunciation to one who has or hasn't attained direct experience of the Self. This semantic assessment can make all the difference between understanding Śaṅkara as emphasizing physical renunciation as a means to, or as a consequence of, direct Self-knowledge. A common meaning of *vidvas* is "meditator." "In the *Upaniṣads*," writes Śaṅkara, "the roots *vid* (to know) and *upas* (to meditate) are seen to be used interchangeably" (BS 4.1.1, 826). Therefore, *vidvas* can be used to distinguish one practicing any form of meditation in contrast with people who perform only rites. This distinction is made, for instance, in MuU 1.2.10–11 (138). There, people who perform only rituals are said to go through the (Southern) path of ancestors at the time of death and to be reborn as humans or beasts; in contrast, forest-dwellers, formal *saṃnyāsins* and *vidvas*—the latter being interpreted by Śaṅkara as "householders who are devoted mainly to meditation (*jñānapradhāna*)"—are said to go through the (Northern) path of gods and to remain in the world of *Brahmā* until complete enlightenment. Thus, a first type of opposition is created here between those who are devoid of knowledge (*avidvas*), because they do not practice the inner cognitive process of meditation, and those who are knowers (*vidvas*) in the sense that they do practice meditation, whatever their way of living (ChU 5.4.2, 480). The meditator is also called a *vidvas* or knower by virtue of his seeking after the Self: "*That itself*, the supreme Self itself, *he*, the *vidvas*, *chooses*, he wishes to attain . . ." (MuU 3.2.3, 157). However, when contrasted with the already enlightened *vidvas*, who sees the scriptures as emerging from himself (AiU intro, 633), the meditating and aspiring *vidvas* will be considered an *avidvas*. This shift occurs for instance when, after justifying the physical renunciation of the enlightened *vidvas*, Śaṅkara declares: "Even the *avidvas* who seeks after liberation has to adopt wandering mendicancy" (Ibid., 636). Yet, a few sentences further, this ignorant seeker-after-liberation regains the status of a *vidvas* when compared with those who do not desire the Self and liberation and who give all their attention to rites and their rewards: "Again, as to the idea that rites extend over the whole of man's life . . . it has been dismissed, since it applies to the *avidvas* . . ." (Ibid., 639).

It follows from this semantic analysis that Śaṅkara's polysemic usage concerning renunciation renders his terminology rather unstable and ambiguous. But a proper contextualization provides evidence of the author's liberality with respect to qualification for Self-knowledge and liberation. In the usage of derivatives from *saṃ-ny* √*as* and √*tyaj*, as well as of other words related to renunciation, we find expressed [1] his primary emphasis on abandonment of doership, and [2] his insistance on physical renunciation as a result of a *direct* Self-knowledge that leads spontaneously to liberation without any additional help from actions. It goes without saying that such a semantic schema will enable us to better understand how later commentators misinterpreted or transformed Śaṅkara's influencial legacy.

PART THREE

Renunciation in Post-Śaṅkara *Advaita Vedānta* and Hinduism

CHAPTER NINE

Post-Śaṅkara *Advaita Vedānta* and Renunciation

After having contextualized, clarified, and reconstructed Śaṅkara's position on renunciation, and yet shown the ambivalence of his terminology on this topic, we are now in a position to enquire into the ways in which post-Śaṅkara *Advaitins* have developped their own interpretations on the basis of the works of the founder of their tradition. As evidenced by a comparison between our findings and the understanding of Śaṅkara's view on renunciation held by most modern scholars and representative followers of *Advaita Vedānta,* a fundamental misinterpretation of his teaching occurred some time in the medieval period. When did this happen? Who were the main protagonists of this shift? How did they redefine the role of renunciation in *Advaita Vedānta* while seemingly remaining faithful to the founder of their tradition? Which terms were central to this new understanding? Can we identify some social motives behind it? And was there any opposition to this trend from some other *Advaitins*? These are the questions before us now.

The very first question to address however concerns Śaṅkara's so-called minor works. Śaṅkara is credited with more than three hundred works by the tradition. As a whole did these play an important role in making Śaṅkara the herald of physical renunciation? Did they serve in emphasizing and popularizing physical renunciation in the name of Śaṅkara, so as to influence the reading of his major works? So let us start with an assessment of the most well-known minor works attributed to Śaṅkara.[1]

THE MINOR WORKS TRADITIONALLY ASCRIBED TO ŚAṄKARA

There exists no reliable datation of the minor works commonly attributed to Śaṅkara. Thus, a synchronic thematic survey seems to be the best means of investigation available at present. Interestingly, one finds in these works both the tendencies of viewing physical renunciation as necessary and unnecessary for Self-knowledge and liberation. We will proceed first with the works which assert the possibility of acquiring Self-knowledge without physical renunciation.

In its description of the fourfold requirement for the discipline of knowledge, the *Aparokṣānubhūti* defines *uparati* as an inner withdrawal: "*Uparati* is the complete turning away from [sense] objects" (Śaṅkara 1925, 1, verse 7). Physical renunciation is not mentioned here as a requirement for the enquiry (*vicāra*) into the Self proposed by verse 10. Again, in verse 106, it is a form of inner renunciation that is valued: "*Tyāga* is the abandonment of the form of the universe through the perception of the Self as [pure] consciousness. It is honoured by great men because it is of the nature of immediate liberation" (Ibid., 9, verse 106).

In the *Ātmānātmaviveka*, the requirement for the discipline of knowledge does not necessarily include physical renunciation: "The word *uparati*," says the author, "means the complete abandonment of prescribed rites, according to the rules. Or it means [continued] focus on hearing and so forth once the mind has been focused on them alone" (Ibid., 407). The author goes to the extent of saying that "even when householders have not acquired the fourfold requirement, they do not incur sin by pursuing the enquiry about the Self. But it is much better [when they do acquire it]" (Ibid., 408).

The *Śataślokī* clearly distinguishes between inner and outer renunciation: "For those who control their mind, there are also two types of renunciation: of the mind-body complex (*deha*) and of the house" (Ibid., 108, verse 14). It adds two verses further: "Even if one lives in the house as head of the family, one who is devoid of the sense of mine-ness is like a guest desiring to go to his native place: he doesn't feel so intensely the sorrows and joys of the mind and body" (Ibid., verse 16). And in the following verses one finds no mention of physical renunciation, but rather of various aspects to be abandoned inwardly, such as desire, anger, greed (verse 18), name and form (verse 41), and fickleness (verse 43).

The hymn *Gurvaṣṭakam* also stresses that no particular way of living is mandatory for liberation: "That virtuous person who reads this octad on the Guru, and whose mind is fixed on the sayings of the Guru—

whether he be an ascetic, king, student, or householder—attains the desired goal, the state which is called Brahman" (Mahadevan 1959, 51, verse 9).

The *Vākyavṛtti* gives "control of mind and so forth" (*śamādi*) as requirements for the discipline of knowledge, without specifying physical renunciation (Śaṅkara 1925, 34, verse 3). Similarly, at the beginning of the *Hastāmalakīyabhāṣya*, no mention is made of physical renunciation as part of the qualification, since the disciple who will receive the teaching of this text is simply presented as "a man who has given up attachment and takes absolutely no interest in transmigratory existence and its means" (Śaṅkara 1982, 455). In the same spirit, the *Ātmabodha* opens with the following words: "This *Ātmabodha* is composed for those who have destroyed their sins through austerities, who are at peace, free from passion and desirous of liberation" (Śaṅkara 1925, 13, verse 1).[2] Verse 40 refers to abandonment of name and form (Śaṅkara 1925, 16), and verse 51 enjoins the giving up of attachment to external happiness (Ibid., 17). While the last verse describes a man "abstaining from rites" (*viniṣkriya*), it also presents him as worshipping the place of pilgrimage of his own Self and as being immortal (Ibid., 18); accordingly, his physical renunciation could very well be interpreted as the result of enlightenment, rather than as a precondition for it.

In the *Ātmajñānopadeśavidhi*, the qualified person is described as a *yati* (Śaṅkara 1953, 1, verse 1.1). Since, in Śaṅkara's usage, the word *yati* can mean either a physical renouncer or a persevering aspirant, it does not clearly indicate that physical renunciation is part of the requirement for Self-knowledge. Later on in the work, it is inner renunciation that is emphasized by a reference to the abandonment (*parityāga*) of the waking, dreaming, and sleeping states of consciousness (Ibid., 35, verse 3.1; 47, verses 4.2–3).

Inner renunciation is prescribed in a number of works with respect to a variety of objects: the knowable things;[3] pride, the thought that one exits in the mind-body complex, as well as speech (*vāda*);[4] and finally "the snare of all the bad inclinations."[5] Similarly, it is declared that when everything (*sarva*) has been abandoned, one attains the *Brahman*.[6]

Other passages are critical of identification with any mode of living, whether it be that of the renunciant or of the householder. The *Svarūpanirūpaṇa* declares for instance: "How can one who knows that he is the *Brahman*—free from all limitations, consciousness devoid of falsehood—be a follower of *varṇas* and modes of living? The wise should abandon things which are connected with *varṇas* and modes of living and bound to regions and birth; he should meditate on his own true being" (Śaṅkara 1978b, 6, verses 11–12). The hymn *Carpaṭapañjarikā* presents a critique of both the householder and renunciant modes of living as mere ways of living (verses 2–4). The renunciant just lives for the sake of his stomach (verse 4) and refuses to give up the chains of false hope (verse 2). The householder will probably be abandoned by his family when old age comes (verse 3). Yet "no one is interested in the supreme *Brahman*" (Śaṅkara 1925, 355, verse 7), and "no one gives up false hopes and anger" (Ibid., verse 9). The reader is then told to "abandon the whole unsubstantial world like the vision of a dream" (Ibid., 356, verse 12). The wandering ascetic depicted in the penultimate verse is one for whom "there is neither I, nor you, nor this world" (Ibid., verse 16). Thus, he seems already enlightened.[7] Hence, even though centered on the value of renunciation as a whole, the hymn *Carpaṭapañjarikā* does not suggest that physical renunciation is necessary for Self-knowledge. The *Sadācārānusaṃdhāna* also insists that "*saṃnyāsa* does not mean wearing the ochre garment, but discipline of the mind-body complex. It is the conviction that one is not the mind-body complex, but the Self" (Ibid., 40, verse 16).

Besides this understanding of renunciation, one finds in Śaṅkara's "minor works" a different trend which holds physical renunciation to be indispensible for Self-realization. The *Sarvavedāntasiddhāntasārasaṅgraha* can exemplify this perspective. It has a long description of the fourfold requirement for the discipline of knowledge—covering verses 14 to 251. The first reference to *uparati* defines it as follows: "By the word *uparati* is meant renunciation, so called because it annihilates actions" (Ibid., 143, verse 152). Later on the author enriches the semantic scope of the word with the sense of inner renunciation. But he specifies as well that the goal will not be achieved without the use of *uparati* as the subsidiary means consisting of physical renunciation:

> The word *uparati* means abstention from occupations with [objects] perceived earlier. And, by semantic status, it is of two kinds, primary and secondary. The primary meaning is the abandonment of objects through one's attitude. The secondary meaning is renunciation of rites—considered as a subsidiary to hearing [and so forth]. A man certainly relies on the subsidiaries for achieving the principal. If the prescribed course of action is without the subsidiaries, the principal is definitely not achieved (Ibid., 147–148, verses 205–207).

At the end of the description of the fourfold requirement, the text goes on saying that the *yati* endowed with these qualifications—including physical renunciation—approaches the master (verse 251). The text proposes an uncompromizing association of the means of liberation with the monastic way of living: "The renouncer is qualified for liberation, the householder, for ritual action" (Ibid., 145, verse 180). Another passage mentions that "engagement in action (*pravṛtti*) and abstention from action (*nivṛtti*) are the two courses taught by the *Śruti*. By engagement in action, man is bound, by abstention from action, he is liberated" (Ibid., 147, verse 201). The opposition and incompatibility between engagement in, and abstention from, action (*pravṛtti* and *nivṛtti*) seems presented mainly in terms of ways of living. Here one finds neither the possibility of attaining liberation without physical renunciation, nor the yoga of action as an intermediary between complete absorption in rites and their complete abandonment: "Because it is not possible to use knowledge and action simultaneously, therefore, the one who desires knowledge should surely make a special effort to abandon rites" (Ibid., 147, verse 203). Later on in the work (Ibid., 150, verse 235), it is the twice-born (*dvija*) that is said to abandon his home, a statement which seems to follow Sureśvara and expands the eligibility to physical renunciation, but which also facilitates the universalization of the prerequisite of physical renunciation for the discipline of knowledge. Thus, in contrast with Śaṅkara's standpoint, this work renders physical renunciation necessary for access to the discipline of knowledge, and opposes *pravṛtti* and *nivṛtti* only in terms of ways of living, an attitude which makes physical renunciation and monasticism the only way of living capable of yielding liberation.

Similarly, in the *Tattvopadeśa*, it is "the one who has renounced rites according to the rules" (Śaṅkara 1981, 176, verse 76) that is described as going to the master for instruction. After several quotations justifying physical renunciation, the *Sanatsujātīyabhāṣya* formally restricts the qualification for Self-knowledge in the same terms: "Moreover, Lord Bṛhaspati says [in the *Mahābhārata*] that only those who have renounced all rites are qualified for knowledge, not others" (Śaṅkara 1982, 215). But, interestingly, the passage of the *Mahābhārata* (12.197.9) mentioned here—and which the author quotes immediately after—only refers to a detached person (*virakta*), and not to a physical renouncer: "One feels sorrow when the senses are carried away, and happiness when they are controlled. For, one given to passion rebounds to his natural trends and the detached man attains knowledge" (Ibid.). Thus, we meet with an overinterpretation of physical renunciation concerning a passage that does not even intend it in the first place.

Given that, in the minor works attributed to Śaṅkara, one can find support for physical renunciation as both a dispensable and indispensible means for entry into the discipline of knowledge and direct Self-knowledge. Thus, it seems that these minor works did not play a determining role in the overemphasis given to physical renunciation by later *Advaitins*.

SUREŚVARA AND SARVAJÑĀTMAN

According to the tradition, Śaṅkara had four main pupils, namely, Padmapāda, Sureśvara, Hastāmalaka, and Toṭaka (or Troṭaka). Hastāmalaka wrote only the fourteen verse poem known as *Hastāmalakaślokas*. The text's single reference to renunciation is when, in verse two, the poet states that he is beyond all categories of *varṇas* and modes of living, including that of wandering mendicancy (Potter 1981, 601). Only two poems are attributed to Toṭaka—*Śrutisārasamuddhāraṇa* and *Toṭakāṣṭaka*—and none refers to our topic. The theme of renunciation will develop mainly on the basis of the sub-commentaries of the two other pupils, Padmapāda and Sureśvara. The sole authentic work known from Padmapāda is the *Pañcapādikā*, which covers only the first four aphorisms of Śaṅkara's commentary on the BS. Among the works ascribed to Sureśvara, three are quite unanimously considered to be authentic: the commentaries (*vārttika*) on Śaṅkara's BṛU and TU, and the independent treatise *Naiśkarmyasiddhi*. The tradition also credits Sureśvara with two commentaries on works attributed to Śaṅkara: the *Mānasollāsa*, a versified commentary on the *Dakṣiṇāmūrti* hymn, and a commentary on the *Pañcīkaraṇa*. But one finds nothing significant with respect to renunciation in these last two minor works.

As pointed out by S. Dasgupta (1975, 47–48), after Śaṅkara, the *Advaita Vedānta* tradition developed around three major ways of understanding non-duality: that proposed by Sureśvara and his disciple Sarvajñātman; that espoused by Padmapāda and commented upon by Prakāśātman in his *Vivaraṇa*—a title which became the name of one of the two major schools of *Advaita Vedānta*; and that put forward by Vācaspati Miśra (around 850) who, unlike the others, was not a direct disciple, and whose *Bhāmatī* on Śaṅkara's BS also gave its name to the second major school of *Advaita Vedānta*.

We will now show that the interpretation of renunciation also developped distinctly along these three channels. But the different perspectives were far from being tightly closed with respect to this issue. The views of Sureśvara and Sarvajñātman on the one hand, and of some *Vivaraṇa* authors on the other, certainly reinforced each other in stressing the necessity of physical renunciation.

In his paper on "Śaṃkarācārya: the Myth and the Man," Karl H. Potter argues that Śaṅkara's position on renunciation was completely reversed by Vidyāraṇya in the fourteenth century. According to Potter, by the concept of *saṃnyāsa*, Śaṅkara emphasized only the renunciation of doership which follows direct Self-knowledge, whereas Vidyāraṇya made physical renunciation necessary for attaining Self-knowledge. Although Potter underestimates the fact that Śaṅkara also stresses physical renunciation as an aid to Self-knowledge, he is right in pointing out that, at some point, a surreptitious reversal occurred within the *Advaita* tradition concerning renunciation. Our contention is that this shift occurred much earlier, in the ninth century, with Sureśvara and Sarvajñātman.

According to T. M. P. Mahadevan, the differences between Sureśvara and his master are "of minor importance" (Sureśvara 1958, xiii). While this is probably true for all other points of the doctrine, it is not the case as far as renunciation is concerned. Some modern scholars see in Sureśvara a more liberal thinker with respect to the requirements for access to Self-knowledge. Patrick Olivelle believes, for instance, that "Śaṅkara was not a radical thinker as evidenced by his insistence that only Brahmins are qualified to become renouncers, a position far more conservative than that of most later Advaitins" (1993, 227).[8] Summarizing Śaṅkara's BS 1.3.34–38 on *Śūdras'* qualification for Self-knowledge, Paul Hacker overlooks the fact that Śaṅkara allows them access to the discipline of knowledge through the *Smṛti* literature, and suggests that for him, the only possible scenario is, "that through the effect of *saṃskāras* [latent impressions] from an earlier existence a *Śūdra* could, in exceptional cases, attain knowledge and thereby its reward (i.e., liberation)."[9] Hacker also refers to the *Vedāntasāravārttikarājasaṃgraha*—a text traditionally attributed to Sureśvara, which holds that *Śūdras* can attain enlightenment[10]—and to Sureśvara's *Naiṣkarmyasiddhi* 2.88, which states that the Self is the seer of both the intellect of the *Śūdra* and of the god Brahmā. Here, Hacker understands that Sureśvara introduces a revolutionary notion according to which the *Śūdras* are qualified for Self-knowledge and liberation as a rule rather than as an exception: "The difference between our text and Śaṇkara's BS 1.3.38 is therefore that Śaṅkara accepts Vidura's case only as an exception which requires special explanation, whereas Sureśvara or Pseudo-Sureśvara cites it implicitely as evidence for a general rule."[11] A similar picture emerges from Mayeda's comparison of the two *Advaitins*. First, like Hacker, disregarding the way to Self-knowledge for Śūdras through *Smṛti* literature, he states that in Śaṅkara's BS 1.3.34–39, "the upper three classes of people, excluding Śūdras, are entitled to the knowledge of *Brahman*" (Upad, transl., 228). And, although rightly saying that Sureśvara rejects Śaṅkara's restriction of physical renunciation to Brahmins alone, Mayeda reduces Śaṅkara's criterion for access to Self-knowledge to being a Brahmin and a monk: "It should be kept in mind in order to understand Śaṅkara's doctrine that he accepts as qualified for his teaching a Brahmin who is in the state of *paramahaṃsa* wandering ascetic" (Ibid.).

Having pointed out the shortcomings of previous comparisons between Śaṅkara and Sureśvara, let us now try to clarify their respective positions. Consciously departing from his master's standpoint, Sureśvara does expand the qualification for physical renunciation to all of the first three *varṇas*. In his commentary on BṛU 3.5.1, he first exposes Śaṅkara's position: " 'Brahmin' is used to identify a distinct qualified person, because there is no prescription of renunciation for *Kṣatriyas* and *Vaiśyas* in the *Śruti*."[12] In the next two verses, Sureśvara then gives his own interpretation: "Since the *Śruti* teaches renunciation to the three [*varṇas*] without distinction, the word 'Brahmin' should be understood as a synecdoche (*upalakṣaṇa*) [mentioning the first type of twice-borns to mean all of them]."[13] According to Ānandagiri's comment on this verse (*Sureśvara* 1990, 3.5.89, 819), Sureśvara refers here to Upaniṣadic statements such as, "one may renounce even from studentship" [*Jābāla Upaniṣad* 4], which do not specify that the invitation to physical renunciation is addressed to Brahmins alone.[14] Sureśvara then points out how restricting physical renunciation to Brahmins alone involves a contradiction, especially in the case of already enlightened people: "When it is agreed that knowledge removes the qualification for rites, why forcibly restrict the qualification for renunciation?"[15]

In the same manner as Śaṅkara, Sureśvara gives everyone access to Self-knowledge. He also states that, in contrast with eligibility to rites, qualification for Self-knowledge is not based on criteria such as *varṇas*, modes of living and external conditions:

> Since (the various things of the transmigratory world) which have arisen from ignorance about (the true nature of) the Ātman are only of the nature of the Ātman (itself), knowledge (about the Ātman) does not expect any (particular) eligible person as does (a ritual) activity (Sureśvara 1993, transl., 1.4.1436, 454).[16]

Elsewhere the pupil comments in quite the same way a similar statement from his master: "And since no man is excluded from qualification [for knowledge], the commentator said 'for all men.' "[17]

On the other hand, Sureśvara clearly states that one has to physically abandon rites in order to start with the discipline of knowledge. In his introduction to the BṛU, Śaṅkara simply says—without mentioning anything concerning physical abandonment—that the *Upaniṣad* is addressed to the detached aspirant (*virakta*).[18] In contrast, at the beginning of his subcommentary, Sureśvara makes physical renunciation necessary for the knowledge taught by the same *Upaniṣad*: "He alone is qualified for *Vedānta*, who has renounced all actions, who wishes to cast off transmigratory existence and to know the Unity."[19] And he gives the same requirement at the beginning of the second part of his *Vārttika* on the TU: "Since knowledge, but not action, is competent to destroy ignorance which makes it (*i.e.*, *mokṣa*) unattained, a person who has abandoned the means (viz., *karma*) mentioned above is eligible for Self-knowledge" (Sureśvara 1984, transl., 2.9, 282).[20] But, again, Śaṅkara does not refer to physical renunciation in his introduction to this section of the *Upaniṣad*.

Sureśvara also interprets *uparati* as physical renunciation: "By 'his mind is controlled, his senses are controlled' [BṛU 4.4.23], the *Śruti* itself has stated that the means to Self-knowledge is connected with abandonment of all [rites]."[21] He points out that, in this passage of BṛU 4.4.23, the word *uparata* specifically denotes physical renunciation: "Since cancellation of the prescription of regular rites is not brought about by the prescription of means such as control of mind, the text states that one must abstain (*uparata*) from [ritual] actions."[22]

Again, in his *Naiṣkarmyasiddhi* 1.52, Sureśvara includes physical renunciation as part of the process of gaining direct Self-knowledge, a sequence that later became the main way of interpreting Śaṅkara himself on this matter:

> From the performance of daily obligatory duties merit arises. From the origination of merit comes destruction of sin; and from this arises purification of the mind, and from this comes the understanding of the real nature of bondage; and therefrom dispassion arises; and from this comes a longing for liberation; and from this comes the renunciation of all actions and their means; then there is the practice of yoga; and from this comes the inclination in the mind towards the inner Self, and then there arises the knowledge of the meaning of the texts such as "*tat tvam asi*" [Thou art That], and from this results the destruction of ignorance . . . (Sureśvara 1988, transl., 1.52, 53).[23]

It follows that while, on the one hand, Sureśvara opened physical renunciation to more people than his master, on the other, he closed the discipline of knowledge to a much greater number of people by making physical renunciation necessary for the latter.

We saw that Śaṅkara did not solve all the logical difficulties involved in stating on the one hand that Self-knowledge is accessible irrespective of conditions such as modes of living and, on the other hand, that physical renunciation is expected as a subsidiary in the case of Brahmins in order for the main means—Self-knowledge—to ripen into its result, namely, liberation. We can now see that far from solving this apparent contradiction, Sureśvara amplifies it. He states first that Self-knowledge is for everybody, irrespective of *varṇas* and modes of living. But he also declares that for twice-borns formal physical renunciation is a necessary requirement for the discipline of knowledge. A peculiar feature of Sureśvara's commentaries is that they not only reinforce the hermeneutical difficulties left unsolved by Śaṅkara concerning physical renunciation, but they extend them to all twice-borns.

Sureśvara's ambivalent position is exemplified by his understanding of Yājñavalkya's famous physical renunciation in the *Bṛhadāraṇyaka Upaniṣad*. First, he suggests that even though possessed of an outstanding intellectual knowledge of *Brahman*, Yājñavalkya had to physically abandon rites and to adopt the renunciant's mode of living in order to obtain liberation:

> Even when he knows *Brahman*, the persevering aspirant (*yati*)[24] who has not given up desire cannot attain liberation; therefore, [the knowledge of *Brahman*] is here combined with renunciation. That is the reason why, although commanding an unsurpassed knowledge, the householder Yājñavalkya attained the abode of Viṣṇu [i.e., liberation] after taking up the monastic mode of living. Indeed, renunciation is the best means of liberation for everyone, since the inner supreme abode of the renouncer can be known by the renouncer alone.[25]

But, elsewhere in his commentary, Sureśvara describes Yājñavalkya as having attained liberation even before physical renunciation, which Yājñavalkya is then said to have done "of his own accord," that is, without being subject to injunction: "Even after he had accomplished the goal (*kṛtārtha*) on account of his proper knowledge of Reality, completely of his own accord, he quickly abandoned rites—which involve the means of speech, mind and body."[26]

We have no explicit statement from Śaṅkara as to whether Yājñavalkya was liberated or not before his physical renunciation. However, in his BṛU 2.4.1 (191), Śaṅkara states that Yājñavalkya is going to adopt "the next mode of living" (*āśramāntara*) consisting of wandering mendicancy. Since there would have been no purpose for an enlightened man to resort to a *formal* monastic mode of living, this comment suggests that Śaṅkara viewed Yājñavalkya as unenlightened before his physical renunciation. But Śaṅkara does not mention that Yājñavalkya needed physical renunciation in order to secure his liberation.

Thus, Sureśvara presents Yājñavalkya's physical renunciation in an ambiguous manner: while, from his perspective, physical renunciation is necessary for liberation, Yājñavalkya may have been liberated even *before* renouncing physically. In sharp contrast with his statements on the necessity of physical renunciation, Sureśvara clearly mentions in a few other places that one can attain liberation without physical renunciation. He writes, for instance, that, "one who has refined his sense organs in the course of numerous transmigratory existences and who has a pure intellect can attain liberation in the very first mode of living" (Sureśvara 1982, 2.4.33, 675). He interprets in the same way the physical renunciation of the ancient Brahmins of BṛU 3.5.1. If they became wandering mendicants, it was not as a result of a prescription, but of their having transcended all matters of qualification through their direct Self-knowledge: "Because renunciation comes from the nature of knowledge, because the Real that is to be known brings [injunction] to an end, and because qualification is annulled, [here] injunction is not required for renouncing."[27] It is also *after* their enlightenment that "the best among the knowers of *Brahman*," are said to be in no need of physical renunciation or rites:

> [The opponent asks:] "Thus having known the Self, should he perform the deeds [enjoined by scripture], or abstain from them? Or, is he free from all restraints?" We reply as follows. Since this [knowledge], not being different from what is known, is in conformity with the known reality, [the man of wisdom] does not even glance at the path of action or that of renunciation (Sureśvara 1988, transl., 4.54, 379).[28]

Thus, Sureśvara left behind him ambiguous relationships between the following aspects of his teaching: [1] the statement of a universal access to Self-knowledge which is independent of *varṇas* and modes of living, including the monastic mode of living; [2] the necessity of formal physical renunciation for the discipline of knowledge in the case of twice-borns; [3] the suggestion that, possessed only of mediate knowledge of the Self, Yājñavalkya needed physical renunciation for liberation; [4] the mention that Yājñavalkya or others attained liberation before physical renunciation.

It was left to Sarvajñātman, a direct disciple of both Śaṅkara and Sureśvara (Sarvajñātman 1985, 2–5), to try to assemble these divergent statements into a consistent picture. He then proposed an explanation which makes Sureśvara's position look more coherent, but which departs even more radically from Śaṅkara's.

Sarvajñātman first specifies in his *Saṃkṣepaśārīraka*, a commentary on Śaṅkara's BS, that those who do not renounce physically are not debarred from the discipline of knowledge. The universal accessibility of Self-knowledge itself is thus respected. But Sarvajñātman adds that these non-renouncers are disqualified from *liberation* as long as they do not adopt physical renunciation. Thus, the latter remains indispensible, since it has to be taken up at some point in time, either in this life or in a future one:

> When hearing and so forth is pursued [only] during the intervals between rites, by hermits, householders, celibates and anyone belonging to a mode of living other [than renunciation], it ripens into [direct Self-] knowledge in a future life [after having been accompanied by physical renunciation]. Nowhere in the scripture are they forbidden this [hearing and so forth], unlike the *Śūdras*.[29]

Now, if physical renunciation is a sine qua non for liberation, how could people such as Janaka reach direct Self-knowledge and liberation without it? Verse 3.361 explains this by assuming that the requirement of physical renunciation has been acquired in a previous life:

> If, in previous lives, the collection of means consisting of hearing and so forth was accompanied by renunciation [but did not ripen into direct Self-knowledge], we do not preclude that anyone could attain [direct Self-] knowledge [in a future life] whatever one's mode of living at that time.[30]

This legitimizes Sureśvara's acknowledgement that Yājñavalkya and others attained liberation before physical renunciation in a given life. But the contradiction remains between Sureśvara's affirmation that Self-knowledge is universally accessible irrespective of modes of living, and his view that, for all twice-borns, physical renunciation is a prerequisite for the discipline of knowledge, a requirement that would normally disallow all those who have not physically renounced to resort to the discipline of knowledge even on a part-time basis.

Being more consistent within itself than Sureśvara's interpretation, Sarvajñātman's theory accounted for all possible cases of access to Self-knowledge and enlightenment, while maintaining physical renunciation as an indispensable requirement for liberation to be fulfilled in any life one can imagine: past, present, or future. Sureśvara's incoherence having been buried, as it were, under Sarvajñātman's theory, most later *Advaitins* believed, as we shall see, that Sarvajñātman's explanation made physical renunciation as a sine qua non for liberation consistent with Śaṅkara's viewpoint. Thus, Sarvajñātman sealed Sureśvara's interpretation in a way that looked more coherent, but which distorted Śaṅkara's perspective on renunciation from the very beginning of his tradition.

PADMAPĀDA'S *PAÑCAPĀDIKA* AND THE *VIVARAṆA* SCHOOL

Padmapāda's *Pañcapādikā* provides the basis for the *Vivaraṇa* school. Yet it covers only the first four aphorisms of Śaṅkara's BS. As a consequence, the most determining issue concerning renunciation in the literature directly connected with the *Pañcapādikā* is how Padmapāda and his commentators interpreted the requirements for the discipline of knowledge—referred to by Śaṅkara in his comment on the first aphorism—and especially the prerequisite known as *uparati* or *uparama* (quietness).

Padmapāda himself does not really comment on the six qualities which include *uparati* and which Śaṅkara refers to by giving only the first two items. The *Pañcapādikā* merely states the names of the other items left understood by Śaṅkara, among which is *uparama* (Padmapāda 1992, 440).[31] Thus, Padmapāda did not play any role in defining the value of renunciation in Śaṅkara's tradition.

Prakāśātman's *Vivaraṇa* on the *Pañcapādikā* was probably written during the first half of the thirteenth century. Prakāśātman does not comment on the meaning of the word *uparama* as mentioned by Padmapāda (Ibid., 434–440). And, in the introduction to his commentary, he only mentions that the investigation about the *Brahman* is for one who has acquired the fourfold requirement (Ibid., 12–13, 18). Later in his commentary, he uses *uparama* to mean cessation of the performance of rites: "Because, once [rites] have resulted in the channel of the mind's inclination toward the Self, *uparama* comes into force."[32] A little furter Prakāśātman anwers a question from the opponent as to how both rites and their abandonment can be said to result in the knowledge of the Self. One of his explanations proposes: "Or one can suppose a separate arrangement for Brahmins, *Kṣatriyas* and others."[33] The author seems to suggest here that, because physical renunciation is for Brahmins alone, it can be said that non-Brahmins attain Self-knowledge while continuing the rites and duties of householders or of other modes of living, and Brahmins do so—or can do so—through physical renunciation and full-time absorption into the discipline of knowledge. Thus, nothing indicates that Prakāśātman departed from Śaṅkara as did Sureśvara and Sarvajñātman. But his comments on renunciation are so rare that their influence seems to have been negligible.

None of the other subcommentators of the *Pañcapādikā* adds anything significant to these few indications about renunciation. In fact, the idea of physical renunciation as a sine qua non for Self-knowledge originated within the *Vivaraṇa* school outside the subcommentaries on the *Pañcapādikā*. It seems to have been held first by Anubhūtisvarūpa, also of the first half of the thirteenth century. Among other works, Anubhūtisvarūpa wrote the *Prakaṭārthavivaraṇa*, a commentary on Śaṅkara's BS that was to exert a major influence in the *Vivaraṇa* school.

We find with him the first clear definition of *uparati* as physical renunciation within the *Vivaraṇa* school: "*Uparati* is, on attainment of purity of mind, the abandonment—as per the rules—of even the regular [rites], as one does with the black horn[34] when its purpose is served."[35] No alternative definition is given by the author. However, in his commentary on *sūtra* 3.4.38, Anubhūtisvarūpa holds the opposite view, namely, that the discipline of knowledge is also accessible to householders and others who have not taken up physical renunciation:

> For [physical] renouncers, the prescription of hearing and so forth is obligatory, because, according to *Śruti*, they incur sin by not doing it. But for others, it will be optional, because prescription of hearing and so forth is with reference to knowledge [which is optional for them], and because there is no prohibition [of hearing and so forth in their case].[36]

Thus, Anubhūtisvarūpa reinstates an inconsistency that Sarvajñātman had not solved in Sureśvara's interpretation of renunciation: on the one hand, Self-knowledge was universally accessible irrespective of modes of living and, on the other hand, physical renunciation as *uparati* was a sine qua non for the discipline of knowledge. Since no one else before Anubhūtisvarūpa in the *Vivaraṇa* tradition seems to have held such a restrictive interpretation of *uparati*, it may very well be that he borrowed his understanding from Sureśvara and Sarvajñātman themselves.

Anubhūtisvarūpa's influence will show in his pupil Ānandagiri (thirteenth century), the most assiduous commentator of Śaṅkara, and it will go up to Govindānanda[37] (second half of the sixteenth century) who wrote the well-known *Bhāṣyaratnaprabhā*[38] on Śaṅkara's BS, and his pupil Rāmānanda (first half of the seventeenth century), the author of the *Vivaraṇopanyāsa*, the last important work of the *Vivaraṇa* School. Like Anubhūtisvarūpa, Govindānanda understands the "quality" consisting of *uparati* to be physical renunciation: "*Uparati* is the renunciation of the prescribed obligatory rites and so forth, for the sake of knowledge" (BS 1.1.1, 37). On the other hand, he writes on aphorism 3.4.38:

> Objection: Let rites be the means of knowledge for the ones who do not belong to modes of living. They are not qualified for hearing and so forth because they cannot renounce. Therefore he says . . . Reply: One who desires knowledge—desire which results in the elimination of the binding ignorance—is qualified for hearing. Performed at some time or other, renunciation is still helpful to knowledge, as it is not a subsidiary to hearing [but to knowledge]. This is the purport (BS 3.4.38, 810–811).

If physical renunciation is subsidiary to Self-knowledge and not to the discipline of knowledge as such, then why does Govindānanda hold *uparati* to be physical renunciation as part of the requirements for the discipline of knowledge? Hence, in the same way as Sureśvara and Anubhūtisvarūpa, Govindānanda indulges in self-contradiction when, on the one hand, he defines *uparati* as the requirement of physical renunciation before beginning the discipline of knowledge and, on the other, he states that people who did not adopt physical renunciation are also qualifed for the same discipline.

Among the authors influenced mainly by the *Vivaraṇa* outlook, Ānandagiri, Vidyāraṇya, and Madhusūdana Sarasvatī—who all adopted formal physical renunciation—proved most aware of the apparent contradictions connected with the theme of renunciation in *Advaita Vedānta*, and each of them came out with original solutions—though far from being always acceptable from Śaṅkara's perspective. Let us now examine their respective contributions to the development of the understanding of renunciation in *Advaita Vedānta*.

ĀNANDAGIRI

Spiritual head of the Dvārakā monastery from Śaṅkara's tradition, Ānandagiri lived around the middle of the thirteenth century. Apart from his works on Sureśvara's *Vārttikas*, almost all his writings are subcommentaries on Śaṅkara's commentaries. *Advaita* scholars usually consider these works to be quite literal and faithful. Still today they often use them as their primary reference for clarifications on the more difficult passages of Śaṅkara's commentaries.

Following his master Anubhūtisvarūpa, Ānandagiri interprets the *uparati* of the fourfold requirement for the discipline of knowledge as physical renunciation: "*Uparati* is the abandonment, as per the rules, of even the obligatory [rites] when purity of mind has been attained."[39] Similarly, in his comment on Śaṅkara's BhG, Ānandagiri sees the author as "desirous of prescribing [physical] renunciation as the only direct condition for hearing and so forth."[40]

To do away with the contradiction between this interpretation and Śaṅkara's statements about access to Self-knowledge without physical renunciation, Ānandagiri divides qualification—apparently for the first time in the tradition—into two types, one being *mukhya*, the other *amukhya*. *Mukhya* and *amukhya* may have various shades of meaning here. They can contrast the two types of qualification in terms of real (*mukhya*)/figurative (*amukhya*), or in terms of full (*mukhya*)/partial (*amukhya*). When Śaṅkara says for instance in his BhG 14.26 (605–606) that both the physical renouncer (*yati*) and the performer of rituals (*karmin*) can cross the *guṇas* and attain liberation through the yoga of devotion—which is said to consist of discriminative knowledge (*vivekajñāna*)—Ānandagiri understands that the author "supposes an option between the really [or fully] qualified people, and the figuratively [or partially] qualified people."[41]

Let us first assess the possibility that Ānandagiri understood *mukhya*/*amukhya* to mean real/figurative. The performer of rites referred to by Śaṅkara can very well be a *Kṣatriya* or a *Vaiśya*. Therefore, physical renunciation cannot even be part of the requirements of his qualification for the discipline of knowledge. Thus, it would be untenable to consider him qualified only in a figurative sense, since no prescription of physical renunciation is even addressed to him. Moreover, Śaṅkara understands that even Yājñavalkya was a performer of rituals, that is, a *karmin* (BṛU 2.4 intro, 190), before his physical renunciation. How could Yājñavalkya not be "really" qualified for the discipline of knowledge because he is a performer of rituals, while being one of the greatest teachers of the *Upaniṣads*?

In fact, it is unlikely that Ānandagiri meant by "*mukhya*" and "*amukhya*" qualification a contrast between "real" and "figurative" qualification, because being "figuratively qualified" is, strictly speaking, not being qualified at all. Thus, Ānandagiri probably intended the opposition between "full" and "partial" qualification. But this opposition is also untenable from Śaṅkara's viewpoint. How can one be partially qualified for Self-knowledge because one is not a physical renouncer when, as a *Kṣatriya*, this is not even required of him? To make sense, full qualification would require that one be born as a Brahmin in the first place. Nor could *informal* physical renunciation outside the monastic mode of living (*saṃnyāsāśrama*) make *Kṣatriyas* and others "fully" qualified for Self-knowledge, because it is not even prescribed by scriptures and Śaṅkara.

Ānandagiri's reasoning appears justified only if one assumes that physical renunciation is a universal prerequisite for the discipline of knowledge or for liberation. This seems to have been Ānandagiri's basic outlook. Although a noticeable attempt at solving apparent contradictions related to renunciation in Śaṅkara's works, the concept of *mukhya* and *amukhya* qualification for Self-knowledge and liberation reveals a basic misunderstanding and adds one more misleading avenue in the interpretation of Śaṅkara. While Ānandagiri did not use this concept extensively, it will be integrated and endorsed in the sixteenth century by Appaya Dīkṣita in the elaborate discussion on renunciation presented by the *Siddhāntaleśasaṅgraha*.

Proceeding along the same line in his commentary on Śaṅkara's TU 1.12.1, Ānandagiri understands that physical renouncers have access to proximate means of knowledge such as the discipline of knowledge, while householders can use only remote means such as rites. In the broader context of this passage, Śaṅkara tries to refute the idea that there exists only one mode of living, namely, that of the householder. As argued by the opponent, "since the emergence of knowledge is the result of rites and since rites are prescribed for the householder's mode of living, there can be only one mode of living" (TU 1.12.1, 435). Following a series of objections and replies, Śaṅkara summarizes his position by pointing out that "since non-injury, celibacy, and the like are [also prescribed for other people as] aids to knowledge. . . . the existence of other modes of living is proven and everyone is qualified for knowledge" (Ibid., 438). While Śaṅkara tries to show that physical renouncers as well as householders are qualified for Self-knowledge, Ānandagiri understands that the proximate means of Self-knowledge are for physical renouncers alone: "Now, to show that the practices of the householder's mode of living are remote means, and the practices of the renouncer's mode of living are proximate means of knowledge, Śaṅkara raises an objection . . ."[42]

If, as believed by Ānandagiri, the proximate means of knowledge were not available to the householder, enlightenment would be practically impossible in his mode of living. This is actually what Ānandagiri suggests in the following comment on Śaṅkara's BhG 5.17: "Thinking that other modes of living are not worthy of being associated with the reward [i.e., liberation] described [here] through a wealth of characteristics, he specifies: 'the yatis.' "[43] While the word *yati* is not used here by the *Gītā* itself, Śaṅkara does introduce it at the end of this comment with reference to the people described in the verse. Yet his comment on this verse and on the two preceding ones does not refer at all to the respective values of the modes of living. In 5.15, Śaṅkara says that people who lack discriminative knowledge (*avivekin*) are subject to unending becoming (*saṃsārin*). In verse 16, he refers to the possibility that ignorance (*ajñāna*) be destroyed by discriminative knowledge and that the supreme Reality be thus illumined. Hence, as suggested by the context, Śaṅkara wishes to convey that direct Self-knowledge eliminates ignorance and brings about liberation from unending becoming. At the beginning of his comment on verse 17, he specifies that it talks about those whose intellect has attained this supreme enlightening knowledge (Ibid., 264). Even if, as it can very well be the case, *yatis* means here physical renouncers, nothing suggests that they became enlightened only after their physical renunciation, and that they could not have renounced after attaining liberation in the householder's mode of living. In a context where enlightened people are described, Śaṅkara most probably uses the word *yati* to suggest that because the liberated person has acheived the goal and is beyond the pale of injunctions, he has nothing to do with rites.

The understanding of physical renunciation as necessary for the discipline of knowledge often leads Ānandagiri to interpret physical renunciation as a requirement for the discipline of knowledge where, in fact, Śaṅkara is describing renunciation of doership only or as accompanied by physical renunciation. Consequently, much more emphasis is given by Ānandagiri on physical renunciation as a prerequisite for acquiring Self-knowledge. In his BhG 5.5 Śaṅkara writes for instance:

> The meaning is as follows. *The state,* called liberation, *which is reached by followers of Sāṃkhya,* by those renouncers who are steadfast in knowledge, *is also reached by yogins.* The yogins are those who perform their duties as a means for the attainment of knowledge, dedicating them to Īśvara, without aiming at results for themselves. They also reach that state, through attainment of knowledge of Reality and renunciation . . . [44]

Does the last sentence mean that, in order to reach liberation, the *yogins* have to adopt physical renunciation after having reached a proper intellectual understanding about the Self, or does it mean that liberation is achieved when one acquires that proper direct Self-knowledge, which enables one to renounce all actions, including the mental ones? To assess how Ānandagiri answered this question, we must first contextualize Śaṅkara's statement.

In his introduction to the following verse (5.6), Śaṅkara specifies Kṛṣṇa's statement as follows: "But the *saṃnyāsa* which is connected with knowledge, I consider to be *Sāṃkhya*; and *Saṃkhya* itself is the true yoga."[45] He then adds that, in verse 5.6, the word *saṃnyāsa* is meant by the word *Brahman*, in the sense of "true" (*pāramārthika*) *saṃnyāsa* (Ibid.), "because it consists of steadfastness in the supreme knowledge."[46] "*Brahman*," pursues Śaṅkara, "is the true *saṃnyāsa* consisting of steadfastness in the supreme Self."[47] Again, is the Self-knowledge referred to here only indirect or direct?

We can identify so far two multitermed equations:

1. *saṃnyāsa* connected with knowledge = *Sāṃkhya* = true yoga;
2. true *saṃnyāsa* = *Brahman* = steadfastness in the supreme knowledge = steadfastness in the supreme Self.

The question arises as to whether these two equations are themselves equivalent in Śaṅkara's eyes. An answer is provided to this as well as to our two previous questions by Śaṅkara's use of "true yoga" (*paramārthayoga*) in BhG 2.53, the only other place where this expression occurs in the commentary. Verse 2.53 explains to Arjuna the condition under which he will attain "yoga." In his introduction to the verse, Śaṅkara refers to this yoga as the "true yoga" (*paramārthayoga*). According to Kṛṣṇa, Arjuna will attain yoga "when [his] intellect remains unmoved and steady in *samādhi*" (BhG 2.53, 112). Śaṅkara glosses *samādhi* by "Self" (*ātman*). Now, verses 2.54–72, which follow, feature the famous description of the "man of steady intellect" (*sthitaprajña*) who has attained liberation-in-life. And, in the introduction to verse 2.54 (113), Śaṅkara refers to him as "one who has attained knowledge in *samādhi*" (*labdhasamādhiprajña*). Hence, the "true yoga" consisting of steadiness in *samādhi* or Self refers quite clearly to stable direct Self-knowledge. Since "true yoga" means steadfastness in direct knowledge of the Self, and since, according to the above equations, it is equal to "*saṃnyāsa* connected with knowledge," it is most likely equivalent to the "true *saṃnyāsa*," which also consists of "steadfastness in the supreme Self." So all the terms of the above two equations seem equivalent from Śaṅkara's perspective.

It follows that, according to Śaṅkara, when verse 5.5 says that the *yogin* attains liberation through knowledge and renunciation, and when 5.6 states that, equipped with the yoga of action, an aspirant soon reaches the true *saṃnyāsa* designated by the word *Brahman,* it does not mean that he attains a stage of mediate Self-knowledge, and that he must take up physical renunciation in order to start with the discipline of knowledge, but that, inasmuch as it is accompanied by cultivation of Self-knowledge, the yoga of action will lead him to immediate knowledge of the Self. This is confirmed by Śaṅkara's following comment on the next verse (5.7): "the one equipped with yoga . . . *who has become the Self in all beings*. . . . who remains in such a state, *though performing* action in order to guide people, *is not tainted,* not bound by actions."[48] Since the "true *saṃnyāsa*" denoted by the word *Brahman* and described here as liberation-in-life is said to be reached by the *karmayogin* without physical renunciation (i.e., as he continues to perform rites for the purpose of guiding people), it must be characterized essentially by renunciation of doership and be coextensive with direct Self-knowledge and liberation.

However, Ānandagiri understands the same "true *saṃnyāsa*" to be physical abandonment of rites as a prelude to the discipline of knowledge. According to him, in the case of *karmayogins* referred to by the verse, the knowledge on which renunciation must be based as a condition for liberation is only mediate, that is, "inducing (*prayojaka*) [to physical renunciation]" (BhG 5.5, 250). In his commentary on Sureśvara's BṛU *Vārttika,* Ānandagiri contrasts "direct realization of Reality" (*tattvasākṣātkaraṇa*) with "knowledge inducing [to physical renunciation and the discipline of knowledge]" (*prayojakajñāna*).[49] His comment on BhG 5.5 leaves no doubt that he expects *karmayogins* to adopt physical renunciation on the basis of their inducing knowledge: ". . . by means of renunciation preceded by true knowledge, by inducing knowledge, even *karmins* reach that state . . ."[50] In contrast with this interpretation, our contextualization shows that Śaṅkara's intention here is not to prescribe physical renunciation as a necessary step after the yoga of action, but to emphasize that liberation comes through a knowledge of the actionless Self, which is characterized by the inner renunciation of doership, even though that knowledge may be reached with the help of practices pertaining to the domain of action.

The understanding that physical renunciation is necessary for direct Self-knowledge also leads Ānandagiri to interpret Śaṅkara's descriptions of physical renunciation accompanied by direct Self-knowledge in the sense of physical renunciation as a requirement for the discipline of knowledge. This again undermines the possibility that one attains liberation without physical renunciation. Towards the end of his comment on ChU 2.23.1, Śaṅkara says that when the householder attains the knowledge of Unity, wandering mendicancy naturally follows. We saw that he means here a direct Self-knowledge. But Ānandagiri sees it only as renunciation of the seeker-after-liberation: "Mediate knowledge of unity is intended here. Because immediate [Self-knowledge] is not possible without wandering mendicancy. It must be viewed in this manner because *Śruti* states that the latter [wandering mendicancy]—called *uparati*—is as much a means as are control of senses and so forth."[51]

We showed that according to Śaṅkara the ancient Brahmins who are said to renounce physically in BṛU 3.5.1 and 4.4.22 were already enlightened, and that they provide an archetypal model for seekers-after-liberation of later ages. However, in BṛU 3.5.1, Ānandagiri describes them as "possessing knowledge leading to enquiry [into *Brahman*]."[52] His position is further elaborated in his comment on Śaṅkara's BṛU 4.4.15. In this passage, Śaṅkara refers to verse 4.4.22 as follows:

> It has been explained that, since ancient men of knowledge, undesirous of progeny, renounced because they held the Self to be their world, their wandering mendicancy comes simply from their knowledge of the world of the Self. Similarly it is proven that the seeker-after-knowledge also can take up wandering mendicancy, because of the statement "desiring this world alone they go on wandering." And we said that rites are addressed to the one who is devoid of [adequate] knowledge [concerning the Self].[53]

Here the already enlightened person is understood to renounce physically as a result of his own direct Self-knowledge, "even without prescription"[54] as specified by Śaṅkara. This is a leitmotif of Śaṅkara's works: the physical renunciation of the man of direct Self-knowledge (*vidvas*) does not come under the jurisdiction of injunctions. But the seeker-after-liberation can also renounce physically out of his desire to know the Self and according to the scriptural prescription. And one who does not even know the Self properly from the intellectual viewpoint—or somehow, should we add, lacks any of the requirements to engage in full-time practice of the discipline of knowledge—is enjoined rites for the purification of his mind. Thus, Śaṅkara distinguishes only two types of renunciation: one which does not depend on an injunction—that of the enlightened—and one which does depend on a prescription—that of the seeker-after-liberation.

Ānandagiri departs from Śaṅkara when he upholds *two* types of unprescribed physical renunciation, that of the man of mediate Self-knowledge—such as the ancient Brahmins of the BṛU—and that of the already liberated person:

> Direct Self-realization is proven to be the sole cause of liberation on the support, already stated, of the [corpus of] reasoning such as the understanding that Self-knowledge leads to immortality. Therefore—because performance of rites is inapplicable to the liberated-in-life—wandering mendicancy which consists of abandonment of all actions follows *without the need of sanction from an authority* [55] (*pramāṇāpekṣām antareṇa*) on the sole ground that a person is doing efforts for obtaining that [knowledge], has studied the *Vedas*, understood the verbal meaning and has indirect knowledge. This is renunciation-of-the-knower (*vidvatsaṃnyāsa*). But for one who has immediate [Self-] knowledge, there is nothing to perform except accepting the results [of actions] which have started to come to fruition. This is the idea.[56]

First, a notable feature of this description is that the expression "renunciation-of-the-knower" (*vidvatsaṃnyāsa*) denotes only the physical renunciation of the man of mediate Self-knowledge. The renunciation of the already enlightened is left unnamed, as if unapplicable even to the present context which refers to the ancient knowers of *Brahman*. This is one of the ways Ānandagiri manages to develop his categories of renunciation in a seemingly faithful manner, while departing quite significantly from Śaṅkara's statement. Second, the interpretation proposed here by him is untenable from Śaṅkara's viewpoint. Because physical renunciation is *prescribed* under the authority of scriptures as a subsidiary for maturation of knowledge, it applies precisely to a person who wants his indirect Self-knowledge to ripen into a direct one. So it is useless to imagine a category of renunciation in which physical abandonment of rites by the seeker-after-liberation is beyond the scope of scriptural authority. Moreover, if the mediate Self-knowledge that Ānandagiri refers to here is what it should be, in other words, if it is correct and detailed, it must obviously include the understanding that scriptures prescribe physical renunciation for the Brahmin who has acquired this mediate Self-knowledge. Thus, the means consisting of renunciation addressed to one with mediate Self-knowledge is known by him and considered authoritative on the basis of scriptures, not out of his personal opinion.

Since, in Ānandagiri's classification, renunciation-of-the-knower (*vidvatsaṃnyāsa*) is already attributed to the man of mediate knowledge—in place of the enlightened man from Śaṅkara's viewpoint—renunciation-of-the-seeker-after-knowledge (*vividiṣāsaṃnyāsa*)—which is meant for any qualified seeker-after-liberation according to Śaṅkara—must be ascribed to a man without mediate knowledge. When Śaṅkara states that "the seeker-after-knowledge (*vividiṣu*) also can take up renunciation" he means that, whatever the depth of his mediate knowledge, any qualified seeker-after-liberation can adopt physical renunciation for the sake of converting his Self-knowledge into a direct experience. But in order to complete his categorization of renunciation, Ānandagiri must contrast his "knowing" renouncer (*vidvatsaṃnyāsin*) endowed with a mediate knowledge—that is, correct, detailed and object of a deep conviction—with a seeking renouncer (*vividiṣusaṃnyāsin*) who has only *general* knowledge of the Self:

> A seeker-after-knowledge is one who has studied the *Veda*, who is endowed with a general knowledge [about the Self] leading him to further enquire, who desires liberation, that is, who looks for direct realization of Reality as the means of liberation. He is said to lack even mediate conviction concerning this.[57]

One of Ānandagiri's justifications for that type of renunciation is that direct Self-knowledge is unattainable without physical renunciation:

> Saying that it is not possible to prohibit abandonment of rites when the desire to know has arisen, he establishes the validity of renunciation-of-the-seeker-after-knowledge. This is connected with wandering mendicancy. It concerns only the men of [general Self-] knowledge who wish to attain direct realization of the Self and who have mediate [knowledge] of it. A [general] understanding of the world of the Self inducing renunciation is also mediate [Self-knowledge]. For, if it were the other [direct Self-knowledge], it would be improper, on the part of one who has reached the stage of the final achievement, to adopt renunciation and the like; and because without the latter, it is impossible to reach that [final achievement].[58]

Thus, in order to do away with the inconsistency between the understanding that physical renunciation is necessary for the discipline of knowledge and the possibility that the model for physical renunciation come from people who attained direct Self-knowledge without—or before—physical renunciation, Ānandagiri is led to interpretations which deviate from Śaṅkara's position on renunciation.

Curiously, this way of understanding Śaṅkara didn't prevent Ānandagiri to acknowledge elsewhere in his subcommentaries that one who has not physically renounced can also have access to the discipline of knowledge and attain liberation. The discipline of knowledge seems also available for householders as is suggested in his comment on *Gītā* 3.20 stating that Janaka and others attained perfection without physically abandoning rites: "He says that even though the man of discrimination who also has control over his senses can always remain in *Brahman* by means of hearing and so forth, yet, being a *Kṣatriya*, you should not abandon the prescribed rites."[59] Ānanadagiri also appears closer to Śaṅkara when he recognizes both the possibilities of liberation without physical renunciation and the importance of the latter in strengthening the path to enlightenment: "Doubt: If both the householder and the renouncer can experience liberation, then what if any is the use of the troublesome renunciation? Reply: Because of the possibility of obstacles for those who are not renouncers, renunciation is desirable for the seeker-after-liberation."[60] We saw earlier Ānandagiri's defence of Gārgī's and Janaka's attainment of enlightenment without physical renunciation in his comment on MuU 3.2.4. Similarly, when Śaṅkara evokes *Gītā* 3.20, Ānandagiri does not object to the possibility of liberation for a householder: "Even though the knowers of Reality engaged in rites by virtue of the operation of their senses towards objects, they were liberated through knowledge alone."[61]

Although, as a commentator of all the authentic works of Śaṅkara, Ānandagiri was in a good position not only to attempt a coherent answer to the pending questions in the master's works, but also to point out the misinterpretations of the previous subcommentators, he did not try to organize the whole conception of renunciation into a really consistent picture. Perhaps for him the notion of *mukhya* and *amukhya* qualification for Self-knowledge and liberation was enough to take care of the apparent contradictions. But, as a whole, Ānandagiri's comments failed in accounting for Śaṅkara's position on renunciation and probably deepened the gap between physical renouncers and others on the path to complete Self-knowledge.

VIDYĀRAṆYA

Vidyāraṇya lived during the fourteenth century, one or two generations after Ānandagiri. Vidyāraṅya's authorship of various works is still controversial (Mahadevan 1938, 1975; Mishra 1992). But there is no evidence so far that the four works quoted below which are usually attributed to Vidyāraṇya and which contain his basic position on renunciation, would be from a different author.

According to Karl H. Potter, Vidyāraṇya was the main protagonist concerning the misunderstanding about Śaṅkara's view on renunciation.

Our findings bring us to an almost opposite conclusion. An original thinker indeed, Vidyāraṇya proposed some unusual interpretations which clearly depart from Śaṅkara with respect to specific aspects of renunciation. But he proved to be quite in agreement with Śaṅkara's perspective as far as the essentials are concerned, namely, qualification for Self-knowledge and for liberation.

In his *Bṛhadāraṇyakavārttikasāra*, a subcommentary on Sureśvara's *Vārttika*, Vidyāraṇya defines *uparati* in a way unheard of before him: "*Uparati* is the understanding that the [ultimate] goal of man is not attained through action."[62] This would rather be included in the second of the fourfold requirement for the discipline of knowledge, namely, the disinterest for the enjoyment of rewards [of rites] in this life and hereafter. But this definition already suggests that Vidyāraṇya does not hold physical renunciation to be necessary for the discipline of knowledge. He actually conveys in the most unequivocal way that both the latter as well as liberation are accessible to people who have not renounced physically:

> The *Smṛti* prescribes steadfastness in knowledge to the householder for the sake of liberation even when it is accompanied by other practices. His wealth honestly acquired, steadfast in the knowledge of Reality, pleasing his guests, performing the *śrāddha* [sacrifice to ancestors], speaking the truth, the householder also is liberated (Ibid., 4.4.428–429, 957).

Vidyāraṇya's position is very well summarized in six verses from his *Anubhūtiprakāśa*, a collection of commentaries on various *Upaniṣads*.[63] The author first makes it clear that, whatever one's mode of living, one can fully know the Self:

> When by way of rites the obstacle which causes disinterest [in Self-knowledge] is removed, one can realize the Self through scriptures whether one is a householder or a wandering mendicant. Otherwise, Janaka, Uṣasta, Gārgī and others wouldn't have acquired knowledge (Vidyāraṇya 1992, 18.304-305, 714).

Yet Vidyāraṇya specifies that physical renunciation makes this realization easier as it allows full-time dedication to the means: "But [knowledge] is easily [attained] by the wandering mendicant, as he is free from numerous mental distractions."[64] Unlike many others before him, Vidyāraṇya does not start with the assumption that physical renunciation is a *sine qua non* for the discipline of knowledge or liberation. Yet he does not underestimate its value. His position is elaborated in the following verse:[65] "When, not even minding the distractions of rites, the householder is able to be mentally one-pointed, he can also know [the *Brahman*]. Otherwise, he must renounce."[66]

Thus, for Vidyāraṇya, physical renunciation is neither a requirement for the discipline of knowledge nor a way to obtain an indispensible unseen potency (*apūrva*). It simply serves in intensifying a practice which may very well have been started in other modes of living. But the author does not address the hermeneutical problem raised by the fact that if the subsidiary of physical renunciation is not used by the one for whom it is prescribed, then it will be missing and will therefore disallow the ripening of all the other means into their result, namely, liberation. Vidyāraṇya chooses to solve the issue in a practical way rather than through the hermeneutical apparatus: physical renunciation becomes indispensable only when one cannot overcome distractions. Thus, he proposes an interpretation unheard of from both Śaṅkara and previous *Advaitins*. Even then, he seems to capture Śaṅkara's basic position better than all other *Advaitins* before him. The statement that one can attain liberation through Self-knowledge applies universally, irrespective of modes of living, while the statement enjoining physical renunciation as a subsidiary to knowledge applies in a specific case only: "Hence the statement 'having known [this alone, one becomes a sage]' is a general one. And the statement '[desiring this world alone the abandoners] abandon everything' is a specific one."[67] The difference between Śaṅkara and Vidyāraṇya is that the master understands the specific case to be that of the Brahmin seeker-after-liberation, while the disciple views it as that of *any* seeker-after-liberation who is incapable of one-pointedness, owing to distractions connected with his way of living.

Vidyāraṇya then gives one more justification for physical renunciation. Verse 306 stated that if one cannot attain knowledge of *Brahman* because of distractions, one has to adopt physical renunciation. Now the author adds that if, even after acquiring the knowledge of *Brahman*, one is not able to make it a permanent direct experience, then one should also take recourse to physical renunciation:

> To know is to apprehend once. To be a sage is to have sustained knowledge. Knowledge removes nescience; being a sage brings about liberation-in-life. When one knows yet without being a sage, one must take up renunciation-of-the-knower.[68]

While Śaṅkara considered Self-knowledge open to everyone but physical renunciation accessible only to Brahmins, Vidyāraṇya makes both

Self-knowledge and physical renunciation accessible to all, including women. Referring to the dialogue between Janaka and the female mendicant Sulabhā in the *Mahābhārata*, he concludes in his *Jīvanmuktiviveka* that women also can study the *Upaniṣads*, adopt the monastic mode of living, carry the emblems of renunciation such as the triple staff, and meditate in seclusion (Vidyāraṇya 1978, 182). But in his *Bṛhadāraṇyakavārttikasāra* and his *Anubhūtiprakāśa*, the author brings some qualifications to his statement, as he tries to show that Śaṅkara himself held this view. There he holds that Śaṅkara disallowed non-Brahmins to adopt the mode of living of renunciation (*saṃnyāsāśrama*)—which is entered *formally*, through a ritual of renunciation, and involves carrying some conventional emblems—but he did not forbid *informal* physical renunciation to anybody:

> Noticing the use of the word "Brahmin" by the *Śruti*, Śaṅkara says that Brahmins alone are qualified for renunciation in the sense of the fourth mode of living. [However], even for Gārgī and Vidura, a woman and a *Śūdra*, Śaṅkara accepts renunciation respectively as a subsidiary to knowledge and as [leading to] the result of the latter [i.e., to liberation].[69]

So when Vidyāraṇya says that "renunciation alone is the best means of liberation for everyone,"[70] he means that, whatever their gender, *varṇa* and mode of living, all have access to physical informal renunciation. But while Śaṅkara distinguished between physical renunciation as a mere means of living and as a subsidiary to Self-knowledge, he never proposed, as Vidyāraṇya does, two types of physical renunciation serving as subsidiaries to knowledge, one being formal—that is, involving the fourth mode of living with all its rules—and the other being informal. On the contrary, as we saw, it is while being presented as part and parcel of the fourth mode of living that physical renunciation is introduced by Śaṅkara as a subsidiary to Self-knowedge.[71] Even if Vidyāraṇya had merely stated what Śaṅkara left understood, there is no ground to see physical renunciation as necessary in his view, since informal physical renunciation is not even prescribed.

Vidyāraṇya distinguishes three major types of physical renunciation: renunciation-of-the-knower (*vidvatsaṃnyāsa*), renunciation-of-the-seeker (*vividiṣāsaṃnyāsa*)—which can both be formal or informal—and physical renunciation as a mere mode of living (*saṃnyāsāśrama*)—where one has not abandoned the desire for the heaven of the Golden Womb and still meditates on it (Vidyāraṇya 1919, 3.5.59–61, 702). Vidyāraṇya probably borrowed his basic understanding of renunciation-of-the-knower and renunciation-of-the-seeker from Ānandagiri. Renunciation-of-the-seeker is for one who has only general knowledge (*āpātajñāna*) about the Self (Vidyāraṇya 1919, 3.5.49, 701), and has not started or mastered the discipline of knowledge. Renunciation-of-the-knower is for one who has already been through the discipline of knowedge: "Renunciation-of-the-knower is carried out by those who have come to know the supreme Reality through proper practice of hearing, reflection, and meditation."[72] But these Self-knowers have not yet converted their discursive knowledge into experience: "And the person qualified for this [renunciation] is one who knows the Reality, [but] is distracted by worldly affairs and wishes for peace of mind."[73] At various places, Vidyāraṇya presents renunciation-of-the-seeker as a means to attain precise and full Self-knowledge, and renunciation-of-the-knower as a means to attain the result of immediate and permanent Self-knowledge, that is, liberation-in-life:[74] "Renunciation of rites is twofold, one relating to the result, the other to the means. The abandonment of the knower is for the result, that of the seeker is for the attainment of knowledge."[75]

According to Vidyāraṇya, hearing, reflection, and meditation are the practices provided in the context of renunciation-of-the-seeker; but the aspirant qualified for renunciation-of-the-knower is to pursue the yogic practices consisting of "dissolution of the mind" (*manonāśa*) and "obliteration of latent desires" (*vāsanākṣaya*) (Vidyāraṇya 1978, 186-187). Unfound in Śaṅkara's works, these terms were borrowed from the *Yogavāsiṣṭha* (ninth–thirteenth century), a philosophical poem often quoted in the *Jīvanmuktiviveka*. In Vidyāraṇya's eyes, the usual *Advaita* discipline of knowledge does not seem to be enough to bring about permanent direct Self-knowledge. It has to be followed by the practice of yoga, leading to direct experience of the Self in the absorption without mental cognition (*asaṃprajñātasamādhi*): "Hearing and so forth are the means for knowing the Reality; yoga is the means for 'dissolving the mind.' "[76] The addition of yoga apart from the discipline of knowledge is obviously foreign to Śaṅkara. For the author of the BS, *nididhyāsana* (meditation) was in itself the yogic aspect of the discipline of knowledge, that is, the practice capable of ripening a merely discursive knowledge about the Self into its direct experience. Thus, the discipline of knowledge comprised all the necessary means to lead the aspirant to liberation. But somehow, for Vidyāraṇya, the usual discipline of knowledge does not seem to be enough to calm down the mind and bring it to the experience of the actionless Self. Hence, as he writes, yoga "is superior even to [mediate Self-] knowledge because it is a [more] proximate subsidiary [of experience] in comparison to [mediate Self-] knowledge, and it is the means to pacify the mind."[77] Yoga leads to the absorption without mental cognition (*asaṃprajñātasamādhi*). And, according to Vidyāraṇya, this absorption is indispensable to eliminate the obstacles to the direct and permanent knowledge of the Self: "Therefore, even for one who knows the Reality, absorption without mental cognition is really necessary to eradicate the causes of 'afflictions.' "[78] Perhaps at the time of Vidyāraṇya the *Advaita* practitioners of the discipline of knowledge had come to overemphasize its intellectual content and to neglect its own yogic practices. In all cases, the goal surely remains the same for Vidyāraṇya and Śaṅkara: the permanent experience of the Self as actionless and non-dual.

Vidyāraṇya also understands that one qualified for renunciation-of-the-knower may have had flashes of direct experience of the Self even before his renunciation. He suggests that the ancient Brahmins of *Bṛhadāraṇyaka Upaniṣad* 3.5.1 and 4.4.22 had already tasted direct Self-knowledge: " 'This world,' means that it is experienced directly."[79] Yet these ancient Brahmins felt the need to make it a permanent experience through renunciation-of-the-knower (Vidyāraṇya 1978, 185–186).[80] In this context liberation-in-life is seen as the result of a safeguard of direct Self-knowledge, for "even though knowledge of Reality may have arisen before, it is well preserved by liberation-in-life."[81] Therefore, "the first purpose of liberation-in-life is to safeguard knowledge."[82]

Vidyāraṇya's interpetation of passages such as those relating to the ancient Brahmins is shaped by these categories of renunciation. Like Śaṅkara, he sees in the physical renunciation of the ancient Brahmin knowers a model for others to imitate in order to reach the same level of knowledge: "Let it be understood here that because renunciation is a characteristic of one in whom right knowledge has arisen, it is also a means for its rise" (Vidyāraṇya 1992, 17.155, 585).[83] But Vidyāraṇya equates the renunciation of the ancient Brahmins to *his* renunciation-of-the-knower—based on mediate knowledge—and the renunciation of their followers to *his* renunciation-of-the-seeker—based on general knowledge (Vidyāraṇya 1978, 183–187). Similarly, according to Vidyāraṇya, Yājñavalkya was not liberated before his physical renunciation, unlike Janaka who acheived liberation-in-life[84] without the need of physical renunciation. Since he wished to attain this state, Yājñavalkya took up physical renunciation as a means to get rid of the distractions of the householder mode of living (Vidyāraṇya 1992, 15.5, 500),[85] to eradicate his impure latent impressions and to make his mind abide in quiescence (Vidyāraṇya 1978, 286–288).[86]

According to Vidyāraṇya, in principle, everyone can qualify for Self-knowledge and yoga, whatever one's *varṇa* and mode of living. In practice, however, only full-time practice of yoga can be considered as the "real" yoga. After explaining how one can gradually increase the time spent on yoga, Vidyāraṇya adds that complete dedication to yoga is incompatible with other activities, "because only one who has given up all other activities is qualified for yoga."[87] It is for this, he adds, that renunciation-of the-knower is required. Perhaps it is also from this viewpoint that, in a way which reminds us of Ānandagiri, the author uses the expression "fully qualified" when referring to the Self-knower of BṛU 4.4.23 who, according to him, would become completely absorbed in yogic practices after having first acquired discursive Self-knowledge: "Desirous [of liberation], endowed with control of mind, control of senses and so forth, the renouncer of actions, being fully qualified, sees the Self in the self."[88] These statements, like those of Ānandagiri, are surely ambiguous, as they make householders and others only "partially" qualified. But since, unlike Ānandagiri, Vidyāraṇa is uncompromizing and explicit about the universal accessibility of Self-knowledge and liberation, this kind of statement probably aims at *emphasizing physical renunciation in spite of the fact that it is not necessary*. And such an attitude brings Vidyāraṇya quite close to Śaṅkara. Thus, Vidyāraṇya's restrictions on qualification do not seem to preclude sincere aspirants from acquiring Self-knowledge, practicing yoga and attaining liberation—even when, for whatever reason, full-time dedication to these means is impossible.

Deeply convinced of the universal accessibility to Self-knowledge and liberation, with or without physical renunciation, Vidyāraṇya recaptured Śaṅkara's basic position on renunciation, though sometimes deviating in terms of specifics. Innovative, consistent and faithful to Śaṅkara on the essentials, Vidyāraṇya provided an outstanding contribution to renunciation in the *Advaita* tradition.

MADHUSŪDANA SARASVATĪ

According to Madhusūdana Sarasvatī (around 1500–1550), liberation is accessible to everyone, irrespective of *varṇas* and other sociоritual conditions. He specifies, for instance, on the use of the word "man" (*mānava*) in *Gītā* 3.17: "Man" is to indicate that any man as such can accomplish the goal, not by way of the superior status of the Brahmin and so forth" (BhG 3.17, 156). Whether he has physically renounced before or after enlightenment, the liberated-in-life can be called a renouncer in the most authentic sense of the term:

> And the supreme renunciation is indeed the direct realization of the self as a non-doer. Although Janaka and others belonged to this type of renouncer . . . their being seen involved in rites is as free from contradiction as wandering mendicancy and so forth on the part of *Paramahaṃsas* with the same type [of inner renunciation].[89]

Madhusūdana also strictly follows Śaṅkara as far as the qualification for physical renunciation is concerned. He rejects Sureśvara's opinion on this in no deferential way: "Understanding that to be the Lord's position, the revered Śaṅkara established that Brahmins alone—and nobody else—are qualified for renunciation. And it should be known that Sureśvara's statement that *Kṣatriyas* and *Vaiśyas* can also renounce is mere arrogant speech."[90] At several places in the *Gūḍārthadīpikā,* his commentary on the *Gītā,* Madhusūdana presents physical renunciation as a step to be taken before entering the discipline of knowledge, without mentioning how non-Brahmins may also attain Self-knowledge and liberation. In the versified introduction of the same work—a summary of the *Gītā*'s teaching highlighting especially the path to be followed for liberation—he includes physical renunciation as part of the fourfold requirement of the discipline of knowledge without additional comments about those who are not qualified for it. After mentioning the first two requirements, he pursues: "Then the acquisition of control of mind and so forth surely leads to renunciation. The abandonment of everything strenghtens the desire for liberation. Then one approaches the master and receives instruction."[91] The author does not mention the word *uparati* and therefore does not equate it explicitely with physical renunciation. But the fact that the latter is placed in the sequence *before* the fourth requirement, namely, a strong desire for liberation, suggests that *uparati* has the value of physical renunciation from the author's point of viewpoint.[92] This is actually confirmed by another passage which describes the third requirement as "control of mind, control of senses and cessation of all rites" (*śamadamasarvakarmoparama*) before approaching the master (BhG 18.10, 687).

Madhusūdhana does not try to reconcile explicitly the universal accessibility of liberation through Self-knowledge, the interpretation that *uparati* as physical renunciation is required for the discipline of knowledge, and the fact that Brahmins alone have access to it. Yet he specifies that "even though renunciation of all actions is not possible for a *Kṣatriya,* his qualification for knowledge still holds good."[93] Madhusūdana gives as exemples non-Brahmins, such as Janaka, who had access to the discipline of knowledge without physical renunciation: "Even though *Kṣatriyas, such as Janaka,* were knowers, that is, Janaka, Ajātaśatru and others, who are well-known from the *Śruti, Smṛti* and *Purāṇas,* they *reached,* they attained, *perfection,* that is, steadfastness in knowledge which is attainable by way of hearing and so forth, *through action alone,* without giving up rites" (BhG 3.20, 159).

But it is only towards the end of his commentary on the *Gītā* that Madhusūdana presents his whole view on the issue of non-Brahmins. Commenting on verse 18.63, he mentions that after attaining purity of mind and the desire to know *Brahman,* the Brahmin takes up physical renunciation in order to start enquiry (*vicāra*) into the Vedāntic scriptures. Madhusūdana then tries to account for the non-brahmins, referring to *Kṣatriyas,* such as, Arjuna or Janaka:

> On the other hand, even after purifying their mind, *Ksatriyas* and others who seek after liberation but are not qualified for renunciation, somehow or other continue to perform rites for the purpose of carrying out the orders of the Lord and guiding people. Yet, since they take the Lord as their sole refuge, they attain liberation either out of the maturation resulting from renunciation and so forth as adopted in a previous life or, without depending on that [maturation], on the analogy of the Golden Womb, through awakening to the knowledge of Reality in this life only by the Lord's grace,[94] or by being reborn as a Brahmin in the next life and awakening to knowledge after renunciation and so forth.[95]

It is significant that in this explanation Madhusūdana resorts to the principle of renunciation in a previous life or in a future one, or to the grace of God, but he does not mention the obvious reason that they could attain liberation through part-time practice of the discipline of knowledge. So even though Madhusūdana insists that non-Brahmins can attain liberation without physical renunciation, he still seems reluctant to grant real emancipating efficiency to the discipline of knowledge, that is, the most proximate means of knowledge, outside the context of physical renunciation. While these are clearly said by the scriptures to be the means of direct Self-knowledge, whether practiced full-time or not, Madhusūdana prefers to refer to unseen causes such as the grace of God and previous or future lives.

A similar passage is found with respect to verse 5.5 of the *Gītā* which declares that the state of liberation is reached by both followers of *Sāṃkhya* and *yogins.* Here Śaṅkara recalls that followers of *Sāṃkhya* are physical renouncers and that *yogins* continue to perform rites. Now, Madhusūdana comments the verse as if *yogins* could reach liberation only with physical renunciation. He writes that they will attain liberation only after they have adopted renunciation in this life or a future one: "Even *yogins* reach that state in this life through purity of mind, through steadfastness in knowledge connected with hearing and so forth, and preceded by renunciation in this life or a future one."[96] But this interpretation disagrees with the meaning of the verse as interpreted by Śaṅkara. If *yogins* have to renounce physically for liberation, then it means that they have to become followers of *Sāṃkhya*. Then the *Gītā*'s statement—in verse 5.5—that *yogins* also can attain liberation would be useless, which is untenable for all these commentators.

In his comment on *Gītā* 18.49, Madhusūdana even seems to contradict himself on the matter of qualification for Self-knowledge by suggesting that the physical renouncer is the only person qualified for reading the *Brahmasūtra*:

> Such a wandering mendicant (*paramahaṃsaparivrājaka*) alone—presented in the *Śruti* passage "the one established in *Brahman* attains immortality" as being different from people belonging to the three divisions of *dharma*—is capable of reflecting on the *Vedānta* statements after having approached the master—a wandering mendicant who has achieved the goal. *It is for him*[97] that the *Brahmasūtra* starting with "Hence thereafter a deliberation on *Brahman*" has been written by the revered Bādarāyaṇa.[98]

Madhusūdana's tendency to view physical renunciation as a sine qua non also shows in the fact that, commenting on Sarvajñātman's *Saṃkṣepaśārīraka*, he does not question the author's recourse to the principle of the unseen potency (*apūrva*): he neither points out that this cannot even apply to non-Brahmins, nor tries to account for the latter (Madhusūdana Sarasvatī 3.357–360, 348–351).

Madhusūdana's assumption about physical renunciation is reflected in his interpretation of the householder's sequence toward liberation given by Śaṅkara in his BhG. From Śaṅkara's viewpoint, this sequence applies to every householder, whether a Brahmin or a non-Brahmin, even though physical renunciation mentioned after enlightenment may not always be actualized. We saw that this sequence can be consistent with Śaṅkara's position only if the step of attainment of Self-knowledge (*jñānaprāpti*) is already direct in nature. But here, for Madhusūdana (BhG 5.12, 257), attainment of knowledge consists only of discrimination between the eternal and the ephemeral (*nityānityavastuviveka*), the first of the fourfold requirement for entry into the discipline of knowledge. While, in Śaṅkara's viewpoint on the householder's sequence, renunciation of all actions is already based on direct Self-knowledge, for Madhusūdana, it precedes full-time absorption in the discipline of knowledge. Thus, from Madhusūdana's perspective, the sequence amounts to: the yoga of action, attainment of purity of mind, "renunciation of all actions, following which knowledge of Reality arises in one who devotes himself to hearing and so forth" (BhG 5.27, 276).

Madhusūdana's misunderstanding of Śaṅkara culminates in his refutation of the master's interpretation of *Gītā* 18.66. The verse reads: "Having abandoned all *dharmas*, take me as your sole refuge. I will free you from all sins. Do not grieve" (BhG, 752). Śaṅkara first specifies that "here the word *dharma* includes wrong actions (*adharma*)" (Ibid.). Thus, in this context, Śaṅkara means by *dharma* and *adharma* right and wrong actions respectively. The same use is found in BhG 9.2 where Śaṅkara states that the knowledge of *Brahman* is the best purifier "because in one instant it reduces to ashes action along with its roots, that is, right actions, wrong actions and so forth (*dharmādharmādi*), which have been accumulated over many thousand births" (BhG 9.2, 411). After quoting, in his BhG 18.66, two passages concerning the abandonment of right and wrong actions, Śaṅkara concludes, "having renounced all *dharmas* means having renounced all actions."[99]

Madhusūdana interprets Śaṅkara's statement simply as a prescription of physical renunciation. And since the adressee of the verse—Arjuna—is a *Kṣatriya*, he finds objection to this objectless injunction. According to Madhusūdana, if the prescription of this verse is to be relevant to Arjuna, it must rule out the possibility that "having abandoned all *dharmas*" means "having physically renounced rites," or "having physically renounced rites as well as wrong actions." It must be complementary to "take me as your sole refuge" and must enjoin indifference to rites rather than giving them up physically:

> Since "take me as your sole refuge" conveys by itself the abandonment of one's refuge in all right actions (*dharma*), the reiteration of the prohibition "having abandoned all duties (*dharma*)" is intended for obtaining that [the Lord] be the cause of [all] actions. . . . That is to say, there is no need of duties (*dharma*) for one who takes refuge in Me, since I am the cause of all prescribed actions. This sets aside the interpretation that because the statement "having abandoned all duties (*dharmas*)" does not convey [literally] the abandonment of wrong actions, the word *dharma* must refer [figuratively] to all actions. It is not abandonment of rites that is prescribed here. What is prescribed is simply taking the Lord as one's sole refuge by being indifferent to rites and duties (*karman*) even as they continue to be performed—which applies universally to students, householders, hermits, and mendicants. "Having abandoned all duties (*dharma*)"

> serves in preventing the possibility that they regard [them] as their own duty (*dharma*). Since wrong action (*adharma*) results in misfortunes, nobody has regard for it. Therefore prescription of its abandonment is simply meaningless. Also because it is [already] met with in other scriptures.[100]

Interestingly, in contrast with Madhusūdana, Ānandagiri understands that "having abandoned all duties (*dharma*)" means physical renunciation as a prelude to the discipline of knowledge. In trying to conciliate this prescription with the fact that it is addressed to a *Kṣatriya*, he proposes the following interpretation: "Since Arjuna is a *Ksatriya*, he is not really qualified for steadfastness in knowledge by way of [physical] renunciation as stated here. In spite of this, since this [steadfastness] is advisable to those who are qualified, Kṛṣṇa uses him as an incidental addressee and, without contradicting himself, says . . ."[101] Madhusūdana clearly rejects this view by pointing out that in this section of the chapter Kṛṣṇa consistently addresses Arjuna alone: "But if the instruction were destined to someone else in the guise of Arjuna, the beginning and the end would not be 'I will tell *you* what is good' [18.64], and 'I will free *you* from all sins. Do not grieve' " [18.66].[102]

At the end of his commentary on this verse, Madhusūdana finally decides to express overtly his disagreement with Śaṅkara. While Śaṅkara writes that the *Gītā* teaches two types of steadfastness, one in action and the other in Self-knowledge, Madhusūdana adds steadfastness in devotion (*bhakti*) as the culmination of these two. He then holds that in this verse Kṛṣṇa concludes the theme of the universally accessible steadfastness in devotion that he developed earlier in various places. And, after boldly disagreeing on this issue with the great master of *Advaita Vedānta*, Madhusūdana finds refuge in humility:

> Now, here, at the end [of the *Gītā*], the statement "having abandoned all duties, take me as your sole refuge" sums up steadfastness in devotion to the Lord as being the means and the result of both [steadfastness in action and in knowledge]. But since, for Śaṅkara, "having abandoned all duties" reiterates [the prescription of] renunciation of all rites (*karman*), he holds that "take me as your sole refuge" sums up steadfastness in knowledge. Who am I, a layman, to delineate the intention of the Lord?[103]

Now, the main question for us is: by renunciation of all actions (*sarvakarmasaṃnyāsa*) does Śaṅkara really mean here renunciation of all rites as a prelude to the discipline of knowledge? Or does he intend a different meaning? A closer look at the rest of his commentary on this verse provides indications that he does point out to a different meaning.

First, Śaṅkara explains that *dharma* includes *adharma* "because it is *naiṣkarmya* (actionlessness) that is meant" (BhG, 752). Now, in verse 18.49, he interprets *naiṣkarmya* as actionlessness based on direct Self-knowledge: "Such a Self-knower *attains*, reaches, the perfection of actionlessness (*naiṣkarmyasiddhi*). One from whom actions have disapeared on account of his perfect knowledge of the Self as the actionless *Brahman* is actionless. *Naiṣkarmya* is the state of the one who is actionless. Actionlessness and the perfection identical with that [actionlessness] is the perfection of actionlessness (*naiṣkarmyasiddhi*)."[104] Indeed, no one can live this "perfection" consisting of actionlessness without directly experiencing the actionless Self. Śaṅkara then gives another explanation which still views *naiṣkarmya* as actionlessness based on direct Self-knowledge: "Or [perfection of actionlessness] is the perfection, *i.e.*, the consummation, of actionlessness which consists of the original state of the actionless Self. *He attains . . . that perfection of actionlessness which is supreme*, superior, different from any perfection resulting from action, and equivalent to the state of immediate liberation."[105]

Further in his comment on verse 18.66, Śaṅkara states that taking the Lord as one's sole refuge should be accompanied by the knowledge that one is the Lord himself. He then adds: "When your knowledge of this becomes resolute, by revealing my true nature as your own self, *I will free you from all sins*, which consist of the bondage of all right and wrong actions."[106] Now, in Śaṅkara's comment on *Gītā* 4.41 one finds a very similar description which provides further evidence that in Śaṅkara's equation between renunciation of all actions and abandonment of right and wrong actions (*dharma* and *adharma*), both imply direct Self-knowledge. The verse reads: "O Dhanaṃjaya, actions do not bind one who has renounced all actions by yoga, whose doubts have been driven asunder by knowledge and who is vigilant" (238). Śaṅkara comments as follows:

> One *who has renounced actions through yoga*, the perceiver of the supreme truth who has renounced actions, namely, right and wrong actions (*dharmādharma*), through yoga, which consists of the perception of the supreme truth. . . . *Whose doubts have been driven asunder by knowledge*, whose doubts have been driven asunder by knowledge consisting of the realization of the unity of the self with Īśvara.[107]

Because the verse puts forward the idea that the Self-knower is not bound by action, the perception (*darśana*) of the supreme truth referred to here by Śaṅkara must be direct in nature. And the abandonment of right and wrong actions (*dharmādharma*) which is said by Śaṅkara to follow that Self-knowledge must be based on it.

This understanding of *dharma* and *adharma* is also supported by other passages of Śaṅkara's commentary in chapter 18. Śaṅkara introduces verse 18.12 by asking: "Now what is the goal which results from the abandonment of all actions?" (690). The verse states that the results of actions do not accrue to renouncers, and Śaṅkara indicates (Ibid.) that here actions "consist of right and wrong actions" (*dharmādharmalakṣaṇa*). Then, in verse 18.17, he further specifies that this freedom from the results of action comes only to those who are without the sense of embodiment: "Thus when the sense of embodiment is impossible for renouncers, their complete renunciation of actions generated by ignorance is possible. Therefore it has been properly said that *the threefold result of actions—wrong actions* and so forth—*does not accrue* [to them] [18.12]."[108] The absence of the sense of embodiment is possible only through direct Self-knowledge. Freedom from embodiment and from the results of actions, whether *dharma* or *adharma*, is thus understood by Śaṅkara to depend on immediate Self-knowledge alone. Śaṅkara then remarks that "this sums up the teaching of the *Gītā* scripture" (BhG 18.17, 701). Since verse 18.66 is the last of the summary verses found in the *Gītā*, the correlation in Śaṅkara's understanding of the summaries of verses 18.17 and 18.66 suggests that, according to him, "having abandoned all *dharmas*" is coextensive with the direct Self-knowledge which frees one from all limitations of actions and of their results.

This interpretation is further supported by the fact that Śaṅkara often introduces freedom from *dharma* and *adharma* as a characteristic peculiar to the state of liberation-in-life. In BhG 4.23, he glosses the word "liberated" by "freed from the bondage of *dharma* and *adharma*" (215).[109] Similarly, when in the comment on verse 9.9, an opponent raises the doubt that Kṛṣṇa may be limited by *dharma* and *adharma*, Śaṅkara explains that because the Lord does not have the sense of being a doer, he is not bound. He then adds in the same vein concerning people who are liberated-in-life: "Hence for anyone else who has no sense of doership and no attachment to rewards, there is no cause of bondage."[110]

Therefore, what Śaṅkara means by "having abandoned *dharma* and *adharma*" in his BhG 18.66 is "having become free from the limitations of all actions, right or wrong." And this state is possible only through direct knowledge of one's identity with the Lord. That is also the essential condition of "renunciation of all actions" (*sarvakarmasaṃnyāsa*) when it includes all mental activity. Thus, when Śaṅkara equates the abandonment of right and wrong actions with renunciation of all actions, he does not mean by the latter mere physical abandonment of rites as a way to the discipline of knowledge. He rather points at that type of renunciation which alone liberates from the limitations of actions and of their results, that is, abandonment of doership—normally accompanied by the physical cessation of rites, which become completely unnecessary when one has attained liberation-in-life. And this meaning of renunciation of all actions is identical with that found in the householder's sequence leading to liberation as expressed earlier in his commentary. Even though it can include physical renunciation, renunciation of all actions occurs here only *after* attainment of direct Self-knowledge, and it may remain only mental for those who do not physically renounce for some reason or other. It can therefore apply to a *Kṣatriya* as a situation already achieved or to be achieved—the latter case being suitable to Arjuna who is still unenlightened.

Although Madhusūdana tried to provide a complete understanding of the path to enlightenment for people who do not renounce physically, his understanding was weakened by major instances of inconsistency. Isn't it ironical that he didn't recognize in the very founder of his tradition the liberal access to Self-knowledge and liberation that he himself defended at least in some places with a remarkable intellectual honesty? This may be seen as one more manifestation of the powerful hermeneutical influence which the implicit assumption of physical renunciation as a sine qua non for complete Self-knowledge had come to exert in the commentaries on Śaṅkara's works by the time of Madhusūdana Sarasvatī.

VĀCASPATI MIŚRA AND THE *BHĀMATĪ* SCHOOL

The most significant way Vācaspati Miśra and the *Bhāmatī* School differ from the prevailing trend in the *Vivaraṇa* School concerning renunciation is with respect to the concept of *uparati* or *uparama* as a requirement for the discipline of knowledge. In his *Bhāmatī* 1.1.1, Vācaspati Miśra indicates: "And in the word "and so forth" are included endurance of objects, withdrawal (*uparama*) from them and faith in Reality."[111] Vācaspati Miśra then quotes BṛU 4.4.23, which enumerates the other "qualities," but he doesn't elaborate further. Nevertheless, for him, the "quality" of *uparama* refers quite clearly to an inner withdrawal rather than to physical renunciation.

Vācaspati Miśra's interpretation of the requirements for the discipline of knowledge shows in the fact that the *Bhāmatī* School puts much less emphasis on physical renunciation and does not seem to hold that it is necessary for acquiring Self-knowledge and liberation. Allālasūri (fourteenth century) glosses Vācaspati's "withdrawal (*uparama*) from them" as "cessation of inclination towards objects of desire" (Allālasūri 1984, 99). As far as the other major subcommentaries are concerned, they do not gloss Vācaspati Miśra on *uparama*.[112] Thus, for the *Bhāmatī* School, the prerequisite quality of *uparati* does not seem to refer to physical renunciation.

The second most significant part of Śaṅkara's BS on physical renunciation is the comment on aphorism 3.4.20 where Śaṅkara explains in what sense, according to ChU 2.23, the man established in *Brahman* (*brahmasaṃstha*) alone is said to attain immortality. Vācaspati Miśra follows Śaṅkara's definition of "being established in *Brahman*." It means for him the exclusive focus on the practice of control of mind and so forth in the context of the renunciant's mode of living, as opposed to the partial focus available in the other modes of living due to the presence of additional duties such as rites:

> This is because the *dharma* consisting of being established in *Brahman* is the exclusive characteristic of the mendicant. Other modes of living are [at times] established in it and [at other times] not established in it. [But] the mendicant is surely established in it. . . . [Being established in *Brahman*] is suitable only for him who is established in it, and for no one else.[113]

Amalānanda's *Kalpataru* (Vācaspati Miśra 1982, 883–884) and *Śāstradarpaṇa* (Amalānanda 1913, 292–297) do not really add anything to this understanding.

Thus, in contrast with the prominent interpretation in the *Vivaraṇa* School, the *Bhāmatī* School does not make physical renunciation a necessary requirement for the discipline of knowledge. Both Vācaspati Miśra and Amalānanda accept that even people who have not taken recourse to physical renunciation have access to the discipline of knowledge. But none of these two authors tries to conciliate their conclusions about the "man established in *Brahman*" and the fact that, elsewhere in the scriptures, people are also said to reach liberation without physical renunciation and exclusive dedication to the discipline of knowledge. This apparent contradiction will be addressed by later sub-commentators of Amalānanda's *Kalpataru*, namely, Appaya Dīkṣita in his *Parimala* and Lakṣmīnṛsiṃha in his *Ābhoga*.

Appaya Dīkṣita's explanation evokes, first, in the case of human beings, physical renunciation in a previous life accompanied by its unseen potency and, second, in the case of gods, the absence of any need for it:

> Because on par with the result of the *citrā* sacrifice and the like, the result [of physical renunciation] has the characteristic of [extending to] the next world, a man who possesses the unseen potency created by renunciation in a previous life and who has done hearing and so forth while being a householder can also attain direct realization of *Brahman*. Therefore, the *Śruti* says that, early, when he was in the womb, even without having adopted renunciation, Vāmadeva reached direct realization. It is known from *Śruti* that even gods[114] and others who didn't even adopt renunciation attained direct realization and therefore liberation.[115]

For Lakṣmīnṛsiṃha, however, physical renunciation in a previous life appears as the universal justification for all cases of enlightenment without it in a given life:

> And it should not be argued that if renunciation is enjoined on a person desiring direct realization of *Brahman*, the fact that [men] like Vāmadeva and gods like Indra attained its direct realization becomes unexplainable. Given that [renunciation's] power to bring about direct realization in this life or in another is like that of the *citrā* sacrifice and so forth, it is possible for them to attain direct realization of the [*Brahman*] by way of a renunciation done in a previous life.[116]

Thus, although the *Bhāmatī* School does not overemphasize physical renunciation as did Sureśvara, Sarvajñātman and the *Vivaraṇa* School as a whole, its attempts at solving the ambiguities and apparent contradictions related to the prescription of renunciation are rather unconvincing. Moreover, at least from the end of the sixteenth century, it may have been influenced by the principle of the unseen potency (*apūrva*) first introduced by Sarvajñātman. This influence becomes conspicuous in most of the major compendiums or their commentaries from the sixteenth to the eighteenth century.

THE COMPENDIUMS AND THEIR COMMENTARIES— SIXTEENTH TO EIGHTEENTH CENTURY

As pointed out by S. Dasgupta (1975, 54), in the *Advaita* tradition, the sixteenth century opens an era of syncretism and a need for compendium literature. Whether an author favors the *Bhāmatī* or the *Vivaraṇa* School as a whole, in terms of renunciation, the greatest influence will come from Sureśvara and Sarvajñātman. Most authors stand between the following two ideas: [1] physical renunciation is necessary for the discipline of knowledge, and [2] it is indispensable for liberation even if the discipline of knowledge is available for householders and the like.

The *Vedāntasāra* of Sadānanda (around 1500–1550) is still today one of the most popular compendiums of *Advaita Vedānta*. It gives two possible meanings for *uparati*: "*Uparati* is the abstention of these withdrawn [external organs] from objects other than the [hearing of scriptures and so forth]; or the abandonment of prescribed rites, according to the rules" (Sadānanda 1949, 12). In his commentary on the *Vedāntasāra* called *Vidvanmanorañjanī*, Rāmatīrtha (around 1520–1620) argues that if *uparati* is abstention from external objects, it becomes redundant with the first two "qualities," namely, control of mind (*śama*) and control of senses (*dama*). He advocates that, "in the same way as control of mind and so forth are necessary for the seeker-after-liberation, so also is [physical] renunciation, because it is a proximate means of Self-knowledge" (Sadānanda 1893, 80). Physical renunciation is indispensable, he believes, "because a person whose mind is distracted by rites cannot ascertain the teaching of *Vedānta*—they being opposite to enquiry."[117] Quite clearly, Rāmatīrtha rejects the first meaning of *uparati* and emphasizes the notion of physical renunciation. Not surprisingly, his quotations include Sureśvara's *Naiśkarmyasiddhi* 1.52 (Sadānanda 1893, 74)—in which the sequence toward liberation includes physical renunciation before the discipline of knowledge—and Sarvajñātman's *Saṃkṣepaśārīraka* 3.666, which states that cessation of rites is the basis of liberation (Ibid., 80).

In contrast with the preceding commentary, the *Subodhinī* of Nṛsiṃhasarasvatī (around 1551–1650) does not show any preference for one of the two meanings of *uparati* (Ibid., 5). On the other hand, a third commentary, the *Balabodhinī* of Āpadeva (around 1600–1700), obviously favors the sense of physical renunciation. It goes to the extent of precluding householders from any access to the discipline of knowledge, as it declares that "the renouncer alone is qualified for hearing."[118] And this is "because, being distracted by rites, the householder cannot engage in hearing."[119] Thus, as a whole, the main commentaries on the *Vedāntasāra* give preference to physical renunciation as a sine qua non for the discipline of knowledge.

In the elaborate discussion on qualification for the discipline of knowledge and liberation proposed in his *Siddhāntaleśasaṇgraha*, Appaya Dīkṣita (1520–1593) seems by and large to favour the position of Sarvajñātman. As pointed out by Suryanarayana Sastri, Appaya Dīkṣita's disposition of the various opinions is such that in most cases the next viewpoint comes as a critique of the earlier one (Appaya Dīkṣita 1935–1937, 1:4). So we can expect to find the author's own opinion at the end of the discussion on any particular topic.

At the end of the section on the qualification of *Śūdras* for hearing and so forth, Appaya Dīkṣita acknowledges, like Śaṅkara, that they can do it through the sections of the *Smṛti* that espouse a non-dualistic outlook (1: 345). But he adds that this may help them to acquire the body of a twice-born in the next life, which will enable them to engage in the discipline of knowledge based on the *Śruti* (Ibid.). Hence, some Self-knowledge is granted to the *Śūdra*, but not direct Self-knowledge and liberation. As far as twice-borns are concerned, Appaya Dīkṣita does not follow Sureśvara: "Thus [physical] renunciation is subsidiary to the practice of hearing and so forth only for Brahmins; for *Kṣatriyas* and *Vaiśyas*, qualification for hearing and so forth is not dependent on that."[120] But he takes recourse to, and seems to endorse, Ānandagiri's distinction between full and partial qualification: "Bereft of renunciation, *Kṣatriyas* and *Vaiśyas* are not fully (*mukhya*) qualified for hearing and so forth."[121] By finally borrowing the notion of unseen potency from Sarvajñātman, Appaya Dīkṣita makes this partial qualification somewhat more hopeful. According to him, one who is only partially qualified in a given life, because he is not a Brahmin and cannot take up physical renunciation, may obtain direct Self-knowledge and liberation in a future life through the working of an unseen potency produced by his part-time practice of the discipline of knowledge and allowing him to be reborn as a Brahmin, to be thus qualified for physical renunciation, and to devote himself completely to hearing and so forth (1: 351–352). Appaya Dīkṣita explains that rites performed by one who is only partially qualified for Self-knowledge can ensure the emergence of the desire for Self-knowledge and the decision to start the discipline of knowledge in the course of a future life through the effect of an unseen potency. So also, he adds, "the very same unseen potency, functioning up to the reward consisting of [direct Self-] knowledge, brings about hearing and makes it helpful for [that] knowledge even in a future life."[122] Since the author repeats the same idea at the end of the discussion on physical renunciation (1: 356), it is reasonable to infer that the theory of the unseen potency corresponds to his own position. This is substantiated by the fact that in his *Parimala* on the *Kalpataru*, Appaya Dīkṣita also uses the principle of the unseen potency to explain why some people attain liberation in a given life without physical renunciation.

As noted by S. Dasgupta (1975, 56), the *Siddhāntasiddhāñjana* of Kṛṣṇānanda Sarasvatī (around 1625–1675) shows more affinity with the *Bhāmatī* than with the *Vivaraṇa* School. But with respect to renunciation, Sureśvara and Sarvajñātman clearly exert the most determining influence on it. In a rather popular style, the author defines *uparati* as "stopping to build castles in the air with desired objects" (Kṛṣṇānanda Sarasvatī 1916, 129). According to this interpretation, householders would not seem to be excluded from the discipline of knowledge. But later on in his work the author brings up Sarvajñātman's idea that those who are not physical renouncers and yet practice the discipline of knowledge can obtain the final result of their efforts only in a future life:

> And, after adopting [physical] renunciation in a future life for the purpose [of practicing the discipline of knowledge], hearing and so forth is practiced as a way to knowledge. Being helped by latent impressions from [earlier] removal of age-old [notions] such as the impossibility [of the existence of the Self], hearing and so forth quickly come to fruition (Ibid., 133).

The author then immediately quotes *Saṃkṣepaśār¥raka* 3.359, which first stated this view in the tradition. Concluding the section on renunciation, Kṛṣṇānanda declares: "Therefore, discrimination, detachment, control of mind, control of senses, renunciation, and so forth are required for starting the enquiry [into *Brahman*]" (Ibid.). He then quotes verse 12 of Sureśvara's *vārttika* on the BṛU, which prescribes physical renunciation for entry into the discipline of knowledge.

Coming later in the period, the *Advaitabrahmasiddhi* of Sadānanda Kāśmīrī (around 1700–1750) does not add any new perspective. Yet it confirms the major influence exerted by Sureśvara, since it also quotes verse 12 of his *vārttika* on Śaṅkara's BṛU in support of the necessity of physical renunciation for access to the discipline of knowledge (Sadānanda Kāśmīrī 1932, 183–184).

The only major compendium to differ from the general trend on renunciation is the *Vedāntaparibhāśa* of Dharmarāja Adhvarīndra (around 1550–1600) along with the commentary *Śikhāmaṇi* by his son Rāmakṛṣṇa Adhvarī (around 1575–1625). In the section on the aim of *Vedānta*, Dharmarāja defines *uparati* simply as "the absence of distractions" (Dharmarāja Ādhvarīndra 1963, 221). The author's justification is quite consistent with Śaṅkara's standpoint as defined earlier by us:

> Here some hold that the word *uparama* means [physical] renunciation, so that [physical] renouncers alone are qualified for hearing and so forth. Others, however, say that the prescription of hearing and so forth is common to all the modes of living, because the word *uparama* does not mean primarily [physical] renunciation, because even householders can be simply free from distractions, and because in the *Śruti* Janaka and others are also described as enquiring about *Brahman*.[123]

Commenting on the first sentence of this passage, Rāmakṛṣṇa, Dharmarāja's son, comes out with the most virulent and personal denunciation of those who hold physical renunciation as a sine qua non:

> Here some mendicants use the word *uparama* to prove that only [physical] renouncers are qualified for the knowledge of *Brahman*; out of confusion about its meaning, they bring up the *Śruti* passage "those who persevere in the yoga of renunciation become pure in mind" [MuU 3.2.6]; they hide *Śruti* passages such as "faggots in hand, [he should go to a teacher] versed in the *Vedas* and steadfast in *Brahman*" [MuU 1.2.12],[124] the stories which tell that Janaka, Raikva and Vasiṣṭha enquired on *Brahman*, and the *Smṛti* text which says that "the householder also is liberated;" and, on that basis, they fallaciously call their own mode of living the "liberation-mode-of-living," they regard themselves as superior just because householders and others do reverential prostrations [before them]. They abrogate the right of householders and others for the enquiry on *Brahman* simply because they hate them. The author gives their opinion . . .[125]

Although this argument is obviously incomplete and not entirely convincing, it expresses a revolt against what we identified as the prominent way of interpreting renunciation in post-Śaṅkara *Advaita Vedānta*. In a unique aggressive tone, it reveals the social tension which probably surrounded the issue of renunciation even among followers of *Advaita*. And this reaction is all the more significant when it comes from a Brahmin.

According to R. N. Nandi (1986) and Patrick Olivelle (1993, 200–201), the restriction of physical renunciation to Brahmins during the Middle Ages was influenced by the fact that this type of renunciation was intimately connected with monasteries, which controlled vast agricultural lands, provided religious legitimacy to political authorities and were dominated by Brahmins. The latter would have been inclined to preclude other *varṇas* from benefiting from these rich and influential institutions. This may well have been a factor in the exclusivistic attitude of most commentators on physical renunciation. But the vigorous critique addressed to formal physical renunciants by Rāmakṛṣṇa Ādhvarī suggests a controversy between householders and monks, whether Brahmins or not. Thus, apart from its socioeconomic motivations, the social tension concerning renunciation was deeply rooted in clashes between hermeneutical presuppositions and between judgments on the usefulness of various ways of living in fulfilling the ultimate spiritual goal of man.

CHAPTER TEN

Śaṅkara and the Value of Renunciation in Hinduism

Prior to examining the controversial and intricate issue of Śaṅkara's interpretation of renunciation, we first constructed a typology of renunciation as a methodological instrument for a systematic, intratextual analysis of all aspects of his works related to this theme. Besides physical renunciation, abandonment of the rewards of action, and the meditative process of inner withdrawal, the last and fourth type identified as renunciation of doership proved to be the most revealing conception in the case of Śaṅkara's works, as it plays the key role in his understanding of the basic path toward liberation.

In brief, according to Śaṅkara, every human being is eligible to liberation through immediate Self-knowledge alone, whatever his position in the system of *varṇas* and ways of living. Contrary to the doctrine of combination of knowledge and action (*jñānakarmasamuccayavāda*), only direct knowledge of the actionless Self can eradicate ignorance of the Self's silent, unbounded, immortal nature, and eliminate the consequent superimposition of an active and mortal nature on it. Direct Self-knowledge can very well be attained by those who adopt the monastic way of living immediately after their studies. For those who do not do so, the basic sequence leading to liberation starts with the practice of the yoga of action. Contrary to a common interpretation about Śaṅkara's viewpoint, the yoga of action can be combined with the discipline of knowledge as well as with various types of meditation, and can lead to direct Self-knowledge. The purity of mind (*sattvaśuddhi*) created by these practices ensures the attainment of a Self-knowledge which is already immediate in nature (*jñānaprāpti*). Thus, direct experience of the Self is the indispensible condition for renunciation of all actions (*sarvakarmasaṃnyāsa*)—mental, oral, and physical—as well as for liberation from their results. This complete renunciation normally includes physical abandonment of rites, there being no use in continuing them for one who has already reached the goal. But even the one who does not renounce physically after enlightenment reaches liberation through Self-knowledge alone and through the inner renunciation of doership and action which is coextensive with that knowledge. Thus, whether one becomes a wandering mendicant or not after one's enlightenment, one ever remains steadfast in that direct Self-knowledge (*jñānaniṣṭhā*) which requires no further action or condition to bring about liberation.

The major consequence of our reinterpretation of the householder's sequence toward liberation is that the expression "renunciation of all actions" (*sarvakarmasaṃnyāsa*) no longer conveys the sense of physical renunciation as a compulsory step toward Self-knowledge and liberation. Appearances notwithstanding, this understanding agrees with Śaṅkara's refutation of the combination of knowledge and action for liberation: while the simultaneous use of ritual actions and meditation can result in direct Self-knowledge through complete purification of the mind, this ensuing knowledge remains the only cause of eradication of ignorance and of liberation from its effects.

According to Śaṅkara, physical renunciation is a subsidiary prescribed to Brahmins alone for full-time absorption in the discipline of Self-knowledge. Śaṅkara accepts the possibility of attaining liberation without recourse to physical renunciation even for those to whom it is prescribed. Yet, he did not address the problem of the missing subsidiary in that case. It is clear, however, that for the seeker-after-liberation the value of physical renunciation and monasticism lies in allowing full-time dedication to the most direct means of Self-knowledge, and not in being the only way of living capable of bringing about that knowledge.

At the time of Śaṅkara, the doctrine of the combination of Self-knowledge and action for the sake of liberation was probably a major prevailing understanding among followers of *Vedānta* Schools as well as followers of the hermeneutical and ritualistic school of *Pūrvamīmāṃsā*. For a good part, Śaṅkara had to convey his teaching by contradicting these thinkers. Therefore, his whole enterprise of establishing the validity of renunciation was part of the process of separating Self-knowledge from action, so that the former could be left as the sole means of liberation. In this context, the type of renunciation to be vindicated most energetically was abandonment of *doership* through direct Self-knowledge. This was because the doctrine of knowledge as a self-sufficient means of liberation logically ensued from demonstrating that [1] direct Self-knowledge automatically results in abandonment of doership, and that [2] the latter is in turn followed by a state of inner silent actionlessness, ensuring liberation from all boundaries without any additional help. Demonstration of the validity of physical renunciation found only a second place. Such argument was not used to prove that liberation is reached through mandatory recourse to monasticism, but to contend, that because scriptures are found to prescribe, for the purpose of Self-knowledge and liberation, a mode of living that is without ritual action, it cannot be claimed that the latter is necessary for liberation. Thus, fundamentally, the basic incompatibility referred to by Śaṅkara to refute the doctrine of the combination of knowledge and action was not between the first three modes of living and the monastic mode of living (*saṃnyāsāśrama*), but between superimposition of doership on the Self, and spontaneous abandonment of that superimposition through direct knowledge of the Self as actionless.

The results of this study are essential to a proper evaluation of Śaṅkara's contribution to Indian thought. This applies first within the *Advaita Vedānta* tradition itself. Our overview of the interpretation of renunciation by major post-Śaṅkara Advaitins brought to light that physical renunciation started to be considered mandatory as early as in Sureśvara's and Sarvajñātman's works—which exerted the most determining influence on the misinterpretation about Śaṅkara's position. In the *Vivaraṇa* tradition, Padmapāda and Prakāśātman do not seem to have departed from Śaṅkara. But Anubhūtisvarūpa set the trend in favor of physical renunciation as a sine qua non—an understanding which was to dominate after him. Although Vācaspati Miśra and the *Bhāmatī* tradition were more liberal and closer to Śaṅkara, for some reason, they did not endeavor to correct current misinterpretations about renunciation in his works. Exceptionnally, Vidyāraṇya, Dharmarāja Adhvar¥ndra and his son Rāmakṛṣṇa tried to counteract the major tendency and proposed interpretations which accounted much more faithfully for Śaṅkara's position.

One reason for this prevailing misinterpretation certainly lies in Śaṅkara's polysemic and even ambiguous terminology concerning this theme. Interestingly, scholars such as Paul Hacker and Tilmann Vetter have showed that Śaṅkara is not always consistent even with the use of important terms. In his study on Śaṅkara's usage of the words *avidyā* (ignorance), *nāmarūpa* (name and form), *māyā* (the illusory cosmic power of manifestation), and the supreme personal God Īśvara, Hacker concludes, in a somewhat ironical fashion, that Śaṅkara lacked interest in unambiguous vocabulary and systematic exposition: "Following this reflection we have to note, as a special feature of Śaṅkara's thinking, an aversion for definitions and a supreme carelessness as far as the systematic use of terms is concerned."[1] As we saw, Śaṅkara remains quite rigorous and consistent in terms of *issues* such as the role of action and Self-knowledge. Yet, for whatever reason, he leaves key *terms* related to renunciation open to polysemy and misinterpretation.

As far as later *Advaitins'* contribution to this misinterpretation is concerned, at least three exegetical predispositions may have played a role. First, Sureśvara's injunction of formal physical renunciation as a prerequisite for access to the discipline of knowledge. Given Sureśvara's reputation as a direct disciple of the founder of the tradition and as one of the greatest exponents of *Advaita Vedānta,* his authority exerted a strong influence on later readings of Śaṅkara's commentaries. The second exegetical predisposition which may explain the misinterpretation is the "previous life" argument. Clearly stated apparently for the first time by Sarvajñātman, it is the rule according to which, when scriptures refer to people who have reached enlightenment in this life without monasticism, one must suppose that they adopted the latter in a previous life and have thus been able to accomplish most of the spiritual purification during this earlier indispensable stage. A third exegetical predisposition may have been connected with the Brahmaṇical hold on the powerful monastic institutions of the medieval period. Some portions of society may have had interest in perpetuating the complete knowledge of *Advaita Vedānta* only within the Brahmin community—which alone has access to physical renunciation according to Śaṅkara—or only amongst the monastic circles of the Brahmaṇical section of society. These exegetical predispositions may have led commentators to overlook the major contradictions that arise when one interprets Śaṅkara as stating that physical renunciation is a sine qua non for full Self-knowledge. They probably disallowed many later *Advaitins* to realize that enlightened people still socially active are not sort of peripheral to an unavoidable monastic path of knowledge, but perfect examples of the very core of Śaṅkara's message, of his emphasis on Self-knowledge and renunciation of doership alone as the universal, correlated, and necessary conditions for liberation.

These findings and hypotheses justify a more in-depth analysis of cultural consequences such as those underlined by Maharishi Mahesh Yogi:

> Misunderstanding itself has taken the shape of a tradition, unfortunately known as Shankara's tradition. . . . [W]hen, in course of time, this teaching lost its universal character and came to be interpreted as for the recluse order alone, the whole basis of Indian culture also began to be considered in terms of the recluse way of life, founded on renunciation and detachment (1969, 14–15).

In his comparison between Śaṅkara and his followers, Hacker concludes that while, for the founder of the tradition, ignorance (*avidyā*) is simply a mental cause of suffering (*kleśa*) equivalent to superimposition (BS intro, transl., 31), it becomes a cosmic power (*śakti*) with later *Advaitins* (Hacker 1951, 250). Thus, according to Hacker, post-Śaṅkara *Advaita Vedānta* proceeds to "a materialization of ignorance into the cosmic substance."[2] This process was perhaps connected with the post-Śaṅkara emphasis on compulsory monasticism: in the same way as the physical universe was to be rejected for being a manifestation of ignorance, life in society had to be outwardly abandoned as the human and social crystallization of the same nescience. The process of monopolization of the path to liberation by the monastic institution transformed Śaṅkara's emphasis on the incompatibility between action and direct Self-knowledge into the opposition between a yoga of action (*karmayoga*) with hardly any proximate means of knowledge for householders, and a yoga of knowledge (*jñānayoga*) with its reserved discipline of knowledge and liberation for monks alone.

Our conclusions also shed a new light on Śaṅkara's interpretation of scriptures and on the understanding of the major periods of Hindu philosophical thought. Let us now identify some directions for further research and propose some hypotheses concerning these issues.

While Śaṅkara has been often criticized for imposing mandatory physical renunciation on liberal texts such as the *Bhagavadgītā*, we contend that he was much more faithful to the spirit of this text than is thought by many critics. As far as renunciation is concerned, in our view, the *Upaniṣads*, the *Bhagavadgītā*, and Śaṅkara's commentaries emphasize the meditative process of inner renunciation as a means to direct experience of the Self, and renunciation of doership—or, at least, of the ego—as an indispensable correlate of Self-knowledge and liberation.

This perspective has a bearing on the understanding of renunciation in Indian history as a whole. The epic period of the *Rāmāyaṇa* and the *Mahābhārata*, commencing around 500 B.C.E., is the common reference point in identifying the rise of Hinduism as distinct from the earlier Brahmaṇism of the *Vedas* and the *Upaniṣads*. In this context, modern scholars tend to see a fundamental break between the Upaniṣadic doctrine of renunciation and its reinterpretation by the *Bhagavadgītā*. It is usually understood that, in the *Upaniṣads*, full inner renunciation and the ensuing liberation entail physical renunciation and the monastic way of living, but that these inner and outer aspects of renunciation become separated in the *Mahābhārata* and particularly in the *Bhagavadgītā*. The earlier ascetical renunciation formulated by the *Upaniṣads* is thus softened, "domesticated," to use Olivelle's expression, and disappears in favor of a universal qualification for inner renunciation even in the midst of social life. Endorsing Madeleine Biardeau's position[3] on this, Charles Malamoud writes for instance that her conclusions

> show how the passage from ancient Brahmanism to Hinduism implies a complete re-evaluation of the initial opposition between the man in the world and the renunciant. . . . [L]iberation—or salvation—is no more a purely individual endeavor, it ceases to be the privilege of the renunciant alone and becomes a future promised to the whole of human race.[4]

Similarly, Patrick Olivelle sets up a radical opposition between the Upaniṣadic mentality and that of the *Bhagavadgītā*. According to him, in the *Upaniṣads*, "where one lives and how one makes a living are inseparable from the aim of one's life. Ascetic life-style and livelihood cannot be separated from the ascetic goal" (1990, 132). On the contrary, "the *Gītā*, in dissociating *mokṣa* from the life-style of renunciation, dissociated it from all life-styles, including that of life-in-the-world. The goal of life is separated from the mode of life" (1978, 33).[5]

According to this theory and to Śaṅkara's common representation as the herald of compulsory physical renunciation, the founder of the *Advaita* tradition would have neglected the viewpoint of the *Bhagavadgītā* and favored the earlier, Upaniṣadic paradigm of liberation through monasticism. But we showed that, with respect to both the *Upaniṣads* and the *Bhagavadgītā*, Śaṅkara emphasizes inner renunciation of doership as the only form of renunciation indissolubly linked with liberation. It is true that one can find a separation of goal and mode of life in the *Bhagavadgītā* as compared, for instance, to the *Saṃnyāsa Upaniṣads*. One also finds a tendency in Hindu culture to associate the last mode of living with liberation as when, for instance, the discipline of the monastic mode of living is called the *dharma* of liberation (*mokṣadharma*).[6] But, as suggested by many stories told in the *Upaniṣads*, there is no conclusive evidence that, as a whole, the *Upaniṣads* indissolubly link liberation with physical renunciation and monasticism; their connection may be privileged, but it is not necessary. And this also turns out to be Śaṅkara's basic interpretation of the value of physical renunciation.

It follows that, with respect to renunciation, one does not find a radical opposition, but both continuity and change in emphasis, in the passage from the *Upaniṣads* to the *Bhagavadgītā* and from the latter to Śaṅkara's commentaries. We can fairly say that Śaṅkara brought out the full consequences of the Vedic principle of sacrificial interiorization by emphasizing renunciation of doership through experience of the Self as actionless. Śaṅkara also took into account the various traditional modes of living. He showed how both life in society and monasticism allow the process of inner renunciation to culminate in the exalted state of absolute freedom from all limitations, which he viewed as the highest goal of human life.

These conclusions have a significant bearing on the modernization of *Advaita Vedānta*. In Indian history, a number of spiritual seekers probably found traditions other than *Advaita Vedānta* more attractive partly because of the exclusivistic monastic mentality of many Advaitin leaders. Today, since a fair number of laymen—Hindus and spiritual seekers around the world—wish to deepen their spiritual life in terms of direct experience of the divine and full awakening to their inner potential, meditation attracts them as a very significant practice. It should now be clear that, at its very roots, in the texts of its founder Śaṅkara, *Advaita Vedānta* encourages such a use of the crucial means of complete Self-knowledge by the layman as well as by the monk.

Notes

PREFACE

1. See also Nakamura 1991, 163.

CHAPTER ONE: ŚAṄKARA AND RENUNCIATION . . .

1. Whether the emphasis on renunciation occurred or not in an organic and unitary manner is still controversial among scholars. J. C. Heesterman (1985, 26–44) favors an organic and unitary perspective on the development of renunciation within the Brāhmaṇical tradition. On the other hand, scholars such as W. O. Kaelber (1989, 101–124) and P. Olivelle (1993, 35–70) propose a model which involves challenge (from both within and without the tradition) as well as assimilation.

2. The dates 788–820 were earlier proposed by K. P. Tiele in 1877 and confirmed by K. B. Pathak in 1882. They remained unchallenged until 1950 when H. Nakamura came out with the dates 700–750 (1983, 48–89). These dates were accepted by scholars such as Louis Renou, (*Journal Asiatique* 143, 1955, 249–251), Daniel H. H. Ingalls (*Philosophy East and West* 3, 1954, 292), and Sengaku Mayeda (Upad, transl., 3). However Tilmann Vetter (1979, 11–12) argues that, according to the material now available, one cannot bring enough evidence for more precise dates than 650–800.

3. See the *Vedāntasāra* (Sadānanda 1949, 12), and the *Vedāntaparibhāṣā* (Dharmarāja Ādhvarīndra 1963, 222).

4. By the expression "discipline of knowledge," I understand the traditional hearing (*śravaṇa*), reflection (*manana*), and meditation (*nididhyāsana*) applied to the *Upaniṣads* and to the Vedāntic knowledge of texts from the *Smṛti* such as the *Bhagavadgītā*.

5. Saway does not try to reconcile this statement with his own recognition that "Śaṅkara does not deny the possibility of a *kṣatriya*'s or other householder's attainment of *mokṣa* without *karmasaṃnyāsa*" (1992, 129).

6. In his study on the contemporary Śaṅkarācāryas (the *Advaita* pontiffs), William Chenkner suggests that in the *milieu* of these modern representatives of Śaṅkara's tradition, physical renunciation is not necessary for the discipline of knowledge:

> A *paṇḍita* of a Śaṅkara Vidyāpīṭha was unequivocal with me in pointing out that there was no absolute requirement for *sannyāsa* in

> order to pursue knowledge, but Ādi Śaṅkara advocated it for easier access to *jñāna*-yoga. The ascetical life releases one from household duties and family ritual. It frees one for a total pursuit of wisdom (1983, 163).

But on the basis of my own conversations with *paṇḍitas* and professors relatively close to the Śaṅkarācārya of Kāñci, I would say that they generally regard physical renunciation to be necessary—either in this life or in a previous one—for complete knowledge of the Self and liberation.

7. Along the same lines, see also Biardeau 1989, 27.

8. See also Saroja 1985, 124–125.

9. My translation. *Stratégie coordonné plutôt qu'éclectisme, la 'méthode' de Maṇḍana laisse ainsi à chacun la possibilité de privilégier celui ou ceux de ces moyens particuliers qui s'adapterait le mieux à sa situation sociale, à son caractère, etc. Avec celui que la tradition nous présente comme un maître de maison à vie nous sommes loin de toute intransigeance sectaire, aux antipodes notamment de Śaṅkara et de son 'hors du saṅnyāsa [sic] point de salut'* (Hulin 1978, 196).

10. A growing number of scholars tend to endorse the authenticity of the *Vivaraṇa* on the *Yogasūtrabhāṣya* traditionally attributed to Śaṅkara (Śaṅkara 1952b), among whom Paul Hacker, Hajime Nakamura, Sengaku Mayeda, and Trevor Legget (Upad, transl., 65). In 1979, Tilmann Vetter also viewed this work as authentic (21–25), but he now considers the matter as yet unresolved (personal letter, 1995). Similarly, according to Wilhelm Halbfass, the authenticity of this *Vivaraṇa* has not yet been completely proven (Halbfass 1991, 223–228). It has also been challenged by T. S. Rukmani (1992). As far as we are concerned here, the *Yogasūtrabhāṣya Vivaraṇa* obviously contains many references to the meditative type of renunciation, but only three references to renunciation as distinguishable from meditation proper. They are found in the comments on *sūtra* 1.16 (with the word *vairāgya*) and on *sūtra* 4.7 (with the words *saṃnyāsa* and *saṃnyāsin*). Yet these three terms also seem to convey the sense of an inner renunciation. Thus, even if the *Vivaraṇa* were an authentic work of Śaṅkara, it does not contain controversial or crucial elements for the understanding of the author's interpretation of renunciation. According to Hacker, Mayeda, and Legget, a commentary on the *Adhyātmapaṭala* of the *Āpastamba-Dharmasūtra* is also rightly attributed to Śaṅkara by the tradition (Upad, transl., 6, and Śaṅkara 1978a, 166–175). But there is even less evidence here than for the *Vivaraṇa*. As we will focus on a controversial issue, for more reliable conclusions, it seems safer to exclude this commentary from Śaṅkara's authentic works.

11. See also BhG 14.25.

12. Jonathan Bader even pointed out wide variations among scholars on how Śaṅkara's thought as a whole may have changed with time (1990, 20–24).

CHAPTER TWO: THE BASIC TYPES OF RENUNCIATION . . .

1. The monastic mode of living or *saṃnyāsāśrama* it often depicted in the scriptures as solitary. But it can also be communal, as some *saṃnyāsins* live in monastic institutions known as *maṭhas*.

2. The passage to the hermit mode of living (*vānaprastha*) involves only a partial physical renunciation, as it maintains some rituals done in the householder's stage, and it is not connected with wandering mendicancy. By physical renunciation we will always mean in this work the physical abandonment which, when formal, leads to the monastic mode of living (*saṃnyāsāśrama*), and when informal, to wandering mendicancy alone.

3. Rites enjoined by the scriptures are classified into four types: [1] the obligatory regular rites (*nityakarmans*), which are performed either daily, such as the oblations in the fire (*agnihotra*), or periodically, such as the full and new moon sacrifices; [2] the obligatory occasional rites (*naimittikakarmans*) performed at particular occasions such as the start of Vedic learning (*upanayana*) and after the death of a parent (*śrāddha*); [3] the desire-prompted rites (*kāmyakarmans*), that is, the numerous rites that one can do to fulfill a personal goal such as the birth of a son or success in business; [4] expiation rites (*prāyaścittakarmans*), which are performed to purify oneself for not having done certain prescribed acts.

4. The vast application of renunciation of the rewards of actions seems to make it incompatible with the obvious requirements of certain types of duties. How, for instance, can a *Vaiśya* engage in trade without seeking some reward, some profit, from his commercial activity? Traditional *Advaita Vedānta* does not seem to have addressed this issue. Perhaps Śaṅkara's response would be: let him do it as an expression of his observance of the ethical conduct required by his profession, and not simply as a means to gain power and gather wealth. And this would also correspond to Kṛṣṇa's teaching to Arjuna: even as he is advised to fight, Arjuna is told not to be motivated by anger or other forms of self-interest, but rather by the good of simply observing the duty prescribed for him. As pointed out by M. M. Agrawal it is "not that one should not be concerned with the results of one's actions, but that one should not make the results of actions one's motive for acting" (1982, 44). Agrawal explains that while no agent or doer can avoid the primary motive that his good actions will benefit others, giving up the reward of action is to disallow the rise of a second motive nourished by the doer's self-interest (45).

5. See also the introduction to the BhG (7) and the comments on verses 2.39, 2.50, 3.19, 3.30, 5.27, 11.55, 14.26, 15 intro, and 18.46.

6. Later *Advatins* such as Madhusūdana Sarasvatī will make a clear separation between yoga of action and a yoga of devotion in which duties become quite secondary and complete abandonment to the Lord is emphasized.

7. . . . *nāhaṃ kartā na me karmaphale spṛhā* . . . (BhG 4.14, 198). See also BhG 9.9, 419.

CHAPTER THREE: FIVE REFERENCE POINTS FOR . . .

1. It should be noted however that, according to these authors, liberation is not a state of pure consciousness, but of absence of consciousness, the Self being devoid of awareness when separated from the mind. See the summary of the positions of the two schools of *Pūrvamīmāṃsā* on this issue in Jha 1942, 36–39.

2. For two succinct and clear summaries of the doctrines of these authors on the combination of knowledge and action, see Potter 1981, 40–44, and Hiriyanna 1980, xiii–xxx.

3. For an account of the perspectives of the two schools of *Pūrvamīmāṃsā* on this point, see Jha 1942, 26–35.

4. The doctrine described here is exposed and criticized at lenght by Śaṅkara in BhG 18.66 (transl., 617–622).

5. See BS 3.4.16.

6. *upacitaduritapratibandhasya hi vidyotpattir nāvakalpate. tatkṣaye ca vidyotpattiḥ syāt tataś ca avidyānivṛttis tata ātyantikaḥ saṃsāroparamaḥ.*

api cānātmadarśino hy anātmaviṣayaḥ kāmaḥ. kāmayamānaś ca karoti karmāṇi. tatas tatphalopabhogāya sarīrādyupādānalakṣaṇaḥ saṃsāraḥ. tadvyatirekeṇātmaikatvadarśino viṣayābhāvāt kāmānupapattir ātmani cānanyatvāt kāmānupapattau svātmany avasthānaṃ mokṣa... (TU 1.12.1, 434–435).

7. *nityalabdhasvarūpatve 'pi saty avidyāmātraṃ vyavadhānam. yathā svarūpeṇa gṛhyamāṇāyā api śuktikāyā viparyayeṇa rajatābhāsāyā agrahaṇaṃ viparītajñānavyavadhānamātraṃ tathā grahaṇaṃ jñānamātram eva viparītajñānavyavadhānāpohārthatvāj jñānasya. evam ihāpy ātmano 'lābho 'vidyāmātravyavadhānam. tasmād vidyayā tadapohanamātram eva lābho nānyaḥ kadācid apy upapadyate* (BṛU 1.4.7, 84).

8. See BS 1.1.1, transl., 8.

9. See BS 1.1.4, transl., 32.

10. For good discussions of the various meanings of *adhikāra*, see Clooney 1990, 179–183, and Halbfass 1991, 66–69.

11. Bhāskara 1931, sections 47–48, 72–74.

12. Widowers are not qualified for sacrifices because one has to be accompanied by his wife during their performance.

13. In his commentary on this aphorism, Vācaspati Miśra describes Raikva as a widower (*vidhura*) (BS 3.4.36, 810).

14. *dṛṣṭārthā ca vidyā pratiṣedhābhāvamātreṇāpy arthinam adhikaroti śravaṇādiṣu. tasmād vidhurādīnām apy adhikāro na virudhyate* (BS 3.4.38, 810–811).

15. *nityam agnihotrādi* ... *brahmādhigamakāraṇatvaṃ pratipadyamānaṃ śravaṇamananaśraddhātātparyādyantaraṅgakāraṇāpekṣaṃ brahmavidyayā sahaikakāryaṃ bhavati* ... (BS 4.1.18, 853–854).

16. *na hy agnihotrādīny eva karmāṇi. brahmacaryaṃ tapaḥ satyavadanaṃ śamo damo 'hiṃsety evamādīny api karmāṇi itarāśramaprasiddhāni* ... *dhyānadhāraṇādilakṣaṇāni ca* (TU 1.12.1, 436).

17. *na hi pratibandhakṣayād eva vidyotpadyate na tv īśvaraprasādatapodhyānādyanuṣṭhānād iti niyamo 'sti. ahiṃsābrahmacaryādīnāṃ ca vidyāṃ pratyupakārakatvāt sākṣād eva ca kāraṇatvāc chravaṇamanananididhyāsanānām. ataḥ siddhāny āśramāntarāṇi. sarveṣāṃ cādhikāro vidyāyāṃ, paraṃ ca śreyaḥ kevalāyā vidyāyā eveti siddham* (TU 1.12.1, 438).

18. What kind of discipline of knowledge would be provided to *Śūdras* is not mentioned by Śaṅkara. But he certainly gives room for such a discipline in this comment.

19. Referring to this passage, Mayeda states that "the upper three classes of people, excluding Śūdras, are entitled to the knowledge of *Brahman*" (Upad, transl., 228). This picture is incomplete and potentially misleading, as knowledge of *Brahman* is

indeed available to *Śūdras*, but simply through sources other than the revealed texts known as *Śruti*. Halbfass misinterprets Śaṅkara's position even more clearly when he states that *Śūdras* "are excluded from the study of the Veda and, consequently, from any legitimate and effectual knowledge of brahman" (1991, 70).

20. *itihāsapurāṇādhigame cāturvarṇyasyādhikārasmaraṇāt. vedapūrvakas tu nāsty adhikāraḥ śūdrāṇām iti sthitam* (BS 1.3.38, 281).

21. *sādhanasādhyād anityāt sarvasmād viraktāya tyaktaputravittalokaiṣaṇāya pratipannaparamahaṃsapārivrājyāya . . . brāhmaṇāya . . . brūyāt punaḥ punar yāvad grahaṇaṃ dṛḍhībhavati* (Upad 2.1.2, 191).

22. *vedārtho niścito hy eṣa samāsena mayoditaḥ* |
saṃnyāsibhyaḥ pravaktavyaḥ śāntebhyaḥ śiṣṭabuddhinā | |
(Upad 1.13.27, 99).

23. Since Mayeda indicates in a note (Upad, transl., 171) that in this passage the prerequisites for receiving Self-knowledge from a teacher start with the second verse quoted here (verse 50), we can infer that, in this particular context, he does not interpret physical renunciation stated in the first verse (verse 49) as part of the qualification for the discipline of knowledge. This tends to go against Mayeda's own understanding of Śaṅkara.

24. *utpādyāpyavikāryāṇi saṃskāryaṃ ca kriyāphalam* |
nāto 'nyat karmaṇaḥ kāryaṃ tyajet tasmāt sasādhanam | |
tāpāntatvād anityatvād ātmārthatvāc ca yā bahiḥ |
saṃhṛtyātmani tāṃ prītiṃ satyārthī gurum āśrayet | |
(Upad 1.17.49–50, 139).

25. A minimal gift traditionally offered by the student to the teacher. These faggots are used as fuel for the sacred fire.

26. Since all other passages concerning qualification for physical renunciation in Śaṅkara's works state that Brahmins *alone* are entitled to it, *viśeṣataḥ* does not mean here "particularly" or "especially" in the sense of "more than others," but *distinctly*, in the sense of "the only one among others."

27. *brāhmaṇasyaiva viśeṣato 'dhikāraḥ sarvatyāgena brahmavidyāyām iti brāhmaṇagrahaṇam* (MuU 1.2.12, 139).

28. . . . *viśuddhasattvasya tu niṣkāmasyaiva bāhyād anityāt sādhyasādhanasaṃbandhād iha kṛtāt pūrvakṛtād vā saṃskāraviśeṣodbhavād viraktasya pratyagātmaviṣayā jijñāsā pravartate* (KeU-P, intro, 18).

29. *evaṃ hi viraktasya pratyagātmaviṣayaṃ vijñānaṃ śrotuṃ mantuṃ vijñātuṃ ca sāmarthyam upapadyate nānyathā* (Ibid.).

30. *tasmād dṛṣṭādṛṣṭebhyo bāhyasādhanasādhyebhyo viraktasya pratyagātmaviṣayā brahmajijñāseyaṃ keneṣitam ityādiśrutyā pradarśyate. . . . kaścidguruṃ brahmaniṣṭhaṃ vidhivad upetya pratyagātmaviṣayād anyatra śaraṇam apaśyan . . . papraccheti kalpyate* (Ibid., 18–19).

31. *yata evaṃ mahāśālā mahāśrotriyā brāḥmaṇāḥ santo mahāśālātvādyabhimānaṃ hitvā samidbhārahastā jātito hīnaṃ rājānaṃ vidyārthino vinayenopajagmuḥ. tathānyair vidyopāditsubhir bhavitavyam. tebhyaś cādād vidyām anupanīyaivopanayanam akṛtvāiva tān. yathā yogyebhyo vidyām adāt tathānyenāpi vidyā dātavyety ākhyāyikārthaḥ* (ChU 5.11.7, 197).

32. *idaṃ vāva tajjyeṣṭhāya putrāya pitā brahma prabrūyāt praṇāyyāya vāntevāsine* (ChU 3.11.5, 100).

33. *śaunako ha vai mahāśālo 'ṅgirasaṃ vidhivad upasannaḥ papraccha* (MuU 1.1.3, 130).

34. *śaunakaḥ śunakasyāpatyaṃ mahāśālo mahāgṛhastho 'ṅgirasaṃ bhāradvājaśiṣyam ācāryaṃ vidhivad yathāśāstram ity etat. upasannaḥ upagataḥ san papraccha pṛṣṭavān* (Ibid.).

35. *ākhhyāyikā vidyāstutaye, priyāya putrāya pitrokteti bhṛgur vai vāruṇiḥ* (TU 3.1.1, 598).

36. See ChU 6.4.5.

37. This is specified by Śaṅkara in his BṛU 6.2.8.

38. This will be substantiated later on. As also noticed by Mayeda (Upad, transl., 228), throughout his works, Śaṅkara consistently maintains his position that the addressee of the injunction of physical renunciation can only be a Brahmin.

39. My translation. "*Une lecture attentive des quatre premiers chapitres de la Manusmṛti, par exemple . . . révèle que le 'deux-fois-né' auquel s'adressent les prescriptions est en fait le brāhmane*" (1976, 32).

40. A similar situation is found in our century: preferring to spread his message mainly in English, the language of a very small fraction of his country, Vivekananda was able to reach a vast national and international audience.

41. *athāprāptasamyagdarśanā janakādayas tadā karmaṇā sattvaśuddhisādhanabhūtena krameṇa saṃsiddhim āsthitā iti vyākhyeyaḥ ślokaḥ* (BhG 3.20, 159).

42. Ibid.

43. *īśvarasamarpitena karmaṇā sādhanabhūtena saṃsiddhiṃ sattvaśuddhiṃ jñānotpattilakṣaṇāṃ vā saṃsiddhim āsthitā janakādaya* . . . (BhG 2.11, 45). For statements on the accessibility of direct Self-knowledge and liberation even for those who have not taken recourse to physical renunciation, see also Śaṅkara's comments on BhG 2.21, 4.15, 4.19–23, and 5.7.

44. *brāhmaṇānām evādhikāro vyutthāne 'to brāhmaṇagrahaṇam* (BṛU 3.5.1, 253).

45. Vidyāraṇya holds that both scriptures and Śaṅkara prescribe *formal* physical renunciation and the monastic mode of living to Brahmins alone, but do not proscribe *informal* physical renunciation to anyone (see chapter 9). Even if this were true, it could not be invoked in support of the necessity of physical renunciation. The reason is that if informal physical renunciation is merely not forbidden rather than prescribed by scriptures, from Śaṅkara's viewpoint, it becomes simply a matter of personal preference and cannot be considered a subsidiary to Self-knowledge.

46. *itaravarṇāpekṣayā vā yāvajjīvaśrutiḥ. na hi kṣatriyavaiśyayoḥ pārivrājyapratipattir asti* (BṛU 4.5.15, 388).

47. *paradharmaṃ ca bhikṣājīvanādikaṃ kartuṃ pravavṛte* (BhG 2.10, 40).

48. *"brāhmaṇo yajeta" ityādīni śāstrāṇy ātmani varṇāśramavayovasthādiviśeṣādhyāsam āśritya pravartante* (BS 1.1.1, 24).

49. *na hi brahmakṣatrādyātmapratyayopamarde brāhmaṇenedaṃ kartavyaṃ kṣatriyeṇedaṃ kartavyam iti viṣayābhāvād ātmānaṃ labhate vidhiḥ* (BṛU 2.4, intro, 191).

50. Here Alladi Mahadeva Sastry (Śaṅkara 1985, 164), and Ramachandra Aiyar (BhG transl., 192) translate *adhikāra* by "duty"; Gambhīrānanda, by "competence" (Śaṅkara 1984, 248); and Krishna Warrier, by "fit to" (1983, 193). All these translations are improper since they cannot apply to the enlightened.

51. *yasyaivaṃ tattvavidaḥ sarvakāryakaraṇaceṣṭāsu karmasv akarmaiva paśyataḥ samyagdarśinas tasya sarvakarmasaṃnyāsa evādhikāraḥ karmaṇo 'bhāvadarśanāt* (BhG 5.9, 254–255).

52. Here Ānandagiri compares physical renunciation with the concluding act of a ritual (*pratipattikarman*), that is, the final disposal of materials used in a ritual. Contrary to a purpose-oriented ritual act (*arthakarman*), the concluding act has no use other than that of disposal itself (Cf. Kane 1974, 5: 1231–1232). Similarly, the physical renunciation of the enlightened person has no purpose other than disposal of what is of no more use. His physical abandonment naturally follows from the fact that prescribed actions have served their purpose (purification for direct Self-knowledge), and it involves no need of something more to be attained through it.

53. *yathoktasya viduṣo vidhyabhāve 'pi vidyāsāmarthyāt pratipattikarmabhūtaṃ karmasaṃnyāsaṃ phalātmakam abhilaṣati* (BhG 5.8, 255).

54. *nanu vidyāpy aviduṣa eva vidhīyate viditavidyasya piṣṭapeṣaṇavad vidyāvidhānānarthakyāt, tatrāviduṣaḥ karmāṇi vidhīyante na viduṣa iti viśeṣo nopapadyate* (Ibid., 73).

55. *na. anuṣṭheyasya bhāvābhāvaviśeṣopapatte.... na tu ... na jāyata ityādyātmasvarūpavidhyarthajñānottarakālabhāvi kiṃcid anuṣṭheyaṃ bhavati* (Ibid.).

56. Ibid.

57. In the whole discussion preceding this statement, Śaṅkara seems to contrast the unenlightened person only with the enlightened one as described in the verse itself. Therefore reference to the seeker-after-liberation in this concluding statement may appear somewhat unjustified. But the fact that there are no rituals to do after apprehension of the Self as actionless through the teaching of the scriptures can be seen to hold good for the deeply convinced seeker as well as for the enlightened. Śaṅkara seems to have this in mind when including the seeker-after-liberation in this conclusive statement.

58. *tasmād viśeṣitasyāvikriyātmadarśino viduṣo mumukṣoś ca sarvakarmasaṃnyāsa evādhikāraḥ* (Ibid.). Here Mahadeva Sastry (Śaṅkara 1985, 45), and Ramachandra Aiyar (BhG, transl., 55) translate *adhikāra* by "have to," and Krishna Warrier, by "are called upon" (Śaṅkara 1983, 46), expressions which suggest the idea of prescription. Gambhīrānanda has a rather confusing translation, wrongly rendering the sentence as if the subject were at the same time enlightened and seeker-after-liberation: "Therefore, the enlightened person distinguished above, who has realized the immutable Self and is a seeker of Liberation is qualified . . ." (Śaṅkara 1984, 66). Y. Saway commits the same mistake: "Therefore, for the enlightened one who sees that *ātman* is unchangeable and who is eager for *mokṣa*, the renunciation of all actions is the only proper course" (1992, 125). Consistent with his erroneous translation, Saway believes that, when compared to statements of physical renunciation of the seeker in Śaṅkara's works, "far rarer is the *vidvatsaṃnyāsa* of the *jīvanmukta*, who has achieved emancipation even before his formal act of renunciation" (1992, 126). As our study will show, physical renunciation of the enlightened is much more frequent and significant in Śaṅkara's works than believed by Saway.

59. *sarvavyāpāroparamātmanaḥ saṃnyāsasyāvikriyātmajñānāvirodhitvāt prayojakajñānavato vaidhe saṃnyāse 'dhikāraḥ, samyagjñānavatas tv avaidhe svābhāvike phalātmani* (BhG 2.21, 75–76).

CHAPTER FOUR: TWO UNFOUNDED EXPLANATIONS . . .

1. *yadi punaḥ kvacid vidhiḥ parikalpyeta pārivrājyasya sa ihaiva mukhyo nānyatra sambhavati* (BṛU 4.4.22, 375).

2. BhG 3, intro, 136.

3. Ibid., 137.

4. See also BṛU, transl., 2.4, intro, 241–243; and 4.4.7, 508.

5. *brahmajñānaparipākāṅgatvāc ca pārivrājyasya* (BS 3.4.20, 796).

6. *sarvaprayoge pravṛttiḥ syāt* (Jaimini 1980, vol. 7, *sūtra* 11.1.16, 2010).

7. *vidyotpattipratibandhakaduritānām anantatvāt kiñcid yajñādyanuṣṭhānanivartyam, kiñcit saṃnyāsāpūrvanivartyam iti . . . tathā ca gṛhasthādīnāṃ karmacchidreṣu śravaṇādyanutiṣṭhatāṃ na tasmin janmani vidyāvāptiḥ, kiṃ tu janmāntare saṃnyāsaṃ labdhvaiva; yeṣāṃ tu gṛhasthānām eva satāṃ janakādīnāṃ vidyā dṛśyate, teṣāṃ pūrvajanmani saṃnyāsād vidyāvāptiḥ* (Appaya Dīkṣita 1935–1937, 2:90).

8. Does this solve all doubts concerning physical renunciation at least with respect to non-Brahmins? In other words, is it already demonstrated that, according to Śaṅkara, they can attain liberation without physical renunciation? No, because some passages in Śaṅkara's works do associate words such as renunciation (*saṃnyāsa*) with non-Brahmins. Hence, we still have to see whether these passages remain consistent or not with Śaṅkara's position in the light of the five points of reference presented in the previous chapter.

9. *na caitan nyāyyaṃ haṭho hy aprasiddhakalpanā* (BS 3.2.32, 662). In his BhG 18.66, Śaṅkara also refutes the opponent's use of postulation in support of the *Mīmāṃsaka* doctrine that the performance of regular obligatory rites produces no effect and that its wearisome aspect is justified by viewing it as the result of sinful acts committed in past lives (transl., 621).

10. The passage is as follows: "Because, the Lord having been proven [to be the ordainer of the results of actions], postulation is ruled out" (BS 3.2.38, 666). A similar comment is found in BhG 18.66 (transl., 621).

11. See also Kane 1974, vol. 2, part 2, 998.

12. Here Clooney translates *guṇamātra* by "only preparatory." But *guṇa* means "secondary" or "unessential," rather than "preparatory." Hence, instead of "only preparatory," we have proposed here "simply not essential."

13. *sarvaśaktau pravṛttiḥ syāt tathāśrūtopadeśāt. api vāpy ekadeśe syāt pradhāne hy arthanivṛttir guṇamātram itarat tadarthatvāt* (Jaimini 1980, vol. 5, 1406, 1408).

CHAPTER FIVE: THE HOUSEHOLDER'S PATH . . .

1. "It has been said that those renouncers who are steadfast in the right perception obtain liberation directly. And, on every occasion, the Lord has already stated and

will be saying that the performance of the yoga of action—after surrendering to Īśvara, the Brahman, with dedication of one's whole being to Īśvara—leads to liberation through the stages of purity of mind, attainment of knowledge and renunciation of all actions."

samyagdarśananiṣṭhānāṃ saṃnyāsināṃ sadyomuktir uktā. karmayogaś ceśvarārpitasarvabhāveneśvare brahmaṇy ādhāya kriyamāṇaḥ sattvaśuddhijñānaprāptisarvakarmasaṃnyāsakrameṇa mokṣāyeti bhagavān pade pade 'bravīd vakṣyati ca (BhG 5.27, 276).

2. "*The man who practices yoga*, the steady-minded man who is resolved that he does actions for the sake of the Lord and not for his own benefit, *having abandoned*, having completely given up, *the rewards of action, attains the steadfast peace*, that is, [a peace] abiding in steadfastness [and] called liberation. To complete the sentence: through the stages of purity of mind, attainment of knowledge, renunciation of all actions and steadfastness in knowledge."

yukta īśvarāya karmāṇi karomi na mama phalāyety evaṃ samāhitaḥ san karmaphalaṃ tyaktvā parityajya śāntiṃ mokṣākhyām āpnoti naiṣṭhikīṃ niṣṭhāyāṃ bhavāṃ sattvaśuddhijñānaprāptisarvakarmasaṃnyāsajñānaniṣṭhākrameṇeti vākyaśeṣaḥ (BhG 5.12, 257).

3. "... *those whose Self is That*, those whose Self is the supreme *Brahman, those who are steadfast (niṣṭha) in That*—steadfastness meaning 'adherence to,' 'absorption in'—those who, having renounced all actions, dwell in *Brahman* alone. ... this kind of people reach [a state] from which there is no return ..."

... *paraṃ brahmātmā yeṣāṃ te tadātmānas tanniṣṭhāḥ niṣṭhābhiniveśas tātparyaṃ sarvāṇi karmāṇi saṃnyasya brahmaṇy evāvasthānaṃ yeṣāṃ te tanniṣṭhāḥ. ... gacchanty evaṃvidhā apunarāvṛttim* ... (BhG 5.17, 264)

4. This kind of misinterpretation is also brought to the fore when Yoshitsugu Sawai translates the *jñānaprāpti* found in BhG 5.27 (list A) and in 5.12 (list B) by "the attainment of the means of knowledge" (1992, 122, 126). Here Saway unduly adds the word "means" to the compound, as if to make it even clearer—though wrongly—that the latter refers to mediate knowledge only. Saway also states that the sequence of BhG 5.12 (list B) describes the path of the *vividiṣāsaṃnyāsin*, that is, of the formal renouncer aspiring to liberation (126). See also Bader (1990, 58, 62) for the same interpretation.

5. *samyagdarśananiṣṭhānāṃ saṃnyāsīnāṃ sadyomuktir uktā* (BhG 5.27, 276).

6. *yasya yathoktadarśinaḥ sarve yāvantaḥ samārambhāḥ sarvāṇi karmāṇi samārabhyanta iti samārambhāḥ kāmasaṃkalpavarjitāḥ kāmais tatkāraṇaiś ca saṃkalpair varjitāḥ mudhaiva ceṣṭāmātrā anuṣṭhīyante pravṛttena cel lokasaṃgrahārthaṃ nivṛttena cej jīvanamātrārtham* ... (BhG 4.19, 209)

7. *yasya tv ajñānād rāgādidoṣato vā karmaṇi pravṛttasya yajñena dānena tapasā vā viśuddhasattvasya jñānam utpannaṃ paramārthatattvaviṣayam ekam evedaṃ sarvaṃ brahmākartṛ ceti, tasya karmaṇi karmaprayojane ca nivṛtte 'pi lokasaṃgrahārthaṃ yatnapūrvaṃ yathā pravṛttis tathaiva karmaṇi pravṛttasya yat pravṛttirūpaṃ dṛśyate na tat karma* ... (BhG 2.11, 44)

8. *Guṇas* or "qualities" pertaining to Nature are its organizing principles. Enlightened people experience the Self as a free silent witness of all the activities of the *guṇas*.

9. *yadi tāvat pūrve janakādayas tattvadido 'pi pravṛttakarmāṇaḥ syus te lokasaṃgrahārthaṃ "guṇā guṇeṣu vartante" iti jñānenaiva saṃsiddhim āsthitāḥ, karmasaṃnyāse*

prāpte 'pi karmaṇā sahaiva saṃsiddhim āsthitā na karmasaṃnyāsaṃ kṛtavanta ity eṣo 'rthaḥ (BhG 2.11, 45).

10. Of course, the conviction that rites are not necessary for liberation must have arisen much earlier during their progress toward enlightenment. And it could have led those who were Brahmins to physical renunciation and full time absorption in the discipline of knowledge. But, in the present context, the realization that action was of no use *after* enlightenment seems grounded in the fact that Janaka and other ancient sages had already achieved the direct Self-knowledge for which rites serve as a subsidiary.

11. *yas tu prārabdhakarmā sann uttarakālam utpannātmasamyagdarśanaḥ syāt sa karmaṇi prayojanam apaśyan sasādhanaṃ karma parityajaty eva, sa kutaścin nimittāt karmaparityāgāsaṃbhave sati karmaṇi tatphale ca saṅgarahitatayā svaprayojanābhāvāl lokasaṃgrahārthaṃ pūrvavat karmaṇi pravṛtto 'pi naiva kiṃcit karoti. jñānāgnidagdhakarmatvāt tadīyaṃ karmākarmaiva sampadyate* (BhG 4.20, 210).

12. *viduṣā kriyamāṇaṃ karma paramārthato 'karmaiva tasya niṣkriyātmadarśanasaṃpannatvāt* (Ibid.).

13. *tenaivaṃbhūtena svaprayojanābhāvāt sasādhanaṃ karma parityaktavyam eveti prapte tato nirgamāsaṃbhavāl lokasaṃgrahacikīrṣayā śiṣṭavigarhaṇāparijihīrṣayā vā pūrvavat karmaṇy abhipravṛtto 'pi niṣkriyātmadarśanasaṃpannatvān naiva kiṃcit karoti saḥ* (BhG 4.20, 210–211).

14. *tyaktvā karmaphalāsaṅgam ity anena ślokena yaḥ prārabdhakarmā san yadā niṣkriyabrahmātmadarśanasaṃpannaḥ syāt tadā tasyātmanaḥ kartṛkarmaprayojanābhāvadarśinaḥ karmaparityāge prāpte kutaścin nimittāt tadasaṃbhave sati pūrvavat tasmin karmaṇi abhipravṛtto 'pi naiva kiṃcit karoti sa iti ca karmābhāvaḥ pradarśitaḥ, yasyaivaṃ karmābhāvo darśitaḥ*. . . (BhG 4.23, 214–215).

15. See for instance Murti 1974, 81–86.

16. See for example, BS 1.4.16–17, 1.4.19, 2.4.20, 3.3.7, and 3.3.17.

17. See for instance BS 1.4.19, and 3.1.5.

18. *"karmaṇy akarma yaḥ paśyet" ity ārabhya . . . ityantair vacanai sarvakarmasaṃnyāsam avocad bhagavān* (BhG intro 5, 241).

19. Emphasis is mine.

20. This renunciation of all actions is referred to specially in verses from chapter 4 on the enlightened man, whose interpretation by Śaṅkara we summarized at the end of the last section.

21. *karmasaṃnyāsāt pūrvoktātmavitkartṛkasarvakarmasaṃnyāsavilakṣaṇāt saty eva kartṛtvavijñāne karmaikadeśaviṣayāt* (BhG intro 5, 245).

22. BhG 5.13, 258.

23. *parakarmaṇāṃ ca parasminn ātmany avidyayāropitānāṃ vidyayā vivekajñānena manasā saṃnyāsa upapadyate* (BhG 5.13, 259).

24. For a short description of this type of renunciation, see BhG 18.7–8.

25. *tacca sarvakriyāsv api samānaṃ kartṛtvāder avidyākṛtatvam avikriyatvād ātmanaḥ* (BhG 2.21, 74).

26. ... *dehādyāśrayaṃ karmātmany adhyāropyāhaṃ kartā mamaitat karma mayāsya phalaṃ bhoktavyam iti ca. tathāhaṃ tūṣṇīṃ bhavāmi yenāhaṃ nirāyāso 'karmā sukhī syām iti kāryakaraṇāśrayavyāpāroparamaṃ tatkṛtaṃ ca sukhitvam ātmany adhyāropya na karomi kiṃcit tūṣṇīṃ sukham āsam ity abhimanyate lokaḥ* (BhG 4.18, 203).

27. *sāttvikasyāpi karmaṇo 'nātmavit sāhaṃkāraḥ kartā* (BhG 18.24, 711).

28. According to Śaṅkara, *Gītā* 18.3 also features the same kind of situation. In verses 18.2–3, says the commentator, "the options concerning renunciation [of desire-prompted rites or of all rites] and abandonment [of the results of all rites] concern only the ones that are qualified for rites. But those who perceive the supreme reality ... are outside the purview of these options" (BhG 18.3, 679).

29. In "being the opposite of the latter" (*tadviparīta*)—the first term in the Sanskrit text of the present passage—the word "latter" (*tad*) stands for "renunciation of all actions," the first nominal form in the context that precedes. Three of the authors of the four complete English translations of Śaṅkara's commentary on the *Gītā* now available completely miss the significance of the word "all" (*sarva*) in the compound "renunciation of all actions," which often distinguishes, in Śaṅkara's usage, the enlightened's renunciation of doership from the aspirant's physical renunciation. Indeed, no one even translates the word *sarva* (all). Alladi Mahadeva Sastry renders "*sarvakarmasaṃnyāsam* ... *tadviparītasya* ... *karmayogasya*" with "Karma-Yoga, the reverse of Karma-Samnyasa" (Śaṅkara 1985, 157); Gambhīrānanda, with "Karma-yoga—which is opposed to renunciation of actions" (Śaṅkara 1984, 236); and Ramachandra Aiyar, with "*karma-yoga*—which is its (renunciation's) opposite" (BhG, transl., 183). A. G. Krishna Warrier, the fourth translator, does not even render the compound "being the opposite of the latter" (Śaṅkara 1983, 184).

30. ... *tadviparītasya mithyājñānamūlakakartṛtvābhimānapuraḥsarasya sakriyātmasvarūpāvasthānarūpasya karmayogasya* ... *samyagjñānamithyājñānatatkāryavirodhād abhāvaḥ pratipādyate yasmāt tasmād ātmavido nivṛttamithyājñānasya viparyayajñānamūlaḥ karmayogo na saṃbhavatīti yuktam uktam syāt* ... (BhG intro 5, 244)

31. It is worth noting that in his BhG 18.11, Śaṅkara also underscores that the possibility and impossibility of renunciation of all actions are function, respectively, of the absence and presence of the sense of doership in the form of identification with the body. The notion usually conveyed by the word "all" (*sarva*) is here expressed by the adverb completely (*aśeṣataḥ*) which is borrowed from the verse:

> ... *for the embodied man*, for the unenlightened, it is not possible *to abandon*, to renounce action *completely*, entirely.... Therefore complete renunciation of action is possible only for one who perceives the supreme reality, who is not *embodied*, that is, who does not regard the body as the Self (... *dehabhṛtā 'jñena na śakyaṃ tyaktuṃ saṃnyasituṃ karmāṇy aśeṣato niḥśeṣeṇa.... tasmāt paramārthadarśinaivādehabhṛtā dehātmabhāvarahitenāśeṣakarmasaṃnyāsaḥ śakyate kartum*; BhG 18.11, 689–690).

In BhG 18.48, the same impossibility and possibility to renounce completely are explained respectively in terms of ignorance (*avidyā*) and direct Self-knowledge, again leaving no doubt that the full renunciation referred to is concomitant with enlightenment:

... it has been said that because action is superimposed on the Self due to ignorance, it is not possible for the unenlightened to renounce action completely "even for a moment" [3.5]. On the contrary, as ignorance has been dispelled by knowledge, the enlightened is indeed capable of abandoning action completely ... (... *karma tadātmany avidyādhyāropitam evety avidvān nahi kaścit kṣaṇam apy aśeṣatas tyaktuṃ śaknotīty uktam. vidvāṃs tu punar vidyayā 'vidyāyāṃ nivṛttāyāṃ śaknoty evāśeṣataḥ karma parityaktum* ... ; BhG 18.48, 732).

32. *evaṃ lokasaṃgrahaṃ cikīrṣuṇāpi kriyamāṇaṃ karma paramārthato 'karma brahmabuddyupamṛditatvāt. tad evaṃ sati nivṛttakarmaṇo 'pi sarvakarmasaṃnyāsinaḥ samyagdarśanastutyarthaṃ yajñatvasaṃpādanaṃ jñānasya sutarām upapadyate.... tasmād brahmaivedaṃ sarvam ity abhijānato viduṣaḥ sarvakarmābhāvaḥ* ... (BhG 4.24, 217)

33. Emphasis is mine.

34. ... *sarvam evāgnihotrādikaṃ karma ... dṛṣṭaṃ nopamṛditakriyākārakakarmaphalabhedabuddhimat kartṛtvābhimānaphalābhisaṃdhirahitaṃ ca, idaṃ tu brahmabuddhyupamṛditārpaṇādikārakakriyāphalabhedabuddhimat karmāto 'karmaiva tat ... bāhyaceṣṭāmātreṇa karmāpi viduṣo 'karma saṃpadyate 'ta uktaṃ samagraṃ pravilīyata iti* (BhG 4.24, 217–218).

35. "... the highest good ... is attained through the *dharma* of steadfastness in Self-knowledge preceded by renunciation of all actions.... The *dharma* consisting of engagement in action ... when practiced with the sense of dedication to the Lord and without hankering for the rewards, brings about purity of mind; and, in the case of one whose mind has been purified, it is even the cause of the highest good, since it is a way of attaining the ability to be steadfast in knowledge and it is the cause of emergence of knowledge" (... *niḥśreyasaṃ ... sarvakarmasaṃnyāsapūrvakād ātmajñānaniṣṭhārūpād dharmād bhavati ... pravṛttilakṣaṇo dharmo ... īśvarārpaṇabuddhyānuṣṭhīyamānaḥ sattvaśuddhaye bhavati phalābhisandhivarjita, śuddhasattvasya ca jñānaniṣṭhāyogyatāprāptidvāreṇa jñānotpattihetutvena ca niḥśreyasahetutvam api pratipadyate*; BhG intro, 6–7).

36. "Attainment of the ability to be steadfast in knowledge" (*jñānaniṣṭhāyogyatāprāpti*) seems to refer to the prerequisite for access to the discipline of knowledge, whereas the "emergence of knowledge" (*jñānotpatti*) which follows, seems to stand for direct Self-knowledge, as in the summaries of chapter 5.

37. Please note that steps 1–3, and 4–6 are taken from two separate places in the text.

38. "... being established in the true nature of the Self alone is the ultimate means of the highest good ... The man qualified [for rites] who has gradually become purified in mind through the practice of yoga of action in the way described above, realizes that he is himself the actionless Self—as he is devoid of changes such as birth. 'Having mentally renounced all actions' [and] remaining 'without acting nor causing to act' [5.13], he attains steadfastness in knowledge which consists of actionlessness ... " ... *ātmasvarūpāvasthānam eva paraṃ niḥśreyasasādhanaṃ ... yo 'dhikṛtaḥ puruṣaḥ pūrvoktena prakāreṇa karmayogānuṣṭhānena krameṇa saṃskṛtātmā san janmādivikriyārahitatvena niṣkriyam ātmānam ātmatvena saṃbuddhaḥ sa sarvakarmāṇi manasā saṃnyasya naiva kurvan na kārayann āsīno naiṣkarmyalakṣaṇāṃ jñānaniṣṭhām aśnute* ... (BhG 18.10, 688)

39. *tasmād yuktam uktam ahaṃkṛtatvabuddhilepābhāvād vidvān na hanti na nibadhyata iti* (BhG 18.17, 700).

40. *nāyaṃ hanti na hanyata iti pratijñāya . . . vedāvināśinam iti viduṣaḥ karmādhikāranivṛttiṃ śāstrādau saṃkṣepata uktvā madhye prasāritāṃ ca tatra tatra prasaṅgaṃ kṛtvehopasaṃharati śāstrārthapiṇḍīkaraṇāya vidvān na hanti na nibadhyata iti* (*Ibid.*, 700–701).

41. BhG intro, 6.

42. In his BS 1.1.4 (72), Śaṅkara considers absence of embodiment (*aśarīratva*) to be synonymous with liberation (*mokṣa*).

43. *evaṃ ca sati dehabhṛttvābhimānānupapattāv avidyākṛtāśeṣakarmasaṃnyāsopapatteḥ saṃnyāsinām aniṣṭādi trividhaṃ karmaṇaḥ phalaṃ na bhavatīty upapannaṃ tadviparyayāc cetareṣāṃ bhavatīty etac cāparihāryam ity eṣa gītāśāstrasyārtha upasaṃhṛtaḥ* (BhG 18.17, 701).

44. As distinguished from terms comprising for instance the negative particles *a-* and *rahita*, both the latter meaning "without."

45. *Pūrvika* and *pūrvaka* can also mean "accompanied by" and could convey this sense here as well.

46. *Sasaṃnyāsa* (with *saṃnyāsa*) is also used with the same meaning, for instance, in BhG 4, intro, 182; BṛU 4.5, intro, 379. Also, *saha saṃnyāsena*, where *saha* is synonymous with *sahita*, occurs, for example, in BṛU 4.4.23, 377.

47. See for example BṛU 2.4, intro; 2.5, intro; 3.5.1. See also BhG 3, intro.

48. BhG 5, intro, 246.

49. BhG intro, 7.

50. BhG 3.20, 159. In his introduction to chapter 3 (137), Śaṅkara also uses *asaṃnyāsin* to qualify the *brahmacārin* (student) who has not yet (physically) renounced ritual actions. In these two cases, the *asaṃnyāsin* is thus a "non-physical-renouncer."

51. *viduṣas tyaktaiṣanasya sthitaprajñasya yater eva mokṣaprāptir na tv asaṃnyāsinaḥ kāmakāminaḥ . . .* (BhG 2.70, 129). In BhG 18.2 (676) and 18.66 (762), Śaṅkara also uses the word *asaṃnyāsin* (non-renouncer) to refer to those who are still subject to the results of their actions and, consequently, to transmigratory existence. In verse 18.12 (691) of the same, *atyāgin* (non-renouncer) is glossed as *ajña* (ignorant). In all these cases, the *asaṃnyāsin* thus appears to be a "non-renouncer-of-doership."

52. We will not discuss here the validity of this interpretation.

53. *tapo 'tra jñānam. liṅgaṃ sannyāsaḥ sannyāsarahitāj jñānān na labhyata ity arthaḥ* (MuU 3.2.4, 158).

54. Ibid.

55. We will discuss these passages later on.

56. As we will see the word "but" should be added here.

57. Here is Ānandagiri's comment: *katham? indrajanaka[gārgī]prabṛtīnām apy ātmalābhaśravaṇāt. satyam. saṃnyāso nāma sarvatyāgātmakas teṣām api svatvābhimānābhāvād asty evāntaraḥ saṃnyāso bāhyaṃ tu liṅgam avivakṣitam* (Ibid.; N.B.: [*gārgī*] is amendment for the misprint *gārgi*).

58. BhG 4, intro, 182.

59. *evaṃ kṣatriyaparaṃparāprāptam imaṃ rājarṣayo rājānaś ca ta ṛṣayaś ca rājarṣayo vidur imaṃ yogam* (BhG 4.2, 183).

60. This teaching principle is stated for instance in BhG 4.34, and KaU 1.2.8. See also MuU where Śaṅkara notices that some of the initial custodians of the knowledge of *Brahman* were householders (intro, 128–129) and acknowledges that they were "endowed with direct realization of the supreme *Brahman*" (*paramaṃ brahma sākṣāddṛṣṭavantaḥ*; 3.2.11, 161).

61. "Their minds" means the minds of the *yatis* evoked by the verse. Śaṅkara glosses the word *yati* simply by "habituated to exertion" (*yatanaśīlāḥ*). Thus, he does not seem to view these people inevitably as physical renouncers.

62. *te ca saṃnyāsayogāt sarvakarmaparityāgalakṣaṇayogāt kevalabrahmaniṣṭhāsvarūpād yogāt . . . śuddhasattvāḥ* (MuU 3.2.6, 158).

63. *saṃnyāsas tu mahābāho duḥkham āptum ayogataḥ.*

yogayukto munir brahma na cireṇādhigacchati (BhG 5.6, 251).

64. *paramātmajñānaniṣṭhālakṣaṇatvāt prakṛtaḥ saṃnyāso brahmocyate* (BhG 5.6, 252).

65. *saṃnyāsena samyagdarśanena tatpūrvakeṇa vā sarvakarmasaṃnyāsena* (BhG 18.49, 733).

66. As noticed by Ivan Kocmarek, Śaṅkara does not see a significant difference between *guṇavṛtti* and *lakṣaṇāvṛtti*: "they seem nothing more than alternative appellations for the general concept of non-primary designation" (1985, 16). It is with Sureśvara and particularly with Sarvajñātman that, along with the famous standard *Advaita* subdivision of *lakṣaṇā* into three types, the distinction between *guṇavṛtti* and *lakṣaṇāvṛtti* was fully developed (Ibid., 18–19). In fact the difference was already given by Kumārila, *guṇavṛtti* being defined in his *Tantravārttika* as the secondary usage based on similar qualities found in the two primary meanings, and *lakṣaṇāvṛtti* being defined as the secondary usage occurring when there remains a connection with the primary usage (Ibid., 15).

67. Here, the inner process of renunciation can be said to be the "cause" of immediate Self-knowledge only in the sense that it serves in eliminating the obstacles to the pure reflection of the Self in the intellect.

CHAPTER SIX: THE MAIN OPPOSITION . . .

1. BhG 3.3, 141. While Mahadeva Sastry (Śaṅkara 1985, 92) and Krishna Warrier (Śaṅkara 1983, 101) do not even translate the gloss, Ramachandra Aiyar (BhG, transl., 106) gives "discipline, intended for steady practice," which wrongly translate *anuṣṭheyatātparyam* as an epithet of *sthitiḥ*. Swāmī Gambhīrānanda (Śaṅkara 1984, 135) is nearest to our translation with "steadfastness, persistence in what is undertaken."

2. *tatra tasmin mārge prayātā mṛtā gacchanti brahma brahmavido brahmopāsanaparā janāḥ. krameṇeti vākyaśeṣaḥ. nahi sadyomuktibhājāṃ samyagdarśananiṣṭhānāṃ gatir āgatir vā kvacid asti . . .* (BhG 8.24, 404–405)

3. *nahi kevalasamyagdarśananiṣṭhā avidyādisaṃsārabījaṃ nonmūlayati kadācid ity arthaḥ* (BhG 18.12, 691–692).

4. As a minimal present.

5. . . . *hitvā sarvakarmāṇi kevale 'dvaye brahmaṇi niṣṭhā yasya so 'yaṃ brahmaniṣṭho japaniṣṭhas taponiṣṭha iti yadvat. na hi karmiṇo brahmaniṣṭhatā sambhavati karmātmajñānayor virodhāt* (MuU 1.2.12, 140).

6. *ayam ātmā balahīnena balaprahīṇenātmaniṣṭhājanitavīryahīnena na labhyo* . . . (MuU 3.2.4, 158).

7. *dhanasahāyamantrauṣadhitapoyogakṛtaṃ vīryaṃ mṛtyuṃ na śaknoty abhibhavitum anityavastukṛtatvāt. ātmavidyākṛtaṃ tu vīryam ātmanaiva vindate nānyenety ato 'nanyasādhanatvād ātmavidyāvīryasya tad eva vīryaṃ mṛtyuṃ śaknoty abhibhavitum* (KeU-P 2.4, 28).

8. See the whole of Śaṅkara's commentary on the same verse (KeU-P 2.4) where it is explained that the Self is really known when it is apprehended not only in the state of absorption (*samādhi*) without mental fluctuations, but also in all mental modifications outside of that state:

> Being the seer of all cognitions and nothing but the true nature of the power of consciousness, the Self is cognized as non-different [even] in the midst of cognitions. There is no other way for its knowledge. When *Brahman* is known as the innermost Self of cognitions, then it is *known*, then is the right perception of it (KeU-P 2.4, 27).

9. By using the phrase "steadfastness in knowledge" to translate *jñānaniṣṭhā*, we are still left even in English with a possible ambiguity between reference to a mediate or to an immediate knowledge of the Self. That is why we will be careful in always specifying the meaning of this word in different contexts.

10. *tasyāsya gītāśāstrasya saṃkṣepataḥ prayojanaṃ paraṃ niḥśreyasaṃ sahetukasya saṃsārasyātyantoparamalakṣaṇam, tac ca sarvakarmasaṃnyāsapūrvakād ātmajñānaniṣṭhārūpād dharmād bhavati* (BhG intro, 6).

11. Human wealth refers mainly to materials and money used directly or indirectly for the sacrifices. Through the latter, it leads to a postmortem temporary sojourn in the world of ancestors. Divine wealth means meditation and leads to the world of gods. More precisely, as elaborated in the comments on verses 11 to 14, mastery of meditation on the qualified *Brahman*—called Golden Womb (*Hiraṇyagarbha*)—leads to identity with the same, and mastery of meditation on the Unmanifest (*avyākṛta*), that is, Nature (*prakṛti*), leads to dissolution in the same.

12. Here "identification with the Self of everything" seems synonymous with liberation.

13. *mānuṣadaivavittasādhyaṃ phalaṃ śāstralakṣaṇaṃ prakṛtilayāntam. etāvatī saṃsāragatiḥ. ataḥ paraṃ . . . sarvātmabhāva eva sarvaiṣaṇāsaṃnyāsajñānaniṣṭhāphalam. evaṃ dviprakāraḥ pravṛttinivṛttilakṣaṇo vedārtho 'tra prakāśitaḥ* (ĪU 15, 13).

14. *abhyudayārtho 'pi yaḥ pravṛttilakṣaṇo dharmaḥ . . . īśvarārpaṇabuddhyānuṣṭhīyamānaḥ sattvaśuddhaye bhavati phalābhisandhivarjitaḥ. śuddhasattvasya ca jñānaniṣṭhāyogyatāprāptidvāreṇa jñānotpattihetutvena ca niḥśreyasahetutvam api pratipadyate* (BhG intro, 7).

15. Śaṅkara defines the *karmayogin* as a seeker-after-liberation (*mumukṣu*) for instance in BS 4.1.18 as well as in BhG 3.30, 4.11, 4.38 and 18.6.

16. T. M. P. Mahadevan makes the same distinction by using the terms *karmamārga* and *karmayoga* (1940, 22).

17. *yo 'yaṃ yogo 'dhyāyadvayenokto jñānaniṣṭhālakṣaṇaḥ sasaṃnyāsaḥ karmayogopāyo yasmin vedārthaḥ parisamāptaḥ pravṛttilakṣaṇo nivṛttilakṣaṇaś ca, gītāsu ca sarvāsv ayam eva yogo vivakṣito bhagavatā* (BhG 4 intro, 182).

18. *athavā jñānakarmaniṣṭhayoḥ parasparavirodhād ekena puruṣeṇa yugapad anuṣṭhātum aśakyatve satītaretarānapekṣayor eva puruṣārthahetutve prāpte karmaniṣṭhāyā jñānaniṣṭhāprāptihetutvena puruṣārthahetutvaṃ na svātantryeṇa, jñānaniṣṭhā tu karmaniṣṭhopāyalabdhātmikā satī svātantryeṇa puruṣārthahetur anyānapekṣety etam arthaṃ darśayiṣyann āha bhagavān* (BhG 3.4, 144).

19. As well shown by Franklin Edgerton (1924), in the context of the *Mahābhārata* and the *Gītā*, the term *sāṃkhya* does not refer to the classical system of *Sāṃkhya*—which will come later on—but to the idea of a path to liberation that is based on contemplative knowledge rather than on action or devotion.

20. To the reading *ātmaviṣayavivekajñānavatāṃ* of the edition we usually use, we prefer here *ātmanātmaviṣayavivekajñānavatāṃ* given in *Works of Śaṅkarācārya*. vol. 2. *Bhagavadgītā*. Delhi: Motilal Banarsidass, 45.

21. The term is *kṛtasaṃnyāsānām*, literally "those who have accomplished renunciation." In medieval times, this term technically refers to formal physical renunciation. The context also suggests this here.

22. *tatra jñanayogena jñānam eva yogas tena sāṃkhyānām ātmaviṣayavivekajñānavatāṃ brahmacāryāśramād eva kṛtasaṃnyāsānāṃ vedāntavijñānasuniścitārthānāṃ paramahaṃsaparivrājakānāṃ brahmaṇy evāvasthitānāṃ niṣṭhā proktā, karmayogeṇa karmaiva yogaḥ karmayogas tena karmayogeṇa yogināṃ karmiṇāṃ niṣṭhā proktety arthaḥ* (BhG 3.3, 141–142).

23. For instance in BS 3.4.17, transl., 770; BS 3.4.20, transl., 777; and BhG 3 intro, transl., 100.

24. See for instance *Mahābhārata* 12.327.61–68 (Dandekar 1974, 3: 2455), where Lord Īśvara describes how, at the beginning of creation, he manifested Marīci's group and Sanaka's group along with the *dharmas* of engagement in, and abstention from, action.

25. *ātmaivedam agra āsīd eka eva so 'kāmayata jāyā me syād atha prajāyeyātha vittaṃ me syād atha karma kurvīy[ety] etāvān vai kāmo necchaṃś ca nāto bhūyo vindet tasmād apy etarhy ekākī kāmayate jāyā me syād atha prajāyeyātha vittaṃ me syād atha karma kurvīyeti sa yāvad apy eteṣāṃ ekaikaṃ na prāpnoty akṛtsna eva tāvan manyate* (BṛU 1.4.17, 112–113). N.B.: *kurvīy[ety]* is emendation for *kurvīy*.

26. *prāg dārasambandhād* (BṛU 1.4.17, 112).

27. *avidvān kāryakaraṇasaṅghātalakṣaṇo varṇī* (Ibid.)

28. *etam eva pravrājino lokam icchantaḥ pravrajanti. etaddha sma vai tat pūrve vidvāṃsaḥ prajāṃ na kāmayante kiṃ prajayā kariṣyāmo yeṣāṃ no 'yam ātmā 'yam loka iti* (BṛU 4.4.22, 370).

29. *dārasaṃgraham akṛtvety arthaḥ* (BṛU 3.5.1, 253).

30. *yasmāt pūrve vidvāṃsaḥ prajādikarmabhyo nivṛttāḥ pravrajitavanta eva tasmād adhunātanā api pravrajanti pravrajeyuḥ*... (BṛU 4.4.22, 374).

31. Śaṅkara is here paraphrasing rather than quoting directly.

32. *"so 'kāmayata"* [BṛU 4.1.17] *ity avidyākāmavata eva sarvāṇi karmāṇi śrautādīni darśitāni, "tebhyo vyutthāya pravrajanti"* [BṛU 4.4.22] *iti vyutthānam ātmānam eva lokam icchato 'kāmasya vihitam. tad etad vibhāgavacanam anupapannaṃ syāt yadi śrautakarmajñānayoḥ samuccayo 'bhipretaḥ syād bhagavataḥ* (BhG 2.11, 43).

33. *atrādyena mantreṇa sarvaiṣaṇāparityāgena jñānaniṣṭhoktā prathamo vedārthaḥ.... ajñānāṃ jijīviṣūṇāṃ jñānaniṣṭhāsambhave... karmaniṣṭhoktā dvitīyo vedārthaḥ. anayoś ca niṣṭhayor vibhāgo mantrapradarśitayor bṛhadāraṇyake 'pi pradarśitaḥ* (ĪU 9, 9).

34. *eṣā yathoktā brāhmī brahmaṇi bhaveyaṃ sthitiḥ sarvaṃ karma saṃnyasya brahmarūpeṇaivāvasthānam ity etad he pārtha, naināṃ sthitiṃ prāpya labdh[v]ā vimuhyati na mohaṃ prāpnoti. sthitvāsyāṃ sthitau brāhmyāṃ yathoktāyām antakāle 'nte vayasy api brahmanirvāṇaṃ brahmanirvṛtiṃ mokṣam ṛcchati, kimu vaktavyaṃ brahmacaryād eva saṃnyasya yāvajjīvaṃ yo brahmaṇy evāvatiṣṭhate sa brahmanirvāṇam ṛcchatīti* (BhG 2.72, 132–133). N.B.: *sarvaṃ karma* is emendation for *sarvakarma* and *labdh[v]ā* is emendation for *labdhā*.

35. *sa evaṃbhūtaḥ sthitaprajño brahmavic chāntiṃ sarvasaṃsāraduḥkhoparamalakṣaṇāṃ nirvāṇākhyām adhigacchati prāpnoti. brahmabhūto bhavatīty arthaḥ* (BhG 2.71, 131).

36. A similar context and use of steadfastness in knowledge (*jñānaniṣṭhā*) is found in the introduction to BhG 4.21, where Śaṅkara refers to one who, even as a student, "has realized that his Self is *Brahman*" (*brahmaṇi... saṃjātātmadarśanaḥ*) and has not embarked upon the path of action (211). "Steadfast in knowledge," says Śaṅkara, "such a man is liberated" (Ibid.)

37. *evaṃ śrutyartham iha gītāśāstre prati[pi]pādayiṣitam* (BhG 3.17, 155–156). N.B.: *prati[pi]pādayiṣitam* is emendation for *pratipādayiṣitam*.

38. *na ca brahmavido vihitāni kāmyatvaśravaṇād etāvān vai kāma iti. brahmavidaś cāptakāmatvād āptakāmasya kāmānupapatteḥ. yeṣāṃ no 'yam ātmā 'yaṃ loka iti ca śruteḥ* (BṛU 2.4 intro, 190).

39. *tasyāṃ paramārthatattvalakṣaṇāyām ajñānanidrātaḥ prabuddho jāgarti saṃyamī saṃyamavān jitendriyo yogīty arthaḥ* (BhG 2.69, 128). N.B.: *ajñānanidrātaḥ* is emendation for *ajñānanidrāyāṃ*.

40. *yasya tu punar niśevāvidyāmātram idaṃ sarvaṃ bhedajātam idaṃ jñānaṃ tasyātmajñasya sarvakarmasaṃnyāsa evādhikāro na pravṛttau. tathā darśayiṣyati "tadbuddhayas tadātmānaḥ" ityādinā, jñānaniṣṭhāyām eva tasyādhikāraḥ* (Ibid.).

41. *sa sarvakarmāṇi manasā saṃnyasya naiva kurvan na kārayann āsīno naiṣkarmyalakṣaṇāṃ jñānaniṣṭhāṃ aśnute* (BhG 18.10, 688).

42. *yaḥ punar adhikṛtaḥ san dehātmābhimānitvena dehabhṛd ajño 'bādhitātmakartṛtvavijñānatayāhaṃ karteti niścitabuddhis tasyāśeṣakarmaparityāgasyāśakyatvāt karmaphalatyāgena coditakarmānuṣṭhāna evādhikāraḥ* (BhG 18.11, 689).

43. *brahma vidvāṃś cet tasmāt paśubhāvāt kartavyatābandhanarūpāt pratimucyate. kenāyaṃ kāritaḥ karmabandhanādhikāre 'vaśa iva pravartate na punas tadvimokṣaṇopāye vidyādhikāra iti* (BṛU 1.4.16, 112). Compare my above translation with that of Swāmī

Mādhavānanda, which does not make evident the repetition of the word *adhikāra*: "If by knowing Brahman he gets rid of that bondage of duty which makes him an animal, as it were, under what compulsion does he take up the bondage of ritualistic work as if he were helpless, and not the pursuit of knowledge which is the means of freedom from that?" (transl, 131). Although the term *adhikāra* can seem to refer to qualification for the discipline of knowledge, Śaṅkara's mention of the knowledge of *Brahman* and freedom from the bondage of duty (which earlier has been connected with superimposition of doership) suggests quite clearly that the man to whom the *adhikāra* with respect to knowledge is attributed, has already attained liberation. Since the translation of *vidyādhikāra* by "pursuit of knowledge" suggests a mediate Self-knowledge, it is not proper in this context.

44. *sarvā hīyam upaniṣad vidyāvidyāvibhāgapradarśanenaivopakṣīṇā* (BṛU 1.4.10, 102).

45. . . . *tasya karmaṇi karmaprayojane ca nivṛtte 'pi lokasaṃgrahārthaṃ yatnapūrvam yathā pravṛttis tathaiva karmaṇi pravṛttasya yat pravṛttirūpaṃ dṛśyate na tat karma* . . . (BhG 2.11, 44)

46. Ibid.

CHAPTER SEVEN: THE YOGA OF ACTION . . .

1. PU 5.1, 190. For similar definitions of meditation, see BhG 6.35, 8.8, 12.3–4, 12.9, and 13.24; BṛU 1.3.9; CU intro and 7.6.1–2; TU 1.3.2–4.

2. *vidyākarmaṇī hi devayānapitṛyāṇayoḥ pathoḥ pratipattau prakṛte. . . . ye na vidyāsādhanena devayāne pathy adhikṛtā nāpi karmaṇā pitṛyāṇe teṣām eṣa kṣudrajantulakṣaṇo 'sakṛdāvartī tṛtīyaḥ panthā bhavatīti* (BS 3.1.17, 612–613). See also BhG 8.24–26.

3. *upāsanāny ucyante kaivalyasannikṛṣṭaphalāni cādvaitādīṣadvikṛtabrahmaviṣayāṇi "manomayaḥ prāṇaśarīraḥ" ityādīni karmasamṛddhiphalāni ca karmāṅgasambandhīni* (ChU intro, 5).

4. . . . *ātmani svahṛdaye hārde brahmaṇi sarvendriyāṇi sampratiṣṭhāpyopasaṃhṛtya* (ChU 8.15.1, 432).

5. *indriyagrahaṇāt karmāṇi ca saṃnyasya* . . . (Ibid.)

6. On the contrary, people who meditate and who, owing to the high quality of their meditation (BṛU 4.2.15, transl., 632), attain the world of Brahmā through the Northern path—or path of gods—may also reach enlightenment in that world without having to return to earth and to a human form (see BS 4.4.22, transl., 912; KaU 2.3.16, transl., 215; PU 1.10, transl., 418–419).

7. *sarvam etad yathoktaṃ karma ca jñānaṃ ca samyaganuṣṭhitaṃ niṣkāmasya mumukṣoḥ sattvaśuddhyarthaṃ bhavati. sakāmasya tu jñānarahitasya kevalāni śrautāni smārtāni ca karmāṇi dakṣiṇamārgapratipattaye punarāvṛttaye bhavanti* (KeU-P intro, 17).

8. See for instance BhG 9.20–21, ĪU 8–9, and 12–14, BS 3.1.7, and 3.3.52.

9. In Upad 2.3.114–116, *parisaṅkhyāna* meditation is described as the process of *nididhyāsana* on the attributeless *Brahman* and prescribed for people who desire liberation alone and do not wish to accumulate new merits. But since the goal referred to here

is sovereignty (*svātantrya*) rather than liberation, and accumulation of merits is given as a means for it, in the present context *parisaṅkhyāna* meditation probably corresponds to meditation on the qualified *Brahman* and not to *nididhyāsana*.

10. Sovereignty seems to mean here the ability to obtain a happy future life as per one's wish.

11. *tasmāt tatkāle svātantryārthaṃ yogadharmānusevanaṃ parisaṅkhyānābhyāsaś ca viśiṣṭapuṇyopacayaś ca śraddadhānaiḥ paralokārthibhir apramattaiḥ kartavya iti* (BṛU 4.4.2, 350–351).

12. The Golden Womb or *Hiraṇyagarbha* corresponds to a form of the lower or modified Brahman and is also known as the god Brahmā. It is the intelligence of the supreme personal God Īśvara as identifying with the seed of creation (AiU 3.1.3, transl., 73). "In Him, as comprising the (cosmic) subtle body, are strung together all creatures" (PU 5.5, transl., 476). The highest level of the Golden Womb's celestial world is the most radiant intelligence of the Golden Womb itself.

13. *tasmād ye gṛhasthā evaṃ agnijo 'ham agnyapatyam ity evaṃ . . . vidus te ca ye cāmī araṇye vānaprasthāḥ parivrājakāś cāraṇyaniṣṭhāḥ śraddhāṃ śraddhāyuktāḥ santaḥ satyaṃ brahma hiraṇyagarbhātmānam upāsate na punaḥ śraddhāṃ copāsate te sarve 'rcir abhisambhavanti* (BṛU 6.2.15, 431).

14. *tasmāt sarvotsāhena yathāśakti svābhāvikakarmajñānahānena dakṣiṇottaramārgapratipattisādhanaṃ śāstrīyaṃ karma jñānaṃ vā 'nutiṣṭhed iti vākyārthaḥ. . . . atrāpy uttaramārgapratipattisādhana eva mahānyatnaḥ kartavya iti gamyate* (BṛU 6.2.16, 434).

15. Commenting on a preceding verse, Śaṅkara defined *kriyāvat* as "one who practices knowledge, meditation, detachment and the like" (*kriyāvāñ jñānadhyānavairāgyādikriyā yasya so 'yaṃ kriyāvān*; MuU 3.1.4, 153–154).

16. See BS 4.1.6, and 4.1.18, ChU 1.1.10, and BṛU 2.1.3.

17. See BS 3.2.21, transl., 619.

18. *Chāndogya Upaniṣad* 3.14.1 refers to the principle of "accomplishment as per one's resolve" *(yathākratu)*. According to this principle, one becomes what one resolves to be. As pointed out by Hiriyanna, "a person who knows the form of a deity mediately can render that knowledge immediate by continued meditation, upon it" (1980, xxiv).

19. *na tu pratīkeṣu brahmakratutvam asti pratīkapradhānatvād upāsanasya* (BS 4.3.15, 890).

20. . . . *devatādisvarūpātmābhimānābhivyaktir iti laukikātmābhimānavat* (BṛU 1.3.9, 43).

21. *yatraita ānandabhedā ekatāṃ gacchanti. dharmaś ca tannimitto jñānaṃ ca tadviṣayam akāmahatatvaṃ ca niratiśayaṃ yatra sa eṣa hiraṇyagarbho brahmā, tasyaiṣa ānandaḥ śrotriyeṇāvṛjinenākāmahatena ca sarvataḥ pratyakṣam upalabhyate* (TU 2.8.3–4, 552).

22. *yadā yasmin kāle te tava mohakalilaṃ mohātmakam avivekarūpaṃ kāluṣyaṃ, yenātmānātmavivekabodhaṃ kaluṣīkṛtya viṣayaṃ praty antaḥkaraṇaṃ pravartate, tat te tava buddhir vyatitariṣyati vyatikramiṣyati. śuddhabhāvam āpatsyata ity arthaḥ* (BhG 2.52, 112).

23. *kiṃ punas tasya grahaṇe sādhanam ity āha. jñānaprasādena. . . . tad yadā . . . ādarśasalilādivat prasāditaṃ svacchaṃ śāntam avatiṣṭhate tadā jñānasya prasādaḥ syāt. tena*

jñānaprasādena viśuddhasattvo viśuddhāntaḥkaraṇo yogyo brahma draṣṭuṃ yasmāt tatas tasmāt tu tam ātmānaṃ paśyate paśyaty upalabhate... (MuU 3.1.8, 155) See also MuU 3.1.9.

24. In BhG 18.70, Śaṅkara mentions that the sacrifice consisting of knowledge (*jñānayajña*) is mental only and therefore amounts to deep meditation.

25. *yajñeneti dravyayajñā jñānayajñāś ca saṃskārārthāḥ. saṃskṛtasya ca viśuddhasattvasya jñānotpattir apratibandhena bhaviṣyati* (BṛU 4.4.22, 372).

26. *jñānaṃ buddhim ātmani mahati prathamaje niyacchet. prathamajavat svacchasvabhāvakam ātmano vijñānam āpādayed ity arthaḥ. taṃ ca mahāntam ātmānaṃ yacchec chānte*... *ātmani* (KaU 1.3.13, 97).

27. *kaścid vidvān vasvādisamānacaraṇo rohitādyamṛtabhogabhāgī yathoktakrameṇa svātmānaṃ savitāram ātmatvenopetya samāhitaḥ sann etaṃ mantraṃ dṛṣṭvotthitaḥ*... (ChU 3.11.1, 99)

28. *udayāstamayakālāparicchedyaṃ nityam ajaṃ brahma bhavatīty arthaḥ* (Ibid.).

29. BS 3.4.38, 810. A doubt may arise as to whether "can succeed" (*saṃsidhyet*) really means "can attain liberation." But the rest of Śaṅkara's commentary on this aphorism refers quite clearly to the "highest goal" (*parāṃ gatim*) as attained by various means. In his commentary on *Manu Smṛti* 2.87 (46), Kullūkabhaṭṭa gives the same meaning to the verb: "*A Brahmin* surely obtains perfection, he can reach liberation, *merely through japa*."

30. *"tapasā brahma vijijñāsasva" ityādiśruteḥ. tapaādividyotpattisādhanaṃ gurūpāsanādi ca karmāvidyātmakatvād avidyocyate. tena vidyām utpādya mṛtyuṃ kāmam atitarati* (AiU intro, 639).

31. *unmānavyapadeśo 'pi na brahmavyatiriktavastvastitvapratipattyarthaḥ. kim arthas tarhi buddhyarthaḥ, upāsanārtha iti yāvat.... na hy avikāre 'nante brahmaṇi sarvaiḥ puṃbhiḥ śakyā buddhiḥ sthāpayituṃ mandamadhyamottamabuddhitvāt puṃsām iti* (BS 3.2.33, 662).

32. *upāsanaṃ nāmopāsyārthavāde yathā devatādisvarūpaṃ śrutyā jñāpyate tathā manasopagamyāsanaṃ cintanaṃ laukikapratyayāvyavadhānena*... (BṛU 1.3.9, 43)

33. *upāsanaṃ nāma yathāśāstram upāsyasyārthasya viṣayīkaraṇena sāmīpyam upagamya tailadhārāvat samānapratyayapravāheṇa dīrghakālaṃ yad āsanaṃ tad upāsanam ācakṣate* (BhG 12.3, 502).

34. *evaṃ vidvān krameṇa sarvātmakaṃ prāṇam ātmatvenopagato bhavati. taṃ sarvātmānaṃ pratyagātmany upasaṃhṛtya draṣṭur hi draṣṭṛbhāvaṃ neti netīty ātmānaṃ turīyaṃ pratipadyate* (BṛU 4.2.4, 296).

35. *loke hi naimittikānāṃ kāryāṇāṃ nimittabhedo 'nekadhā vikalpyate. tathā nimittasamuccayaḥ teṣāṃ ca vikalpitānāṃ samuccitānāṃ ca punar guṇavadaguṇavattvakṛto bhedo bhavati.... kvacij janmāntarakṛtaṃ karma nimittaṃ bhavati yathā prajāpateḥ. kvacit tapo nimittam.... kvacit*... *ekāntajñānalābhanimittatvaṃ śraddhāprabhṛtīnām. adharmādinimittaviyogahetutvāt. vedāntaśravaṇamanananididhyāsanānāṃ ca sākṣājjñeyaviṣayatvāt. pāpādipratibandhakṣaye cātmamanasor bhūtārthajñānanimittasvābhāvyāt* (BṛU 1.4.2, 59–60).

36. See BhG transl., intro, 5; 3.16, 117; 18.45, 726; 18.46, 727–728; 18.49, 733; 18.50, 734; 18.56, 744.

37. *evaṃ satatayuktā nairantaryeṇa bhagavatkarmādau yathokte 'rthe samāhitāḥ santaḥ pravṛttā ity arthaḥ. ye bhaktā ananyaśaraṇāḥ santas tvāṃ yathādarśitaṃ viśvarūpaṃ paryupāsate dhyāyanti ye cānye 'pi tyaktasarvaiṣaṇāḥ saṃnyastasarvakarmāṇo yathāviśeṣitaṃ brahmākṣaraṃ* . . . (BhG 12.1, 500).

38. Saway reports on his part that, even in the context of the *Śṛṅgeri Maṭha*, only a few physical renouncers practice *nididhyāsana* (1992, 177).

39. *ke punas te ya evaṃ vidur gṛhasthā eva. . . . ye cāmī araṇye vānaprasthāḥ parivrājakāś cāraṇyaniṣṭhāḥ . . . upāsate* . . . (BṛU 6.2.15, 430–431) See also ChU 5.10.1 for a similar description.

40. *indriyasaṃyama*, which is equivalent to *dama* and is said to be a proximate means to Self-knowledge in BṛU 4.4.22.

41. *bahulāyāsāni hi bahūny āśramakarmāṇi yajñādīni taṃ prati kartavyatayopadiṣṭāny āśramāntarakarmāṇi ca yathāsaṃbhavam ahiṃsendriyasaṃyamādīni tasya vidyante* . . . (BS 3.4.48, 818–819).

42. *evaṃ śrautasmārteṣu nityeṣu karmasu yuktasya niṣkāmasya paraṃ brahma vividiṣor ārṣāṇi darśanāni prādur bhavanty ātmādiviṣayāṇīti* (TU 1.10.1, 418).

43. . . . *karmayogānuṣṭhānād aśuddhikṣayahetukajñānasaṃcchinnasaṃśayo na nibadhyate karmabhir jñānāgnidagdhakarmatvād eva* . . . (BhG 4.42, 239).

44. *asakto hi yasmāt samācarann īśvarārthaṃ karma kurvan [paraṃ] mokṣam āpnoti puruṣaḥ sattvaśuddhidvāreṇety arthaḥ* (BhG 3.19, 158). N.B.: *param* is added, following *Works of Śaṅkarācārya*. vol. 2. *Bhagavadgītā*. Delhi: Motilal Banarsidass, 1981, 52.

45. *samatvabuddhiyuktaḥ san svadharmam anutiṣṭhan yat phalaṃ prāpnoti tac chṛṇu buddhīti. buddhiyuktaḥ samatvaviṣayayā buddhyā yukto buddhiyuktaḥ, sa jahāti parityajatīhāsmiṃl loke ubhe sukṛtaduṣkṛte puṇyapāpe sattvaśuddhijñānaprāptidvāreṇa* . . . (BhG 2.50, 109–110)

46. See also BhG 3, intro, for a similar definition.

47. . . . *buddhir ātmano janmādiṣaḍvikriyābhāvād akartātmeti prakaraṇārthanirūpaṇād yā jāyate sā sāṃkyabuddhiḥ, sā yeṣāṃ jñāninām ucitā bhavati te sāṃkhyāḥ, etasyā buddher janmanaḥ prāg ātmano dehādivyatiriktatvakartṛtvabhoktṛtvādyapekṣo dharmādharmavivekapūrvako mokṣasādhanānuṣṭhānanirūpaṇalakṣaṇo yogaḥ, tadviṣayā buddhir yogabuddhiḥ, sā yeṣāṃ karmiṇām ucitā bhavati te yoginaḥ* (BhG 2.11, 42).

48. See for instance BhG 2.48, 2.49, 10.5, 13.9, 18.57.

49. See for instance BhG 5.29, MuU 3.1.2, and BṛU 4.4.23.

50. See for instance BhG 2.51, 5 intro, 6.9, 6.29, 7.18, 7.29–30, 12.4, 12.14, 15.11.

51. In his translation of Śaṅkara's commentary, Ramachandra Aiyar glosses quite rightly *samādhiyoga* by "(meditation)" (BhG 2.39, transl. 70). Also in support of *samādhiyoga* as practice of meditation within the wisdom of yoga is the fact that when *samādhiyoga* is used for the definition of yoga in 2.39, it is presented as complementary to a yoga of action that already comprises performing actions without attachment (*niḥsaṅgatayā*). On the contrary, when evenness of mind (*samabuddhitva*) and wisdom of evenness (*samatvabuddhi*) are used in the definition of yoga (2.50 and 5.4), they are complemen-

tary to "performance of one's *dharma*" (*svadharmamanutiṣṭhan*) and to "mere yoga of action" (*karmayogaṃ ca kevalam*) respectively. Thus, evenness of mind (*samabuddhitva*) and wisdom of evenness (*samatvabuddhi*) seem to mean non-attachment as added to the mere performance of actions, while yoga of absorption (*samādhiyoga*) adds another dimension apart from non-attachment, which is most likely meditation.

52. *sāṃkhye paramārthavastuvivekaviṣaye buddhir jñānaṃ sākṣācchokamohādisaṃsārahetudoṣanivṛttikāraṇam* (BhG 2.39, 96–97).

53. *yoge tu tatprāptyupāye niḥsaṅgatayā dvandvaprahāṇapūrvakam īśvarārādhanārthe karmayoge karmānuṣṭhāne samādhiyoge ca imām anantaram evocyamānāṃ buddhiṃ śṛṇu* (Ibid., 97).

54. *taj jñānaṃ svayam eva yogasaṃsiddho yogena karmayogena samādhiyogena ca saṃsiddhaḥ saṃskṛto yogyatām āpanno mumukṣuḥ kālena mahatātmani vindati* (BhG 4.38, 235–236). In the comment on verse 2.49, wisdom of yoga is also said to lead to wisdom of *Sāṃkhya*: "Since this is so, therefore *seek shelter* . . . *in the wisdom* of yoga, or rather in the wisdom of *Sāṃkhya* which arises when yoga attains maturity" (*yata evaṃ yogaviṣayāyāṃ buddhau tatparipākajāyāṃ vā sāṃkhyabuddhau śaraṇam* . . . *anviccha* . . . ; BhG 2.49, 109).

55. See for instance BS 3.4.17, 770 and BhG 2.11, 37.

56. *jñānamātre yady api sarvāśramiṇām adhikāras tathāpi saṃnyāsaniṣṭhaiva brahmavidyā mokṣasādhanaṃ na karmasahiteti bhaikṣyacaryāṃ carantaḥ saṃnyāsayogād iti ca bruvan darśayati. vidyākarmavirodhāc ca. na hi brahmāikatvadarśanena saha karma svapne 'pi sampādayituṃ śakyam* (MuU intro, 128).

57. *yat tu gṛhastheṣu brahmavidyāsampradāyakartṛtvādi liṅgaṃ na tat sthitanyāyaṃ bādhitum utsahate. na hi vidhiśatenāpi tamaḥprakāśayor ekatra sadbhāvaḥ śakyate kartuṃ kim uta liṅgaiḥ kevalair iti* (MuU intro, 128–129).

58. *ata eva ca vidyāyāḥ puruṣārthahetutvād agnīndhanādīny āśramakarmāṇi vidyayā svārthasiddhau nāpekṣitavyāni* . . . (BS 3.4.25, 801)

59. To use another analogy: clouds give rain which makes the mango tree grow, following which the latter yields its fruit independently, as if out of its own nature; so also all *karmans* (all practices) generate purity of mind which in turn give rise to immediate Self-knowledge, the latter spontaneously and independently leading to liberation by virtue of its exclusive ability to cancel ignorance.

60. *yathā ca yogyatāvaśenāśvo na lāṅgalākarṣaṇe yujyate rathacaryāyāṃ tu yujyate. evam āśramakarmāṇi vidyayā phalasiddhau nāpekṣyanta utpattau cāpekṣyanta iti* (BS 3.4.26, 803).

61. See BhG 18.11, transl., 556, and 18.48, transl., 587. Of course, with support from the scriptures, Śaṅkara also claims that, before enlightenment, when complying with the prerequisites for the discipline of knowledge, a man of the Brahmin *varṇa*, and he alone, would preferably abandon ritual actions in order to devote himself entirely to hearing, reflection, and meditation on Vedāntic knowledge.

62. *karmaniṣṭhāyā jñānaniṣṭhāprāptihetutvena puruṣārthahetutvaṃ na svātantryeṇa, jñānaniṣṭhā tu karmaniṣṭhopāyalabdhātmikā satī svātantryeṇa puruṣārthahetur anyānapekṣety etam arthaṃ darśayiṣyann āha bhagavān* (BhG 3.4, 144). In his comment on the same verse,

Śaṅkara gives as synonymous with "steadfastness in the yoga of knowledge (*jñānayoga*)" the words "actionlessness," "state of non-action," "absence of action," and "remaining in the true nature of the actionless Self." All these suggest renunciation of doership as a result of immediate knowledge of the Self (Ibid., 145).

63. Our interpretation of Śaṅkara's standpoint certainly differs from the understanding criticized by Ramachandra Aiyar, since we recognize that, in Śaṅkara's works, the Brahmin can, and is encouraged to, "embrace the *saṁnyāsin*'s life" based on physical renunciation as a means for Self-knowledge.

64. A conclusion endorsed by Saway (1992, 122).

65. Emphasis is mine.

66. *kriyāsādhyaṃ purā śrāvyaṃ na mokṣo nityasiddhataḥ* (Upad 1.18.19, 149).

CHAPTER EIGHT: SELF-KNOWLEDGE AND PHYSICAL RENUNCIATION

1. *na ca sa niyoktuṃ śakyate kenacit. āmnāyasyāpi tatprabhavatvāt. na hi svavijñānotthena vacasā svayaṃ niyujyate* (Ibid., 633). Śaṅkara also writes in BṛU 2.1.20: "When the transcendent *Brahman* is realized as the only existence, there is neither instruction nor instructor nor the result of receiving the instruction, and therefore the *Upaniṣads* are useless—it is a position we readily admit" (transl., 219).

2. *kāmaprayuktatvād gārhasthyasya* (Ibid., 635).

3. However, Śaṅkara does oppose the monastic mode of living with that of the householder just before mentioning the Golden Womb as the result of steadfastness in action: "And the integral practice of means of knowledge such as celibacy is possible [only] for those who are beyond the modes of living [but] impossible in the householder stage" (*brahmacaryādividyāsādhanānāṃ ca sākalyenātyāśramiṣūpapatter gārhasthye 'sambhavāt*; Ibid., 636). What does he mean by this contrast? Let us first clarify the expression, "those who have gone beyond the modes of living" (*atyāśramin*). A few lines before the above citation, Śaṅkara introduces it within a quotation from *Śvetāśvatara Upaniṣad* 6.21. In this verse, a master is said to teach *Brahman* to students who have gone beyond the modes of living (*atyāśramin*). Since Śaṅkara also attributes integral practice of celibacy to these *atyāśramins*, he seems to see them as monastic seekers-after-liberation. Yet Śaṅkara's description of the limited means of householders in the passage quoted above does not necessarily imply his self-contradiction with respect to the universal availability of Self-knowledge and liberation. It can very well be that, in accord with the intent of the whole AiU's introduction, the spiritual limitations of the householder are mentioned to prove that there exists a mode of living based on physical renunciation of ritual actions and prescribed for Self-knowledge, and that, as a consequence, it cannot be claimed that liberation comes from Self-knowledge as combined with ritual actions. Besides, Śaṅkara specifies that it is "the integral practice" of the mentioned disciplines that cannot be pursued by the householder, implying that the latter also has access to these means.

4. *na. tanniyamasya pūrvapravṛttisiddhatvāt tadatikrame yatnagauravāt* (Ibid., 636).

5. *arthaprāptasya vyutthānasya punar vacanād viduṣaḥ kartavyatvopapattiḥ* (Ibid.).

6. *tathāpi prārabdhakarmāyattas tvaṃ lokasaṃgraham evāpi lokasyonmārgapravṛttinivāraṇaṃ lokasaṃgrahas tam evāpi prayojanaṃ saṃpaśyan kartum arhasi* (BhG 3.20, 159–160).

7. Opinions of modern scholars on the meaning of "the man established in *Brahman*" (*brahmasaṃstha*) are varied. Patrick Olivelle believes that it means a "renouncer," a category of persons "who set their mind on liberation" (1974, 34). But in his *History of Dharmaśāstra*, Pandurang Vaman Kane favours an interpretation similar to Potter's:

> The last clause about 'brahmasaṃstha' differentiates the three āśramas from him who has knowledge of brahma and holds fast by it. That portion says that the consequence of the knowledge of brahma is immortality; but it does not say expressly or impliedly that the stage of parivrājaka is a means of attaining the knowledge of brahma. So one may doubt whether saṃnyāsa as an āśrama is spoken of here . . . (1974, 2:1:420–421)

8. *jñānotpatter ūrdhva ca brahmavidaḥ karmābhāvam avocāma "brahmasaṃstho 'mṛtatvam eti" ity atra* (ChU 6.14.2, 282).

9. *tasmād avidyādidoṣavata eva karmāṇi vidhīyante. nādvaitajñānavataḥ. ata eva hi vakṣyati—"sarva ete puṇyalokā bhavanti. brahmasaṃstho 'mṛtatvam eti" iti* (ChU intro, 5).

10. *tapa iti kṛcchracāndrāyaṇādi tadvāṃs tāpasaḥ parivrāḍ vā na brahmasaṃstha āśramadharmamātrasaṃstho* . . . (ChU 2.23.1, 76)

11. *tapa eva dvitīya ity atra tapaḥśabdena parivrāṭtāpasau gṛhītau. . . . teṣām eva caturṇāṃ yo brahmasaṃsthaḥ praṇavasevakaḥ so 'mṛtatvam etīti* (Ibid., 77).

12. The word *parivrāṭ* is somewhat confusing in this passage, since it seems to refer to the enlightened man established in *Brahman*, even if it was used earlier to mean the wandering mendicant merely following the *dharma* of his mode of living. A tentative explanation will be provided later.

13. *yac coktaṃ tapaḥśabdena parivrāḍ apy ukta iti. etad asat. kasmāt? parivrājakasyaiva [nivṛttabhedapratyayasya] brahmasaṃsthatāsambhavāt* (Ibid., 82). (N.B.: *nivṛttabhedapratyayasya* is taken from *Works of Śaṅkarācārya*. vol. 1. *Ten principal Upaniṣads*. Delhi: Motilal Banarsidass, 1964, 407).

14. *aviśiṣṭas tv anuktaḥ parivrāḍ brahmasaṃstho brahmaṇi samyak sthitaḥ* (ChU 2.23.1, 77).

15. *brahmasaṃstha iti hi brahmaṇi parisamāptir ananyavyāpāratārūpaṃ tanniṣṭhatvam abhidhīyate* (BS 3.4.20, 795).

16. *tatraivaṃ sati yaṃ bhedapratyayam upādāya karmavidhayaḥ pravṛttāḥ sa yasyopamarditaḥ* . . . *vākyapramāṇajanitenaikatvapratyayena sa sarvakarmabhyo nivṛtto nimittanivṛtteḥ, sa ca nivṛttakarmā brahmasaṃstha ucyate* (ChU 2.23.1, 79).

17. *na. svasvāmitvabhedabuddhyanivṛtteḥ. . . . tasmāt svasvāmitvābhāvād bhikṣur eka eva parivrāṭ. na gṛhasthādiḥ* (Ibid., 81).

18. *Pārivrājyam arthasiddham* is variously translated as "he has to resort to monasticism as a matter of course" (ChU, transl., 155); "he also naturally attains the position of a Wandering Mendicant" (Potter 1982, 124); "his *saṃnyāsa* is really implied therein" (Warrier, 1981, 426). Because in the next sentence the opponent mentions the sin of nonperformance of rites, *pārivrājya* must include physical renunciation and mean the (for-

mal or informal) monastic mode of living. Another interpretation could be that wandering mendicancy (*pārivrājya*) is "self-evident" (*arthasiddha*) even if the householder does not really take recourse to it. But then it would be out of place on the opponent's part to bring in the question of physical abandonment immediately after. Therefore, this interpretation is untenable. In addition, since the word *arthasiddha* usually means "self-evident," it cannot imply a prescription. Hence, our translation: "wandering mendicancy follows naturally."

19. *tasmād vedāntapramāṇajanitaikatvapratyayavata eva karmanivṛttilakṣaṇaṃ pārivrājyaṃ brahmasaṃsthatvaṃ ceti siddham. etena gṛhasthasyaikatvavijñāne sati pārivrājyam arthasiddham* (ChU 2.23.1, 83).

20. *śamadamādis tu tadīyo dharmo brahmasaṃsthatāyā upodbalako na virodhī. brahmaniṣṭham eva hi tasya śamadamādyupabṛṃhitaṃ svāśramavihitaṃ karma yajñādīni cetareṣāṃ tadvyatikrame ca tasya pratyavāyaḥ* (BS 3.4.20, 795).

21. *na. bubhukṣādinaikatvapratyayāt pracyāvitasyopapatter nivṛttyarthatvāt* (ChU 2.23.1, 81).

22. BS 3.4.20, 795.

23. *tac ca trayāṇām āśramaṇāṃ na sambhavati* (Ibid.).

24. *nātaḥ paraṃ puruṣārthasādhanam asti* (BṛU 2.5.16, 210).

25. For Śaṅkara's most detailed discussion of these issues, see BU 4.5.15, transl., 544–552. See also BU 4.4.22, transl., 527–528.

26. See also BS.4.20, transl., 777, and BU 4.5.15, transl., 551.

27. See also AiU intro, transl., 17–18, and BhG 3 intro, transl., 85.

28. Śaṅkara also writes: "Accordingly, in the case of those who are detached owing to tendencies created in previous lives, it is desirable to resort to the other mode of living [i.e., the monastic one]" (TU 1.12.1, 437).

29. For instance, Kauṭilya asks to first make provision for one's wife and sons before entering the monastic mode of living (Kane 1974, 2:1:932).

30. A major symbol in the life of the performer of Vedic rites.

31. *tadvyatirekeṇa cāsty āśramarūpaṃ pārivrājyaṃ brahmalokādiphalaprāptisādhanaṃ yadviṣayaṃ yajñopavītādisādhanavidhānaṃ liṅgavidhānaṃ ca* (Ibid., 256).

32. See for instance BS 3.4.17–20, transl., 770–778; BṛU 2.4.1, transl., 243; AiU intro, transl., 17–18; TU 1.12.1, transl., 436–438; BhG 3 intro, transl., 100–102; BhG 6 intro, transl., 214.

33. As early as the eighth century C.E., the *saṃnyāsins*, belonging to Śaṅkara's tradition, are called "single-staffed" (*ekavaiṇavinaḥ, ekaveṇupāṇayaḥ*) by Bhāskara (Olivelle 1986, 1:52).

34. *pratyagātmāvikriyasvarūpaniṣṭhatvāc ca mokṣasya. na hi pūrvasamudraṃ jigamiṣoḥ prātilomyena pratyaksamudraṃ jigamiṣuṇā samānamārgatvaṃ saṃbhavati* (BhG 18.55, 743–744).

35. *etam eva lokam iccanta ity avadhāraṇān na bāhyalokatrayepsūnāṃ pārivrājye 'dhikāra iti gamyate. na hi gaṅgādvāraṃ pratipitsuḥ kāśīdeśanivāsī pūrvābhimukhaḥ praiti* (BṛU 4.4.22, 373).

36. See also BṛU 4.5.15, transl., 551, and TU 1.12.1, transl., 280.

37. *māyety evamādayo doṣā yeṣv adhikāriṣu brahmacārivānaprasthabhikṣuṣu nimittābhāvān na vidyante tatsādhanānurūpeṇaiva teṣāṃ asau virajo brahmaloka ity eṣā jñānayuktakarmavatāṃ gatiḥ* (PU 1.16, 170).

38. BS 3.4.47, 817.

39. Olivelle comes to the same conclusion. See Olivelle 1986, 1: 55 and 1993, 224–226.

40. *apicaike vidvāṃsaḥ pratyakṣīkṛtavidyāphalāḥ santas tadavaṣṭambhāt phalāntarasādhaneṣu prajādiṣu prayojanābhāvaṃ parāmṛśanti. kāmakāreṇeti śrutir bhavati vājasaneyinām* . . . (BS 3.4.15, 788)

41. *brahmavidaś cāptakāmatvād āptakāmasya kāmānupapatteḥ. yeṣāṃ no 'yam ātmā 'yaṃ loka iti ca śruteḥ* (BṛU 2.4 intro, 190).

42. See also BS 3.4.9, transl., 765, and AiU intro, transl., 7.

43. Here the text of the *Upaniṣad* says only "they leave everything." Śaṅkara provides various reasons to substantiate his reading an injunction of physical renunciation even when the Upaniṣadic text has no explicit indication—such as the optative mood—for it. He argues for instance that, following the *Upaniṣad*'s statement of renunciation, "they leave everything," the eulogy (*arthavāda*) introduced by "This is [the reason for it]" can be justified only if the statement of renunciation is understood as a prescription (transl., 527). Moreover, argues Śaṅkara, since, two sencences before the statement of renunciation, the *Upaniṣad* mentions that "Brahmins seek to know It [the *Brahman*] through the study of the *Vedas*," since even the opponent can but recognize this sentence as an injunction, and since the subject of all verbs stated in this context refer to the same grammatical subject (i.e., the Brahmin), the statement of renunciation must be also an injunction (Ibid.). It may be noted that the argument of a common grammatical subject is also used by Śaṅkara as a key point in BṛU 3.5.1 (transl., 338, 341).

44. *tasmād ātmānaṃ lokam ichantaḥ pravrajanti pravrajeyuḥ* . . . (BṛU 4.4.22, 374).

45. *yasmāt pūrve brāhmaṇā etam ātmānaṃ asādhanaphalasvabhāvaṃ viditvā sarvasmāt sādhanaphalasvarūpād eṣaṇālakṣaṇād vyutthāya bhikṣācaryaṃ caranti sma. dṛṣṭādṛṣṭārthaṃ karma tatsādhanaṃ ca hitvā. tasmād adyatve 'pi brāhmaṇo brahmavit* . . . . *eṣaṇābhyo vyutthāya* . . . (BṛU 3.5.1, 257). See also BṛU 4.5.15, transl., 550–551.

46. See *Manu Smṛti* 6.35–36.

47. Śaṅkara never mentions the first three categories of *saṃnyāsins* stated by various *Upaniṣads*, namely the *Kuṭīcaka*, *Bahūdaka* and *Haṃsa* types. For a description of these categories, see Kane 1974, 4:230.

48. For another example, see BhG 6.10.

49. BhG 2.11, 45.

50. For another example, see BhG 3.3.

51. *nāpi saṃnyasanād eva kevalāt karmaparityāgamātrād eva jñānarahitāt siddhiṃ naiṣkarmyalakṣaṇāṃ jñānayogena niṣṭhāṃ na samadhigacchati na prāpnoti* (BhG 3.4, 145). *Kevala* is often found with a similar context in BhG 5.2–5.

52. Students perform some rituals, but not the worship of the fire god Agni who is reserved for householders.

53. *na hy agnikāryādyakaraṇāt saṃnyāsinaḥ pratyavāyaḥ kalpayituṃ śakyo yathā brahmacāriṇām asaṃnyāsinām api karmiṇām* (BhG 3 intro, 137).

54. *ātmajñānavataḥ saṃnyāsa evādhikāraḥ* (BhG 2.21, 75). See also the absolutive *saṃnyasya* with the same meaning in BhG 2.72, 233.

55. Śaṅkara often uses the word *saṃnyāsin* to mean the enlightened person, whether he has physically abandoned all practices or not. See for instance MuU 3.1.4, transl., 150; BhG transl., 5.25–26, 206–207; 9.22, 307; 15.5, 491; 18.2–3, 444–448.

56. In Śaṅkara's BS 3.4.36, Raikva is presented as one who does not follow any mode of living (*anāśramin*). Vācaspati Miśra specifies that he is a widower (*vidhura;* Ibid., 810).

57. For other ambiguous usages of *saṃnyāsin*, see MuU 3.1.4–5, transl., 150–152; BhG transl., 5.28, 208; 8.11, 276; 14.1, 464.

58. For *karmasaṃnyāsa* as formal physical renunciation, see also BhG transl., 6 intro, 213; 6.37, 240.

59. BhG 2.11, 45.

60. BG 18.56, 744. Śaṅkara understands in the same way the use of the compound *saṃnyāsayoga* in verse 9.28 of the *Gītā* (436).

61. A similar description is found in BG 12.11, 509.

62. As glossed in BG 12.7, 507–508.

63. A similar usage is found in MuU 2.2.7, 149.

64. *yo hy ādita eva saṃnyasya karmāṇi jñānayoganiṣṭhāyāṃ pravṛtto yaś ca karmayogena tayoḥ sthitaprajñasya prajahātīty ārabhyādhyāyaparisamāptiparyantaṃ sthitaprajñalakṣaṇaṃ sādhanaṃ copadiśyate* (BhG 2.55, 114).

65. . . . *kartṛtantratvāt pravṛttinivṛttyor vastv aprāpyaiva hi sarva eva kriyākārakādivyavahāro 'vidyābhūmāv eva* . . . (BhG 4.18, 200)

66. *saṃkalpair varjitāḥ mudhaiva ceṣṭāmātrā anuṣṭhīyante pravṛttena cel lokasaṃgrahārthaṃ nivṛttena cej jīvanamātrārtham* . . . (BhG 4.19, 209)

67. *tam etam īśvaram ātmānaṃ ye nivṛttabāhyavṛttayo 'nupaśyanti ācāryāgamopadeśam anu śākṣād anubhavanti dhīrā vivekinaḥ* . . . (KaU 2.12, 114).

68. . . . *ity ātmajñāne saṃjāte sarvakarmaṇāṃ nivṛttiṃ darśayati. atas tasminn ātmajñānārthe sāṃkhye kṛtānte vedānte proktāni kathitāni siddhaye niṣpattyarthaṃ sarvakarmaṇām* (BhG 18.13, 694).

69. *tasya karmaṇi karmaprayojane ca nivṛtte 'pi lokasaṃgrahārthaṃ yatnapūrvaṃ yathā pravṛttis tathaiva karmaṇi pravṛttasya yat pravṛttirūpaṃ dṛśyate na tat karma* . . . (BhG 2.11, 44)

70. *pravṛttiṃ ca pravṛttiḥ pravartanaṃ bandhahetuḥ karmamārgaḥ. nivṛttiṃ ca nivṛttir mokṣahetuḥ saṃnyāsamārgaḥ* (BhG 18.30, 714).

71. For a similar connection between *pravṛtti* and bondage as well as between *nivṛtti* and liberation, see ĪU 14, transl., 23.

72. *atra cātmeśvarabhedam āśritya viśvarūpa īśvare cetaḥsamādhānalakṣaṇo yoga ukta īśvarārthaṃ karmānuṣṭhānādi ca. ... "te prāpnuvanti mām eva" iti akṣaropāsakānāṃ kaivalyaprāptau svātantryam uktvetareṣāṃ pāratantryam īśvarādhīnatāṃ darśitavāṃs teṣām ahaṃ samuddharteti. yadi hīśvarasyātmabhūtās te matā abhedadarśitvād akṣararūpā eva ta iti samuddharaṇakarmavacanaṃ tān praty apeśalaṃ syāt* (BhG 12.13, 511–512).

CHAPTER NINE: POST-ŚAṄKARA *ADVAITA VEDĀNTA* . . .

1. As found mainly in Śaṅkara 1925, Śaṅkara 1981, and Śaṅkara 1982.

2. The same verse is found at the beginning of another work ascribed to Śaṅkara, the *Adhyātmavidyopadeśavidhi* (Śaṅkara 1952a, 1, verse 3).

3. Śaṅkara 1925, 42, verse 38.

4. Ibid., 353, verse 3.

5. Ibid., 362, verse 25.

6. Ibid., 365, verse 1.

7. Other hymns attributed to Śaṅkara describe the physical renouncer either as a seeker-after-liberation or as liberated. For instance the *Dvādaśapañjarikā* (Ibid., 358–359) advocates inner renunciation of avidity, desire, anger, greed, delusion, and of the cosmic illusion (*māyā*) in the context of wandering mendicancy as depicted by verse 6. The *Dhanyāṣṭaka* (Ibid., 359–360) describes the physical and spiritual detachment of a wandering mendicant. The *Kaupīnapañcaka* (Ibid., 354) evokes the enlightened wandering mendicants "who rejoice day and night in *Brahman*."

8. Actually, Olivelle's position appears somewhat self-contradictory on this issue, as he suggests elsewhere in the same work that most writers after Śaṅkara were not less conservative than him: "The vast majority of prominent medieval writers, beginning at least with the Advaita theologian Śaṃkara (eight to ninth century C.E.), supported the position restricting renunciation to Brahmins males" (1993, 196). A little further, Olivelle also identifies an "increasing tendency in medieval Brāhmaṇical theology to limit asceticism to the Brahmin community" (200). One comes to wonder, from Olivelle's account, who was more conservative than the other. A more precise study of this question would be welcome.

9. *". . . dass durch Wirkung der Saṃskāras aus einem früheren Dasein in Ausnahmefällen ein Śūdra zur Erkenntnis und damit zu ihrer Frucht (der Erlösung) gelangen könne"* (Hacker 1950, 11)

10. In support of his interpretation, Hacker (1950, 11) quotes the following excerpt from the *Vedāntasāravārttikarājasaṃgraha*: "Vidura, from the *Śūdra* caste, is also liberated in every way." In the introduction to his commentary on Śaṅkara's BṛU, Sureśvara also states that the *Śūdra* is qualified for liberation, even though his *varṇa* deprives him from eligibility to heaven through rites such as the *agnihotra* (Sureśvara 1958, 147, verses 292–293).

11. *"Der Unterschied zwischen unserem Text und SBh 1,3,38 besteht demnach darin, dass Śaṅkara den Fall Viduras nur als besonders zu erklärende Ausnahme gelten lässt, während Sureśvara oder Pseudo-Sureśvara ihn implicite als Beleg für die Regel anführt"* (Hacker 1950, 11).

12. *adhikāriviśeṣasya jñānāya brāhmaṇagrahaḥ* ।
na saṃnyāsavidhir yasmāc chrutau kṣatriyavaiśyayoḥ ।।
(Sureśvara 1990, 3.5.88, 819).

13. *trayāṇām aviśeṣeṇa saṃnyāsaḥ śrūyate śrutau* ।
yadopalakṣaṇārthaṃ syād brāhmaṇagrahaṇaṃ tadā ।। (Ibid., 3.5.89). The respective impact of Śaṅkara and Sureśvara on the concrete policies concerning qualification for formal physical renunciation during the medieval and modern periods is yet to be clarified. According to Y. Saway, there is no evidence that Sureśvara's qualification of all twice-borns for physical renunciation "was ever accepted as authoritative in *Śṛṅgeri Maṭha*" (1992, 131). As noticed by David M. Miller and Dorothy C. Wertz, the *daśanāmī saṃnyāsins* of Bhubaneswar are "mainly Brahmans" (1976, 76). Dolf Hartsuiker observes that the contemporary *daśanāmī saṃnyāsins* are not all Brahmins (1993, 31). And, as reported by Wade H. Dazey, they include people from all categories of twice-born (1990, 302).

14. For a discussion of the various opinions found in *Dharmaśāstra* about qualification for renunciation in terms of *varṇas*, see Olivelle 1984, 111-115, and Kane 1974, 2:2:942–946.

15. *karmādhikāravicchedi jñānaṃ ced abhyupeyate* ।
kuto 'dhikāraniyamo vyutthāne kriyate balāt ।।
(Sureśvara 1990, 3.5.90, 819).

16. *ātmāvidyāsamutthānām ātmayāthātmyamātrataḥ* ।
karmavat kāṅkṣate jñānaṃ viśiṣṭaṃ nādhikāriṇam ।।
(Sureśvara 1993, 1.4.1436, 453).

17. *sarveṣām api ca nṝṇām adhikāro'nivāritaḥ* ।
yato 'taḥ sarvato nṝṇām iti bhāṣyakṛd abravīt ।।
(Sureśvara 1982, 1.1.1025, 185).

18. BṛU intro, 7 and 9.

19. *tyaktāśeṣakriyasyaiva saṃsāraṃ prajihāsataḥ* ।
jijñāsor eva caikātmyaṃ trayyanteṣv adhikāritā ।।
(Sureśvara 1982, 1.1.12, 17).

20. *tadanāptikṛdajñānadhvastaye 'laṃ na kārakam* ।
pratyagjñāne 'dhikāry asmāt tyaktapūrvoktasādhanaḥ ।।
(Sureśvara 1984, 2.9, 282).

21. *śānto dānta iti tathā sarvatyāgapuraḥsaram* ।
upāyam ātmavijñāne śrutir evābravīt svayam ।।
(Sureśvara 1982, 1.1.216, 53).

22. *nityakarmavidher yasmāc chamādividhinā hatiḥ* ।
na saṃprāptety ato yatnāt prārabdhoparataśrutiḥ ।।
(Sureśvara 1990, 4.4.1226, 1264).

23. *nityakarmānuṣṭhānād dharmotpattiḥ, dharmotpatteḥ pāpahāniḥ, tataś cittaśuddhiḥ, tataḥ saṃsārayāthātmyāvabodhaḥ, tato vairāgyaṃ, tato mumukṣutvaṃ, tatas tadupāyaparyeṣaṇaṃ, tataḥ sarvakarmatatsādhanasannyāsaḥ, tato yogābhyāsaḥ, tataś cittasya pratyakpravaṇatā, tatas*

tat tvam asy ādivākyārthaparijñānaṃ, tato 'vidyocchedaḥ... (Sureśvara 1988, 1.52, 53) Shoun Hino compares this sequence with a similar one found in Sureśvara's *Vārttika* on BṛU 2.4.2–5 (Sureśvara 1991, 8–15). But Hino is mistaken when he states that Śaṅkara equally holds "the necessity of [physical] renunciation for liberation" (Ibid., 15).

24. The word *yati* is somewhat ambiguous here. As we saw, for Śaṅkara, it can mean generally a physical renouncer or a disciplined person aspiring to liberation. The present context highlights a model for adjoining physical renunciation to the knowledge of *Brahman*. Hence, the *yati* who is here advised to renounce physically must be an unenlightened persevering aspirant who has not yet taken up physical renunciation.

25. *saty api brahmaveditve nāsaṃtyaktaiṣaṇo yatiḥ* |
muktibhāg iti cehoktaḥ saṃnyāsena samuccayaḥ | |
nirastātiśayajñāno yājñavalkyo yato gṛhī |
kaivalyāśramam āsthāya prāpa tad vaiṣṇavaṃ padam | |
tyāga eva hi sarveṣāṃ mokṣasādhanam uttamam |
tyajataiva hi taj jñeyaṃ tyaktuḥ pratyak paraṃ padam | |
(Sureśvara 1982, 2.4.21–23, 673–674).

26. *samyagvijñātatattvatvāt kṛtārtho 'py akhilaṃ svayam* |
tatyāja karma tvarayā vāṅmanaḥkāyasādhanam | |
(Sureśvara 1990, 4.5.26, 1282).

Sureśvara glosses in a quite similar fashion the statement of the ancient Self-knowers of BṛU 4.4.22 who did not marry after completion of their studies: "And we do not engage in action because we have achieved the goal" (*asmākaṃ na pravṛttiḥ syāt kṛtārthatvāc ca kāraṇāt* |; Sureśvara 1990, 4.4.1112, 1251). But, when summarizing Sureśvara's passage on Yājñavalkya's physical renunciation, Karl H. Potter and S. Subrahmanya Sastri seem to bring up a third interpretation of the relationship between enlightenment and physical renunciation in Yājñavalkya's story. Here, Yājñavalkya appears to be *both* enlightened by direct Self-knowledge and in need of physical renunciation to secure liberation: "though Yājñavalkya has acheived the supreme knowledge he had to take up *saṃnyāsa*, without which liberation is not attainable" (Potter 1981, 483). This interpretation does not correspond to either Śaṅkara's or Sureśvara's position.

27. *jñānasvabhāvād vyutthānaṃ jñeyavastūparodhataḥ* |
vyutthāne codanāpekṣā nādhikāropamardataḥ | |
(Sureśvara 1990, 3.5.104, 821).

28. *evam ātmānaṃ jñātvā kiṃ pravartitavyam, uta nivartitavyam, āhosvit muktapragrahatā? ity. ucyate.*
jñeyābhinnam idaṃ yasmāj jñeyavastvanusāryataḥ |
na pravṛttiṃ nivṛttiṃ vā kaṭākṣeṇāpi vīkṣate | | (Sureśvara 1988, 4.54, 379).

29. *vānaprasthagṛhasthanaiṣṭhikajanair anyaiś ca varnāśramaiḥ karmavyadhvaniṣevitaṃ bhavati vai janmāntare pācakam* | *vidyāyāḥ śravaṇādilakṣaṇaṃ idaṃ na hy etad eṣāṃ kvacit śāstreṇa pratiṣiddham īkṣitam idaṃ śūdrasya dṛṣṭaṃ yathā* | | (Sarvajñātman 1985, 3.359, 664).

30. *janmantareṣu yadi sādhanajātam āsīt saṃnyāsapūrvakam idaṃ śravaṇādirūpam* | *vidyām avāpsyati janaḥ sakalo 'pi yatra tatrāśramādiṣu vasan na nivārayāmaḥ* | | (Ibid., 3.361, 665).

31. Also the "quality" called faith (*śraddhā*) is left unmentioned in this enumeration.

32. *cittasya pratyakpravaṇatādvāraphalam avagamyoparamasiddheḥ* (Padmapāda 1992, 417–418).

33. *brahmakṣatrādiviṣayatayā vā vyavasthā kalpyate* (Ibid., 421).

34. To avoid any contact with impurities during sacrifice, a black horn is used instead of the fingers when one needs to scratch a part of one's body.

35. *uparatir iti kṛtaprayojanakṛṣṇaviṣāṇasyeva sattvaśuddhisiddhau nityānām api vidhita eva parityāgaḥ* (Anubhūtisvarūpa 1935–1939, 1.1.1, 28)

36. *saṃnyāsinām śravaṇādividhir nitya eva, akaraṇe pratyavāyaśravaṇāt; itareṣāṃ tu kāmyo bhaviṣyati, vidyoddeśena śravaṇādividhānāt, pratiśedhābhāvāc ca* (Ibid., 3.4.38, 977).

37. See Mahadevan (1968, 190–193) for the various influences exerted by Anubhūtisvarūpa.

38. However, according to R. Thangaswami (1980, 282) and S. Revathy (1990, 4), the author of the *Bhāṣyaratnaprabhā* is Rāmānanda and not Govindānanda.

39. *sattvaśuddhau nityānām api vidhita eva tyāga uparatiḥ* (BS 1.1.1, 37).

40. *sākṣād eva śravaṇādihetuṃ saṃnyāsaṃ vidhitsur* (BhG 15 intro, 609).

41. *mukhyāmukhyādhikāribhedena vikalpaḥ* (BhG 14.26, 605–606).

42. *idānīṃ gṛhasthāśramakarmaṇāṃ bahiraṅgatvaṃ saṃnyāsāśramakarmaṇāṃ tv antaraṅgavidyāsādhanatvam iti viśeṣaṃ darśayituṃ codyam udbhāvayati* (Ibid.).

43. *uktaviśeṣasaṃpattyā darśitaphalaśālitvam āśramāntareṣv asaṃbhāvitam iti manvāno viśinaṣṭi—yataya iti* (BhG 5.17, 265).

44. *yat sāṃkhyair jñānaniṣṭhaiḥ saṃnyāsibhiḥ prāpyate sthānaṃ mokṣākhyaṃ tad yogair api jñānaprāptyupāyatveneśvare samarpya karmāṇy ātmanaḥ phalam anabhisaṃdhāyānutiṣṭhanti ye te yoginas tair api paramārthajñānasaṃnyāsaprāptidvāreṇa gamyate ity abhiprāyaḥ* . . . (BhG 5.5, 250)

45. *jñānāpekṣas tu saṃnyāsaḥ sāṃkhyam iti mayābhipretaḥ. paramārthayogaś ca sa eva* (BhG 5.6, 251).

46. *paramātmajñānaniṣṭhālakṣaṇatvāt* (Ibid., 252).

47. *brahma paramārthasaṃnyāsaṃ paramātmajñānaniṣṭhālakṣaṇam* (Ibid.)

48. BhG 5.7, 253–254. A very similar description is found in Śaṅkara's introduction to verse 4.42, which closes chapter 4 and is thus separated from 5.5 by only four verses: "Because he who, by practicing the yoga of action, gets his impurities destroyed and thereby obtains the knowledge that cuts his doubts to pieces, 'is not bound by actions,' his actions having been burnt solely by the fire of knowledge . . ." (239). BhG 9.28 is glossed in a similar spirit, as the verse is addressed to Arjuna: ". . . *having your self*, your internal organ, *equipped with the yoga of renunciation, liberated*, that is, from the bonds of action, even while living. And when this body will fall, *you will come to*, arrive at, *Me* . . . " (436–437).

49. Sureśvara 1990, 3.5.104, 821.

50. . . . *prayojakajñānaṃ paramārthajñānaṃ tatpūrvakasaṃnyāsadvāreṇa karmibhir api tad eva sthānam prāpyam* . . . (BhG 5.5, 250)

51. *ekatvavijñānaṃ parokṣaṃ vivakṣitaṃ. aparokṣasya pārivrājyam antareṇāyogāt. tasyoparatiśabditasya śamādivat sādhanatvaśruter iti draṣṭavyam* (ChU 2.23.1, 83).

52. *vicāraprayojakajñānavantaḥ* (BṛU 3.5.1, 253).

53. *tathā ca vyākhyātam etat "yeṣāṃ no 'yam ātmā 'yaṃ loka" iti hetuvacanena. pūrve vidvāṃsaḥ prajām akāmayamānā vyutthiṣṭhantīti pārivrājyaṃ viduṣām ātmalokāvabodhād eva. tathā ca vividiṣor api siddhaṃ pārivrājyam. "etam evātmānaṃ lokam icchantaḥ pravrajanti" iti vacanāt. karmaṇāṃ cāvidvad viṣayatvam avocāma* (BṛU 4.5.15, 387).

54. *vacanam antareṇāpi* (Ibid., 386).

55. Emphasis is mine.

56. *ātmajñānasyāmṛtatvahetutvābhyupagamād ityāder uktanyāyād ātmasākṣātkārasya kevalasya kaivalyakāraṇatvasiddheḥ sati tasmiñ jīvanmuktasya karmānuṣṭhānānavakāśāt taduddeśena pravṛttasyādhītavedasya viditapadapadārthasya parokṣajñānavatas tanmātreṇa pramāṇāpekṣām antareṇa siddhaṃ sarvakarmatyāgalakṣaṇaṃ pārivrājyam eṣa eva vidvatsaṃnyāso na tv aparokṣajñānavataḥ prārabdhaphalaprāptim antareṇānuṣṭheyaṃ kiṃcid astīti bhāvaḥ* (Ibid.).

57. *vividiṣur nāmādhītavedo vicāraprayojakāpātikajñānavān mumukṣur mokṣasādhanaṃ tattvasākṣātkāram apekṣamāṇas tasmin parokṣaniścayenāpi śunyo vivakṣitaḥ* (Ibid.).

58. *satyāṃ jijñāsāyāṃ karmatyāgo na śakyate niṣeddhum iti vadan vividiṣāsaṃnyāsaṃ sādhayati. etat pārivrājyam iti saṃbandhaḥ. viduṣām ātmasākṣātkārārthināṃ tatparokṣaniścayavatām iti yāvat. ātmalokasyāvabodho 'pi vyutthānahetuḥ parokṣaniścaya eva. satītarasmin phalāvasthasya vyutthānādyanuṣṭhānāyogāt tadantareṇa tatprāptyabhāvāc ca* (Ibid., 387).

59. *yady api jitendriyo 'pi vivekī śravaṇādibhir ajasraṃ brahmaṇi niṣṭhātuṃ śaknoti tathāpi kṣatriyeṇa tvayā vihitaṃ karma na tyājyam ity āha* (BhG 3.20, 158).

60. *gṛhasthaḥ saṃnyāsīty ubhāv api cen muktibhoginau kiṃ tarhi kaṣṭena sarvathaiva saṃnyāsenety āśaṅkya saṃnyāsivyatiriktānām antarāyasambhavād apekṣitaḥ saṃnyāso mumukṣor ity āha* (BhG 2.70, 132).

61. *indriyāṇāṃ viṣayeṣu pravṛttidvārā tattvavidāṃ pravṛttakarmatve 'pi jñānenaiva teṣāṃ muktir ity āha* (BhG 2.10, 45). See also Ānandagiri's comment on BhG 4.23, 215.

62. *pumarthaḥ karmaṇā neti dhīr eṣoparatir bhavet* |
(Vidyāraṇya 1919, 4.4.462, 964).

63. The first five verses quoted below are also found in the *Bṛhadāraṇyakavārtikasāra* 4.4.432–436, although verse 434 has a different wording than the corresponding one (18.306) in the *Anubhūtiprakāśa*.

64. *sulabhaṃ tu parivrājo bahuvikṣepavarjanāt* |

(Ibid., 18.305, 714).

65. In the *Bṛhadāraṇyakavārtikasāra*, this verse reads differently: "When, not even minding the distractions of rites, the householder remains steadfast in knowledge, he is also liberated. Otherwise, he takes up [physical] renunciation" (Vidyāraṇya 1919, 4.4.434, 958).

66. *soḍhvāpi karmavikṣepaṃ cittaikāgrye kṣamo yadi* |
tadā vettu gṛhastho 'pi pravrajatv anyathā pumān | |
(Vidyāraṇya 1992, 18.306, 714).

67. *ato viditveti vākyaṃ sāmānyaviṣayaṃ bhavet* |
pravrajantīti vākyaṃ tu viśeṣeṇa pravartate | |
(Ibid., 18.307, 714).

68. *sakṛd bodho vedanaṃ syān munitvaṃ jñānaśīlatā* |
ajñānahānir bodhāt syāj jīvanmuktir munitvataḥ | |
buddho 'pi na muniḥ syāc ced vidvatsaṃnyāsam ācaret |
(Ibid., 18.308–309, 715).

69. *brāhmaṇagrahaṇaśrutyā viprāṇāṃ eva bhāṣyakṛt* |
saṃnyāse 'dhikṛtiṃ prāha caturthāśramarūpy asau | |
vidyāṅgatatphalātmānaṃ gārgīvidurayor api |
strīśūdrayor bhāṣyakāraḥ saṃnyāsam anumanyate | |
(Vidyāraṇya 1919, 3.5.37–38, 698). The same verses are found in the *Anubhūtiprakāśa* (Vidyāraṇya 1992, 17.162–163, 587). Elsewhere in his *Bṛhadāraṇyakavārtikasāra*, the author also argues along the same lines:

> Maitreyī abandoned her wealth, as a means of knowledge. Since, after renouncing, her intellect was concentrated, she was qualified for knowledge. Objection: The fourth stage of life is not for women. Reply: Then let it not be for them! Still they are allowed to abandon everything as a subsidiary to knowledge, for it is not forbidden (Vidyāraṇya 1919, 2.4.12–13, 582).

70. *tyāga eva hi sarveṣāṃ mokṣasādhanam uttamam* |
(Ibid., 3.5.52, 701).

71. See for instance BS 3.4.17–20, transl, 770–778; BhG 3 intro, transl, 100–102; BhG 6 intro, transl., 214.

72. *samyaganuṣṭhitaiḥ śravaṇamanananididhyāsanaiḥ paraṃ tattvaṃ viditavadbhiḥ saṃpādyamāno vidvatsaṃnyāsaḥ* (Vidyāraṇya 1978, 4).

73. *tasmiṃś ca viditatattvo lokavyavahārair vikṣipyamāṇo manoviśrāntiṃ kāmayamāno 'dhikārī* (Ibid., 149).

74. The result of this Self-knowledge is explicitly referred to as liberation-in-life in Vidyāraṇya 1978, 194.

75. *dvividhaḥ karmasaṃnyāsaḥ phalasādhanabhedataḥ* |
phalāya jñāninas tyāgo jijñāsor jñānasiddhaye | |
(Vidyāraṇya 1992, 15.4, 500). The same verse appears in Vidyāraṇya 1919, 2.4.9, 581. See also Vidyāraṇya 1992, 17.159–160, 586–587; Vidyāraṇya 1978, 186, and 194.

76. *tattvajñānasya śravaṇādikaṃ sādhanaṃ, manonāśasya yogaḥ* (Vidyāraṇya 1978, 41). Although Vidyāraṇya also mentions the necessity of obliterating latent desires (*vāsanākṣaya*) in addition to dissolving the mind, when the latter is completely acheived through yoga, the former is also automatically ensured, resulting in liberation-in-life (Ibid., 364–365).

77. *jñānaṃ praty antaraṅgatvāc cittaviśrāntihetutayā ca jñānād api adhikaḥ* (Vidyāraṇya 1978, 116).

78. *tasmāt tattvavido 'pi kleśakṣayāyāsty evāsaṃprajñātasamādhy apekṣā* (Vidyāraṇya 1978, 118).

79. *'ayaṃ lokaḥ' ity aparokṣeṇānubhūyamāna ity arthaḥ* (Vidyāraṇya 1978, 6). Referring to Yājñavalkya, he also specifies that his knowledge before physical renunciation was neither general (*āpāta*), nor only mediate, but direct, though not yet permanent:

> Objection: Although his knowledge was correct, it was only mediate. Reply: No. Because in passages such as '[explain to me] the *Brahman* that is directly and not indirectly cognized' [BṛU 3.4.1], one comes across specific questions about the foremost direct [Self-knowledge] alone.
> (*nanu samyaktve 'pi parokṣajñānam eveti cen na, 'yat sākṣād aparokṣād brahma' iti mukhyāparokṣaviṣayatayaiva viśeṣataḥ praśnopalambhāt;* Vidyāraṇya 1978, 72).

80. Vidyāraṇya mentions elsewhere that the renunciation of these ancient Brahmins is out of their desire for liberation-in-life (Vidyāraṇya 1919, 4.4.437, 959).

81. *tattvajñānaṃ pūrvam evotpannam api jīvanmuktyā surakṣitaṃ bhavati* (Ibid., 146).

82. *seyaṃ jñānarakṣā jīvanmukteḥ prathamaṃ prayojanaṃ* (Ibid., 137).

83. The same principle is stated in Vidyāraṇya 1919, 3.5.66, 704.

84. Cf. Vidyāraṇya 1919, 2.4. 11, 581, and Vidyāraṇya 1978, 302, where the author uses the term *jīvanmukti* with respect to Janaka.

85. The same verse is found in Vidyāraṇya 1919, 2.4.10, 581.

86. Vidyāraṇya also illustrates this need by quoting a passage from the *Laghu-Yogavāsiṣṭha* where Rāma is said to know everything that is worth knowing, yet to be short of quiescence (*viśrānti*) (Vidyāraṇya 1978, 366).

87. *luptetarakṛtsnavyāpārasyaiva yoge 'dhikārāt* (Ibid., 112).

88. *rucimān karmasaṃnyāsī yuktaḥ śamadamādibhiḥ |*
mukhyādhikārī bhūtvāsāvātmany ātmānam īkṣate | |
(Vidyāraṇya 1992, 18.313, 717). After quoting BrU 4.4.23, Vidyāraṇya also specifies in the introduction to his *Aitareyopaniṣaddīpikā* that the Self-knower, referred to by the verse, is endowed with "the real qualification" (Vidyāraṇya 1980, intro, 1).

89. *paramārthasaṃnyāsaś cākartrātmasākṣātkāra eva. janakādīnām etādṛśasaṃnyāsitve 'pi . . . karmadarśanaṃ na viruddhaṃ paramahaṃsānām īdṛśānāṃ bhikṣāṭanādivat* (BhG 18.17, 701).

90. *etādṛśabhagavadabhiprāyavidā bhagavatā bhāṣyakṛtā brāhmaṇasyaiva saṃnyāso nānyasyeti nirṇītam. vārtikakṛtā tu prauḍhivādamātreṇa kṣatriyavaiśyayor api saṃnyāso 'stīty uktam iti draṣṭavyam* (BhG 3.20, 160).

91. *tataḥ śamādisaṃpattyā saṃnyāso niṣṭhito bhavet | |*
evaṃ sarvaparityāgān mumukṣā jāyate dṛḍhā |
tato gurūpasadanam upadeśagrahas tataḥ | | (BhG intro, 4).

92. For other passages where Madhusūdana gives physical renunciation as a prerequisite for the discipline of knowledge, see BhG 3, intro, 135; 3.20, 159; 5, intro, 242; 5.5, 250–251; 18.12, 692.

93. *sarvakarmasaṃnyāsābhāve 'pi hi kṣatriyasya jñānādhikāraḥ sthita eva* (BhG 6.44, 337).

94. Perhaps this evokes the cosmological account according to which the Golden Womb decides to take the creation in charge inasmuch as he can rely on God for his own liberation. Similarly, the devotee continues his activities and leaves his spiritual fate in the hands of the Lord.

95. *kṣatriyādes tu saṃnyāsānadhikāriṇo mumukṣor antaḥkaraṇaśuddhyanantaram api bhagavadājñāpālanāya lokasaṃgrahāya ca yathā kathaṃcit karmāṇi kurvato 'pi bhagavadeka-śaraṇatayā pūrvajanmakṛtasaṃnyāsādiparipākād vā hiraṇyagarbhanyāyena tada[na]pekṣaṇād vā bhagavadanugrahamātreṇehaiva tattvajñānotpattyā 'grimajanmani brāhmaṇajanmalābhena saṃnyāsādipūrvakajñānotpattyā vā mokṣa iti* (BhG 18.63, 750). N.B.: The emendation is from the edition by Lallurama 1912, 1287.

96. *tair yogibhir api sattvaśuddhyā saṃnyāsapūrvakaśravaṇādipuraḥsarayā jñānaniṣṭhayā vartamāne bhaviṣyati vā janmani saṃpatsyamānayā tat sthānaṃ gamyate* (BhG 5.5, 250).

97. Emphasis is mine.

98. *etādṛśa eva 'brahmasaṃstho 'mṛtatvameti' iti śrutyā dharmaskandha-trayavilakṣaṇatvena pratipāditaḥ paramahaṃsaparivrājakaḥ paramahaṃsaparivrājakaṃ kṛtakṛtyaṃ gurum upasṛtya vedāntavākyavicārasamartho yam uddiśya 'athāto brahmajijñāsā' ityādicaturlakṣaṇamīmāṃsā bhagavatā bādarāyaṇena samārambhi* (BhG 18.49, 733).

99. *sarvadharmān parityajya saṃnyasya sarvakarmāṇīty etat* (Ibid., 753).

100. *atra mām ekaṃ śaraṇaṃ vrajety anenaiva sarvadharmaśaraṇatāparityāge labdhe sarvadharmān parityajyeti niṣedhānuvādaḥ tu kāryakāritālābhāya. . . . tathā ca mamaiva sarvadharmakāryakāritvān madekaśaraṇasya nāsti dharmāpekṣety arthaḥ. etenedam apāstaṃ sarvadharmān parityajyety ukte nādharmāṇāṃ parityāgo labhyate 'to dharmapadaṃ karmamātraparam iti. na hy atra karmatyāgo vidhīyate api tu vidyamāne 'pi karmaṇi tatrānādareṇa bhagavadekaśa-raṇatāmātraṃ brahmacārīgṛhasthavānaprasthabhikṣūṇāṃ sādhāraṇyena vidhīyate. tatra sarvadharmān parityajyeti teṣāṃ svadharmādarasaṃbhavena tannivāraṇārtham. adharme cānarthaphale kasyāpy ādarābhāvāt tatparityāgavacanam anarthakam eva, śāstrāntaraprāptatvāc ca* (BhG 18.66, 753).

101. *arjunasya kṣtriyatvād uktasaṃnyāsadvārā jñānaniṣṭhāyāṃ mukhyānadhikāre 'pi taṃ puraskṛtyādhikāribhyas tasyopadidikṣitatvād avirodham abhipretyāha* (BhG 18.66, 753–754).

102. *arjunavyājenānyasyopadeśe tu 'vakṣyāmi te hitaṃ' 'tvā sarvapāpebhyo mokṣayiṣyāmi mā śucaḥ' iti copakramopasaṃhārau na syātām* (Ibid., 754).

103. *bhagavadbhaktiniṣṭhā tūbhayasādhanabhūtobhayaphalabhūtā ca bhavatīty anta upasaṃhṛtā 'sarvadharmān parityajya mām ekaṃ śaraṇaṃ vraja' ity atra. bhāṣyakṛtas tu sarvadharmān parityajyeti sarvakarmasaṃnyāsānuvādena mām ekaṃ śaraṇaṃ vrajeti jñānaniṣṭhopasaṃhṛtety āhuḥ. bhagavadabhiprāyavarṇane ke vayaṃ varākāḥ* (Ibid., 755).

104. *ya evaṃbhūta ātmajñaḥ sa naiṣkarmyasiddhim nirgatāni karmāṇi yasmān niṣkriyabrahmātmasaṃbodhāt sa niṣkarmā tasya bhāvo naiṣkarmyaṃ naiṣkarmyaṃ ca tat siddhiś ca sā naikarmyasiddhiḥ . . . adhigacchati prāpnoti* (BhG 18.49, 733).

105. *naiṣkarmyasya vā siddhir niṣkriyātmasvarūpāvasthānalakṣaṇasya siddhir niṣpattis tāṃ naiṣkarmyasiddhiṃ paramāṃ prakṛṣṭāṃ karmajasiddhivilakṣaṇāṃ sadyomuktyavast-hānarūpāṃ . . . adhigacchati* (Ibid.)

106. *ahaṃ tvā tvām evaṃ niścitabuddhiṃ sarvapāpebhyaḥ sarvadharmādharma-bandhanarūpebhyo mokṣayiṣyāmi svātmabhāvaprakāśīkaraṇena* (BhG 18.66, 753–754).

107. *yogasaṃnyastakarmaṇaṃ paramārthadarśanalakṣaṇena yogena saṃnyastāni karmāṇi yena paramārthadarśinā dharmādharmākhyāṇi taṃ yogasaṃnyastakarmaṇam. . . . jñānenātmeśvaraikatvadarśanalakṣaṇena saṃchinnaḥ saṃśayo yasya sa jñānasaṃchinnasaṃśayaḥ* (Ibid.)

108. *evaṃ ca sati dehabhṛttvābhimānānupapattāv avidyākṛtāśeṣakarmasaṃnyāsopapatteḥ saṃnyāsināṃ aniṣṭādi trividhaṃ karmaṇaḥ phalaṃ na bhavatīty upapannam* (BhG 18.17, 701).

109. For other instances where freedom from *dharma* and *adharma* is associated with the state of liberation, see BṛU 4.4.23; BhG 3.31, and 6.27.

110. *ato 'nyasyāpi kartṛtvābhimānābhāvaḥ phalasaṅgābhāvaś cābandhakāraṇam* (BhG 9.9, 419).

111. *ādigrahaṇena ca viṣayatitikṣātaduparamatattvaśraddhāḥ saṃgṛhyante* (Vācaspati Miśra 1982, 73).

112. Cf. the *Bhāṣyabhāvaprakāśikā* (Śaṅkara 1933, 742) of Citsukha Muni (1200–1250), the *Kalpataru* (Vācaspati Miśra 1982, 73) of Amalānanda (around 1250), the *Parimala* (Vācaspati Miśra 1982, 72–74) of Appaya Dīkṣita (around 1575), the *Ṛjuprakāśikā* (Śaṅkara 1933, 742) of Akhaṇḍānanda Sarasvatī (between 1600 and 1700), the *Ābhoga* (Lakṣmīnṛsiṃha 1955, 94) of Lakṣmīnṛsiṃha (around 1675–1725).

113. *eṣa hi brahmasaṃsthālakṣaṇo dharmo bhikṣor asādhāraṇaḥ, āśramāntarāṇi tatsaṃsthāny atatsaṃsthāni ca, bhikṣus tatsaṃstha ity eva. . . . tatsaṃstha eva tatrāñjasī nānyatra* (Vācaspati Miśra 1982, 884).

114. In his *Siddhāntaleśasaṅgraha,* Appaya Dīkṣita argues that since gods do not have to perform sacrifice, they are naturally in a position to devote themselves completely to the practice of meditation and attain liberation without physical renunciation (Appaya Dīkṣita 1935–1937, 1:352).

115. *brahmasākṣātkāraś ca citrāyāgādiphalavad āmuṣmikasādhāraṇaṃ phalam iti janmāntarasampannasaṃnyāsāpūrvasya gārhastyadarśāyāṃ kṛtaśravaṇādikasyāpi bhavati. ata eva vāmadevasya garbhasthasya prāg akṛtasaṃnyāsasyaiva sākṣātkārodayaḥ śrūyate. devādīnām apy akṛtasaṃnyāsānām eva sākṣātkāras tena muktiś ca śrūyate* (Vācaspati Miśra 1982, 885).

116. *na ca brahmasākṣātkārakāmaṃ prati saṃnyāsavidhāne, kathaṃ tadrahitānāṃ vāmadevādīnām indrādidevānāṃ ca tatsākṣātkāra iti vācyam. saṃnyāsasya tasmin janmani janmāntare vā sākṣātkāre janakatvaṃ citrāyāgādivat ity abhyupagamena pūrvajanmakṛtasaṃnyāsād eva teṣāṃ tatsākṣātkāropapatter iti bhāvaḥ* (Lakṣmīnṛsiṃha 1955, 3.4.18–20, 773–774).

117. *karmavikṣiptacittasya vedāntārthanirṇayāśakteḥ karmaṇāṃ vicāravirodhitvāt* (Ibid.).

118. *saṃnyāsina eva śravaṇe 'dhikāra iti* (Āpadeva 1911, 26).

119. *gṛhastasya karmavyagratayā śravaṇakartavyatānupapatteḥ* (Ibid.).

120. *evaṃ ca brāhmaṇānām eva śravaṇādyanuṣṭhāne saṃnyāso 'ṅgam, kṣatriyavaiśyayos tannirapekṣaḥ śravaṇādyadhikāraḥ* (Appaya Dīkṣita 1935–1937, 2: 91).

121. *saṃnyāsarahitayoḥ kṣatriyavaiśyayor na mukhyaḥ śravaṇādyadhikāraḥ* (Ibid., 92).

122. *tad evāpūrvaṃ vidyārūpaphalaparyantaṃ vyāpriyamāṇaṃ janmāntarīyāyām api vidyāyāṃ svakāritaśravaṇasyopakārakatāṃ ghaṭayati* (Ibid., 93).

123. *atra uparamaśabdena saṃnyāso bhidhīyate tathāca saṃnyāsinām eva śravaṇādāv adhikāraḥ iti kecit. apare tu uparamaśabdasya saṃnyāsavācakatvābhāvāt vikṣepābhāvamātrasya gṛhastheṣv api sambhavāt, janakāder api brahmavicārasya śrūyamāṇatvāt, sarvāśramasādhāraṇaṃ śravaṇādividhānam ity āhuḥ* (Dharmarāja Ādhvarīndra 1963, 222).

124. How this passage supports the idea that householders and others also have access to full Self-knowedge is far from obvious, especially since, in his comment on this verse, Śaṅkara writes that the author of the *Upaniṣad* uses the word Brahmin because the latter is especially qualified for Self-knowledge through (physical) renunciation.

125. *atra saṃnyāsinām eva brahmavidyāyām adhikāra ity atroparamaśabdaṃ pramāṇayantaḥ "saṃnyāsayogād yatayaḥ śuddhasattvāḥ" iti śrutiṃ tātparyabhramād upodbalayantaḥ "samitpāṇiḥ śrotriyaṃ brahmaniṣṭham" ityādiśrutiṃ janakaraikvavasiṣṭhānāṃ brahmavicārapratipādikām ākhyāyikām "gṛhastho 'pi vimucyate" ity smṛtiṃ cācchādayantas tadupodbalatayā ca svāśramasya mokṣāśramanāmadheyādikayuktyābhāsaṃ vadanto gṛhasthādikṛtasāṣṭāṅgapraṇāmamātreṇa svātmānam adhikaṃ manyamānā brahmavicāre gṛhasthādīnām adhikāraṃ teṣu pradveṣamātreṇa kecid bhikṣavo dūṣayanti teṣāṃ matam āha* (Rāmakṛṣṇa Ādhvarī 1985, 375).

CHAPTER TEN: ŚAṄKARA AND THE VALUE OF RENUNCIATION . . .

1. My translation. Nach dieser Betrachtung müssen wir als allgemeine Eigentümlichkeit des Denkens Ś[aṅkara]s eine Abneigung gegen Definitionen und eine souveräne Sorglosigkeit gegenüber begrifflicher Systematik festhalten . . ." (1951, 285).

2. "*Die Materialisierung der Avidyā zum Weltturstoff*" (Hacker 1951, 266; cf. also Mayeda's comments in Upad 77–79). It should be noted, however, that Śaṅkara also considers the illusory cosmic power of manifestation (*māyā*), as constituted of the three *guṇas*, to be ignorance (*avidyā*) (BhG 9.10, 419). Hence, with respect to this, the difference between Śaṅkara and his followers may be due to the emphasis of the latter on the illusory nature of the world rather than to a completely new interpretation.

3. See Biardeau 1989, 23–24, and 114.

4. My translation. ". . . *montrent comment le passage du brâhmanisme ancien à l'hindouisme implique une réévaluation complète de l'opposition initiale homme dans le monde/ renonçant. . . . [L]a délivrance (ou le salut) n'est plus affaire purement individuelle et cesse d'être l'apanage du renonçant pour devenir la perspective promise à l'humanité entière*" (Malamoud, 1976, 12–13).

5. See also Olivelle 1990, 146.

6. Ibid., 146 and 1984, 106.

Bibliography

Agrawal, M. M. 1982. *The Philosophy of Non-Attachment*. New Delhi: Motilal Banarsidass.

Allālasūri. 1984. *Bhāmatī Tilaka*. Edited by V. S. V. Guruswami Sastrigal. Madras: Adi Sankara Advaita Research Centre.

Amalānanda. 1913. *Śāstradarpaṇa*. Srirangam: Sri Vani Vilas Press.

Ānandagiri. 1917. *Tarka-Saṅgraha of Ānandajñāna*. Edited by T. M. Tripathi. Baroda: Central Library.

Anubhūtisvarūpa. 1935–1939. *Prakaṭārthavivaraṇam*. Edited by T. R. Chintamani. 2 vols. Madras: Madras Sanskrit Series.

Āpadeva. 1911. *Vedāntasāra of Sadānanda with the Commentary Balabodhini of Āpadeva*. Edited by K. Sundararama Aiyar. Srirangam: Sri Vani Vilas Press.

Appaya Dīkṣita. 1935–1937. *The Siddhāntaleśasaṅgraha of Appaya Dīkṣita*. Edited by S. S. Suryanarayana Sastri. 2 vols. Madras: University of Madras.

Bader, Jonathan. 1990. *Meditation in Śaṅkara's Vedānta*. New Delhi: Aditya Prakashan.

Bhagat, M. G. 1976. *Ancient Indian Asceticism*. New Delhi: Munshiram Manoharlal.

Bhāskara, Laugākṣi. 1931. *Arthasaṃgraha*. Edited and translated by S. S. Sukthankar. Delhi: Bharatiya Vidya Prakashan.

Bhattacharya, Kokileswar. 1979. *Introduction to Adwaita Philosophy: A Critical and Systematic Exposition of Śaṅkara School of Vedanta*. 2nd Ed. Varanasi: Bharatiya Publishing House.

Biardeau, Madeleine. 1989. *Hinduism. The Anthropology of a Civilization*. Oxford: Oxford University Press.

Biardeau, Madeleine and Charles Malamoud. 1976. *Le Sacrifice dans l'Inde ancienne*. Paris: Presses Universitaires de France.

Bos, Mike. 1983. "After the Rise of Knowledge." *Wiener Zeitschrift für die Kunde Südasiens* 27:165–184.

Chandraśekhara Bhārati. 1988. *Śrī Śaṁkara's Vivekacūḍāmaṇi. With an English translation of the commentary of Śrī Candraśekhara Bhāratī*. Translated by P. Sankaranarayanan. Bombay: Bharatiya Vidya Bhavan.

Chenkner, William. 1983. *A Tradition of Teachers: Śaṅkara and the Jagadgurus Today*. Delhi: Motilal Banarsidass.

Clooney, Francis X. 1990. *Thinking Ritually. Rediscovering the Pūrva Mīmāṃsā of Jaimini*. Vienna: Publications of the De Nobili Research Library.

———. 1993. *Theology after Vedanta: An Experiment in Comparative Theology*. Albany: State University of New York Press.

Dandekar, R. N. 1974. *The Māhābhārata Text as Constituted in its Critical Edition*. 19 vols. Poona: Bhandarkar Oriental Research Institute.

Dasgupta, Surendranath. 1975. *A History of Indian Philosophy*. Vol. 2. Delhi: Motilal Banarsidass.

Dayzey, Wade H. 1990. "Tradition and Modernization in the Organization of the Daśanāmī Saṁnyāsins." In *Monastic Life in the Christian and Hindu Traditions. A Comparative Study*. Edited by Austin B. Creel and Vasudha Narayanan. 281–321. Lewiston: The Edwin Mellen Press.

Deutsch, Eliot. 1968. *The Bhagavad Gītā*. New York: Holt Rinehart and Winston.

Dharmarāja Adhvar¥ndra. 1963. *Vedānta-Paribhāṣā*. Translated by Swāmī Mādhavānanda. Belur Math: The Ramakrishna Mission Saradapitha.

Dumont, Louis. 1980. *Homo Hierarchicus. The Caste System and its Implications*. Translated by Mark Sainsbury, Louis Dumont, and Basia Gulati. Chicago and London: The University of Chicago Press.

Edgerton, Franklin. 1924. "The Meaning of Sāṃkhya and Yoga." *American Journal of Philology* 45: 1: 1–46.

Eliade, Mircea. 1954. *Le Yoga. Immortalité et liberté*. Paris: Petite bibliothèque Payot.

Hacker, Paul. 1950. *Untersuchungen über Texte des frühen Advaitavāda*. Vol 1. *Die Schüler Śaṅkaras*. Wiesbaden: Akademie der Wissenschaften und der Literatur.

———. 1951. "Eigentümlichkeiten der Lehre und Terminologie Śaṅkaras: Avidyā, Nāmarūpa, Māyā, Īśvara." *Zeitschrift der Deutschen Morgenlandischen Gesellschaft* 100:246–286.

Halbfass, Wilhelm. 1980. "Karma, *apūrva* and Natural Causes." In *Karma and Rebirth in Classical Indian Traditions*. Edited by Wendy Doniger O'Flaherty. Berkeley: University of California Press.

———. 1991. *Tradition and Reflexion. Explorations in Indian Thought*. Albany: State of New York University Press.

Hartsuiker, Dolf. 1993. *Sādhus. Holy Men of India*. London: Thames and Hudson.

Heesterman, J. C. 1985. *The Inner Conflict of Tradition. Essays in Indian Ritual, Kingship, and Society*. Chicago: The University of Chicago Press.

Hiriyanna, M. 1949. *The Essentials of Indian Philosophy*. London: George Allen and Unwin Ltd.

———. 1952. *Popular Essays in Indian Philosophy*. Mysore: Kavyalaya Publishers.

———. 1980. *The Naiṣkarmya-Siddhi of Sureśvarācārya*. 4th ed. Poona: Bhandarkar Oriental Research Institute.

Hulin, Michel. 1978. *Le Principe de l'ego dans la pensée indienne classique. La Notion d'ahaṃkāra*. Paris: Collège de France, Institut de Civilisation Indienne.

Jaimini. 1980. *Mīmāṃsā Sūtras*.Translated by Mohan Lal Sandal. Delhi: Motilal Banarsidass.

Jha, Ganganatha. 1942. *Pūrva-Mīmāṁsā in its Sources*. Benares: Benares Hindu University.

Kaelber, Walter O. 1989. *Tapta Mārga: Asceticism and Initiation in Vedic India*. Albany: State University of New York.

Kalyanasundara Sastri, V. R. 1989. "Śaṅkara on jñāna-Yoga." In *Perspectives of Śaṅkara. Rashtriya Śaṅkara Jayant¥ Mahotsava Commemoration Volume*. Edited by R. Balasubramanian and Sibajiban Bhattacharya. 297–306. Department of Culture Ministry of Human Resource Development Government of India.

Kane, Pandurang Vaman. 1974. *History of Dharmaśāstra*. 5 vols. 2nd Ed. Poona: Bhandarkar Oriental Research Institute.

Kocmarek, Ivan. 1985. *Language and Release. Sarvajñātman's Pañcaprakriyā*. Delhi: Motilal Banarsidass.

Kṛṣṇānanda Sarasvatü. 1916. *Siddhāntasiddhāñjana*. Trivandrum: Superintendent Government Press.

Lakṣmīnṛsiṃha. 1955. *Ābhoga-Kalpataru-Vyākhyā*. Edited by Rāma Sastri and S. Subrahmanya Sastri. Madras: Government Oriental Manuscripts Library.

Lallurama, Jeevarama. 1912. *Shrimad-Bhagvad-Geeta, with eight commentaries*. Bombay: Gujarati Printing Press.

Madhusūdana Sarasvatī. 1925. *Sārasaṅgraha*. In *Saṅkṣepaśārīraka by Sarvajñātma-Muni*. Edited by Bhau Sastri Vajhe and P. Sitaram Sastri Kelkar. Benares: Kashi Sanskrit Series.

Mahadevan, T. M. P. 1938. *The Philosophy of Advaita, with Special Reference to Bhāratītīrtha-Vidyāraṇya*. London: Luzac and Co.

———. 1940. *The Two-Fold Path in the Gītā*. Madras: Swāmī Nityananda.

———. 1959. *Homage to Śaṅkara*. Madras: Ganesh and Co Private Ltd.

———. 1968. *Preceptors of Advaita*. Edited by T. M. P. Mahadevan. Secunderabad: Sri Kanchi Kamakoti Sankara Mandir.

———. 1974. *Invitation to Indian Philosophy*. New Delhi: Arnold-Heinemann Publishers (India) Private Limited.

———. 1975. *The Pañcadaśī of Bhāratītīrtha-Vidyāraṇya*. Madras: Centre for Advanced Study in Philosophy.

Maharishi Mahesh Yogi. 1969. *Bhagavad-Gītā: A New Translation and Commentary Chapters 1–6*. New York: Penguin Books.

Mainkar, T. G. 1969. *A Comparative Study of the Commentaries on the Bhagavadgītā*. 2nd Ed. Delhi: Motilal Banarsidass.

Malamoud, Charles. 1976. "Village et forêt dans l'Inde brâhmanique." *Archives européennes de sociologie* 17:3–20.

Manu. 1983. *Manusmṛti. With the Sankrit Commentary Manvartha-Muktāvalī of Kullīka Bhaṭta*. Edited by J. L. Shastri. Delhi: Motilal Banarsidass.

Marcaurelle, Roger. 1987. "Śaṅkara's Hermeneutics on Renunciation in the *Gītā*." In *New Essays in the Bhagavad-gītā. Philosophical, Methodological and Cultural Approaches*. Edited by Arvind Sharma. 98–126. New Delhi: Books and Books.

———. 1988–1989. "States of Consciousness and Meaning in the *Bhagavadgītā*: The Contribution of Maharishi Mahesh Yogi." *The Journal of Studies in the Bhagavadgītā* 8–9:25–45.

———. 1994. "The Basic Types of Renunciation in Hinduism with Special Reference to Śaṅkara's *Gītā-bhāṣya*." In *Hermeneutical Paths to the Sacred Worlds of India*. Edited by Katherine K. Young. 104–122. Atlanta: Scholars Press.

Mayeda, Sengaku. 1964–1966. "Ādi-Śaṅkarācārya's Teaching on the Means to Mokṣa: Jñāna and Karman." *Journal of Oriental Research* 34–35:66–75.

———. 1988. "Śaṅkara and Nārāyaṇa Guru." In *Interpreting Across Boundaries. New Essays in Comparative Philosophy*. Edited by Gerald James Larson and Eliot Deutsch. 184–202. Princeton: Princeton University Press.

Miller, David M., and Dorothy C. Wertz. 1976. *Hindu Monastic Life: The Monks and Monasteries of Bhubaneswar*. Montreal: McGill-Queens's University Press.

Mishra, Kamalakar. 1981. *The Significance of the Tantric Tradition*. Varanasi: Arddhanārīśvara Publications.

Modi, P. M. 1955. *The Bhagavadgītā: A Fresh Approach with Special Reference to Śaṅkarācārya's Bhāṣya*. Baroda: P. M. Modi.

Murty, K. Satchidananda. 1974. *Revelation and Reason in Advaita Vedānta*. Delhi: Motilal Banarsidass.

Nakamura, Hajime. 1983. *A History of Early Vedānta Philosophy*. Vol. 1. Delhi: Motilal Banarsidass.

———. 1991. *Ways of Thinking of Eastern Peoples. India China Tibet Japan*. Edited by Philip P. Wiener. Delhi: Motilal Banarsidass.

Nandi, R. N. 1986. *Social Roots of Religion in Ancient India*. Calcutta: K. P. Bagchi.

Olivelle, Patrick. 1974. "The Notion of Āśrama in the Dharmasūtras." *Wiener Zeitschrift für die Kunde Südasiens* 18:27–35.

———. 1975. "A Definition of World Renunciation." *Wiener Zeitschrift für die Kunde Südasiens* 19:75–83.

———. 1976–1977. *Vāsudevāśrama Yatidharmaprakāśa: A Treatise on World Renunciation*. 2 Vols. Vienna: Publications of the De Nobili Research Library.

———. 1978. "The Integration of Renunciation by Orthodox Hinduism." *Journal of the Oriental Institute of Baroda* 28, 1:27–34.

———. 1981. "Contributions to the Semantic History of Saṃnyāsa." *Journal of the American Oriental Society* 101, 3:265–274.

———. 1984. "Renouncer and Renunciation in the *Dharmaśāstras*." In *Studies in Dharmaśāstras*. Edited by Richard W. Larivière. 81–151. Calcutta: Firma KLM Private Limited.

———. 1986–87. *Renunciation in Hinduism: A Medieval Debate*. 2 Vols. Vienna: Publications of the De Nobili Research Library.

———. 1990. "Village and Wilderness: Ascetic Ideals and the Hindu World." In *Monastic Life in the Christian and Hindu Traditions. A Comparative Study*. Edited by Austin B. Creel and Vasudha Narayanan. 124–160. Lewiston: The Edwin Mellen Press.

———. 1993. *The Āśrama System. The History and Hermeneutics of a Religious Institution*. New York: Oxford University Press.

Padmapāda. 1992. *Pañcapādikā*. Edited by S. Subrahmania Sastri. Mount Abu: Mahesh Research Institute.

Potter, Karl H. 1981. *Encyclopedia of Indian Philosophies*. Vol. 3. Delhi: Motilal Banarsidass.

———. 1982. "Śaṁkarācārya: The Myth and the Man." *JAAR Thematic Studies* 18/3–4:111–125.

Radhakrishnan, S. 1929. *Indian Philosophy*. Vol. 2, 2nd Ed. New York: The MacMillan Company.

Rāmakṛṣṇa Adhvarī. 1985. *Vedānta-Paribhāṣā of Dharmarāja Adhvarīndra with the Śikhāmaṇi Commentary by Rāmakṛṣṇa Adhvarī*. Edited by Svāmī Amaradāsa. Varanasi: Chaukhamba Amarabharati Prakashan.

Renou, Louis. 1966. *L'Hindouisme*. 4th Ed. Paris: Presses Universitaires de France.

Revathy, S. 1990. *Three Little Known Advaitins*. Madras: University of Madras.

Rukmani, T. S. 1992. "The Problem of the Authorship of the *Yogasūtrabhāṣya-vivaraṇa*." *Journal of Indian Philosophy* 20: 419–423.

Sadānanda. 1893. *Vedāntasāra of Sadānanda*. Edited by G. A. Jacob. Varanasi: Chaukhamba Amarabharati Prakashan.

———. 1949. *Vedāntasāra or The Essence of Vedānta*. Translated by Swāmī Nikhilananda. Mayavati: Advaita Ashrama.

Sadānanda Kāśm¥r¥. 1932. *Advaitabrahmasiddhi*. Calcutta: University of Calcutta.

Śaṅkara. 1925. *Works of Shankaracharya*. Vol. 4. *Minor Works*. Edited by H. R. Bhagavat. Poona: Ashtekar and Co.

———. 1933. *Brahmasūtra-Saṅkara-Bhāṣyam with Nine Commentaries*. Calcutta: Metropolitain Printing and Publishing.

———. 1952a. *Adhyātmavidyopadeśavidhi*. Bombay: Nirnaya Sagar Press.

———. 1952b. *Pātañjala-Yogasūtra-Bhāṣya Vivaraṇam of Śaṅkara-Bhagavatpāda*. Edited by Polakam Sri Rama Sastri and S. R. Krishnamurthi Sastri. Madras: Government Oriental Manuscripts Library.

———. 1953. *Vākyavṛtti and Ātmajñānopadeśavidhi*. Translated by Swāmī Jagadānanda. Madras: Sri Ramakrishna Math.

———. 1978a. *The Chapter of the Self*. Translated by Trevor Legget. London: Routledge and Kegan Paul.

———. 1978b. "Svarūpanirūpaṇa." In *Prakaraṇāṣṭakam*. Edited by S. Subrahmania Sastri. Mount Abu: Mahesh Research Institute.

———. 1981. *Complete Works of Sri Sankaracharya*. Vol. 2. Madras: Samata Books.

———. 1982. *Complete Works of Sri Sankaracharya*. Vol. 5. Madras: Samata Books.

———. 1983. *Srīmad Bhagavad Gītā of Sri Saṃkarācārya*. Translated by A. G. Krishna Warrier. Madras: Sri Ramakrishna Math.

———. 1984. *Bhagavadgītā: With the Commentary of Śaṅkarācārya*. Translated by Swāmī Gambhīrānanda. Calcutta: Advaita Ashrama.

———. 1985. *The Bhagavadgītā: With the Commentary of Śaṅkarācārya*. Translated by Alladi Mahadeva Sastri. Madras: Samata Books.

Saroja, G. V. 1985. *Tilak and Śaṅkara on the Gītā*. New Delhi: Sterling Publishers.

Sarvajñātman. 1985. *The Saṁkṣepaśārīraka of Sarvajñātman*. Edited and translated by N. Veezhinathan. Madras: University of Madras.

Saway, Yoshitsugu. 1992. *The Faith of Ascetics and Lay Smartas: A Study of the Śaṅkaran Tradition of Śṛṅgeri*. Vienna: Publications of the de Nobili Research Library.

Sureśvara. 1958. *The Sambandha-Vārtika of Sureśvarācārya*. Edited by T. M. P. Mahadevan. Madras: University of Madras.

—— 1982. *Bṛhadāraṇyakopaniṣad-Bhāṣyavārtikam: With the Commentary Shāstraprakāshika of Shri Ānandagiri Aacharya*. Edited by S. Subrahmanya Shastri. Vol. 1. Varanasi: Mahesh Research Institute.

———. 1984. *The Taittirīyopaniṣad Bhāṣya-Vārtika of Sureśvara*. 2nd Ed. Edited and translated by R. Balasubramanian. Madras: University of Madras.

———. 1988. *The Naiṣkarmyasiddhi of Sureśvara*. Edited and translated by R. Balasubramanian. Madras: University of Madras.

———. 1990. *Bṛhadāraṇyakopaniṣad-Bhāṣyavārtikam: With the Commentary Shāstraprakāshika of Shri Ānandagiri*. Edited by S. Subrahmanya Shastri. Vol. 2. Varanasi: Mahesh Research Institute.

———. 1991. In Shoun Hino, *Sureśvara's Vārtika on Yājñavalkya Maitreyī Dialogue*. 2nd Ed. Delhi: Motilal Banarsidass.

———. 1993. *Sureśvara's Vārtika on Puruṣvidha Brāhmaṇa*. Edited and translated by K. P. Jog and Shoun Hino. Delhi: Motilal Banarsidass.

Suryanarayana Sastri, S. S. 1961. *Collected Papers*. Edited by T. M. P. Mahadevan, Madras: University of Madras.

Thangaswami, R. 1980. *Advaita-Vedānta Literature. A Bibliographical Survey*. Madras: University of Madras.

Tiwari, Kapil N. 1977. *Dimensions of Renunciation in Advaita Vedānta*. New Delhi: Motilal Banarsidass.

Vācaspati Miśra. 1982. *Brahmasūtra Śaṅkara Bhāṣya with the Commentaries Bhāmatī, Kalpataru, and Parimala*. Edited by Anantakrishna Sastri. Varanasi: Chaukhamba Sanskrit Series Office.

Vetter, Tilmann. 1979. *Studien zur Lehre und Entwicklung Śaṅkaras*. Wien: De Nobili Research Library.

Vidyāraṇya. 1919. *Bṛhadāraṇyakavārtikasāra with Commentary Laghusaṅgraha by Maheshwar Tirth*. Edited by Bhau Sastri Vajhe. Benares: Chaukhamba Sanskrit Series Office.

———. 1978. *Jīvanmuktiviveka*. Edited and translated by S. Subrahmanya Sastri, and T. R. Srinivasa Ayyangar. Madras: The Adyar Library and Research Centre.

———. 1980. *Aitareya Upaniṣad with Śaṅkara's Commentary*. Poona: Ananda Asrama Sankrit Series.

———. 1992. *The Anubhūtiprakāśa of Vidyāraṇya: The Philosophy of Upaniṣads: An Interpretative Exposition*. Edited and translated by Godabarisha Mishra. Madras: University of Madras.

Warrier, A. G. Krishna. 1981. *The Concept of Mukti in Advaita Vedānta*. Madras: University of Madras.

Wilson, Boyd Henri. 1982. *Śaṅkara's Use of Scripture in His Philosophy*. Ph.D. Dis., University of Iowa.

Index

Abandonment: *see* renunciation
Absorption (*samādhi*), 116, 122–123, 183, 238n. 51; devoid of mental cognition/construct (*asamprajñātasamādhi*), 18, 192–193, 231n. 8
Abstention from action (*nivṛitti*), ix, 156–157, 169, 232n. 24, 243n. 71; as steadfastness in Self-knowledge, 88–93, 96–97, 103–104. *See also* steadfastness in Self-knowledge
Action (*karman*): definition according to Śaṅkara, 98; effects of, 27–28, 145
Actionlessness (*naiṣkarmya*), 200, 239n. 62
Adhikāra, 62; definition of, 29, 220n.10, 223n. 50, 223n. 58, 234n. 43; as "having to do with," 41–43, 101–102; as qualification, 38, 41, 44
Advaita Vedānta, ix–xi, 219n. 4; liberation in, 4; renunciation in, 4, 45, 145, 165–208, 211–213, 217n. 6, 253n. 2
Advaitin(s), 11, 48–49, 68, 159, 165, 170–171, 219n. 6
Agrawal, M. M., 219n. 4
Akhaṇḍānanda Sarasvatī, 252n. 112
Allālasūri, 205
Amalānanda, 203, 252n. 112
Ambiguity: *see* Śaṅkara
Ānandagiri, 42–43, 76–77, 179–188, 192–194, 199, 206, 223n. 52
Ancient Brahmins/sages/men, 45, 94–95, 99, 146–148, 150, 175, 185–186, 193, 226n. 10, 246n. 25, 250n. 80
Anubhūtisvarūpa, 178–180, 211, 247n. 37
Āpadeva, 205
Appaya Dīkṣita, 47, 181, 203, 205–206, 252nn. 112, 114
Arjuna, 3, 17, 41, 134, 196, 198–199, 202, 247n. 48
Austerity/asceticism (*tapas*), 3, 76, 86–87, 116, 119, 129, 136–137, 155
Attainment/emergence of knowledge (*jñānaprāpti/jñānotpatti*), 25, 27, 30, 75, 117–118, 122; as listed in the householder sequence toward liberation, xi, 55–56, 61–63, 71–73, 80–81, 89, 182, 197, 209, 225n. 4, 228n. 36

Bader, Jonathan, 218n. 12
Balasubramanian, R., 120
Bare maintenance of life, 58, 151, 154–156
Bhagavadgītā/Gītā, 3, 4, 6, 35, 46, 57, 72–73, 78, 88–89, 92–93, 95, 99, 102, 106, 108–109, 134, 199, 213–215, 217n. 4, 232n. 19
Bhāmatī School, 5, 170, 202–204, 206, 211
Bhartṛprapañca, 22–23
Bhattacharya, Kokileswar, 8
Biardeau, Madeleine, 39, 214, 253n. 3
Bliss, 18, 20, 23, 96, 98, 114, 116
Brahmadatta, 22
Brahmasūtras, 4, 103